TRY AND TRY AGAIN A PIONEER'S TALE OF THE GREAT STATE OF
FLORIDA, AS TOLD BY JAMES HIRAM LEE

© 2013 by The Habitation of Chimham Publishing

http://www.chimhampublish.com

Paperback
All rights reserved

Library of Congress Cataloging-in-Publication Data

Doudney, Douglas S.

ISBN-13:978-0-9899696-0-4
Library of Congress Control Number 2013950141

PS36-
813 Dou

12	11	10	9	8	7	6
7	6	5	4	3	2	1

Legal Disclaimer
This is a work of historical fiction. Any resemblance between the characters in this novel and actual people is purely coincidental.

Try and Try Again

A Pioneer's Tale of the Great State of Florida

As Told by James Hiram Lee

Al,

Hope you enjoy this as much as I have.

Best Wishes!

By Douglas S. Doudney

Habitation of Chimham Publishing
La Vergne, TN
www.chimhampublish.com

Table Of Contents

Try, Try Again

'Tis a lesson you should heed,
Try, try, try again.
If at first you don't succeed,
Try, try, try again.

Then your courage should appear,
For if you will persevere,
You will conquer, never fear,
Try, try, try again.

Once or twice though you should fail,
Try, try, try again.

If you would at last prevail,
Try, try, try again.

If we strive 'tis no disgrace,
Though we may not win the race;
What should you do in that case?
Try, try, try again.

If you find your case is hard,
Try, try, try again.
Time will bring you your reward,
Try, try, try again.

All that other people do,
Why, with patience should not you?
Only keep this rule in view,
Try, try, try again.

-Anonymous

Dedication

Myra Ann Southward Doudney
September 23, 1929 - June 1, 2013

I treasure the way you enjoyed reading the rough drafts as this work slowly evolved. I appreciate your loving encouragement to continue and deeply regret I wasn't able to put a finished copy in your hand. Thanks, Mom.

Acknowledgements

The author's gratitude is owed to so many who contributed to *Try and Try Again*, here are just a few. To:

Charles Lee, 1892-1991, for dictating the "Lee Family History," a genealogical study of the Lee family line which became the author's bible and outline throughout this project;

Thelma Lee Clonts, 1925-2009, for the wonderful work she did in organizing, compiling, composing and producing the above-referenced work with her father, Charles;

Robert and Jane Lee, for opening their files and treasure trove of pictures, documents, anecdotes and memories of their family;

William S. Morgan V, for his encouragement, friendship and sharing his encyclopedic knowledge of American history in general, Civil War history specifically, and for sharing his incredible talent for genealogic research, and ability to find long-buried facts from the many databases he accesses;

Erin Fish, for her editing expertise reflecting a confident knowledge and command of our quirky English language well beyond her young years;

Bob MacLeish, Sr., for his steadfast support, encouragement, critiquing and friendship throughout this project.

Thomas Tart, for sharing his thorough knowledge of the Civil War and its times, especially as it relates to and the impact it had on the great State of Florida;

Doug Doudney, Jr., the author's weapons consultant, for his surprisingly thorough knowledge of the weapons used during the Civil War;

The author's family, especially Julie, for selfless encouragement and patience as the work evolved;

Numerous other friends and Lee Family members who took interest and gave time, encouragement, anecdotes and materials to the author in his curious and unlikely adventure as a novelist;

Thank you all.

Preface

About twenty-five years ago, the author read and was fascinated by a genealogy of the Lees, a pioneer family of Florida. More recently, when reading a history novel of a different family, he had an epiphany and knew the Lee family history had to be told, not in the form of sterile genealogy but in the form of a novel to bring long-dead people, their lives, times, adventures and accomplishments back to life.

All the key characters in *Try and Try Again* are real people. Likewise, all major events of the story are ones in which the characters participated in real life. Thus, Volume I of the story unfolds as an accurate and colorful history of the state from pre-Territory days into Reconstruction. The Lee family is composed of ordinary folks who lived in extra-ordinary times.

The title is chosen for two reasons. First, the theme of trying again fits so well with the development of Florida, hinting of the repetitive cycle of life and death through successive generations, as well as the cycle of success, failure, striving and learning.

Second, the author's Great-great-great-grandfather, the Rev. David Alfred Doudney, a minister of the Church of England, authored and published a book of the same name in 1864. His auto-biographical work of his personal joys, struggles, successes and failures in England occurs simultaneously with the story of the Lee family half a world away. The author is fascinated by the parallels between the lives and times of the two un-related families at such a distance and gets personal joy from borrowing a title from his ancestor.

Hope you enjoy,

Doug Doudney

Early St. Marys

Great-granddaddy Levi Lee, born in Virginia in 1748, fought in the Revolutionary War. Not much is known of him except he married a woman who was one-quarter Indian. Now the fact of his wife's heritage didn't set too well with the staid bunch of Virginia Lees, so Levi decided to head south, thus beginning the southward migration of this branch of Lees, setting us apart from those who settled thick in the Virginia woods and mostly tended to stay put.

I guess you could say he had to try again!

Levi, his wife and young family moved to South Carolina and farmed, as Lees are known to do. Over the course of his life he drew several land grants from South Carolina and Georgia. I'm guessing he'd wear out one farm and move on to another like so many of the early planters did. No use trying to steward the land; just crop it heavy as you can, exhaust the ground and move on. Land was free or very near-free so no use taking care of it 'cause there was always new ground opening up just a little down the road. In those days, it was a point of pride to wear out several farms in a lifetime to prove you're a real farmer.

I, for one, am glad he did keep moving, for with each new farm and uprooting of his family, Levi got closer to Florida. His name might have better been Moses instead of Levi because he spent his life wandering. He got real close, but never quite made it to the Promised Land. Levi started his family on a multi-generational trail of trials, full of hope and full of fears; full of faith and full of folly. His life was a journey so typical of the mass early-American migration south, leaving the prosperous settled colonies to trek into God-forsaken wilderness, always looking for better land and a new beginning.

The reasons these Americans migrated were many, but key was the brand new U.S. Constitution, which became effective in 1788 and was unlike any the world had ever seen. It established human rights and freedoms were "Endowed by our Creator," not by any man, and placed severe limits on the powers the central government could exercise over those rights. Our Founders were inspired by the writings of the likes of Adam Smith, Edmund Burke, John Locke and others; all with strong teachings of the virtue of free markets, free practice of religion, rule of law, "enlightened self-interest," private property rights and generally, maximum personal liberty.

The folks who populated the big migration were as varied as they were numerous. A common thread among the settlers in this new land was the uniquely famous American

Protestant work ethic. Overwhelmingly, the land was settled by deeply committed Protestants, mostly Methodists and Baptists. Their faith drove them to work with a purpose never before seen in men, free or bond. They wore themselves out six days a week, then got bolstered up on Sundays by absolutist, fire-breathing preachers who drove themselves to deliver a perfect balance of condemning fear and glorious hope to keep the faithful going another week. Even the few who didn't practice a Protestant faith, or even had no faith at all, couldn't help being influenced by the drive and commitment of their faith-filled neighbors.

It wasn't only dreams of earthly gain and heavenly reward driving these folks, but also the moral compass implanted in each believer. The Biblical admonitions "Do unto others as you would have them do unto you" and "Greater love has no man than this, that he lay down his life for his friend" were engraved on the hearts of the faithful. This foundation created a virtuous cycle of man helping fellow man while helping himself. The result, though not flawless, was so glorious even Jefferson's grand vision for the country fell far short of what was actually achieved.

Already motivated to build a better life than they left behind, these folks were stirred into action by their government, or, better said, lack of government. They were unfettered and enabled to "go forth, be fruitful, multiply and subdue the earth," armed with no guarantee other than personal liberty and the assurance some king or feudal lord was not going to take away from them everything they'd gained for themselves. Add to this vision millions of acres of virgin land begging to be settled and improved, with the new government giving it away to those intrepid or foolish enough to dare try.

The result is America.

New towns, cities and farms popped up across the land from Maine to Georgia. May this same spirit of building and growing be on our land forever!

Levi didn't migrate to escape grinding poverty, as was fairly common of the day. He also didn't leave to escape the law, which was just common enough to cause trouble and add a little bit of fly in the ointment to the new communities. He left a very well-established family who simply disapproved of his bridal choice. I don't know of anything wrong with my great-grandma except her heritage, but can only assume Levi's straight-laced family was very judgmental. I think it was wrong but can only be thankful because it caused my life to take place in a brand new and very exciting world.

Levi's known offspring were two girls and one boy. First was Sarah, number two was John, and the baby was Susannah. Shortly after Susannah was born, Levi up and died at fifty-one, leaving his squaw a widow in a land not known for taking too kindly to her type.

John was about six when Levi died in 1800, so he grew up quickly, being the only man for his sisters and Indian mother. Living had to be tough in this area, which was just getting shed of Indians and had plenty of reason to worry about them coming back to visit, and on not-so-friendly terms. John's part-squaw mother was partially accepted because she had white children and was a converted Methodist. She was raised in white ways and was committed to teaching her young the same faith, fear and work ethic to keep them on the straight and narrow path.

It was very hard for a woman to legally hold land in early America. It would also be very hard for a single woman to hold on to and operate a farm. Further, if said woman happened to be an Indian, you could assume her property rights as a widow were pert' near nothin'. It wasn't uncommon for widows to be taken great advantage of in those days, even by family. So it's a safe assumption Levi's widow was forced off her farm with little or no money for it.

Thus, very shortly after Levi died, the family moved to St. Marys, Georgia. They had only a pittance of money from Levi, so the widow had to do what she had to do to raise a small family in a rough and tumble early-nineteenth-century boomtown. She found support, encouragement and some assistance from her new friends and surrogate family at St. Marys Methodist Church.

St. Marys was a thriving new port town at the very southern boundary of Georgia. Founded in 1789, it wasn't a real big natural port, but if your ship needed provisions, this was your southernmost chance to get 'em in the U.S. St. Marys was a small but bustling town in the coastal low country, built in what was a beautiful Live Oak grove. However, the hungry settlers didn't have much use for beauty because they lived constantly on the edge of life and death. The majestic, spreading oaks quickly became firewood. By 1800, the town had been pretty much stripped of trees and had several loading docks, storage yards, shipping offices and a boarding house covering the waterfront. To the widow Lee, it looked to be the type of place she could earn enough to get by while raising her family all alone. She offered seamstress services, washing, housecleaning and any moral, legal job she could get. This town was sure to grow. The businesses did well by supplying the farmers just getting started outside of town and the sailors who came in by river.

The river was a little too wide, and the current usually too strong to swim. If you felt an urge to try, the currents would probably get you. If the currents didn't get you, there was a pretty good chance either the sharks from the ocean or the alligators from upriver would be there to ruin your day.

The other bank of the St. Marys River was the territory of La Florida. It was Spanish country. Its port town closest to the inlet was Fernandina, which was bigger and older than St. Marys. St. Marys was growing, though, just like all the rest of America. Fernandina, though a very old town, seemed to just be there to support Florida's trade with Spain. Once you got inland from the coast, Spain really didn't much care about the land, or developing it to its potential, or protecting its people.

In 1763, Spain traded Florida off to the British in a swap for Cuba, only to get it back after the Revolutionary War by virtue of the Treaty of Paris in 1783. Well, we Americans would rather have the Spaniards as neighbors than the British, but again, Spain was pretty neglectful of its land. America used inland Florida as its dumping ground, pushing Indians further south to get our southern states free of the native threat. It was also a haven for fugitive slaves and outlaws.

When the Lees moved to St. Marys about 1800, young John was six years old and without a father in his house. Even at his young age, he knew he wanted to make something of himself, provide for his Momma and sisters and vindicate the good name of his family, not to mention his strong drive to live the good life of the farmers and traders he saw around him in the early prosperity of South Georgia. Add an extra drive to show those unknown relatives in Virginia a thing or two to vindicate his dead father, and you've got a highly motivated youngster. The ambition he showed made his Momma proud but also got her worrying about him falling into the wrong crowd and taking foolish risks.

Following Levi's dying instructions, John's Momma faithfully had her children at St. Marys Methodist Church every time the doors opened. Through the church, John had a variety of father figures in some of the church-men. One of those was Mr. Jacob DeLoach, the local butcher.

Opportunity Strikes and Young Love

St. Marys was a rare small town of the day because it was prosperous enough to support a butcher. In most of the newer towns, if you wanted meat, you had to raise it, catch it, shoot it, or steal it yourself. Once you did, you'd better know how to dress it and cure it in a hurry, or it would rot in the hot, humid swelter of the South. Most country folks possessed these skills, but your more prosperous St. Marys-ites would come to Jacob to buy their meat all wrapped and ready to cook. The traders and shippers were all Jacob's customers, and they paid him very well to do a job most anyone could do for himself. Even though John wanted to be a planter someday, he was pretty sure he wanted to get started in the type of business which allowed him to make his money daily instead of seasonally like the farmers. Jacob was amused how young Mr. Lee would ask him questions of how to run a butcher shop, even on Sundays when talk was supposed to be focused on more heavenly things than dead animal flesh.

Butcher DeLoach was a kind man for the type of town he lived in, but he shrewdly saw St. Marys was a place where most anyone would do well by being the first of anything. So, he decided he'd be the first butcher in town. He sold his shop in Charleston to reinvest in his big chance. His first few years there were slim, but by 1800 he had a steady business and watched it grow every month. He lived alone at the town's only boarding house at the time. His butcher shop, a simple rough-log affair, had an unfinished second floor he planned to make into his residence someday.

Jacob had a soft heart for the poor and hungry; even more, though, he had an eye for hungry talent and a gift for making a good deal for himself. When John Lee had just turned eight, in 1802, Jacob approached John's Momma after church and asked if her son would like to be an apprentice. "I can teach him the business and pretty soon he can start helping you make ends meet. If he does a good job, I should be able to send a little meat home with him every now and then. I can't pay him any money to start with, but I can feed him for you, and you know he's about to hit the age where it's real hard to fill a boy. After a couple of years, I should be able to feed him *and* pay him a little something."

Mrs. Lee asked, "He's so young; do you think he can do the job?"

"Yes I do, and I believe he'll learn it quickly. He's in third grade, he's learned enough to be able to figure anything he needs. I see the way he looks at the meat in my store and I like the hunger in his eyes. He wants to make something of himself, and the younger he can start, the better he'll be. I'm sure of it. Whattaya say?"

Widow Lee thought just a minute and said, "'Idol hands *are* the Devil's workshop,' and I figure if you can make John busy before he's old enough to have all those other urges, I might just have a shot at raising a righteous man. Thank you, Mr. DeLoach."

If Momma needed little convincing, John needed even less. He was ready to start the next day, but Jacob insisted he wait 'til he finished third grade to go full time. If he had his lessons done, though, he could come in on school day afternoons and clean up the shop so he could have a feel for it before he went full-time. John couldn't sleep all night thinking about his new career in butchering and all the good things it would bring him.

John thought this venture would be just about perfect. He'd only had enough store-bought meat to know he liked it. He'd never handled money, but knew he could do it. He'd never worked with knives, and had never done more than whittle sticks, once nearly slicing off his thumb, but he was ready. He could just see himself with the big apron on, butcher knife in hand, greeting the customers and showing off the prettiest cuts of beef you ever saw. Maybe Mrs. Sylvia Campbell would come in, and she and her daughter Julia would swoon at his newfound skills.

The DeLoach meat market was a simple thing. It consisted of the showroom, which held cases of salt and sugar-cured and smoked meats of all kinds for the local ladies to inspect. Behind the counter, against the wall, was hung a wall full of quarters of cow, lamb, goat and all kinds of game animals from the local hunters. The hunters would bring in their kill, and for every two pounds of dressed meat they turned in, they'd get credit with Jacob for one pound of similar finished meats.

Behind the showroom was the cutting room, where the animals were dressed out for curing and aging. This room was where most of the work got done - the skinning, quartering, deboning, fat removal and all; next, the rubbing with the salt and sugar mix, and maybe some pepper or other spices when available, used to preserve meats while they aged. Once ready for aging, they'd be carried out back to the smokehouses, hung there for about thirty days (maybe more) 'til they were ready to go home with some lucky customer.

Before the school bell rang the next morning, John asked his teacher, Mrs. Duggar, if he could talk with her. He wasn't sure how to tell her his exciting news, because he always fancied himself her favorite student and knew she would be very disappointed to lose such a fine pupil. He thought she was hard on him, harder than on the others, but she always made him get his work right. He tended to be sloppy and impatient when he thought he could get away with it, but for some reason he always felt good about himself when he put in the effort and did good work as she always demanded. Come to think of it, maybe she wasn't going to miss him, but he was going to miss her. At first she acted very sad, saying, "John, you may not think so, but you're going to need to know more than you know now if you're going to do all you say you want to." His eyes drooped, and he got a big lump in his throat because he couldn't bear thinking Mrs. Duggar didn't believe he could conquer the world and wasn't already smart enough to do so.

Then she smiled and told him Mr. DeLoach had already talked to her, and together they'd arranged for her to continue giving him his work after third grade, and he would be able to apprentice, do his schoolwork at night, and still finish the sixth grade with his friends! Furthermore she said she told Mr. DeLoach she would only give the idea her blessing if he and John both promised they would make sure he did get a full sixth grade education. She said she knew he'd do just fine.

Now, how would he tell his friends of his good fortune, that he had a job? Especially, would this be the way he could finally impress Miss Julia Campbell? He'd tried everything since he met her to make her see how perfect he was for her; that is, of course, except for telling her. He'd already tried catching frogs, lizards and snakes, and shaking them in her face, but finally he may have just landed the big one! Maybe if he was gainfully employed she'd finally see how much he owned her heart. Or was it the other way around?

Julia didn't talk much to the boys, but her big brown eyes said it all for her. When her eyes smiled she could warm up a room; but when she was unhappy, her look could burn you from clear across the same room. She was needle thin, and her worn-out homemade clothes were always cleaner and a little sharper than the worn-out homemade clothes of the other girls in school. The Campbell clan was full of good folks who worked hard. John knew Julia'd make a good wife someday, but he just didn't know how to tell her and was too busy to bother. He knew this to be a mighty serious thought for an eight year old, but John was serious about life and knew someday he was going to be more than just a third-grader. John called her "Cami," short for Campbell. He thought it befitting because "Julia" was so formal, while "Cami" seemed to match her spunk and sparkle. She didn't mind, so it stuck with her.

Well, Cami must've been impressed, 'cause she told him she thought it was ". . . Nice" that John had a job, but there was something different about the way she blushed and sparkled when she said ". . . nice." John was confused but so excited about his job that it didn't matter.

When the school let out that day, he was first out the door and didn't stop running 'til he got to the butcher shop halfway down to the river.

John's first day as a butcher's apprentice was less than glorious. By time he got to DeLoach's, the usually happy Jacob was already in a foul mood because he'd just gotten in a big argument with Mrs. Brewer, who ran the local boarding house, over the hog bones he'd sold her for soup.

DeLoach didn't seem at all happy to see his new apprentice and just growled at him, "Clean up the cuttin' room." John set out to clean the place up with no instruction and no real idea what the finished product was supposed to look like. He saw blood everywhere and was pretty sure it all had to go, but wasn't sure where. He saw a bucket and knew Jacob had a well with a pitcher pump outside the back door. He guessed it might not be a bad idea to put some water in the bucket and swill it around on the bloody mess and maybe it would go away. So he primed the pump, filled his bucket, and went to work. Well, after far too long of working breathlessly to please his new boss, and making the mess worse before it was better, John successfully completed his first of many cleanups.

After inspecting John's work, Jacob just told him he took too long. "It's clean, but better make it quicker tomorrow." No instructions, no helpful hints.

When John walked into the schoolhouse next day, he came in all smug, sure the class desperately wanted to hear from their resident man-of-the-world. Surely Miss Cami would cling to every word of wisdom gleaned from the newly-minted eight-year-old fount of wisdom. At first they did, turning in their seats as he entered the room, anxious to hear from the world of employment. After all, John was the first third-grader to enter the working world that year. As he walked the aisle to his seat, though, he could hear coughing and gagging progressing through the room commensurate with his passing. Turns out ol' Jacob neglected to teach him how to get the stench of dead animal off his hands and clothes every day. John couldn't smell it on himself because he'd been wearing it for over twelve hours by then - not a very good way to advertise his new job at the butcher shop.

Then he heard Cami say, "Eeeeeewwww." He was crushed.

Embarrassed, he looked at Mrs. Duggar and asked if he could leave. She said, "No. You're here to learn, and you're going to learn. The rest of you are here to learn also and the first one I hear making fun of a man who's been working is going to get the hardest whack I've ever given with my hickory paddle. I will do us all a favor, though, and open the shutters so we can get some air in here." As she walked toward the shutters, she couldn't contain herself any longer, letting go with a snicker the whole class could hear. Then the class erupted, even John, who just learned a most valuable lesson: You might want to be a butcher, but you never want to smell like one! He would have to regale Cami with his stories of meat prowess another day.

That afternoon, Jacob smelled John right when he came in, and let out a hoot. "I guess I forgot to tell you butchers have to bathe more than once a month, unlike the rest of the townfolk." He showed John the bleach and soap and how to stretch the soap, which was also a valuable by-product of the store. He didn't want his hired help using up all the profits.

Then Jacob confessed, "I wasn't really angry yesterday when you came in, I just wanted you to figure things out for yourself. Mrs. Brewer and I made up our little spat 'cause I din't want you to think you can come and ask me every little thing around here. It'll drive me crazy and do you no good. You'll learn better, and faster if you'll use your eyes as much as you can. Watch me and see how I do, then try it. There's certain tricks of the trade I'm gonna pass on when time's right, but lots of it is just plain common sense, and I know you've got enough common sense to figure out a meat store. Heck, you might just figger how to do some things better'n I do. I might be needin' to worry about you openin' up your own shop across the street and puttin' me out of business!" John assured him he'd never do such a thing, but Jacob wisely knew how often an ambitious young man goes in competition with his mentor. I guess he was willing to take the risk.

Mr. DeLoach turned out to be a pretty good old guy to work for after all and must've been happy with the work he got from John. After two full years of apprenticeship and lots of lessons learned from one of the best and only butchers in South Georgia, John was made an employee and began to earn a decent wage *plus* plenty of leftover meat to take home to his Momma.

The butcher shop was a very resourceful enterprise. DeLoach raised some of his own livestock, including a few chickens, pigs, goats, sheep and cows. He bought from local farms when they had excess animals, and did a custom butcher and curing business for customers who supplied their own meat. He tanned and sold hides for shoes and other leather goods and rendered the carcasses for lard, soaps and oils for sale. He told John, "You see that little pig in the back yard? We're going to grow him up, and when we're done with him we're gonna sell everything but the squeal! Now, if you can figure how to sell that derned squeal too, we'll really be on to something!"

DeLoach had a good business going, but John couldn't understand how you'd earn a living just selling such a luxury as store-bought or store-cured meat to the tiny village of St. Marys. Then he saw the kind of money he could make selling cheap cuts of salt-cured animal parts to the ships coming in and out of port every day when the weather was fair enough to sail. On days the weather was too foul, he did a fine business supplying meat to sailors who'd give what was left of their meager wages (after it was mostly gambled, drank, or womanized up) for some of his best cuts. It was the kind of meat they would never receive in ship's rations, and he had a special price for the sailors.

He sold lots of jerky 'cause it never went bad. He also moved a lot of live hogs. What better way to keep meat fresh on board than to keep it on the hoof? Many boats on long trips at sea would take a hog or two on board. The hog would eat leftover food scraps until about halfway through an ocean crossing, then he'd become a good supply of fresh meat for the captain and crew. This was quite a treat for men sailors or passengers who'd been weeks with no meat other than tough ol' jerky and salted fish.

Now John understood why the curing room was so huge. It was 20 feet by 20 feet and always stacked floor to ceiling. He marveled at the volume this one man was doing all alone; DeLoach needed more help than John alone could give. John made a pledge to himself: if there was any possibility Ol' Jacob might ever entertain thoughts of bringing in a partner, his first thought would be of John Lee.

There was one very special breed of sailor DeLoach saved his very best cuts for: pirates. St. Marys was a frequent visiting point for the scum of the sea gang, because the Spaniards in Florida had made clear all known pirates would be hanged on sight. Of course, this law only applied to English and French pirates, but that was most of them. Since St. Marys was the first non-Spanish port for a stretch of about three-hundred miles, it was a welcome sight for weary pirates. Our laws said we didn't tolerate them either, but the pirate business meant so much because they spent so much. You could normally find the sheriff needed to take an afternoon off and go inland for some real important law business whenever the right pirates came to town. By time they got to St. Marys, if they had any money, they were ready to spend it; and they usually had money.

Mr. DeLoach was an honorable man, but he sure did like the pirate money. Even though they were pirates, they normally behaved when in port, and were even gentlemen, mostly, because they preferred causing their trouble on the high seas, out of reach of the law. But we knew who they were and what they were up to.

One of the most notorious pirates of high seas history was Jean Lafitte. As you can imagine, he was one Frenchman who found himself quite unwelcome in Spanish La Florida. Ol' Jean needed a friendly port and found he was limited to New Orleans, the Bahamas and St. Marys for the safety of himself and his men. In order to keep his head firmly attached to his shoulders, he would frequent St. Marys for his provisioning and shore leave. When in town, he would be sure to visit Jacob's store and usually bought out all the best cuts, and never haggled over price. He was always friendly and usually tipped John nicely for his very attentive service. Since he had so few places of refuge, you can bet Mr. Lafitte was a model citizen when in our port.

Jean Lafitte

I've already told you Jacob DeLoach was an upright, God-fearing Methodist, and I'd be remiss to forget telling you he ran his business thattaway. There's no way he could ever open his doors on a Sunday, it being the Lord's day and all. In fact, he wouldn't allow John to lift a finger in the shop on a Sunday, and there were no exceptions . . . unless, well, maybe if one of the ships happened to be leaving port on the Lord's day and had to do a little last-minute provisioning. Now what kind of Christian would let sailors go off to sea without adequate food? So, while he wasn't open on Sunday, Jacob did have a small side door to which a needy ship's cook could bring his dollars or gold if he was just so desperate.

Seemed the Christian thing to do, right?

Of course Methodists don't drink either. Never. But they did have a customer or two who imbibed. You know how those Episcopalians are. Well, sometimes a customer might just demand a little rye to help him with his decision, and Jacob found a way to accommodate such customers.

There were the poor subsistence farmers from out in the boondocks. They rarely came to town and didn't need a lot of store bought meat. But when they did make the trip, those poor folks almost never had any money to buy food. So, Jacob would do just a little bit of barter business when they brought in their home distilled "tonics" for trading. He called it an "outreach to the poor."

John noticed from time to time one of the tonic bottles would be missing from the shelf when he arrived for work, but Jacob always maintained that stuff was just for some of those weak-willed customers who might like the devil's brew.

Jacob's word was all John needed.

Life Lessons

John got through the sixth grade, and life seemed to be shaping up for him. Looked as if he'd found a place to plant roots, but something else was stirring inside.

Shortly after his 'graduation' from Mrs. Duggar's protective care and nurture, John was starting to feel really big. After all, he was twelve years old by then. Like all good teachers, Mrs. Duggar gave lots of valuable lessons involving more than just readin', writin', and figgerin', and so did Jacob DeLoach. One in particular stuck with John for life.

"You're done with sixth grade now, John," Jacob said. "I'm guessin' I should say congratulations or make a big deal, but I'm not gonna. That's because you're still in a school, and you're never going to get out of this school; it's called LIFE. And your teacher isn't Mrs. Duggar, and it's not me. It's everybody you see every day of your life. You learn from them and they learn from you. Some are going to teach you by showing you what you want to be. Others will show you exactly what you DON'T want to be, or think, or do. But everybody has something to teach you.

"In the same way," he went on, "you are teaching everyone around you, young and old. The main thing, maybe the only thing, you want most others to learn from you is they can trust you. If you don't have the people around you knowing they can trust you, you've got nothin'."

Jacob continued, "You see this meat scale over here?"

"Yes, sir."

"See this weight?"

"Yes, sir."

"How much is this weight?"

"One pound."

"How 'bout this one?"

"Quarter pound."

"And this?"

"One ounce."

"How do you know what you just told me?"

A little nervous now because he couldn't see where the conversation was going, John stuttered, "B-b-because you taught me."

"Well, that's right. And every time a customer comes in this store and I flop one of those weights on my scale, I'm telling Mrs. MacLeish or ol' Mrs. Green it's a weight she can rely on, and these customers only 'know' it because they trust me. Do you know how easy it would be for me to make a set of weights I could use to double my profits?"

"No, sir," seemed the proper answer.

"If I just made my weights ten percent lighter no one would know it, and if my profits are about ten percent after all my costs of doing business come out, the extra ten percent would be a double in profits, mighty nice, wouldn't it, boy?"

"No, sir," seemed to fit this occasion, too.

"Why not?" DeLoach just kept pressing.

"Because it wouldn't be honest, even if the customer didn't know."

"Good answer. And if I was to cheat a customer, and she didn't know, it would leave only me knowing, and it would eat my innards from the inside out, and it'll do the same for you. It's called conscience, and you always want your conscience clean because it's always doin' one of two things: it's either leavin' you alone, or it's eatin' at your innards. Maybe I don't know much, but I do know you don't want your innards eaten from the inside out, do you?"

John confidently replied, "No, sir."

"Let me show you another thing." John sure did wish he'd just say 'Now get to work,' but no such luck.

Slapping a piece of smoked venison on the scale, he asked, "What's this weigh?"

John read the scale and said "One pound three ounce, sir."

Jacob yanked it off the scale, thrust it at John saying, "Now you weigh it."

Placing it carefully just as he'd been taught - part of the show, the all-important "presentation" for the customer, John said, "Why, it's an ounce short of a pound."

Jacob smiled, "You didn't watch my thumb, did you?"

"Your thumb?" John quizzed.

"Yup, oldest butcher trick since invention of the scale. Come around my side of the counter and take a look."

As John obeyed the latest command, he could easily see DeLoach's fat thumb barely pressing the scale to make the meat grow. "You can make this old piece of a dead deer carcass weigh most anything you want. But you only want it to be the true weight for two reasons. First is, these are good people here, and they're going to be good to you if you're good to them. And you wanna always be able to look 'em straight in the eye and know you never lied or cheated anyone. Second is your innards. Don't ever forget yer innards. It's real hard to sleep at night when yer innards are getting' eaten out."

Jacob continued, "You know the Golden Rule?"

"Yes, sir."

"Mrs. Duggar teach it to ya?"

"Yes, sir, and my Momma."

"Say it." Jacob demanded softly.

"Do unto Others as You Would Have Them Do unto You," John easily recited.

"If, when you close up this shop every night, you look in that mirror, saying the Golden Rule to yourself, then say, 'I did it,' then you're running your business right."

"Now get to work," he said abruptly.

John almost ran to the cutting room, but as he was half out the door he heard old Jacob say, "Someday I'll teach you how some of the guys add water to the sausage. You don't have to sell much water at the sausage price to be doing real well." John was real sure he'd learned enough for one day as he sprinted to the smokehouse to pack an order for Mrs. O'Donnell.

Off To War

Having grown up in a hard-scrabble way, separated from his deep-rooted, almost noble, family back in Virginia, John, now eighteen, was hungry to get himself started in life. Though a master butcher, he wanted some new experience away from St. Marys and had a very strong desire to prove himself a man, and things were stirring in the bigger world. He said "Good bye" to a tearful Cami and promised he'd be back, but she really didn't believe him. She knew he was going to have to settle his wanderlust and figured she'd be an old woman before he ever came back to St. Marys.

Now a master butcher, John had just enlisted to fight in what became known as the War of 1812, when England and America got all tangled up yet again. Because he was a young man, he felt the urge of so many young men to test himself on the battlefield. Once done, he'd come back to St. Marys, become a half owner of *DeLoach and Lee*, marry Julia Campbell, and build his life in St. Marys. There would be time for settlin' down later.

To most folks, the War of 1812 was a mix-up between America and England with a little bit of French and Canadian involvement thrown in. Most of it happened up North, but if you look to the South, it got even messier down there. In Florida, the setting of the lesser-told story, we managed to get the Spaniards, Indians, and even Florida's numerous fugitive slaves involved in the fray.

In due course, John came under the spell of John McIntosh, a wealthy, charismatic Florida planter with powerful connections to Washington, DC. This opportunity was not to be missed, and John was to take part in taking over Florida and becoming a soldier in the "Patriot War." Though a lowly private, he was promised he'd be a wheel in the establishment of the "Republic of Florida," all in the name of service to the United States of America. McIntosh was convinced he could become President of the new country of Florida and had just about recruited enough young and hungry foot soldiers to launch him into his rightful place in history.

Spanish Florida was getting to be a problem for the U.S. We didn't mind Spain owning the spit of land to the south as long as it was nothing more than a mosquito-infested backwater with nothing to offer but Indians, rattlesnakes, cotton-mouths and gators. In 1693, Spain's King Charles II announced he would harbor fugitives on the peninsula, thus allowing Florida to be a refuge for runaway slaves, maroons, they were called. His invitation was just fine as long as most slaves had to run from at least as far as the Carolinas, and had no idea where Florida was or the fact they could gain freedom there. Well, as farming grew and prospered further south, slavery followed, and came closer and closer to, yes, Florida. Now, with huge cotton plantations in coastal South Georgia, the runaways were sometimes just a good day or two walk to freedom!

Additionally, the mosquito-infested backwater was starting to develop and Florida was showing a lot more potential than it used to. Just a few years earlier, we'd decided we needn't worry about Spain being our neighbor because the entire territory was living in depraved subsistence. Then, Florida began to show potential as an exporter of lumber to Europe. It was well established that upland cotton could grow there, and the new cotton gin made it possible to grow it profitably. Florida was starting to look like something to those who could see through its current shambles.

By 1812, we were getting worried about Spain as a neighbor. Though Florida was an unimportant outpost for King Ferdinand VII, we really didn't know how hard Spain would or could fight against a hostile force wanting to take it. We worried said hostile force wouldn't want Florida for Florida, but as the back door into our growing, prospering, newly-wealthy land called America.

How long before England's King George III would come calling from the south? What if Napoleon was not as broke as he seemed, or some new Napoleon of his same ilk decided he wanted to control the world again?

America was still very young, but it was already showing the world a thing or two about how to produce and grow a new country. How long could America's farmers afford the steady drain of their slave-property running down through the Okefenokee to freedom? How long could America be safe without controlling and protecting entire Atlantic and Gulf shoreline?

John McIntosh knew he had the answer, and his answer was . . . John McIntosh! John Lee and about three hundred other dirt-poor and hungry Southern lads were each promised five hundred acres and a chance to gain glory by hitching to Mr. McIntosh's wagon and taking Florida from the Spaniards. By enticing the Seminole Indians and the maroons to take arms, McIntosh was able to mount a formidable force relative to the forces Spain had encamped to protect its interests. McIntosh had only to hope Spain didn't decide to reinforce its garrisons, mostly in Fernandina, St. Augustine, Apalachicola and Pensacola. If it did, the rag-tag army of invaders would be swamped quickly unless McIntosh could convince the U.S. to come to the rescue.

Maybe through Andrew Jackson, President Madison could be influenced to intervene.

The invasion of Florida was a fairly easy victory over a small part of Middle Florida. A piece from roughly Gainesville north to the state line, west to somewhere around Live Oak and east to somewhere close to Cowford was ceded over by Spain in 1812 to the Republic of Florida, with McIntosh as its President. As history tells, though, it was to be very short lived.

Because of his skills at butchery, John Lee was initially charged with feeding the troops instead of killing the enemy. He groused mightily about it, but when he saw a few of his friends come back to camp all mutilated Indian-style, he thought maybe he was where he ought to be. Not that there was a whole lot of regular meat to feed this army, but since so many of the soldiers were woodsmen, they had a steady supply of the bounty of the Florida woods: deer, eagles, hawks, turkeys, rabbits, squirrels, coons, otters, hogs, gators, snakes, gopher turtles, soft shell turtles, wild cattle, fish of all kinds; whatever moved they could kill and eat. John was expert at butchering, cooking, and preserving all of the bounty with minimal waste. His preserving skills had little chance to shine, though, 'cause the meat was usually gone as soon as it came into camp.

John Lee and his small band of fellow McIntosh mercenaries were beginning to pick out their five hundred acres and plan for new lives in the untamed land of flowers. What promise it showed! In one of his forays, John had fallen for the settlement at Upper Mineral Springs, perched on the beautiful Suwannee River, with a crystal clear spring, vast virgin heart pine forests, huge cypress heads and good soils for farming. What a perfect place to stake a claim and build a life! There was nothing there yet but for a few raggedy settlers around the spring and along the river. John saw where the river and its high bluffs would provide safety from flood and enemies. Couldn't the land around Upper Mineral Springs grow up to be just like St. Marys? He could already see the vast farms, fat cows and a yard full of happy young'uns underfoot. Oh, the spoils of war! What more could an eighteen-year-old soldier of fortune hope for? Made him think of Cami and settling down.

But maybe it wasn't supposed to be so easy.

Remember the Indians and fugitive slaves McIntosh used to beat the Spanish? Well, seems they didn't want to go back to living in the swamps under McIntosh any more than they liked being under Spanish rule. It was a big problem. And there were lots of these folks. And they weren't happy because they didn't think we'd treated them too well.

Turns out, McIntosh wasn't much more than a useful pawn for America, and James Madison couldn't be bothered by McIntosh's antics with his hands so full of fighting the *real* War of 1812. Madison only kept forces in Florida to keep the Brits at bay. He really couldn't be bothered by the Indian squabbles, runaway slave problems, and all the other problems McIntosh had used to catapult himself into royalty. Real U.S. forces came in to clean up the mess, but their only real objective was to push the Indians far enough south into Spanish Florida to make life safe for Americans all the way down to the southern boundaries of Georgia.

Once the northernmost Indian outposts were at least fifty miles south of the Georgia and Alabama lines, Madison was happy the U.S. borders were secure enough for peaceful settling to resume to the 31st latitude.

As soon as the Republic of Florida requested aid from the Motherland, it faded into historic obscurity, and the land went back to Spain, but only temporarily. The U.S. soon began a diplomatic campaign to convince Spain it really didn't need the filthy, insect- and Indian-infested peninsula called "Land of Flowers." America could defend it better and we would always be friends to Spain, anyway.

While in Florida, John witnessed some expeditions in which some of the innocent settlers were treated pretty shabbily by this army of Mr. McIntosh. There's reason to believe John and his fellow soldiers of fortune were ordered to do some things to these people he wasn't very proud of, but we'll never know because John never spoke of it.

Under pressure of several fierce attacks of retribution by Indians and maroons, John Lee and most of his fellows soldiers of fortune made a hasty retreat back to St. Marys in 1814. Some of the tougher American boys, and the ones who had nothing to go back to, stayed to take their chances in the Land of Flowers.

Young Adulthood in St. Marys

John wasn't deterred. He knew he was young, and it was simply time to try again. He would return home to St. Marys, get back to work in the butcher shop and claim Cami for his own, and life would go smoothly.

His mother was ailing badly when he arrived home, and she passed away quickly thereafter. It was as if she was hanging on to see her John one last time. She had built as good a life as she could and got to see her three children reach adulthood. She'd faithfully upheld her promise to Levi to raise their children well and equip them to make their way in the world. The Rev. Jim Spencer told John since St. Marys Methodist didn't have its own graveyard, arrangements had been made for her final resting place to be in the Green - Miller Cemetery on Cumberland Island, the place she loved so and dreamed of someday living. This arrangement seemed odd to John, but he knew how his Momma loved the island, and he figured she would be happy. About two weeks later, Levi's very old Uncle Henry from Virginia sent ten dollars with a note saying, "This should be enough to cover the funeral costs and just a little to spare." John never knew how Henry knew of her passing, nor why he sent the money. Maybe not all those Virginia folks were as opposed to his Momma as he'd assumed. He vowed to one day meet his Virginia kinfolks and find answers to so many questions he had about his people.

Cami seemed to have other plans as well. While John was off on his war-time adventure, she went and promised her hand to a new man in town, a sea captain's son who worked with his father on the tall ships.

Now John had lost his two life-loves: his Momma and Cami, whom he figured was just gonna be his someday. Yes, she'd make a good wife, and things should be just fine with her, but maybe in this new, burgeoning town there could be a real love match for John. Strangely, he felt alright about his new reality. He'd just try again. He set off to work.

At least the butcher shop was there for him. It was still every bit the opportunity it was before he went off to war. DeLoach had a new apprentice: a skinny redheaded lad named Jimmy Jones, who reminded John of himself when he was ten. He thought they'd get along just fine. John returned none too soon for Jacob, though, because the old man was beginning to slow down a bit, and really didn't know how he'd handle the work as it came in faster while he moved slower and wore out easier.

DeLoach and Lee Butchery was off and running. John was able to buy into his part with a combination of his meager savings and yet another gift from his unknown great uncle Henry. How Henry knew John was ready to buy into a business and why he supported a grand-nephew he never met was a mystery, but John was very grateful. Had Henry been helping the family all along? Was he an invisible hand of support his Momma never divulged? John vowed to someday meet this man and find out.

The three butchers made a great team. John could get all the heavy work done, and Jacob was still great at chewin' the fat with his customers, the one thing John felt he just didn't have time for anymore. Jimmy just filled in at every job there. Business was good and they were on their way. Jacob didn't pocket Lee's investment, but plowed it back to expand the operation so it could handle more volume, and hopefully stay just dominant enough in St. Marys to ward off the constant threat of a new competitor.

Competition's alright, but no self-respecting businessman is gonna invite it. Lee figured he had to always offer the best service and keep the overhead trimmed to the bone, just like the meat. This way he might make sure any new butcher thinking about coming to St. Marys would just keep moving on to the next town. It would devastate Jacob if he ever heard St. Marys had a great opening for a new butchery because the old one had gotten fat and lazy and took the customers for granted. May it never be so!

Young Jimmy was valuable to John as more than just an employee. Once John got over his loss of Cami, he found his eye turning toward another. John's new love was Jimmy's sister Elizabeth. She was only fifteen and John had just turned twenty-two. She was old enough to be legally wed so long as her father vouched for her. John felt like he was falling hard for her, yet all he'd done was flirt with her a few times at the store and escorted her to Sunday dinner on the grounds a time or two. He knew it was too soon and knew he was insane, but he felt sure he was going to be asking her father for Lizzie's hand.

He knew he liked everything about her. She had a natural feminine shape and her beautiful almond-shaped eyes could cut holes in his heart. She wasn't just pretty, though. She just oozed of the pioneer spirit of "Let's go build this world." She'd finished sixth grade six years behind John and was sure she was one of Mrs. Duggar's best students. Of course John was too big to pay much attention to her when she was six and he was a working man of the world at twelve, but they had been in the same one-room schoolhouse together, if for only a short time.

One day Mr. Jones was in the store. Upon seeing him, John told Jacob he'd handle this customer. Visibly nervous, John tended Mr. Jones' meat needs. When it was all packed up, John asked him into the backyard so he could show him something. Once there, nervous as one of his pigs in the butcher's pen, John said, "Sir, I don't have anything to show you, 'cept I want you to see I have a heart full of love for your daughter and I'm real sure she's the one for me. I'd be real honored if you'd allow me to ask Lizzie for her hand, as I know I could make her a real fine home."

The sweat beaded on John's brow.

He continued, "We've got this business going here, and Jimmy can tell you I'm honest with him, and a good boss. Jimmy has a good shot at being a part of it, and it would be a great family business, and if Lizzie doesn't say 'Yes' to me, or if you forbid me, I don't know what I will do or how I could go on. I've got savings, probably more than any of the other fellas in town except the rich boys. I know I haven't courted Lizzie long enough to be asking a man for his daughter, but I really do love Lizzie more than I can say, and we'll have a real big family and give you lots of grandkids."

By this point, his shirt was soaked.

"And I'm going to buy a farm so we can supply more of our own meat, and when we do, I'm gonna build a big house for Lizzie and all the kids, and the house is going to have glass windows and a big porch, and you and Mrs. Jones can come live with us if you want, and I know I love her because I'm here babbling to you like an idiot, and you're just letting me rattle on! I gotta shut my mouth, but all I can say is PLEASE, Mr. Jones, PLEASE!"

Jones just stared back at him. He forced himself to pause and intensify John's agony as much as humanly possible. He knew this young man better than John thought because the whole town had been able to watch him working the butcher shop since he was eight. He knew how John had run off and fallen into the folly of McIntosh's army, and how he'd come home. He knew John because he was one of the men at St. Marys Methodist who had been on the ready to help his family in their tenuous circumstances; but he'd never had to because John, with all his human faults, had worked himself tirelessly to make sure their needs were met. John had no idea he had a safety net from the Methodist men and was sure his Momma was far too proud to accept if they had tried to help.

In short, James Jones was having one of the proudest moments of his life. To make it humorous, he also well knew John Lee was a young man of few words. Oh, he could talk, but he was much more the strong, silent type than this babbling idiot Jones just witnessed.

"John," he said, "You're one of the finest young men I know, and I think I know you better than you think I do. I've watched you grow up. I've seen your impulses, mistakes and successes. You've got a lot of 'em for your age. I also watched how you honored your Momma while she was alive, and how you've been watchin' after your sisters since your momma's been gone. And because of all this, I couldn't be happier to approve of you asking Lizzie for her hand. She's young, but just like you, she's chompin' at the bit to get started in her life, and I have a hunch you're the one she has her designs on. Of course you have my approval!"

With that, the two men embraced. Neither of them were the hugging type, so they were glad no one saw. Jacob, Jimmy, and Mrs. Brewer didn't let on how wrong they were about their "nobody saw" assumption.

As they parted, James told John, "One more thing. Jacob tells us proudly how you make extra effort to treat your customers by the Golden Rule."

"Yes, Sir."

Then James Jones got suddenly stern, even curt, "Never forget, the Golden Rule applies to your wife, too."

John didn't know if he'd been warned, threatened, or encouraged by Jones's final admonition. All in all, though, he thought the meeting went pretty well.

If you think John was nervous when he asked Jones for his daughter's hand, he was just learning what nervous was when it was time for him to ask Lizzie. He planned it all out. After Sunday dinner on the grounds he was going to take her on a walk down Osborne Street to St. Marys Street.

They'd walk along the river, holding hands, and eventually, when the time was just right, he'd say something just right, she'd melt in his arms, and they'd live happily ever after.

But, "OH, GOD, what are the right words?" Every time John thought of this horrible moment, his mind would go blank and he had no idea what words to say. Even if he'd have enough control of his body to make words - the *right* words - how in the world could he force them out in any sort of meaningful sequence?

He'd rather be taking his chances in the middle of an Indian massacre! How could this strapping young adult man with all his life experiences be so afraid of a little morsel of a person, who weighed under one-hundred pounds soaking wet, and was six years his junior? How could she be making him feel like he was burning up with fever? Was she evil? "Dear God, are you telling me to run away and she's not right for me?" Now, John was a good Methodist, so he'd done lots of praying in his time, and he felt like he'd seen some pretty direct answers to prayers before, but never ANYTHING like this. Could God Himself be sending a message? Poor John had never sweat so much in his life, and it was still early spring.

Sunday arrived. Church bells pealed, calling all the faithful to worship.

John got dressed in his good pair of pants and his good shirt.

His sister Susannah was ready early (Sarah was married by then and met her siblings at the church each Sunday). Susannah seemed perkier that day than she'd been since Momma died. John thought, "How could she possibly be more annoying?"

It was time to go.

John felt strangely like he did when it was time to walk to the church for Momma's funeral: lump in throat, pit in stomach. Why dread this so much?

Once the church was in sight, he thought he'd hurl, but fortunately he hadn't eaten anything since Thursday night, and there was nothing left in him to hurl. He reminded himself at least he didn't smell like a butcher, or did he? No, he only made some mistakes once.

Walking in the door, he spotted the Jones pew. Lizzie turned just in time to see him. Their eyes met and suddenly there was no one else in the church, no one else in the world but Susan Elizabeth Jones and John Levi Lee. How could even God himself make a creature so beautiful? And it being Sunday, of course Lizzie was wearing her good dress. Now her Sunday dress musta been something special, 'cause it sure 'nuff put a spell on ol' John. Even in his old age, he'd talk dreamily about his Lizzie in her nice dress, but even then, he could never be any more descriptive than to choke out, "It was . . . yellow."

Of course, with one look she could tell something was wrong with John, and felt sorry for him. She worried something really bad might have happened. Was he carrying a heavy load of sin? He looked for all the world like he'd gotten some really bad news or eaten some really bad food.

The organist was playing "How Firm a Foundation" on the little pipe organ as one of the church youngsters turned the crank to pump the bellows full and ready to send just the right amount of air in just the right pipe to make all those wheezy yet glorious sounds, but John could hardly hear it today. He did remember praying "God, please make this a firm foundation I'm laying here today, and help me get through this day, and help Lizzie think this is as good an idea as I do. Amen."

Strangely, he did feel better now, since he was sitting beside Lizzie. Maybe they would take their walk and maybe the right words, laced with just the right amount of sweetness, and maybe a dove will fly by as a sign from above, and maybe, maybe, maybe . . .

John always tried to pay attention to the sermon so he could discuss it with the older folks at dinner on the grounds. They always liked quizzing him at the store later in the week, and he liked being ready. Today, he couldn't even pretend. Midway through Brother Jim's sermon, when Lizzie slyly slipped her hand into his, his heart just about gave out. With his clubby right and her tiny left hands locked together and hidden between their two legs, he thought surely he was having a foretaste of heaven right there in the pew!

The faithful recessed to "Oh, For a Thousand Tongues to Sing," while John prayed simply to keep his one tongue from saying something really stupid. Dinner on the grounds was its usual Sunday success. John made excuses for not eating of the bounteous feast in a manner befitting a twenty-two year old. He was only able to choke down a little smoked turkey from *DeLoach and Lee Butchery* and had a little of Mrs. Jones's peach cobbler. It calmed him a bit.

The day was beautiful, with spring springing and birds chirping. The whole town, with one exception, was relaxed. John's knees were wobbling at the thought of the fearsome task he had ahead, but he knew he had to do it. He'd already let Cami slip through his fingers, and now he saw it was for the best. The only strength he had remaining came from remembering his Momma shaking her crooked little worn out finger at him saying, "Remember, the faint heart never won the fair maid." Now he knew what she meant and knew it was time to be a man, but it still wasn't easy.

As soon as they could leave, John and Lizzie took the planned route to the river and enjoyed the glorious day. They walked the loading dock as far as they could without getting wet, then turned around and headed back with nothing more important accomplished than skipping a few stones. Finally they turned back up Osborne Street toward St. Marys Methodist, all the while passing any number of convenient places to sit and have a chat.

John finally decided he just had to do it. If she said, "No," it would just have to be.

"Lizzy?" He had to start somewhere.

"Yes," she said sweetly, still looking forward as they walked.

"What do you think about . . . life?" ("CRAP!" he thought, "Not what I planned to say!")

"I guess . . . I'm all for it."

They kept walking. John picked up the pace.

"But, what about . . . your . . . life?"

She turned and curiously set her gaze into his eyes and whispered, "I'm all for that one, too."

He managed to choke out, "Good" . . . and with both of them now in an eye-lock, he suddenly blurted, "Do you think I could spend the rest of my life with you and you spend the rest of yours with me, and we'd have a house and I'd provide for us real well, and we'd have kids and horses, and dogs, and . . . and now I'm blathering just like when I talked to your father!"

Silence. Awkward silence.

"You talked to my father? And what did you talk about?"

Suddenly, remembering how well his talk with James Jones went and how he finally got his tongue under control, he felt more comfortable and knew he had the ability to pour his heart to Lizzie, and could even form coherent words. He felt a strength and confidence suddenly welling up inside him, a strength he couldn't explain, but a real strength nonetheless.

"Lizzie, I told your father last week how much I love you and want to spend my life with you and provide for you and make you the happiest lady in all of America." Now with confidence bordering on boldness, he added, "I've thought about this a lot and I know it's too soon, but I really think you and I are meant for each other and we can live our lives better together than we can live 'em apart.

"Elizabeth Jones, have you ever thought about life in those terms?"

Lizzie teared up as you might expect, and said, "Of course I have! I've dreamed about you since you were such a big sixth grader and you didn't know I existed. I prayed you'd pay attention to me, even if it was just by you being mean to me. I craved to know you were aware of me, and now I guess I can feel pretty sure at least you know who I am, and it makes me the happiest girl in the world."

Just then their walk brought them back to the church yard. Expecting everyone to have gone home, they were surprised to see the yard still full and more surprised to see the entire congregation looking their way. Reverend Spencer stepped out of the crowd asking, "Well?"

"Well, what?" John queried.

"Well, did she accept your offer?"

"I don't rightly know yet. We had a pretty nice talk, but I never got a straight answer. Maybe I should try again." Without hesitation, John took Lizzie's hand, got down on one knee and asked her to marry him, right there in front of God and the entire congregation of First Methodist. Then he noticed half his friends and customers from First Presbyterian and First Baptist were in the mix, too.

"OF COURSE I WILL," shrieked Lizzie! And the whole place, led by Reverend Spencer, let out the whoopingest "HALLELUJAH" you ever heard.

Next ensued the biggest frenzy of hugging and kissing St. Marys ever witnessed. You'da thought all those straight-laced Protestants were auditioning for parts in a naughty French tease show! But all with perfect decorum, of course.

Just then, Susannah lunged at John from the crowd and gave him a huge hug, another rare public display of affection for these straight-laced folks. She said, "I've been bursting to tell you this all week. Everybody in town knew except you two! We're so happy for you and just know you will have a wonderful life together. I know if Momma were here to see you and Lizzie so happy, she would be happy, too, and would bless you two in your new lives together."

When it was all over, on his way home with the Joneses, it occurred to John his father-in-law to be must've let a cat out of the bag, otherwise why was the church lot still full and waiting to hear Lizzie's verdict? When asked, Jones just started laughing.

"You know the big hug we did, and were both real happy no one saw?"

"Yes sir."

"Well, we were wrong. I kept my pledge, didn't even tell Mrs. Jones. But DeLoach, Jimmy, and Mrs. Brewer made no promises. Unknown to us, they were watching from the big crack in the cutting room door. They not only saw it, but heard every word. Jacob and Jimmy never gave it another thought until Thursday when customers came in and started asking about the big question on Sunday. Mrs. Brewer was careful to tell only a few people; just the ones she thought would be sure to tell everybody else!

"Turns out this whole town except Lizzie was in on the drama of your big question. More than anything else, if I was you, I'd take it as a sign this whole town loves you and really cares for you. Even though they're not related, that's family, and it's what family can do for you. In your shop you're never gonna know for sure if they like you just 'cause you put up a good cut of meat, or do they like you for who you are?

"What you saw here is real life. These folks care for you and your new little family, and don't you forget it. You're blessed if you have a big family of your own, but even if you have no kin and no money, you can still have a rich life. You're an ambitious fellow, and it's especially important for you to keep this in mind. If you can learn this lesson young, you'll be sure to not end up as the old miser who wakes up and sees how wretched he is in his old age with all his gold but no warm folks to be his friends.

"Life's like a wild stallion, John, and it's an especially hard ride in these new lands. You'd do real well to remember this lesson your entire life."

John was starting to like his future father-in-law already.

John promised Mr. Jones he wouldn't marry Lizzie until he had a place for them to stay. This promise proved a challenge because of the boom going on in town. He was disheartened. Mrs. Brewer was chock-full with a waiting list. She said she'd put the Lees on top of her list but none of the tenants looked like they'd be leaving anytime soon. And every homeowner in town with a spare room had it rented out in this burgeoning burg. The future Lees were in a big hurry to "set up housekeeping."

John complained about his problem to Mr. DeLoach, who said "Why don't you just move in above the shop? I'm getting too old to mess with building it out, and I'm just as happy three blocks away at Mrs. Brewer's. You're going to be putting a lot of hours in here. Nothin' better than living at your work if you're going to make a go of it, especially when you start having your young'uns. Our ol' pitcher pump can supply all the water you and the butcher shop can use. You got the privy out back, so what else do you need?"

John was real excited about the idea and said he'd get started building it out right away.

To this Jacob howled, "What are you talking about? To make it right for your little lady will take you weeks, maybe months, I thought you were in a hurry! Any couple I ever saw in a hurry didn't need anything but a bed and a couple of sea chests for storage, and they didn't really need the sea chests. Maybe a table would be nice, too. You outfit the place like I just said and if Lizzie ain't ready to take her vows soon as you show it to her, then maybe she's not the one for you. You've got room up there to make a bedroom and a sitting area, but why not live there just a while before you start building so you can decide just how you want to do it? I may be just an old fool bachelor, so I may not know anything. But if you two think you're right, and the time's right, there ain't nuthin' wrong with being in a hurry."

John borrowed the meat wagon, hitched it up to the old swayback mare, and raced through town to his old house. There he got Momma's old bed and the chest of drawers Levi built for her. The old mattress had gone kinda flat, but they could stuff more Spanish moss in it and fluff it up some. He loaded the furniture and galloped the poor horse all the way back to the shop. Mrs. Brewer added a spare two foot round table one of her tenants had left years ago. Jacob threw in a couple of homemade bowback chairs from the shop. The new apartment looked done!

Needless to say, Lizzie was sold. She'd been raised in a pretty nice house but she knew her parents started just about the same way. Besides, she knew with all this free furniture, John would still have all the money he'd saved in his few years in business. He told her it was getting near to two-hundred dollars, so why should they set their savings back by buying furniture and paying rent somewhere when this would do just fine?

She got so excited at seeing her new house, she grabbed hold of John and locked her arms around him and he around her. They were giddy . . . Giddy led to frisky . . . and frisky led to . . . Lizzie pushing John back yet still holding on in a way that seemed to say, "We've gone far enough" and "Whatever you do, don't let go" all at the same time. Breathlessly, she said, "We gotta go see Reverend Jim."

The good Parson was just about to close up the church when they careened up in the meat wagon. "Don't you two look like a couple of lovebirds?" He said, not expecting to hear what came next.

Lizzie said, "Rev, we want you to marry us,"

"NOW!" John blurted.

Spencer knew both of them well and knew they had the character he looked for in young folks. He also knew how foolish it was to take the leap so quickly, because he also knew just why they were in such a hurry.

As they rushed into the church, Lizzie reminded the reverend, "You know I've just turned sixteen, don't you," as if to offer proof of her full maturity and ability to make her own decisions.

After about an hour of trying to throw buckets of emotional cold water on these two to cool them off at least a little, Reverend Spencer was either fully convinced of their love or fully worn down by their pleas. He remembered how he felt when he met his Sally and how maybe they shouldn't have waited so long. He was sure their engagement of a whole three months was nothing but a waste of time!

He conjured a plan to go with them to see Mr. and Mrs. Jones. His deal was if Daddy approved, well then, he would tie the knot. He also told John his sisters Susannah and Sarah must be part of it and must approve, or they would have to find another Parson.

John and Lizzie Lee enjoyed their first night above the butcher shop to the fullest. No fancy wedding trip necessary.

The nearest thing to a wedding gift was, John confided in Lizzie, "You know how I told you I had almost two-hundred dollars saved?"

"Yeah."

"Well, I didn't tell you everything. When I add it up, it comes to $235.47. Baby, we're on our way! Someday we're going to own this town, or some other town anyway!"

The honeymoon continued.

Growth in So Many Ways

The sun came up.

As usual, Mr. DeLoach wandered into the shop right after his breakfast of grits and *DeLoach's* ham with Mrs. Brewer at the boardinghouse. What a creature of habit he was.

The only thing different this morning was, as he walked in, John and Lizzie were walking down the stairs from above.

John had practiced how he was going to say something grand like, "Mr. DeLoach, meet Mrs. John Lee," but you know John well enough now to know he was no master of eloquence when excited. He just stood there all tongue-tied and blurry-eyed, and Lizzie's smile said it all. She ran the last half of the stairs and jumped into Jacob's arms and kissed his cheek, saying, "Thank you for all you've done for John - and for me. We love you and want to make the rest of your life easy because you took a chance on John when he was just a whip of a boy. We're going to make sure putting your trust in John was the best investment you ever made."

DeLoach thought he liked what he saw, but he had to ask, "Y'all did this right, didn't you? You let Spencer take part in it before you . . . you know what I mean."

John was working on another noble statement when Lizzie jumped right in and said, "Of course we did. You know John'd be shot dead this morning by my Daddy if we weren't all proper, don't you?"

Jacob, replied, "Well, yeah. He's white as a ghost, but I don't think he's dead." They all laughed.

Word travelled, and all of St. Marys just happened to drop by today. Not to be nosy and check out the new couple, you know, but to "buy just one more pork chop we needed for 'guests' tonight," or some such excuse. It was the best day of sales for a whole year. The Lees took it as a good omen for good things to come.

Mrs. Brewer and Reverend Spencer almost had to call a town meeting to squelch the rumors flying about the new Lees, but they got it simmered down, and the new couple was handily accepted by the town; well, at least four months later they were accepted when it became obvious Lizzie wasn't gaining any weight yet. As busy and bustling as the town was, it seemed never too busy to stir up a scandal.

What a team they were. Lizzie made the store look more like a market. She added display windows and a feminine touch. When John and Jacob made fun of her for adding all the "silly stuff" around their shop, she'd look square at them and ask, "Is it the men, or women who bring the money in here to you?" This retort would cause both of them to nervously wipe their hands on their aprons and suddenly remember they had some more meat cutting or curing to do.

Lizzie worked with the wives, young and old, teaching them new ways to fix the great cuts of meats they could get from *DeLoach & Lee*. She introduced the idea of dinner parties to St. Marys, a town heretofore too busy prospering to worry about the finer things of life.

Lizzie even had a set of silver candelabras and serving dishes shipped down from Boston for the wives to borrow and dress their tables for the finer affairs, but only so long as the table was also graced with the finest cuts of *D & L* meats.

How they prospered, and how they loved their lives! John had worked hard all his life, and he always knew hard work had its rewards, but never had he felt so rewarded for his work as since he and Lizzie became a team.

It wasn't too long before Lizzie began to gain a little weight, then a little more. She was strong, but Doc Borden told her to slow it down a little to protect the baby. She tried, but she still had so many ideas and loved working with her John and Jacob, whom she called her father-in-law, in the store.

In 1817, little Nancy Lee was born. The three Lees were happy, healthy and growing!

And pretty soon later, Lizzie was growing again to produce Wiley Lee, born 7 November 1818, barely over a year after Nancy. Could life possibly get any better?

Old Doc Borden pulled John aside and said, "Congratulations, son, but be a little more careful, next time. You're putting a lot of stress on Lizzie with the way you've got her throwin' pups and running your business and all. I know you think she hung the moon, but if you want to keep her around, you might think about slowing her down a little.

John listened but didn't speak.

As the family grew, so did *D & L Butchery*. Jimmy Jones became a partner in addition to Jacob, John and Lizzie; with Jacob holding 40%, John 30%, Lizzie and Jimmy 15% each, but they each had one equal vote. There were now three apprentices being worked silly by the four partners. This business was in high cotton. Lizzie continued operating her business for the townfolk, but the men had all they could handle running the ship provisioning business.

As sailing ships got ever bigger, *D & L* found they had to stay ever busier to supply the demand of all those hungry sailors. And the pirate business? Oh my!

Sales grew reliably each year. Even though there were now two butcher shops in town, John found St. Marys has grown enough to support both of them better than he would have expected. John and Jacob were both grateful for all Lizzie had done to make the *D & L* meats the preferred brand for most of the locals.

It couldn't be any better, or could it? John thought he had reached the top of St. Marys ladder. He'd gone from fatherless lad to simple butcher, to partner in a growing enterprise. He'd grown with his town and his business. It was clear he was on his way to success. He had a good name, a good business, and a growing family. You could say he had it all.

One day John asked, "Jacob, why did you never move out of the boarding house? I know you've made enough money."

"Well," Jacob said reflectively, "you know I never married; got no kids, no heirs. I used to want to have the finest house a Georgia boy could own, a real, 'hey, look at me' kind of house - red bricks, big white columns. It was a good dream because it motivated me for a lot of years, but if I had it today it would just be a big lonely house. Now I can afford about any house I want, but I find I just don't want it. Isn't life funny thattaway?" John never got tired of learning wisdom from his almost-father, and decided then and there he was going to keep the family cramped in its little free space above the shop and save up piles of money. But then Jacob added, "But if I had a beautiful young gal like Lizzie, I'm not so sure I wouldn't buy her one of those places if I could really afford it while I was still young."

Now John was confused.

John and Lizzie worried about St. Marys, and how it just wasn't a place to raise children anymore. And wasn't it getting to be too busy? The streets were getting noisy, the sailors seemed to outnumber the residents, and too often, they caused trouble when they came ashore on leave. There were more bars and other kinds of places they didn't want their children to go.

This wasn't the same town anymore.

Change Always Happens

In 1822, America finally completed its purchase and takeover of Florida, and that southern peninsula became a territory of the United States. Tallahassee was picked to be the territorial Capitol, and the same year, the town of Cowford changed its name to Jacksonville, in honor of Andrew Jackson, who took office in 1821 as the 'Military Governor' from March of '21 through the end of the year. Spain was finally fully out of the picture. The land John was so enamored by during his run with John McIntosh was now where it belonged, under stable rule with the U.S. Constitution as its framework. The new territory had every chance of becoming something.

John and Lizzy had Levi II in early '22, and James joined the family just before the year was out. His Uncle Jimmy Jones couldn't have been prouder to have a namesake.

By July, 1824, the oldest two, Nancy and Wiley, were students at Mrs. Duggar's school. Due to the town's growth, the school had grown to two classrooms, but it still offered a fine basic education to all who came through its doors.

The people of St. Marys grew with their town. Some of the scrapping farmers from the boondocks turned into wealthy planters, with their cotton and tobacco going through St. Marys port; some traversing up North, some going straight to Europe. The more successful plantations were beginning to look more like the big ones around Savannah and Charleston.

Needless to say, the shipping industry bloomed along with the farms and St. Marys. The young city was now served by four times the freight traffic of just ten years ago plus several passenger ships stopping here every week. Those folks on the passenger ships ate a whole lot more and a whole lot better than the sailors on the cargo ships. The town's prosperity had been very good to the first butcher shop in town.

The Lees bought themselves a place on Wheeler Street, a modest but nice house for the growing family. Some tongues were buzzing, "John might be livin' a little too high now," and "worried" he wouldn't be able to handle a $750 house. What they didn't know was he had it all saved up. He didn't, and wouldn't, borrow a dime for such an extravagance. His life had been steeped in frugality from his Momma, from Jacob, from his deep Methodist roots, and from the good people of the town, and he was beginning to reap the benefits.

He also saw the folks coming in daily to pay up for his finest cuts when he knew he could almost give them dirt cheap parts to make a perfectly good stew, just as his Momma made.

He still missed Momma. He'd even try to help some understand how to "stretch" the meat and was always amazed when most of them went ahead and bought the more expensive cuts, which *D & L* was more than happy to sell.

They loved this place, but every time John and Lizzie would snuggle together to do their dream talking, John would find himself telling her wistfully of a little settlement built around beautiful Upper Mineral Springs, by then renamed White Sulphur Springs, on the banks of the Suwannee. People said the spring was going to become a health attraction for wealthy Northerners. The settlement was sure to grow, but maybe not grow quite as crazy as St. Marys did. The young couple would ask themselves, "How can we raise our kids in this town with all the distractions of the fast life here?"

Though the meat business had been good to him, John had a real itch to be a landowner, a farmer, or better yet, a "Planter." A planter might be best described as a farmer who somehow managed to make some money. But even his considerable savings wouldn't buy him any sizable coastal farmland in Georgia. The land was already too prosperous and valuable for a starting farmer to afford. The coastal lowland farms where all the long staple cotton was grown were pretty well taken up, and such fortunes had been gleaned from them that the already wealthy planters were competing against each other to buy whenever a farm came available.

Every time John would get halfway into one of those dreamy White Springs talks, he'd realize he had some job to do at the shop, dreaming time was over, and he had to go do his job and make some more money. It wasn't all bad, though, because his and Lizzie's savings continued to grow, even after buying the house. He owed nobody, and his share of the butcher business had to be worth maybe three times the house, but he always had to go back to work.

In early 1825, news came of a Congressional Act to encourage settlers to come to Florida. It decreed a farmer cultivating land in the new Territory of Florida by January 1, 1826, would "be entitled to the right of pre-emption in the purchase thereof." This meant the farmer working any given piece of land would have a hold on the land as long as he farmed it continuously for six full years. When the time was complete, he could by his land, up to 640 acres, for $1.25 an acre. This deal was good for everyone involved because no man in his right mind would pay such a price up front for raw land still in need of clearing and developing into a farm in a brand new area which still needed to be civilized. However, if you could work it free for six years and have it nicely improved and productive, paying the $1.25 price in the seventh year became real cheap.

John and all the migrating settlers were very pleased with the direction their young country was taking. How wise it was for the United States to acquire whole territories, quickly break it up and push smaller parcels into private hands, then watch as wild lands flourished. When individuals take ownership, they protect and preserve their land so much better than any government body could. It seemed to fit right in with those "Self-evident" truths our country's Founders spoke of.

Never before had any government anywhere been so dedicated to fostering private property rights. Ownership was available to anyone, at least any white male, who would work the land. No longer was land just for those who had done special service to some monarch; it was available in full, irrevocable title to anyone willing and able to make the land produce.

The experiment of the American Republic was still less than fifty years old, but it was working, and its people were working with an industrious vigor never before seen anywhere. The results were already astonishing.

John was already in love with Florida and excited about its potential. He imagined what a better place it would be as a U.S. Territory, than as the questionable 'Republic of Florida,' with John McIntosh as its Monarch, or as some unwanted appendage of Spain.

The partners of *DeLoach and Lee* had their business meetings every Wednesday morning at the boarding house, but one sultry summer day in early July 1825, Jacob said he wanted to meet with John alone. He started by saying he couldn't be happier he'd hired a skinny little eight-year-old about twenty years ago, but it was getting time for him to bow out. He said he didn't need another dime from the store because it had supplied him with more dimes than he could count. He wanted to have no regular hours anymore, but be able to work when he wanted to work. As long as he was making a contribution, he wanted to be welcome there, but John must pledge to tell him when he got in the way so he'd know when it was time to walk out for good.

Jacob cut his interest in *D & L* to 25%, adding 5% to each of the other shareholders. Lawyer Humphries had drawn the papers and they were already signed and sealed.

Jacob then told John he'd written up a will. Since he had no heirs, he wanted his money to go to the church, but his property and his remaining shares of the business were to go to John. John and Humphries were the only two souls to know it before his death, and they were not to tell anyone about it until after his funeral. That was, if they felt the need to even have a funeral. He then asked John if he had any questions, to which John said "No, sir," an address John was forbidden to use for Jacob since the day they became partners. John was overwhelmed but managed to say, "I will do your wishes, and I hope I'm a very old man when I have to carry them out. Thank you for all you've been to me and done for me, and . . ."

As John began welling up, Jacob quickly interjected, "I think this meeting's over. Thank you, John."

For land's sake, he couldn't tell Lizzie, or Jimmy, or Jim Spencer? Well, it was the way this fabulous man wanted it, and he will have it his way, John thought to himself.

The next Wednesday, the partners assembled at the boarding house for Mrs. Brewer's breakfast and their weekly business meeting. The other partners were aware of Jacob's new work schedule, but not of the confidential arrangements.

It was after 7:00. Jacob always started the meeting at 7:00, because he was sure punctuality was one of God's favorite virtues. When the big St. Marys clock struck 7:00, all were expected to be seated. This time, however, Jacob himself was not in attendance. John took the meeting over and said, "We'll get started because Mr. DeLoach is exercising his much-deserved new right to be late, and he's probably testing us to see if we can manage without him."

By 7:15, Mrs. Brewer slipped upstairs. She was sure Jacob had no real intention of working any less, and certainly no thought of being less punctual. She knocked lightly, with no answer; next she knocked harder to no response. Now panicked, she ran downstairs, got her master key and breathlessly, yet quietly, charged back upstairs trying not to be noticed.

When she barged in the room, the old butcher put down his *Georgia Messenger* newspaper, folded it neatly, placed it in his lap, and asked Mrs. Brewer with a twinkle, "Why did you wait 'til I was so old to break into my room? When I was a younger man, I wished you would, and now I couldn't . . . oh, never mind," he said in a rare playful moment, forcing himself to stop before he broke his perfect record of perfect decorum with his landlady. Now, laughing hard at himself, he didn't notice how un-funny Mrs. B thought he was.

After her tirade, the old man apologized and said he was just trying to be sure the young partners would carry on the business if he didn't show up. He was "proud to notice they hadn't interrupted their business meeting to bother with the old goat" and was just a little apologetic to Mrs. Brewer for upsetting her, but not as much as he was tickled at himself for pulling off a real funny joke. He'd spent his entire life observing straight-laced, Victorian Methodist manners, a true by-the-book - uh, the Good Book, of course - gentleman.

"Please tell them you checked, and I'm just fine, and tell 'em how happy I am they can run the business without me. I think I'm going to spend the day NOT living by the town clock for the first time in my old, over-planned, over-worked life. Tell them I'm not coming in today."

"I will, you old bat!" Mrs. Brewer said angrily before melting into a big smile. She congratulated him on deciding to enjoy the rest of his life.

True to his word, he didn't go to the shop that day, or any other day, ever again.

Sometime after Lady Brewer closed the door to his room, the Good Lord snuffed out Jacob's candle. After he missed supper, he was found in the same chair with the same newspaper folded in his lap. From that very day forward, Jacob DeLoach would be living by the Almighty's time clock and would never again worry about his own schedule.

A Fitting Sendoff?

The next day, his funeral drew friends and customers from miles around. Reverend Spencer had to open all the shutters and doors of the church, and the overflow stood crowded outside at every door or window clear around the building.

Now Reverend Spencer didn't mind giving a sermon, and this one was going to be special because he knew a lot about the kindnesses Jacob had done during his life, but even he didn't know the half of it. After sermonizing a solid one hour and twenty minutes, having to shout everything twice so those on both sides of the outside of the church could hear, he opened up the floor to those who might want to speak of Jacob. Then he sat down exhausted.

At first, only lawyer Humphries stood up. After saying, "Thank you, Reverend Spencer, for your wonderful sermon, I coulda listened to you all day long . . . and for a while there, I thought I might have to!" The crowd roared as the tone was set for a celebration of a good man's life.

Suddenly a line of no less than twenty formed on the left side aisle, all anxious to pay tribute. Even though everyone tried to be brief, it was clear this memorial would take a while. Seemed when one person finished, two more stood up to tell of the kindnesses of this quiet man.

Now remember, this was middle of July. It was 99 degrees according to the thermometer hung to the giant Magnolia in the churchyard. What slight breeze there was came from the hot farm land, not a cooling seabreeze. This church was packed like a box of farmer Hooper's summer peaches, but it didn't smell like any box of peaches. All the hand fans were pumping hard, but they were just kind of moving the sweaty odor around.

After about thirty tributes to Jacob, those in the front row started noticing maybe the honored guest was getting a little hot, too, but he didn't have a fan, and it wasn't sweat we were smelling. By time brother Robert Bryan had his say, the odor reached clear to the balcony. There weren't enough flowers in this town to mask what the congregation was smelling.

The teenage girls started giggling, the boys laughing, the babies crying and the old folks just started gagging because they couldn't breathe.

John knew he had to take charge. It was already established he would be the last to speak, so he abruptly stood up at his place in the front row, turned around and said, "Brothers and Sisters, we all loved this man; he was a father, friend, and so much more to me. Even though he lived his life a single man with no known relatives, he was a part of the big family which is St. Marys town and Camden County, Georgia. His kindness will be long remembered, but now we gotta do somethin' with him real fast!"

On close examination, as close as one dare get, it was easy to see the problem. Old Jacob, being the good Scotsman he was, had pre-purchased his coffin years prior to need. You get a better deal that way, y'know. You'd get a really great deal if you bought the simple pauper's casket, and DeLoach wasn't about to let someone else go and buy some fancy box for his remains to spend eternity in. Since this box was the very bottom-of-the-line, and had been sitting in wait far longer than advisable, the pine wood had dried and contracted, leaving some pretty hefty gaps between the boards. In fact, if you held a candle up looked between the boards, you could clearly see the old butcher, but not a single soul said "My, he looks so natural," because he neither looked nor smelled very natural. With Jacob's sendoff party happening on one of the hottest days St. Marys had ever seen, and with the unintended ventilation feature of the coffin, well, things were ripe for a big smelly surprise, and a huge party for all of St. Marys flies!

As the organist quickly played "On Jordan's Stormy Banks," the pallbearers quickly whisked him out to the waiting *D & L* meat wagon. Nobody sang, though, because none dared breathe more of the rank air than they had to for survival! Those sitting in the window sills just turned around and slid out the window. The ladies were breaking out their kerchieves and smelling salts to help out the fainters.

It was just the risk you took when you had to have a funeral on a hot day back in those days.

During the four-block meat wagon ride to the Oak Grove Cemetery, John was briefly taken back to his second day of work with Mr. D. and his first butcher mistake. Jacob treated it like a joke to this mortified, smelly young man, but today old Jacob played the same joke on himself, only Jacob was mortified for real this time.

Some of the men passed around a not-so-quiet joke that they better watch to make sure the meat wagon went straight to the cemetery and didn't make a stop at *D & L* along the way. They'd say things like, "The old tightwad never wasted that much meat in his whole lifetime!" Or, "We might better find ourselves a new meat store next couple of weeks!" There was more knee slapping and har-dee-har-ing at this solemn farewell than St. Marys had seen since the traveling comedy show came to town. More than one of the men got his head rapped by his wife's parasol for such irreverence.

No one would confess to starting the jokes, but most assumed they came from Reverend Jim himself!

One would've thought it was a New Orleans funeral with all the merriment around the procession. I think it's the way ol' Jacob DeLoach would have wanted it.

The mood abruptly changed as the congregation watched the coffin go down, down, down into the hole where it would rest forever. Then John tearfully said, "Good bye, my friend," as he tossed the first shovel full of dirt onto the casket. "Good bye."

He felt sure his good bye at Jacob's grave was more than just farewell to a friend. So many chapters were closing in his life. He wondered if it was just the same old wanderlust so prevalent in the frontier lands. Had he inherited it from his Daddy? Was it something about Methodism? Protestants so often repeat, "This world is not our home." Maybe we were becoming gypsies, sentenced to wander the world in search of a home.

We keep looking to a promised land in heaven, but is it causing us unrest here on earth?

He knew as soon as he met with Humphries he was going to be a near-wealthy man, but why wasn't he excited? Why wasn't he knocking on the lawyer's door to hear Jacob's will? It surely wasn't disrespect for his departed friend. Maybe it was the final good bye he worried about. Maybe as long as Jacob still was owner of 25% of his company, surely he couldn't really be dead. Or something like that.

About a week after the funeral, John got to the shop early as always. Humphries was waiting at the front door. "Morning, counselor. I guess you're not here for a pound of pork chops, are you?"

"No," he said, "Lizzie told me you were dreading this and I can tell you from all my years, it's a normal thing you're going through. It's funny, some folks can't wait to see what's in it for themselves, and others feel they're re-burying the dead. I prefer to work with the latter type, so let's read the letter, my friend."

The letter had all the usual legal language of the day. As promised, John left all personal cash and gold for the Rev. Jim Spencer, or his successor at First Methodist Church, to do the Lord's work as he saw fit. But then Jacob dropped the formal tone and got personal from beyond the grave.

"John, I'm happy for you. It's yours and Lizzie's and Jimmy's now, all of it. It's grown a lot, mostly due to you and your ambitious hard work, but it's only a shadow of what you can make it, if you so desire.

We learned to do a lot with those poor animals, but we never did figure how to make a penny out of the darned old squeal, did we?" John choked tears and laughed at the same time. "Now do with it as you want. I've seen a restlessness in you for some time now. We loved what we did together, but I could see you looking to the horizon. I felt you were staying and growing the business for me, out of loyalty. I appreciate your loyalty, and the store's been good to both of us, but the fact you're reading this means I'm gone where I'm going to, and I'm hereby setting you free to go and do what you want. Again, your loyalty to me is appreciated, but you have to know loyalty to the store does me nor you a wit of good anymore.

Go on to the next frontier. I know you love Florida, and you can do things there you can only dream about here. Take your money and stake a big claim there. Make the woods thick with Lees. But only do it if it's what you really want to do. Good bye, God bless, and don't forget to have fun along the way."

John took to heart the load of advice by Jacob, and he knew it was his final sign he needed to go to Florida. But how would he tell Lizzie?

Leaving It All Behind

Telling Lizzie turned out to be easy because she was more aware of John's Florida dreams than he was. Maybe it was the "women's intuition" thing.

With Lizzie's blessing, John took a scouting trip. On returning one week later, he was more excited than ever. He was sure. He'd seen several tracts he thought would be just fine to get started but fell in love especially with one. It surely was going to be a lot of work, but work was all John had ever known, so he looked forward to taming the wild land. Lizzie asked what was holding him back. He said, "Honey, you've finally got this town half as civilized as you, and now I'm talking about ripping you away from it. I need to know this is good for you."

"Well, Doc Borden tells me we have another one on the way about June," She said sweetly, "Why don't we make this one a real, live Florida native?"

John responded, "I didn't know how to tell you, but I put my dibs in on one piece, 160 acres of virgin pine, live oak, red oak, some cypress and the occasional wild hickory, pig nuts we call 'em. It's beautiful and has a nice roll to it with a beautiful little creek running through it. There are three or four other families in the settlement, and it's built around a Methodist church! It's ours if I can get on it first. I put a reservation in, but I can't claim it if somebody gets there before us and squats on it. And I have to be farming it by the first of January, 1826."

Not a word was said, but Lizzie's eyes gave full approval.

"I must see Jimmy right away," he said as he kissed Lizzie and ran out the door. "Did she just tell me I'm going to have another baby?" he asked himself while running to the store.

He made arrangements for Jimmy to take over his shares, paying for them over time from the earnings of the business. Jimmy would buy John's and Lizzie's piece of whatever of the other operations he wanted (the tannery, saddler, soap factory, and butcher shop itself) or sell off any he didn't want, get a fair price, and send John his portion. John told Jimmy, "I'm going to start over. I'm going to try again and do even better this time!"

Plans were made as quickly as was the decision to move. John would move immediately. He would buy two experienced slaves (without letting Reverend Jim know), and they would move with him to the land right away.

He sent ahead to the land agent in White Springs and wrote, "Set me up to homestead the 160 ac. tract in Genoa. I'm on my way." The land was an almost free grant from the U.S. government for men who would actively farm it and get commerce going in the untamed lands. Even though John had more means than most pioneer settlers, he was still hungry for the new start and to begin life in the Florida frontier.

Reverend Spencer told John and Lizzie of the Johns family of four children. They'd been motherless for years, but were recently orphaned and in desperate straits. Lizzie approached John about taking them in. It would be perfect; Avarilla, the oldest, was eighteen, another adult who could be a great help with the Lee kids during the move and the rigors of getting settled. The two boys were already strapping teenagers and could help on the new farm once they arrived. The baby, Lillie, was a girl of ten, and should fit right in with the rest of the family. John didn't need much convincing because it was the right thing to do, and he knew one of the many challenges he would face in the new land would be getting enough labor. The Lees became custodians of the four Johns children.

Avarilla was hopelessly shy at first. She couldn't look Lizzie or John square in the eye, and had no idea if she could trust them, or if they would accept her as anything more than an obligation and an act of charity. Or they might simply treat her as cheap property and work her to death. Would she be not much more than a slave as was too often the case with older adopted orphans of the day. Her clothes and her whole appearance were tattered from the use and abuse of trying her best to make her siblings presentable while neglecting herself. Lizzie was anxious to introduce Avarilla to a good life.

The land John chose was at Genoa, which was little more than nothing at the time. It was about three miles from the White Sulphur Springs settlement, where he would build a butcher shop at a later date, well after the farm was established. He liked having the house a distance from the butcher shop because it allowed him to concentrate his efforts on farming. He planned to bring one of the experienced butchers from *D & L* to run the daily operation of the new shop, a new way of doing business. More importantly, his children would not grow up in the town, but on the farm with plenty of room. Life was going to be hard, and the family would miss the city comforts they'd gotten used to. Further, John and Lizzie agreed that by raising the new generation of Lees on the farm, their young would be the product of their upbringing. In St. Marys, the parents worried their broods were become products of bad influences of the city.

It would surely be worth it all . . . wouldn't it?

John knew, if history was any guide, White Sulphur Springs would be growing, and just like DeLoach, he was going to start again with a small butcher shop to serve the needs of the settlers around there and be ready to grow with the town. Since a traveler could now get from New York to Middle Florida in only about ten days of travel, places like White Sulphur Springs were going to be busting at the seams.

His farmland was loaded with mature timber, and he knew he'd have a great market at St. Marys and Fernandina, but there was no way to get it there, and he was forced to sell it to a local farmer with a sawmill. All he would get for all his beautiful wood was its removal from his land and enough rough-hewn logs to build his house, barn, cook shack and slave quarters. John would use the local logs to frame his house, but planned to bring in fine lumber from St. Marys for the inside walls and floors to make it a fine house for Lizzie. After all, she deserved it with all she was leaving behind.

Genoa was a delight for John. It had three or four families already established, and steady flowing water from Swift Creek, and was centered around the Swift Creek Methodist church. He believed Lizzie would be happy, and he knew she would be happy to raise their young'uns in this spot.

Genoa isn't far from White Springs, and White Springs isn't but about thirteen miles from the nearest big town, Alpata Telophka, meaning "Alligator Village." Well, it's actually not a big town, but it used to be a pretty good-sized Indian settlement. Only a few Indians remained, and they were the ones who were too weak to leave or had some white blood or some reason to believe the Army would tolerate them staying.

John realized that might just make Genoa in the middle of nowhere. John gulped. Nobody knows if ol' John or any of those early settlers really thought about what they were leaving behind and what wasn't awaiting them when they arrived. However, like his Daddy Levi, John wasn't leaving squalor and poverty as many frontiersmen were. He left the comfort and prosperity he'd worked hard for since age eight, but something pushed him on.

John Lee, like so many other Southern pioneer spirits, was driven by the desire to try again, to start over. There must have been some magic to the notion of taming new lands.

Alligator Village probably included some of the same poor natives John Lee and John McIntosh used to stir up trouble for the Spaniards during Lee's last, ill-fated Florida adventure. He hoped the new attempt would have better results than the last. He also hoped none of his old friends recognized or remembered him because he wasn't real sure how fond those recollections might be for them. Even though Alligator Village was a good fifteen miles away, he knew the Indians would be around to see every new settler (whether the settlers saw them or not) and would make it their business to know something about each of their new neighbors.

Now the road linking Fernandina to Pensacola was indeed the best road in all of the Florida territory of the day, but that wasn't saying much. It was cobbled together from a series of Indian trails and cattle trails in a general east-west direction, but in 1825, there was nothing "fine" about it. It was "maintained" by the beating down it got from horses, wagons, foot traffic and cattle drives, all of which used it only because it was the easiest way to go from one end of Florida to the other.

One man traveling on it might benefit from the crude bridges built over small creeks by earlier travelers, but they were so rickety as to sometimes cause trouble for the traveler who trusted them with too heavy a load. Most of the smaller fording spots eventually became piles of debris stacked up high enough to allow safe passage. If you didn't like the looks of one of these sorry structures, you might just add enough debris of your own to shore it up and make it suitable to get your own cargo across. So long as you got across, whether or not your improvements actually improved the structure was the next traveler's dilemma, not yours.

The high spots were nearly as much of a problem as the low spots. In dry times the creeks got easier to cross, but the hills got harder to scale. In Florida, a hill might not have an elevation change much more than ten feet, but said ten feet of altitude could make the difference between dense swamp and sugar sand hill. As the sand got drier, the sand ruts got deeper. Suddenly a one-horse wagon might need two very stout horses to pull it through the dry hills.

When the terrain was either too dry or too wet, the road got a natural widening, as the travelers would hug one side or the other of the trail, seeking either firmer mud or firmer sand, as the need may be. If the area was heavily treed, it wouldn't get widened because no one was going to stop long enough to fell and stump a tree to widen the road. In the heavily forested areas where the user couldn't easily sneak one side of his wagon onto newer, firmer ground, repeated use of the road just made it ever sandier or ever muddier.

The creeks and rivers which were too deep, wide or swift to ford safely generally had a ferry. These were flat little barges you'd walk, ride your horse, or drive your wagon onto. Then you'd paddle or pull the barge on a rope to get across. There was supposed to be a rowboat kept on the side of the river where the barge was not, so a traveler could always either get right on the ferry-barge, or at least have a way to get to it. The last one to cross was to make sure to leave the rowboat and barge on opposite banks. It was not unusual, though, to find the rowboat and barge on the same side of the river. Worse, it was not unusual for those two boats to be on the side of the river you needed them not to be on. Sometimes you could just wait for someone to come from the other direction, but that could be days, even on the main road. Most times it meant somebody had to get wet retrieving the barge.

On the larger and more traveled rivers and creeks, the barges were tended by local ferrymen. The ferryman would pull you across on a rope strung from one bank to another or pole you to the other side, for a small fee, of course. Once there, you'd get off and be on your way.

Some improvement would be made to the road over the next few years. The territorial government would hire teams of slaves from their owners to dig the road's sandy hills lower with shovels and buckets. Usually, the sand would gain clay content as you dug down a few feet. The clay, mixed with the sand, added stability to the road, making the road harder and easier to traverse in dry weather, but not too slick in wet times. The spoil sand was taken by wagon or bucket, depending on how far, downhill to the lower lands and used as fill to begin building up a graded road.

The slaves, supplied with good timber by the government, would also be used to build less crude bridges where they were needed most. These changes would be great improvements on the road, but might as well be a century away for those who had to travel it in 1825.

Settling a Wild Land

Swift Creek Methodist Church sat on a placid, gently rolling knoll with the newly-built church building on the high point looking across a wagon trail to where the cemetery would one day be. It was a plain, simple affair, a thatched roofed log building with no sign of frivolity and devoid of architectural features. It just invited in plain old pioneer language, "Come unto me, ye who are weary and heavy-laden, and I will give you rest." The churchyard and future cemetery were both generously sprinkled with graceful, ancient live oaks, red oaks, magnolias and a few wild hickories adding to the placid feeling as the creek gurgled peacefully as it made its way to the Suwannee.

This setting was perfect for John and his family.

Wasn't it?

John's arrival was dead of winter, at least as dead as winter gets in Florida. His challenge was to get enough land cleared, stumped and turned to have ten acres plantable by spring. The first crop wouldn't be a cash crop but a canning crop for the Lees to live from. Food would be much more important than money this first season. John had the advantage of his savings and the money he'd made from selling his business and house, which allowed him to buy the tools and equipment needed to make this raw land into a farm. He was amazed how many of the squatters staked their claims with nothing but an axe, a shovel, a hoe and maybe a mule, but hardly a cent of money.

He chose to commence clearing at a spot where five giant live oaks spread their arms out over an area of at least five acres. Because of the shading, there was very little under the oaks to be cleared, so once they were removed, he had a pretty well cleared, farmable piece of land. Of course, cutting down any one of those trees was a monstrous task. Once they fell, each one had several limbs the size of a big tree themselves. He knew the land under such trees was going to be rich and deep.

The first round of crops would include lots of corn, sugar and beans for the staples, and the new farm would grow all the family could use of summer vegetables, melons and strawberries for fresh eating and preserving. After the first field was readied, logging and clearing would take a back seat to managing the planted crops. It would be many years before John would clear all he planned to farm.

The land clearing had to be done all by hand with axes, men and mules. John had some black powder bombs to use for stumping, but he knew to use those reservedly, for they were not only in short supply but real expensive. The original clearing, then, would only involve felling the trees, sorting them to go to either the sawmill or keep for firewood. The sawmill would haul off the lumber trees, and the firewood trees were to be mule-dragged over to the house for eventual cutting and stacking for cooking and heat.

The smaller stumps could be grubbed out with axes and mules, while the larger ones would be left in place. The farmer would just work around the stump for the first season or two until it got soft and rotten enough for easy removal. This system didn't make for real pretty farms and high yields, but it did make land-clearing go faster. Of course, an old, sappy fat pine stump would never soften and never rot enough to easily remove, so someday, it would have to be taken out the hard way.

One extra feature John envisioned for his new estate was to dig out a swimming hole in Swift Creek. Once the first twenty acres and homesite were cleared, he figured on having the men spend a couple of days widening and deepening a spot for bathing and playing, using nothing but shovels and buckets. Eventually he wanted to build a dam there so he could have enough water to stock it with panfish and bass.

John was really excited about showing his new pond to Lizzie and was already planning to show it to her some warm midnight while the kids were in bed.

On his third day as a Genoan, John was working at clearing along with the two Johns boys, Joseph and Joshua; the two slaves, Robert and Daniel; and the two mules, Sloppy and Stupid. The homesite would be in the middle of the first field for safety. John had already been advised to clear around his homesite first and create as much visibility as possible as quickly as possible to take away cover for marauding Indians or other vagabonds with ill intent. Although life was pretty peaceful between the Indians and the whites at the time, some were concerned the land rush of settlers would un-settle the natives. John wasn't worked up too much about the warning, but since he had to clear the land anyway, he figured he might as well take the precaution and do as advised.

In fact, a few of the Indians from Alligator Town came over and volunteered their labor services for twenty-five cents per day. John and they understood they would work day-to-day, and only if there was work to do. They would work only if they showed up at sun-up, but they wouldn't obligate themselves to feel like working every day. It was sort of the Indian way of doing business.

A day's work meant a full day of work. The only time our labors stopped was for a short dinner break at the noon hour. Each morning John would place a time stick at the edge of the field. This stick, stuck upright in the ground, with a line drawn in the sand heading due north, would tell us it was noon time when its shadow perfectly lined up with the line in the sand. After the noon break, the laborers knew their day didn't stop until dark.

The Indians taught the settlers how to make suitable flour out of the coontie root. Coontie is a low-slung wild-growing native plant. It looks sort of like a palmetto relative, but it's not. It grows well on well-drained sands of all types, and if you're hungry enough you could make a paste, then a flour, then bread or custard out of it. Like most things, if you added enough sugar or molasses to it, it didn't taste all bad. You'd better do it right, though, 'cause it's deadly poison if you don't ferment the root long enough. Many's the hungry pioneer who heard you could eat the coontie root, tried it and got very sick, or died, or wished he would die, just because he hadn't fermented the poison out of it.

The Indians also cautioned to be very careful working the coontie plants because that other prominent native species, rattlesnake, really like the small critters who took refuge in the dense bushes. It was not uncommon for a settler to reach into the coontie, thinking he was grabbing onto a root, then find he'd grabbed a handful of fang-faced varmint with evil on his mind. When this happens, a man knows he's got a real tough couple of days on his hands before he gets better. Or he may never get better, and that might take a couple of days, too.

Most of the Lee farm consisted of the good, rich soils of the Suwannee Valley, but there was a higher, sandy hill in the northeast corner. It was loaded with strong mature pines and a thick undergrowth of coontie. John designated it as the turpentine farm. He also decreed none of the coontie root would be cleared from the turpentine patch because it was going to be the emergency food supply only. White men didn't like coontie very much. Even Robert said, "Dat stuff ain't fittin' to eat, bossman." If there was a crop failure sometime in the future or for some reason times got really hard, John wanted to know we had coontie root to eat so we could keep on living 'til things improved.

Saving the turpentine patch was a smart move. John wasn't trying to go into the turpentine business, but he wanted his farm to be able to supply itself of that very important brew. Besides, the sandhill was a very light, sandy soil, and John thought it didn't have what it needed to grow good crops.

Turpentine comes from pine sap. It's harvested by cutting an open face on one side of the pine tree. A worker would cut thin grooves into the newly exposed wood, then the sap oozed out of the cuts like a man's bleeding sore to be gathered into a small cup hung to the tree. Over time, the workers cut fresh grooves in the scarred area so the tree would continue producing the sap through its fresh wounds. The resulting scar on the side of the tree is called a "cat face."

Once collected, the sap is distilled into turpentine and rosin and is one of the very most useful things on the farm. As a cleaner, just mix with water to make it as strong or as light as you want. It's a great medicine when mixed with various other country cures, like alcohol and maybe a little opium with some honey and sugar. Nothing gets rid of chiggers like a turpentine bath. A light sprinkle of turpentine and water will keep the bed bugs at bay for days on end. It can also varnish and polish furniture and makes a great paint solvent.

The heavier byproduct, rosin, would be used to fill holes in barrels or in a wall. It was a fine preservative to protect ropes and wood products from the elements. It was also valuable for spreading in hulls of boats and ships to make their bilges water-tight.

Lizzie wanted to build the turpentine still in the cook shed, but John insisted on building it separate from the house right on the piney hill. He said something about how the turpentine was better the quicker it got distilled; besides, distilling was a craft, and it was a man's job. It shouldn't be confused with women's work like cooking.

It wasn't 'til years later the women figured out John and the boys were also be distilling a little bit of the farm's corn supply at the turpentine still, and that was probably for medicinal purposes, too.

One day when John was about half-through with clearing his first ten acres, he saw two horsemen approaching. He put down his axe and went to greet his new neighbors. They were both big men on big horses and both had rifles in their saddles and pistols tucked in their belts.

"Howdy. Name's Lee . . . John Lee."

"Pleased to meet you, but this isn't a social call," the lead horseman said abruptly. "My name's E.T. Roux, and this here's Judd O'Connor. I've been livin' here ten years now, and we're here to tell you somethin' and you need to pay good attention. As you know, next year these parts are going to be their own county. In a little over a year, in 1827, it's going to be called Hamilton County, and it's being carved away from Duval County. It's about 515 square miles and there's nothing here yet except suddenly there's a lot of you land-hungry fools comin' in to stake your claims. I hear you were part of ol' John McIntosh's folly. Well, I was, too. 'Til now, we've had it pretty good out here. We didn't have much problem except an occasional Indian stealing an occasional horse or pilferin' a little of our produce, but we generally got along pretty well 'til now."

"Well, Mr. Roux," John said tensely, "it sounds like you don't much cotton to my being here, but I'm here to earn a livin' just like I s'pose you are, and if you're here to interfere with my intentions of doin' just that, then we're gonna have a problem, and we might just as well settle it right here and right now."

"No, Mr. Lee, I don't mean to cause you no trouble, and I'm happy to have you here. I'm jest here to tell you this: Duval County knows it's losing us, so it's pullin' out all its lawmen, figurin' it might as well save its money and not waste law service on us since it's getting the last of its revenues from us next year. All we'll have for law protection around here will be the U.S. Marshall, and you prob'ly know how thin he's stretched. The new county will take a while to get organized after its formed, so we're kinda on our own out here for a while. We never had much law here and didn't need much, but now with all y'all comin' in here, and the whole outlaw world knowin' the law's leaving, we've got new problems. I'm hearing stories about some white gangs plunderin', stealin', rapin', murderin' and burnin' places to the ground in other parts of Florida, and they seem to be concentrating on areas where the new settlers are coming in most. We could be ripe for the pickin'.

"I hope you'll forgive me if I sounded a bit hostile, but I'm sure the threat is real, and we need to work together. I really needed to make my point, and I have a long way to go to spread the word. Out here, the very closest neighbors are about a half mile apart. A gang can pick us off one by one, and we'll never know what's happening 'til it's too late. We're gonnna have to make some kind of system to spread the word if there's a threat.

My house and farm is about a mile the other side of Genoa from you. It's the one with the pecan tree and the weeping willow in the front yard. Y'all have a good day."

John could only say, "I appreciate your concern, Mr. Roux, and good day to you, too."

With that, E.T. Roux and Judd O'Connor turned and left galloping just as hard as they'd come. O'Connor had yet to say a word.

Daniel looked at John almost crying, and said, "Missuh Lee, dey ain't a gonna be no bad white men out here, is dey?"

"Of course, not, Daniel. This guy Roux is crazy as a bedbug. You'll see. We won't have any problems out here."

"Well Robert an' me, we know what type folks Missuh Roux be talkin' of, and dey's special mean to us niggah men, and dey do awful things to our womenfolks, too." Robert just stood and nodded with fear lighting up his saucer-wide eyes.

The most trouble John had seen in his life from white men was from the drunken sailors in St. Marys. Their little barroom brawls, pranks, and petty thievery were pretty harmless by comparison. He'd heard from time to time of bad gangs doing their evil from house to house and town to town, but he had never considered it for such a peaceful, virgin place as his little settlement in Genoa.

"Mr. Roux is a fear-monger. Now get back to work."

But secretly he was confirming to himself, "We *will* be safe out here . . . won't we?"

Since the family was going to be moving in soon, he had to put up a squatter's shack for a first house until the main house could be finished. It was a one-room affair, about twenty by twenty with a thatched roof and a packed dirt floor. It was Just a place to stay dry and keep supplies dry, but not much else, it would serve as a tack room after the big house got built. John quickly saw how much smaller it was than the bare little love nest above the butcher shop where he and Lizzie had been newlyweds, and there were going to be six Lees and four Johnses living in this thing. He figured he'd better get started on the big house right away. Wisely, he decided he would use some of the money from the sale of his house in St. Marys to build the new one framed and supported with heart pine and finished with walls and floors of planed and painted or varnished cypress boards. It would also have real glass windows and glass panes in the doors, the first house of its type in Hamilton County.

Even though it was going to be a fancy house with glass windows, the first roof was to be made of simple thatch. There was plenty of palmetto in the area, and thatch was quick and cheap to build. By time it wore out, John figured the farm should be profitable enough to replace the thatch with real cypress roofing shingles. The outside walls were to be simple, just half-cut logs with a grout made of local clays, sand, and water. The rounded half of the logs would face outside, with the rough, flat side facing in. The fine, finished lumber would be overlain in the interior to cover the mortar and roughness of the logs and give it a more finished look than most houses in the area. The interior walls and ceiling could be finished with plaster, but on a later day.

If all went right, John figured by time Lizzie got there, he could sleep the girls in the downstairs of the new house and boys in the squatter's shack. With a little more luck, the upstairs could be finished and everybody might be under one roof. He thought It could be completed by mid-summer. He contracted Jack Walls, a skilled local carpenter, to build the house first.

"Can you have it built by end of April, Mr. Walls?" John asked his new contractor.

"I sure could have the house up and the roof on if I could get the lumber, Mr. Lee. But it's going to have to be ordered and I expect it's going to take a while to get the fine wood you're spec'ing for your house. We could get local lumber, but it's all rough boards nowadays. The local stuff will be good for your frame, stringers, rafters, floor joists and roof trusses, but nobody's building anything fancy out here today. For your finish boards, you're asking for something that's gotta come from the coast. And I can assure you the windows won't be ready by then because the glass has to come out of Savannah or Charleston. We can make the window frames here, but it'll take some time. There's a lot of building going on and I think we're going to find the sawmills too busy to take your special order."

This set John back. He knew Lizzie was coming in the spring whether he was ready or not. If he didn't even have the house livable yet, he was going to have to convince her to come later, and he really didn't want that. John decided life was better for him when Lizzie was around, and he knew how Lizzie wanted this baby born in Florida.

He wrote to his friend Robert Bryan, back in St. Marys (you met him at the DeLoach funeral). Robert was a successful planter who also ran a sawmill he'd developed when timbering his own land. The Bryan mill made the fine lumber for the plantation houses of Camden County. In the letter, John told Robert of his predicament and asked if there was any way he could help. Just in case he could, John sent a list of all the good lumber he'd need for the entire house.

In these times, letters were sent and had to get to their destinations as best they could. Because it was a shipping port, St. Marys had a post office in a corner of the General Store. The proprietor of the General Store was also the postmaster for the town. John's letter to Robert was addressed simply "*Bryan's Lumberyard*, St. Marys, Georgia." The official carrier of mail between Fernandina and Pensacola only came through rarely. If the local postmaster could trust the driver, sometimes the letter would simply be put on the next wagon or horse headed in the direction indicated on the mailbag. There was a high likelihood it would go to Fernandina first, then get ferried across the river to its destination.

Robert got John's letter four days later. He immediately responded and had his office boy run the return letter to the St. Marys post office/ General Store. There it would wait for a horse or wagon headed west in the general direction of White Sulphur Springs settlement. Of course, neither White Sulphur Springs nor Genoa had a full-fledged post office yet, so the letter would go to the designated "post," which was the White Sulphur Springs blacksmith shop. The blacksmith-postmaster was an albino chap playfully dubbed "Blackie" by the locals. His skin was lily white and his unruly hair looked like it'd been powdered white. The only color in him was his eyes, which appeared blue and red at the same time.

When Blackie received a letter, he'd put out the word he had a letter addressed to "John Lee, Genoa, Florida," for instance. The next time a Genoan would be in town, he'd probably be the one to take the mail to his neighbor. Given the nosiness of so many of the neighbors, most folks used a very thick paper for envelopes in those days.

Shortly after receiving the order, Mr. Bryan had his first load of Lee lumber all stacked on his delivery wagon. He'd never sent a loaded wagon on a one-hundred-mile trek before, and hoped the old wooden axles and wheels would hold up. He knew once it got on the road between Fernandina and Alligator Village, his equipment would be traveling the finest road in all of Florida. He also knew "the finest road in all of Florida" was nothing to brag about, so he sent his best delivery man, and by that he meant the man who could best fix whatever was bound to go wrong on the journey. For the special job he decided he'd send ol' Flathead. Flathead was given his name by his fellows at the sawmill because he had, well, a very flat head. They used to joke he could carry five glasses of beer all day up there and not spill a drop. He proved 'em wrong because the most any of 'em could make stand was three.

Robert Bryan knew to send him off with plenty of nails, twine, wire, rope, a hammer, saw, blocks, and a good lever. Finally, he loaded some extra boards and one spare wooden axle so Flathead could make any kind of repair he needed. Bryan knew Flathead could get the wagon to Genoa and back, and the two strong Clydesdales could pull it through whatever sandhills or mud holes they might encounter on the finest road in all of Florida. Clydesdales were the best workhorses in the land - not very fast, but huge, muscular, and powerful. They could pull the heaviest wagons and drag the deepest plow of any breed of horse. They can work day and night if you need 'em to.

If all went well, *Bryan Lumber Company* might just be able to make the delivery date Robert pledged in the letter he'd previously sent.

"Flathead, get movin', you need to get a start before sundown, but don't forget to stop by the post office to see if you can carry some mail," Robert instructed.

At the post office, Flathead said he was headin' west. "Got anything for me to carry?" The clerk handed him one heavy satchel with "Tallahassee" handwritten on the paper tag, and a lighter one with "White Sulphur Springs" on it. "This should be it. Hope you have good travels." Flathead was on his way with the first of several loads John Lee was going to need to build his dream house in paradise.

The trip was fairly uneventful, with only three stops for minor repairs. Flathead found himself being real thankful his route took him on such a long stretch of Florida's finest road. Judging by what he saw, he wasn't anxious to do a delivery on one of Florida's rough roads.

Once at White Sulphur Springs, Flathead pulled up to the town water pump and horse trough, left his horses, then walked into the blacksmith's shop hollerin', "I got some mail, and I need some directions." Blackie stopped his smithing and came outside, taking a quick double look at this deliveryman.

"M'name's Flathead," he said, as if to let his curious new acquaintance know he was aware of his own unique attribute. He tossed down the two mail satchels. The contents of the White Springs bag would be distributed by the blacksmith-postmaster, and the Tallahassee bag would have to wait there for another sojourner to take it another hundred miles west.

"Blackie's mine," was the retort as if to let it be known his name wasn't quite so self-evident as Flathead's.

Flathead said, "Goin' to Genoa. Can you tell me how to get to Lee's place?" Now with full directions in his flat head, Flathead returned to the trough to fill his own canteen at the public pump. As he was fixing to gee the now-refreshed horses on the final leg of the delivery journey, Blackie came running out, yelling, "Hey, Flathead, I gotta letter for Lee for you. It was the only thing in the White Springs bag. How 'bout killin' two birds with one stone while you're out there?"

John saw a heavy wagon ambling up to his homesite, which now included a rough settlers' shack, a lean-to horse shed, and a crude cook shed which amounted to not much more than a firepit. The place was nothing more than a camp.

As the wagon approached, John let out a yelp, shouting excitedly, "Flathead, what you doin' out here?" Flathead told him truthfully, "I think I got some lumber for you here. I hope you like it, 'cause if'n you reject it I gotta haul it back to St. Marys, and I don't think this poor ol' wagon will make it back with a full load on it."

"It's beautiful wood," John said admiringly, "but I wish I'da known it was coming. I'da had the foundation up and some carpenters ready to go. I can use it, though, and I will send payment with you- better to send it with you than put it in the mail."

With that, Flathead remembered he had another delivery for John. "Speaking of mail, I almost forgot to give you this letter. It's U.S. Mail from somebody in St. Marys."

By the handwriting John could tell it wasn't from Lizzie, but he was still hoping for news from home, which he craved nowadays. The letter only said, "Be ready for first shipment ten days after date on this letter. Full order will be complete within three weeks. Good luck with your house. Sincerely, Robert Bryan." Looking at the date atop the letter, he did some figuring and sure enough, to the day, the lumber had been milled, shipped and delivered in the precise time his lumberyard friend had estimated. As he looked at his first shipment and the letter intended to foretell of same, he just started laughing. His lumber itself got there just as fast as the mail! "Stay with us tonight, Flathead. Rest those animals and I will arrange payment and give you another couple of letters to take to St. Marys."

Builder Jack Walls was on the hook now! He promised he could deliver the house if he had the lumber, but he couldn't dream of really getting it so soon. He had another problem, though: labor was just as tight for him as for everybody else. John recommended a planter in Fernandina who he thought could rent him some slaves to do the manual labor while Jack and his other skilled carpenter worked furiously to try to deliver. There was a growing trend of folks in the growing, labor-starved interior lands renting slave labor from the owners of the established coastal plantations. The older plantations were finding themselves with a surplus of labor as the plantation workloads were reducing since the plantations were fully developed and the planters were moving toward less labor intensive crops.

At the same time, even though the international slave trade was outlawed in 1808, meaning slaves could no longer be imported, the slave population was growing dramatically through birth. Slave owners found a new way to profit was to rent their labor out. It was a good deal for slave-owners and for the temporary slave-renters. I guess it was a good deal for everbody involved 'ceptin' the slaves.

For Mr. Walls and John Lee, "delivery" of the house meant the outside walls, floors, and roof were to be up, outside doors and shutters on, fireplaces and chimneys up, front porch, overhang, front and back outside steps all in place, and the inside staircase built. All the lathes for plastering the inside walls were to be in place, but no plaster on the walls or ceiling. The cook shed would be in about the same condition: a sturdy frame, walls and floor in place, but the shelves would have to wait. Of course the windows would not be in. Jack would try to have all inside doors hung, but he guaranteed John and Lizzie's bedroom door would be in and the privy out back built prior to her arrival.

John wrote four letters that night:

To Robert Bryan: "Thank you, Robert, for a fine load of lumber. Please take the enclosed letter to St. Marys bank for payment in full from my account." The letter was addressed to Mr. Jack Burden, Pres., St. Marys Bank. It said, "Please take this letter as authorization to pay *Bryan's Lumberyard* $23.60 for one load of lumber. The funds are in my account. Sincerely, John Lee." This was as much of a check as John needed at his St. Marys Bank.

To Lizzie he wrote a brief note expressing how much better Genoa would be after she arrived.

To Jimmy Jones at *D & L Butchery*: "Please immediately deliver twenty-five pounds of your finest cuts to *Bryan's Lumberyard* with instructions for Mr. Bryan to enjoy and share it with his men. Please send me the bill, but don't forget the family discount!"

John fully believed that being able to present his bride with a good house on her arrival (or at least a good start on one) was key to her being able to adjust to the stark new setting, considering all she was leaving behind.

The cook shed was built in back of the house. It was just a shack made of rough-hewn pecky cypress, a cypress board roof (because thatch would catch fire too easily), a packed dirt floor, and a brick fire pit with a small chimney. A horse stable and some cow pens, chicken coops, and a hog shed were quickly assembled. A well would soon be needed, but they had the luxury for a while of plenty of good water from Swift Creek to meet their needs. They wouldn't need a privy until about April when Lizzie, Levi, and James moved in. Ever the romantic, John got the idea to build it just before the arrival date, so he could assure Lizzie she was the first to use it, an honor which wasn't as impressive to Lizzie as John thought it might be, thus proving the age-old story about men and women and how they really can't understand each other.

Nancy and Wiley stayed in St. Marys with Lizzie's parents until school finished for the year. John couldn't wait for the whole family to be intact again on its new farm. He loved being back to his usual old, busy self.

The number five child, Mary Lee, was born in May, the first of many, many Lees to be born in Florida. Life was tough but couldn't have been better for all. It would have been toughest on Lizzie if she hadn't had the help of Avarilla. They were becoming very good friends. Ava loved Lizzie not only for taking her in, but for all the motherly instruction she got from her so late in her life since Ava's mother died when she was very young. Mr. Johns, God rest his soul, did the best he could, but suffice it to say, he wasn't equipped to raise a young lady.

The Lees settled in to settling in. All loved the new land, and John knew he was living his long time dream. The land let loose of its bounty, and life was good.

By September, the sparkling new glass windows looked wonderful on the finally complete Lee house. This house was to be home for multitudes of folks for many years.

Disaster in the New Land

After a couple years of settling in, you shouldn't be surprised to hear Lizzie was going to have another baby. She seemed to have more trouble this time than during her prior pregnancies. John attributed it to the fact she had so much going on with five children, four step-children, and feeding all of them plus two slaves. Even though the Lee family had been in Hamilton County two years, they were still getting settled, and life still wasn't easy. John didn't notice, but Ava was a Godsend to Lizzie, because she was so capable and got along so well with her new family. Ava and all the ladies of the Genoa settlement were watching Lizzie, taking care of the youngsters, and coaching Lizzie along. John just stayed out on the farm except for mealtimes and bedtime because by this time they were planting 120 of the 160 acres in the farm, leaving a little for wildlife around the creek and the homestead.

When the time came, little Elizabeth came real slow. Lizzie was getting fatigued the likes of which John had never seen. John figured the best thing for him to do was . . . go to work. Besides, he knew the women could handle it all, and he'd always just kind of been in the way during the deliveries of the other five. With any luck they would be able to finish planting the summer vegetables before nightfall.

After working all day, John realized Lizzie had been in labor for twenty hours and thought maybe he should check on her. Just then he saw Wiley riding out at a gallop on his favorite horse.

"Dad, you better come quick! It's not going well." In his usual stoic way, John responded "I'll be right there."

"NO! NOW!" Shouted the normally respectful Wiley.

John got home in no time, running his horse in a beeline to the house through the freshly planted field, then through the next field, horse trampling shin-high cotton plants with every gallop-step, a fire-able offense if John had seen anyone else doing such a trick.

Once at the house, he raced upstairs to the bedroom to see Baby Elizabeth sleeping calmly. Lizzie was drained and sweating all over. She could barely speak, and what she said was kept secret by John forevermore. He told her he loved their new little girl and he promised her life was going to be easier.

The next morning Lizzie was dead.

For reason of blood loss, simple fatigue, internal damage from childbirth, or a combination of all three, John's beautiful Lizzie was ripped away from him. It's un-knowable if her ailment could have been addressed by a real doctor, like Doc Borden back in St. Marys, but it was sure there was no doctor around, just a few home remedies in Genoa, Florida in 1828.

John could have just buried her on the Swift Creek Church grounds, but it didn't yet have an official cemetery. I guess to keep her from feeling too alone, she was buried in the Prospect Primitive Baptist Cemetery and was one of the earlier occupants of that winsome but sorrowful little patch of ground. If she had died in St. Marys, the church would have been packed and she would have had a fitting sendoff. At Prospect she had a few families, including her own. There wasn't even a circuit-riding preacher to officiate because he only came one weekend a month; and since nobody wanted a repeat of ol' Jacob DeLoach's funeral, Lizzie was promptly carted the ten miles to the Prospect Cemetery where she was quickly planted.

Instead of the modern pump organ at the St. Marys church, Lizzie's funeral had a decrepit harpsichord for her farewell service, at which daughter Nancy did her best to play a fitting rendition of Lizzie's favorite hymn, "Amazing Grace."

Since there was no stone mason for miles around, John himself carved out a crude wooden marker for his beloved. Since it was wooden, it soon disappeared, likely a victim of the unforgiving Florida elements. By time I was a boy old enough to remember these things, all anyone knew was, "Your Grandma Lizzie's buried somewhere over round here." I thought it quite a shame.

John's life would've been ripped away from him by the loss of Lizzie if he didn't have so many people depending on him. He was haunted by the memory of how lost the Johns kids were when they were orphaned. For his children, for the Johns kids, for Lizzie, and for himself, He pressed on. He vowed he would do all he could and continue being the father his family needed, at least to the best of his ability. He was convinced the best of his ability came from doing his work and keeping his chin up for the others.

For the rest of his life John had a nagging doubt left by the little lecture he'd gotten from Doc Borden about being so hard on Lizzie. Would she be alive today in St. Marys? She was so devoted and committed to the family needs and all John's wants, but did John make her happy? She was so willing to follow John "to the ends of the earth," even to Genoa, Florida, but was she happy there? John would never know, and couldn't know because he was so busy at his work he really didn't have the luxury of idle time to think about it all. He didn't like all this reflection and soul-searching the loss of his wife caused him. He found the only thing he could do to keep from thinking about, and desperately missing, Lizzie was . . . work.

Fortunately, Ava was a fabulous nanny for the other children. During the preciously short time she had with Lizzie, she learned so many things and became just like a sister to the younger Lee children as John was throwing himself back into his work with Wiley, the Johns boys, Robert, and Daniel all working alongside him. Ava was finding herself feeling very fulfilled; she just sort of stepped right into Lizzie's shoes.

John tried very hard to fill the holes in the hearts of the rest of his family, but it was very hard. When he looked at Nancy, all he could see was Lizzie's graceful movements, and her smile was her mother's.

John knew he'd been hard on Wiley, but he was the oldest son, and it was a father's duty to be hard on his sons, especially the oldest, right? Levi, James, and Mary might grow up without a memory of their sweet mother, but John could hope she would live on in them and all would cling to the belief she was "up there," wherever "there" was, interceding for them and helping them through their daily troubles and sorrows, helping them through the "Dangers, Toils and Snares" (as we'd sing in Lizzie's favorite hymn) of life which afflicted them each and every day, but to which she was no longer victim.

The Johns boys had become strongly attached to their adopted mother in the few years they were with her and had special pains of having lost not one, but two mothers in their short lives.

Even Robert and Daniel would get melancholy and start wailing whenever the name of "Mizz Lizzie" came up. Though they were her property, and the world would think they should hate her and hope only to spit on her grave, they loved the woman because she treated them with the respect they deserved as humans, even though so many mistresses of her day treated slave people lower than dirt. They respected John because he treated them fairly, if such was possible in such a relationship, but they loved Lizzie for her genuine care and concern for them. "Dat Sweet Chariot dun swung real low for Mizz Lizzie, but dat don' stop me from missin' her a whole bunch," Robert would say.

Baby Elizabeth was the glue to hold the clan together. She never knew her mother, but from her earliest days she reflected Lizzie's calm grace and concern for all around her. She took on the name L'il Lizzie. For her, life was a glorious thing, and she was grateful for every second she had.

Eventually, the ship of life righted itself and life became normal again for the Lees. John knew if he was going to make a go of his farming enterprise, he was going to need to grow it beyond the 160 acre patch he had and keep expanding. Sure, a quarter section was more than plenty for him to live and prosper on for all his years, but if this was all the land the family had when there was seven Lee and maybe a few Johns families, he knew he must expand. Time flew for John, and he was reaching the age where most men notice time speeding up just when you might like to see it slow down a little. He was soon to be thirty-five, almost the full life expectancy of his day. He'd seen a lot of his friends die by every cause from measles to mule-kicks, from pneumonia to polio. He was especially amazed at the women, who seemed to live forever if they could only make it through the child-bearing years.

Wiley, at almost twelve years old, was proving to be quite a worker. A lot like his father, he didn't show a lot of emotion. If you watched carefully, the only sign he'd ever show of anything bothering him would be to just work harder. There were times his co-workers would almost expect him to unhitch the mule, ol' Sloppy, and pull the plow himself. It wasn't known if he was hearing his Momma saying, "Time is money," or if he was he trying to gain approval of his father, which he thought he never achieved. Was it just that same inner drive which was populating the entire Southeastern United States and making fabulous farms and cities bloom out of nothing in this great young country?

Daniel liked to tell him, "Massuh Wiley, 't'aint right for no Massuh to be outworkin' de slave. I'se twiced yo' size an' I knows how to woik, but I just can't woik like you. Don't go killin' yoself now, and don' go 'spectin' me to woik like you. If I'se gonna be havin' to woik like you, bossman, you might'n jes' as well start a-whuppin' on me now. But you might wanna think about easin' up on yo sef if'n you don' wanna have yo sef a heart attack b'fore yore sixteenth birthday." Wiley seemed to get the point and would try to pace himself better when he got one of his lectures from his good friend Daniel.

"Work with purpose," his father would tell him, trying to encourage him. But was he encouraging or just giving a boost to the inner devils already driving poor Wiley? If he reached success due to his insatiable drive, would he be able to recognize it? Enjoy it?

Wiley was the eldest son of a driven man, and he was expected to carry on the family name with honor and take over when John saw fit to pass the reins his way. In the meantime, he was supposed to keep his nose to the wheel and be a "good boy" in the eyes of all around.

Wiley played his role very well. He was never any trouble, always a leader at Swift Creek Methodist, even though he wasn't even twelve yet. Preachers saw potential in him and would ask John if he'd thought of grooming Wiley for the seminary, to which John groused, "Too much work on the farm." Wiley stayed content doing what he knew and driving himself ever harder.

The one way Wiley was able to escape the backbreaking work on the farm was through his hunting and fishing. John even approved because it was productive. At least it produced meat for the family, and Wiley was really good at it. John was never much of a hunter because, as you remember, he'd been working six days a week since eight years old, and hunting and fishing were strictly forbidden on the Lord's Day. He enjoyed outdoor sports through Wiley but kept himself too busy on the farm to allow himself the time to hunt and fish.

Wiley even saw where he might make a little money with his sport. He planned someday when John opened up his meat shop, and he'd shot or caught more than the family needed, he could sell excess to the butcher shop and make a little money. He could leave the house about an hour before sun-up, steal away on his horse, Sugar, and be back by breakfast with a bag of birds, a big buck, a mess of fish, or whatever the kill of the day was. He could have it all cleaned, dressed out, ready for the girls to cook for dinner and still be in the field to do his day's work by 8:30 or so. Though John never said it, this made him proud, too; his boy was a worker and a provider.

John, of course, noticed how responsible and productive his son was, and marveled at the young man he was becoming. He surely was proud of Wiley, but it wouldn't be very John-like to say so, would it? So Wiley worked on.

Wiley's soft spot in his life seemed to be Ava, who reminded him so much of his Momma, but she was also very confusing because she was still a young lady, and he was now a young man. He wondered if maybe it was meant to be for his part-nanny, part-adopted sister to . . . never mind.

Wiley just couldn't get Ava off his mind. He'd had crushes before, with his foray into puppy love with the little Hillhouse girl at the farm next door. He understood how those were just passing fancies, but this felt more like real love. He grappled with her being so much older than he, but he was just real sure Ava couldn't find herself any better man in the frontier.

Love Blooms

Every time John saw E.T. Roux, he'd get a new report on the bad men running wild in the Florida territory. How does this man do any farming, when he was so busy chasing after mirages? As far as John could see, this new land was working out just fine and he saw no reason to be worried about anything. Roux made John promise he would make sure everybody in his family, particularly the girls, knew how to handle a rifle and a pistol. John, though, didn't see the point because he just wasn't worried about gangs in Hamilton County.

Wiley was happy to take charge of this project, and he was just the one to teach shootin' to the rest of the family. The one pleasure he allowed himself was his great enjoyment of the outdoors, particularly hunting. He was a self-taught expert marksman and could reload and be on the ready for another shot quicker than any of his hunting pals. He loved passing these skills on to his family.

He would particularly enjoy teaching Ava to shoot and felt so chivalrous in doing so because of the hum of fear going through the countryside on account of all the worry over the white gangs, which never seem to appear. Just in case, though, Wiley was clear he was going to protect all the women and children.

John took great pride in his son's hunting prowess. John felt the outdoors was something he missed out on since his father died so young and he went to work at only eight years of age. John didn't resent a minute of his working hours because he felt it was so much more productive to cut the jugular of a fattened cow than to stalk a lean and wary deer in the woods for hours and still not get take a shot. John was going to have Wiley show him how someday, but it wouldn't be any day too soon; he was too busy, don't ya know? But father and son had some good times together when Wiley would patiently tell his Dad about the hunt for a particular deer, hog or other critter.

You certainly got more and better meat out of a nice fat cow than a deer or wild hog, but John was thrilled when he could get meat for the family for just the price of a little powder and lead as opposed to all the work, time, herding, and feeding it took to grow up a calf to eating age.

As you can see, work was the daily focus on the farm, but a few times a year the neighbors would gather for some sort of occasion. One of those events was New Year's.

On New Year's Eve the whole Genoa settlement, now ten families, had a tradition. Or at least they figured someday it might become a tradition, of meeting at the church for a grand covered-dish gathering to usher out the old and ring in the new. The whole Lee gang, even Li'l Lizzie (though she knewnot why) was excited to ring in 1829, since '28 had been such a trial with the Lee's loss of their matriarch. Absent that one big blow, it had been a pretty good year for all since they pulled together as a family and did as families do in adversity. It was a strong maturing experience for the children, and maturity is something you can't come about too early on the frontier.

The latest addition to the settlement was the James Hiram McDonald family. They had just moved in and were camping on their ground, starting the whole painful, painstaking process of civilizing their patch of ground, and molding it into a family supporting machine. They were worn out from travel and the rigors of setting up a camp they'd be living in for months. They were from a large clan and came straight to Hamilton County from Scotland, supposedly wealthy and very refined folks. The McDonalds weren't your typical squatters of the day. Why someone with wealth in Scotland would want to come halfway across the world to squat on land in Genoa, Florida, with bad roads, no schools, only one little church, was beyond all the other settlers. They seemed nice people, though, and the neighbors at the New Year celebration were willing to give a fitting welcome to other nice people who wanted to try to stake their claim and make it go here in the new world.

The oldest McDonald girl was Alice. She was only a couple of years older than Wiley, so she seemed to be just about right. She was as cute as a bug's ear to Wiley. He thought it would be good for him to come over and make a proper introduction and show her just how refined and charming the good residents of Genoa could be.

After all got their fill of supper the New Year festivities continued. The square dance was called by Mercer Henry, a decent caller and as fine a man as you could meet. He was barkin' to swing your partner and promenade and dosey-doe 'til the church felt it was going to sway off its foundation. Wiley still couldn't figure if he wanted to dance with young Hilary Hillhouse or Ava Johns, whom he was now convinced were *both* the loves of his life. But to play hard-to-get, every now and then he'd grab the arm of the new McDonald girl and show the other two just how independent he could be. He kinda liked having three women anyway, two older and one younger.

It turns out another Lee man was having same thoughts about Ava; talk about confusing!

John had no idea if he was in love with Ava for how she'd helped him with the kids in such a trying time; or was he in love with her because she stepped into Lizzie's shoes so gracefully; or was he lonely; or was he just needin' to have more young'uns around? Regardless, his feelings started pretty quickly after Lizzie's death. Oh, his heart still ached for Lizzie, but his house was full and happy again already largely thanks to the way Ava so sweetly filled the void for each family member, even Robert and Daniel. John hadn't dared to breathe a hint of these feelings to anyone. For most pioneer men, there wasn't a whole lot of time or reason to talk about feelings, so it was best to just keep 'em to yourself.

It was more than amazing how Ava gained confidence and blossomed as a woman, first under Lizzie's care and teaching, then on her own with the sudden responsibility of a large family. She grew into herself overnight, and was quite sure her place in the world was right there in Genoa as the surrogate mother for the Lee family and her own siblings. She would do it for Lizzie, if for no one other reason.

Well, when it was time to do the final promenade and find your best partner and usher her out the door, John instinctively jumped to Ava's side, linked her arm and said "You with me? If you are, I promise a good ride."

Ava looked into his eyes and all the way through to his soul and said, "I think I'm with you, plowboy!" Both stunned by this little exchange, they quickly broke the gaze and continued walking arm-in-arm speechlessly toward the wagon. Neither of them knew or understood what just happened, but they were both surprised by what they felt.

Then they had to go home to where they both lived under the same roof, cared for the same kids, and worked together day and night. It wasn't shaping up to be a traditional courtship.

1829 was going to be another bell-ringer for the Lees.

Now make no mistake, John was still working hard, but he could easily be distracted by any excuse to come back to the house to check on a sick young'un, pick up another tool or get water for the working men. His best line was, "I'm letting Wiley run the crew now; he needs to learn how to be a foreman while I'm tending to business." No one had ever seen John around his own house so much, which was a nice change for him, because Lizzie's absence, he'd been stayin' as far away from the house, especially his bedroom, as he possibly could, whenever he could.

The children found John's new habits fortunate for them because he'd finally gotten to be pleasant to be around again. Not to say he was unpleasant before, but it was real hard to tell if he was distant because he was so wrapped up in making a go of his farm, or if he was busy missing his Lizzie and had no better way to handle it than to withdraw. Until now, the always-reserved John Lee was going so deep into his shell that nobody thought he'd ever come out again. Suddenly it all changed.

By now, John was experienced in love. He loved and lost Cami, and he loved and won Lizzie, just to lose her all too soon. Since he was considering romance again, it seemed he'd be pretty good at it, but don't underestimate John's ability to be a klutz at affairs of the heart. It's probably a man problem in general more than just a John Lee problem.

You see, we men tend to learn our lessons about women the hard way, and we always seem to be applying our last lesson to our next love. Most pioneer men didn't have much choice in women; they kind of had to take what was available. Many of the big families had a girl or three who didn't get married, and there was normally a real good reason they became old maids, if you know what I mean. Though I guess it works about the same for the women folks, too, 'cause lots of the big families also had a son or two who never took a bride.

By comparison, John would have been a pretty good catch; he was a promising farmer, well established and ambitious to grow beyond what he already had, with a nice family and the finest house in the county (although it was crude by the standards of any coastal town). He was a pretty good package there in the newly-settled Suwannee Valley. But John never did feel he was much of a catch. In fact he never gave it much thought. He was built like a stump with slightly dark, leatherized skin from working in the Florida sun, and dark eyes. Many believed each of those attributes came from his partial Indian heritage.

While a city girl might have needed a better dancer, more courtly manners, softer hands, a smoother complexion, or better coifing, the pioneer girl saw "I'm not afraid to work, and don't get in my way of getting a job done." The pioneer lady would see John's features and swoon because there were plenty of men, even there and in those times, who only wanted to do what they had to just to get by. There was another plenty of men who were going to spend every spare minute with a jar of their homemade hooch, and plenty of them were getting real good at finding more and more spare time. I guess this is kinda true everywhere, isn't it? But John was different, and it looked like his boy Wiley was shaping up to be cut from the same bolt of cloth.

All that's to say poor John found himself in a new predicament. He was falling for a girl who first, was his adopted daughter; second, was the nanny of his children; and third, already lived under his roof.

He was thankful he was no longer in St. Marys 'cause there was a group of well-intended ladies there who could stir up a great big scandal over this one. One more reason he loved Hamilton County was because most folks were just too busy scraping a living out of the land to stick their noses where they didn't belong. Whatever happened on the Lee farm would probably stay (he dearly hoped) right within his house. What could've be more convenient?

It was really a flat-footed, pioneer-type arrangement for John. One evening he told the younger kids to finish cleaning up the supper dishes and asked Ava to come outside. He escorted her politely, but not romantically, to the new two-seater swing hanging from the big oak tree. They were seated facing away from the house and overlooking the expanse of farmland for which John and all had labored so hard. They enjoyed the light dusky breeze, and John saw how winsome she was with her auburn hair in strands pulled behind her and twisted somehow or another to make it look like a rope. He couldn't figure why a woman would want her hair to look like a rope. Even more, he couldn't understand why something so simple could make a man's heart flutter and cause him to lose his mind. It always seemed some women just knew what they were doing with what they had and just how to drive us fellas crazy. It was a huge disadvantage.

He started by telling her how much he appreciated all she'd done for the family since Lizzie died and how well his kids were doing, all to her credit. He was glad she fit in so well and gave so much of herself to everyone right down to Robert and Daniel.

Now here's where you might want to hold the hand of the target of your affection, if for no other reason than to symbolically capture your prey, but John was approaching the whole thing in far too businesslike a manner. He sounded like a good salesman who knew his subject well and was out to make his best offer and close the deal.

He carried on like this for a while until Ava decided to make it easy for him. In her common sense way, she said, "John, we've been through a lot, and I can never thank you enough for adopting my family and keeping us together. I can never thank Lizzie enough for teaching me to be a lady. The only way I know to thank you is to continue helping you in whatever way I can. If you see fit to make it official, since I am only your adopted daughter, I think it's the most natural thing in the world, and it would make me the happiest girl in all Genoa" (giggling) "or maybe the whole world! I'd love to spend the rest of my life with you making you happy. And you know, don't you, your daughters are going to need a lot of advice you're not going to be able to give them?" Seemed the salesman was getting outsold by his intended customer.

John's heart was all aflutter now. He tried to keep his composure as he made his final disclosure because he wasn't sure she'd thought of, shall we say, everything. She'd even said it herself, she wanted to continue throwing herself into the family. Did she realize it would include John throwing himself at her? Surely it never dawned on this beautiful young flower to think of them being married in *that* way. How could she? If she understood the hint, John figured she'd run screaming back into the house to barricade herself in her room and never want to see him again, he thought, now in a full panic. "It will be so natural," he managed to say, "all we've got to do is re-arrange the furniture a little - you know - move your chest into my room," looking at her quizzically, as if to say, "Are you sure you're aware of all we're talking about here?" Nervously he continued, "And doesn't Nancy deserve to maybe have a room of her own for a while until she's fully grown?" Silently and with mind racing, he slowly turned his head to look at her to see if she was red with anger or shocked with fear. He could conceive no other options at this point.

What he saw melted him. She was looking straight into him with a calm, confident smile. Her face said it, but just to be sure John understood, she figured she'd better say it in plain English. "Yes, John. I can't wait to be your wife, and if the good Lord will bless us with a few more kids I will be even more thrilled to be Momma to not only your kids, but to our kids, too. And I pledge to you I will never treat our kids any different than I do your kids because they're all God's children, and we only have them for a while and need to treat everyone as we'd like to be treated ourselves." John finally relaxed; they embraced, had their first kiss, then just held on tight and enjoyed a moment they'd both been apparently dreaming of for some time with only one thin wall separating them. It was a good thing each didn't know what the other was thinking, or the heat just might have burned a hole in the thin dividing wall.

The embrace might have lasted longer, but they were interrupted by sudden yelps coming from inside the front window. The older children were trying hard to keep the younger ones silent so they could watch the whole thing and see how it played out, but it wasn't to be. All the kids ran outside, the older ones to congratulate Ava and John for doing what they had all prayed for since right after Momma died, and the younger ones just wanted to tease them for getting caught in the act of kissing.

Wiley, real manlike, went to his Pa, stuck out his hand and said, "Congratulations," with a mixture of goodwill, jealousy, and concession. He knew he really shouldn't have a crush on a woman twice his age, but when young love gets stabbed in the heart, it has a real special pain. Wiley would quickly see the new arrangement made more sense than his plans ever did.

The sun set, and the next day, like all days on the Lee farm, would bring lots of work to be done.

Wedding day came just a couple of weeks later. The family loaded up both wagons and took all the Lees - bride and groom; the six Lee kids; Ava's three siblings, Joe, Josh and Lillie; and Robert and Daniel - up to the church. Having a church wedding was uncommon in that day, and kind of trendy. John hadn't even thought of it, but Ava wanted it, so he happily obliged. She said it made the good Lord more a part of the wedding, and that's a good way to start a marriage. The rest of the settlement was all invited and, of course, came. The church was the center of, or, better said, the sum total of social life for the settlers.

Of course Reverend Gerry was happy to perform the joyful occasion for the Lees, after so recently sharing in the pain of the loss of Lizzie, so the wedding date was set for his next rotation there. It was a very special day for the Reverend because he got to preach the wedding of his friend and also do a baptism for little Nancy Johnson, the latest addition to Genoa's population.

After Nancy was "sealed into God's Kingdom forever," the bridal party was all ready to go. Having heard of another new wedding trend in the big cities, Ava decided to have "attendants." The Lee boys were all "best men," and the girls were all "maids of honor." Now if the reader is confused, thinking, "The Lees are not trendy people," the reader would be right. However, John thought it harmless enough to let the family stand up with the bride and groom. Besides, if all of Genoa showed up, the little church was going to run out of room anyway. Therefore, if somebody was gonna have to stand up, why not let the Lees stand up front so nobody has to stand in the back? A Lee man was always practical, even if it meant he had to be trendy to do so.

The boys all had on whatever their best clothes were. Being the oldest boy, Joseph Johns had a pretty decent set of pants and shirt. It was handmade and homemade, but he was dapper. As the boys ages decreased, their clothes got successively more tattered, clear evidence the Lees were a hand-me-down family and no article of clothing was too old or tattered. The Lees made darn sure every piece of clothing was well worn out before it was re-assigned to the rag bin. No one cared, and all seemed to enjoy "dress-up occasions," not necessarily because they liked looking their best, but maybe because a day in the good clothes meant a day not in the field.

Since several of the girls' dresses were in tatters, Ava and the girls quickly sewed up three or four new white dresses, each nearly identical to the bride's. Even li'l Lizzie, who wasn't walking very well yet, was in her baby bride dress and stood up front as a maid of honor. The bride, of course, wore the customary white flowers arranged like a crown in her hair, while the other girls did not.

Ava was never prouder of her family or of the work of her hands.

She tried to insist John get himself a new, real suit of clothes, but it would mean a trip all the way to St. Marys or Fernandina for measurements and another trip for fitting. They realized that unless they wanted to delay the wedding, the new groom's suit was just not possible. Both agreed wild horses could not stop them from having this wedding on the very first day they could get the Reverend. Thus, John's threadbare "good" pants were starched and ironed real straight, and his shirt, well, it probably didn't look too bad if you were sitting in the back row.

Robert and Daniel were ushers. Their job was to stand at the front door of the church and give everybody a real warm welcome, thank them for coming, and thank 'em again when they left the church. It added a bit of a formal touch. Ava had been working with them on their speech and grammar, so they had an opportunity to show off their new social skills.

Simple vows were spoken. After a booming "What GAAAWWD hath brought together, let NO MAN put asunder," the crowd cheered, and all hurried outside for dinner. The guests gave their best advice for the new couple, including E. T. Roux, who just said, "Congratulations, John, we're all going to need to work together if we're going to protect these families of ours."

That day, Wiley noticed Alice McDonald. The dress she wore was not made by some country girl out of whatever cloth she could get her hands on. Wiley never noticed dresses much before, but it was either the dress or the person in it, or a combination thereof that caught his eye. Something was stunning about Alice. He couldn't explain it, but he was real sure he liked it. Alice had a lilting Scottish brogue he was pretty sure could tame a wild bear. Her folks were giving her lots of education, with music training and even Latin, a language not spoken for about a thousand years and surely never heard around Genoa, Florida.

He was too nervous to talk to her much, so he mostly teased her about talking so funny. Her little sister, all of four years old, was named Mary Ann Elizabeth McDonald. He didn't understand why you'd give anybody four names, especially a girl, 'cause she was likely to add yet another name down the road sometime. After teasing Alice about her sister's many names, he said he especially liked one of them: Elizabeth. It was just like his Momma Lizzie's name.

Wiley loved Ava, and he was real happy about this new arrangement where he could love Ava like a Momma and still have room in his heart for someone else. Maybe this Alice girl, even though she was older, too, would be a little more his vintage.

Shortly after the wedding, Daniel, Robert, and Wiley came to John to talk business. It was early, and they were all leaning on the fence at the cow pens. "Dad," Wiley said, "Daniel and Robert have come to me with a proposal I think makes sense. They think you need more help, and they think you're going to keep on needing more help, and they see a way that with just a little bit of an up-front investment, you can have a growing labor force to keep you set for all you need."

"How's that work, Wiley?"

"Well, you see, I guess it was the wedding made them start thinking how lonely they are, er, I mean how much they'd be able to expand the work crew for you for free if you'd buy a wife for each of them."

John just about bit his tongue. "What? You know slave women are expensive. The slave trade has stopped and so they don't just come in by the shipload anymore."

"And that's why we're here, Dad," pled Wiley. "And the only way to get more labor is to grow it here or pay a high price for the slaves the plantation owners don't want. Further, you know how hard freeman labor is to get out here. We all thought labor would be in good supply by now, but the land keeps opening up and every bit of labor just gets taken up as soon as anyone gets wind there might be a hire available. If we're gonna expand our fields, we may have to expand our labor force right here."

Daniel chimed in, (with his new and improved English Ava taught him), "Mista Lee, the only thing I beg is please, please, promise us we will be able to stand as a family, and you won't sell no kids, . . . I mean, *any* kids. My wife and me, I, we will grow you the best farmhands you ever seen, *saw*. I think you agree, too, Robert and I have learned how to farm your way, and we can teach it real good" (his language wasn't perfect yet) "to another generation. We can set up Mr. Wiley with the best farmhands in Hamilton County."

Robert decided to give it a try, too. "Missah Lee, We know you . . . have . . . a . . . new baby on the way, and another thing yousa, YOU ARE, gonna need is mo hep for your ladies. I just be knowin' Miz Ava gonna need mo' hep if you gonna keep havin' babies, I just know she do, WILL. And Missah Lee, if you's be needin' mo hep 'round here, I 'gree wit' Missah Wiley, and I promise, if'n you'll jus' provide the womenfolk, Me and Daniel, we'll take real good care of the breedin', you won't have to worry none 'bout dat." Robert still wasn't as smooth as Daniel, especially when he got excited.

John looked all three men in the eye, took a long pull on his pipe, and said, "Thank you, gentlemen. This has been an interesting meeting, and I will get back to you soon."

Wiley stayed back and said, "Thanks, Dad. We all know what Robert and Daniel want, and we both want good things for them, too, but think about it cold and hard. There's so much running away going on, and we know our guys are hearing from those pot-stirrers out there. I don't think we ever have to worry about either of those fellas laying harm to any of us, but if they have to continue being so lonely, they may just run off in search of a family. Even more, I just think they deserve it."

Since John was the one who shelled out his hard earned money for Robert and Daniel, he saw them as more of a business deal. Wiley, though, grew up with them, worked shoulder-to-shoulder with them, and saw them as brothers, sort of back-yard brothers. What he said seemed to make sense. John, like so many slaveholders, had to keep himself from thinking of slaves as flesh and blood rather than just property. Besides, he bought them fair and square, didn't he?

Or to look at it another way; what fool cowman would have a perfectly good bull without making him into a breeding pair?

He also knew some of the coastal plantations were hiring out or selling slave labor nowadays. As those farms were converting away from cotton to the lower intensity grain crops, slaves, particularly breeders (women), were losing value for the first time since 1807, when the importation of slaves was outlawed. Even more, the cotton gins were getting so good, the need for slave labor was plummeting. A modern gin of this day could run one thousand pounds of cotton per hour, and only fifty years ago the same half-ton would take about one thousand slaves four or five hours each.

The planting, cutting, weeding and harvesting still took huge amounts of man-hours, and we'd been lucky to get enough extra hired labor when we had to have it, but it was always a struggle to get enough hands I our busy times.

John continued thinking to himself, "I think my teenage son and my two African slaves have just made me a good proposal!"

The White Sulphur Springs settlement enjoyed steady, plodding growth. Several folks had plans to build a hotel down near the spring and thought it would be a big attraction for wealthy wintering Northerners. There were rumors of a second hotel in the works, too. Some town leaders began to suggest it might be worth organizing into an official town soon.

In 1831, the Hooker Brothers (William and James), James Prevatt, Joseph Bryant and John Lee joined together and took the legal steps necessary to make a real town, incorporating and naming it Jackson Springs in honor of Andrew Jackson, of course. It wouldn't be long before the healing powers of White Sulphur Springs were known across the country. It wasn't many years later the name was changed to White Springs to help bring attention to its main attraction.

To help make it a real town, John decided to go ahead and open his butcher shop as soon as Jackson Springs was incorporated. Though there was probably not enough customers to support it yet, John thought it would help attract folks who might be thinking of moving in, and it might discourage another butcher who might have his eye on John's town.

Life couldn't have been better for the Lees. There was a four-year run wherein everything grew: beans, corn, cotton, cows, hay, indigo, melons, pigs, tobacco, even the wives. Several of 'em grew real big then dropped a new young'un and went right back to work.

You remember how John told Ava she oughta move into John's bedroom so Nancy Lee could have the luxury of her own bedroom? Well, Nancy did have it . . . for about a minute!

Ava quickly had little John Jr., and if he wasn't the king of the house! His laugh never stopped. Never, that is, until he got the whooping cough and his sweet little laugh was never heard again. John, Jr. was buried in the new Swift Creek Cemetery.

Then came another John Jr. in 1831. He didn't see life quite as humorously as his deceased older brother, but he was a keeper. He mighta been a little too guarded by his siblings on account of his older brother's demise, but John knew he'd be alright. And Sarah Lee joined the family in '33. Li'l Sarah had John wrapped around her little finger. John's sister Sarah and her husband moved in from St. Marys, too. Mr. Walls had been back to the Lee place twice to add on to the now rambling (but not so stately) Lee farmhouse, but nobody was real sure when we were going to have enough bedrooms for the couples or when the sleeping porches would be big enough for all the young'uns.

Joshua Johns was engaged to marry one of Farmer Jeffrey Murphy's girls. They planned to move to Murphy's to start out, but Wiley told him he'd make room somewhere for 'em if they changed their minds. Ava joked they might have to stay in the barn, "But y' know our Lord was born in a barn, and probably not as fine a stable as we have here!"

After almost four years, Daniel and Robert just couldn't quit smilin' since they met Josie and Mamie, slave sisters from the Morgan plantation all the way up in Charleston. John issued them their wives and told them to figure out which one belongs to which. "Get all cleaned up," he said, "Come up to supper at the house. When we're done, we'll have a 'Jump the Broom' ceremony, and you'll be married." Robert and Daniel decided they both loved both of them so much, they just couldn't decide, so they were gonna have Josie and Mamie do the decidin'. It's still unknown how the girls came about their decision, but that night Josie and Daniel, and Mamie and Robert became men and wives. When John was blowing out his last candle for the night, he looked out at the slave quarters, then back at Ava, saying, "If we have to listen to this every night, we'll never get any sleep around here again." Ava just laughed. John was very happy for his friends, er, property.

Josie and Mamie were great around the house, helping with the children and teaching the older girls a thing or two of how things were done on the fine coastal plantations. Ava hoped these slave women could teach the girls more about the finer things in life so they might attract fine gentlemen for husbands.

In their short time with us, Josie and Mamie already had five young'uns between them.

Just like the extended Lee clan, all of Hamilton County was growing. New families were always moving in, and progress was making life better for all.

Vigilant Vigilantes

John went into the butcher shop which he named *D & L Meats* in order to keep a remembrance of old Jacob DeLoach, about twice a week. He spent about a half day each time, more if he was needed. It ran pretty well, but just didn't make money like he was used to at the original shop. Truth be told, I think John really liked his long horse ride into town and the peace and quiet of the butcher shop. His butcher and shop manager, Tom, was a sliver of a kid when he went to work for John in St. Marys. At only twenty-one, he was proud to be in charge of his own store. John thought him honest and kinda had to trust him because he wasn't around enough to know if he was shorting John or shorting the customer. Jacob would've never let John out of his sight long enough to cause any doubts, but now John had a whole different enterprise running down the road at the farm, and he was much more interested in assuring the farm's success than worrying about his two bit butcher shop which might never really pay him back.

In 1835, things finally started growing in earnest around White Springs. Bryant Sheffield, who owned the spring and land around it finally opened the first hotel for health tourists and wintering Northerners. John thought maybe this development would be the one to launch the growth he was predicting when he left St. Marys years ago. He had to wonder, though, was he better off to have pioneered White Springs or to have stayed in much more civilized St. Marys. He knew it was a sure waste of time to second-guess a ten-year-old-decision. He loved the land and loved the accomplishment of earning a living out of newly developed earth from pure scratch.

One fine day, about mid-day, John was at the shop when a new customer came in, a burly man with a big scowl on his face and a bunch of scars. Though he was real dirty and all-around unpleasant, the sight of him wasn't too unusual in these parts because there were lots of men who worked real hard and weren't the prettiest sights to see, but this one was different.

After the stranger got his package of goat ribs, which he paid for from a huge wad of cash, John thought he'd be a little friendly to him and maybe break the ice with a newcomer.

"You're not from here, are you?" He inquired, then, offering a handshake, he said, "M' name's Lee, John Lee . . . what's yours?"

"None o' yore bidness," was all he said, turned and walked out. John gulped.

Soon as the door shut, John started laughing, "No wonder he's no friendlier than a rattlesnake, he's got the personality of one, too." After a couple of big har dee hars, he looked at his butcher, Tom, who was just standing with his cleaver, white as a ghost.

Tom paused, then said, "His first name's same as yours. That was John Murrell. He showed up in town yesterday, had a horse shod at the blacksmith, then left. It's what he does when he's scouting out a new area. He tries to act like he's doing business, but he's figurin' out who everybody is, where they live, and what they've got that he might want. He has a gang of criminals, misfits, fugitive slaves, and Indians he recruits to go on his raids, then he disappears somewhere in the swamps, I guess. Has a sidekick named Callahan. The gang, known as the Murrellites, works a big area. They've been murdering men, raping women, stealing cattle, money and slaves, and burning farmsteads from as far south as Hogtown settlement all the way to Madison to the west. He won't tell anybody his name. We thought he might be who he is, but weren't able to confirm it 'til Mr. Roux came in and listened to a description of him. Now I think we know, and it's not good. With all due respect, Mr. Lee, he now knows who you are, and I just bet you he already knows where you live and what you've got, what with those fine windows on your house, this store, and everything."

John, with no more joking, in fact, downright somber, said, "I know, Tom, I know. I just didn't think you knew so much and didn't want you to be afraid. I knew of the rascal when we were in the Army together in the War of 1812. I didn't remember his name, but I'd remember that face anywhere. He was no good then as a soldier, and he's no good now. He's one of the ones who had nothing waiting for him back in the U.S., so he just stayed out here and took his chances against the Indians, fugitives, and what was left of the Spanish Army. Desperate men like him do what they have to for survival. I know he knows me, too. It hasn't been very long. Seein' him around here makes me worry for my family and the farm.

I heard ol' E.T. Roux talk of him. He said the Murrell gang was the main group of outlaws we need to worry about here. I couldn't let myself believe him, or I guess I just didn't want to. I figured he was nothing more than a two bit thief, but I don't like what I just saw. If Roux is right, this one's a real rotten egg, and we might have our hands full. I guess I wish I'd paid more attention. I fear I've been a fool."

Lee left the shop real quickly and went straight to Roux's farm. "E.T., I guess I owe you an apology. I saw John Murrell today."

Roux responded, "Never mind the apology, John. How do you know it was Murrell?"

"Recognized his face from the Army, didn't remember the name, but this'ns no good. He was in my butcher shop today. My man, Tom, said he was snooping around town yesterday. He's a bad egg alright, I think I just didn't want to believe you, E.T."

Roux said, "I know he was here yesterday, but this is the first I hear of him being around today. He and his gang are some of the worst lowlifes anywhere in the country. Those bastards are terrorizing farms and small towns everywhere. He doesn't make a lot of mistakes, so there's some reason he's pokin' aroun' here. You can bet he's up to no good"

Then with a deadly serious expression, Roux continued, "John, we have a U.S. Marshall now, and we've got a Sheriff, but you know how thin they're spread, and I know the law's more scared of Murrell than Murrell is of the law. If, and I mean if, we could all get deputized, we couldn't do anything unless it was under Sheriff Shaddrack Sutton's command. We've got to be able to respond right away or somebody we know or love is gonna get killed, and I don't want it to happen. I know you and most of the rest of the county think I'm an idiot, and I don't mind, but I hope I've repeated the warnings enough so now the folks around White Springs will respond and rally. We got good riflemen and good hunters. We know this land better'n they do, but they are cagey. They've been renegades a long time and they don't mind dyin'.

"John, assuming you're in, we need to go to all the farms and tell each one of the farmers what we're facing. Get an inventory of horses, guns, men, boys, and slaves. And, oh, yes, and how many of the women can shoot. Them what can't shoot have got to learn to load. To every farm you go to, have each farmer go to five more. Have them write it up best they can. Try your best to keep it from the women and children until we're organized, then they *need* to know 'cause they're going to be part in this also. Bring in your inventory sheets tomorrow afternoon. It won't be perfect, but it'll give us an idea what we've got to work with. Start at your farm and get Josh, Joe, and Wiley on their horses right away. I know those boys will get right on it, and I know they can write. Tell 'em be real smart. No heroes yet. If we can find Murrell's camp or hear tell of where they might be, we'll have a big jump on 'em, 'specially if they don't see us seein' them. But any one man or small group of men, who tries to take him on are just making business for the undertakers.

"Make sure every farm knows to give 'em anything they want for now. Don't put up a fight, and they've got a chance. If ol' John's in a lovin' mood, it's gonna get real ugly if the man's around. They'll tie him up and torture him while he's doin' his evil on the wife. If the farmer's not around, tell the women don't resist. I hate this part, but the women who fought back have come out real bad. Not all will join us, but make sure they all know to get any information about the band to the nearest farmer who's in our group. If we can get a sightin' of him, we can track his ass down. Next time he comes to White Springs, we'll have a tracker on him.

"There's a pretty good group of folks don't think I'm as looney as you do, and they've done some work to get ready. Their women are trained, and all their slaves know how to shoot, or at least load. Of course, that could be its own problem someday, but for now we need 'em all on our side. They're fearin' for their women because Murrell lets his idiots have their way with the slave women sometimes and they're all talking about it." John had heard tell of such events. Roux continued, "Some of the slaves are real scared of shooting or even pointing a gun at a white man, but they have no problem goin' after the Indians and blacks in Murrell's motley gang. We need everybody. They know he's stealing slaves, and even the ones that ain't happy know they don't want the treatment they'll get from whoever he resells 'em to.

"You in, John?"

"E.T., I'm in, and I have a whole new respect for you. I'm sorry to say I only believe you because I looked the man in the eye today, and I suddenly understand. He's a bad one. "

"We'll have time for all your respectin' later on. I hope it's not at our funerals. Since you and, I'm assuming, your boys are with us, our recruitin' should get a lot better. You carry a lot of influence around here, Mr. Lee. There's a whole lot more everybody has to learn. All our squad meetings will be Saturday mornings; Murrellites are a hard-drinkin' bunch of cusses, and they haven't yet made a raid on an early morning. It might be the only advantage us God-fearin' Protestants have over them."

John and his horse were gone on a flat run. He was glad to see all the boys, including Robert and Daniel, were together working the cows near the house, but far enough away to not be heard by the women.

"Boys, your jobs just changed."

He reconstructed everything as best he could, but his head was spinning from all he heard and couldn't believe he was telling this to his boys. Even young Levi and James happened to be at the cowpens, so they got a good dose of growin' up that day. John passed some instructions ET had printed up four years ago for when (not if) this happened. He'd gone in secret to the Fernandina newspaper, befriended the owner, and they worked together at night to print them up. E.T.'s handbills got to be real well known around these parts.

John, Joe, Josh, and Wiley went four different directions on a White Springs version of Paul Revere's more famous ride of less than sixty years before. Wiley, of course, went straight to the McDonald farm.

Robert and Daniel watched them ride off. Looking at each other they agreed, "If we have to, we's gonna die for our women and our babies and for the Lee women, too."

The boys all got home well after dark and were disappointed they weren't able to get the word out further, but John told them it would be all right, and they would see tomorrow when they got their results.

Of course, if it went according to plan and the four Lee boys each went to five farmers, who then went to five more farmers, half the county would be quickly covered. In his wisdom, Roux knew it wouldn't be so easy, but he would surely get enough names of volunteers to have a force to overwhelm Murrell and his band of miscreants, who at last report were about twenty strong.

Saturday morning, farmers started showing up at the Roux house. Per instructions, every farmstead sent only one man to this meeting, the others would stay home to protect the property and womenfolk just in case. On arrival, each man was instructed to give his information sheet to John Lee so they could begin tallying the available resources. Every farmer for miles with a Scotch or Irish last name was there and ready for blood. Almost all the Welsh were there, too. Something about the blood from the folks in that corner of Europe was always ready for a fight, especially if it meant protecting family and property.

The meeting began on a humorous tone when Mr. McCree observed how unlikely it was for all these Scotch-Irish and Welshmen to be gathering to follow the lead of a Frenchman. A roar rose from the crowd, then the men settled and the meeting started.

John Lee called the men to order, saying, "Make no mistake, gentlemen, this is a secret vigilance committee we're launching today. We're a raggedy army, and the law's not going to like us any more than the Murrellites are. We're choosing this route because we think it's the only way we can protect our people and property."

"KINDA LIKE PUTTIN' THE BIT IN YOUR OWN MOUTH, AIN'T IT, LEE?" Shouted a voice from the back of the room.

Some muttered agreement while others just stared blankly at Lee.

John just said, "Well, maybe so, but we're here today to listen to Mr. E.T. Roux and his plan. He's been preparing for this day a long time now, and thanks to him, we stand a chance of giving John Murrell a push back. Anybody who thinks he has a better idea can bring it up when E.T.'s through. I think we need to say a prayer before we get started on this."

Next, John called on the Rev. Thomas Robinson Barnett, a Methodist circuit rider based in the little turpentine settlement of Sanderson, up on the main road between Alligator and Jacksonville. He'd been passing through town on the Lord's business. Asked to lead an opening prayer and beg for grace, the Reverend started with, "Let's bow our heads for a season of prayer," then he set in to invokin', blessin', protectin', hedgin', shieldin' and condemnin' the demon enemy, and pleadin' with the almighty to rain down glory from above to overcome, just as in the days of Moses - and more. John worried he was going to miss his harvest season if Barnett didn't button up his season of prayer sometime soon. John really did appreciate, though, the man's fervor, integrity, and commitment. He knew the local boys had a big advantage over Murrell if Thomas Barnett would just keep on praying like he did that morning.

When he finished, every one of the new vigilante troops hooted out a real big AMEN!!! and settled in for the one-hour boot camp before taking vows and going into battle. Reverend Barnett excused himself because he really had to be getting back to God's work.

Well, with a roomful of Irish and Scotsmen, and suddenly no preacher in attendance, you won't be surprise what happened next. No sooner had the door slammed behind the preacher than bottles started appearing out of pockets, corks started popping out of bottles, and bottles started passing around like a baby at a nun convention.

Roux took charge with the manner of a Field Marshall. He was a little annoyed by the sudden party atmosphere, but he figured as long as it didn't get out of hand, a little imbibing might just help to lubricate the troops and stir them into service. He had the plan, he would be able to coordinate the troops, and Hamilton County may just achieve what the U.S. Marshalls could not yet: to bring about the demise of the Murrell-Callahan gang. Here were the rules as laid out by E.T. Roux:

"First: Absolute secrecy. If Murrellites catch wind of any of our strategies, they might use them against us. Know who you're talking to at all times, and make real sure he or she is trustworthy.

"Second: No more blasting." All the farmers were still using black powder bombs to clear land. "This must cease right away. From now 'til Murrell is dead or gone or safely under the jail, the only bomb blasts or gunshots are to be a cry for help. Everyone in earshot is to take his men and rifles riding or running in the direction of the sound. If evil is going on at any farm, neighbors will defend neighbors. If you need meat, trap it. If you still don't have enough, eat beans. Gentlemen, this system is our only chance; we must make it work.

"Third: Same for your daily burning: it must cease. Another call for help is to build a fire. Have your bonfire built with turpentine rags at the ready. If you have trouble or see trouble coming, set 'em ablaze at the first sign of any kind of mischief. False alarms are tolerated, because we want you alive, not dead. Again, if you see anything suspicious, set off a bomb and light the fire. We'll be there for you. Use a lot of Spanish moss on your fire - it makes a lot of smoke.

"Fourth: If you can trust your slaves, teach 'em to shoot. If you don't trust them, teach 'em to load. Teach your women to shoot and load, but do it today because there's no more firing after sundown. If you can be in your house with rifles loaded, and if one rifleman can have two or three reloaders, then you've got the advantage over them. They have to reload themselves, and they have garbage for weapons. They never clean their guns, and they misfire all the time. I'm guessin' two straight-shootin' men with reloaders, shootin' from a shelter, should be able to handle ten Murrellites out in the open."

"Fifth: Only a few of them are good aims. They win by making you more fearful than they are. If you can stay calm and take good shots, you'll hit a few and they'll likely run, leaving a trail of hooves and blood. With a sure trail, we can get 'em. They're cagey woodsmen, but so are we.

"Sixth: Don't be trusting, but don't shoot 'til you know it's trouble. A Bible salesman got killed in Welaka because a nervous settler didn't believe him. We're working on getting all the salesmen to quietly leave town, but there's always new ones coming in. Murrellites will pose as salesmen, tradesmen, even laborers. I hear once six of 'em hired on to work a man's farm. After a couple of hours the farmer left, they sneaked into the house, robbed it, bound and gagged the women and got away clean. Lee, that fancy glassed up house of yours might be a target for one of those hired-hand ploys, 'cause they're not gonna waste breakin' a sweat if they don't think there's money or valuables inside. A real salesman is going to leave when he sees you're armed and you don't want his goods, but a Murrellite is going to try to get your confidence and get in your house; then you're in trouble.

"Seventh: Bury your gold and valuables, and don't leave anything looking like a fresh-dug hole. They know the trick, but you gotta say, 'We have no money, we just paid the mortgage, my husband drinks up every dime he earns, hail hit our cotton last year, we just bought two new horses and we're broke,' be creative. Everybody say something different. Leave a few of your good things out if you have any, and let 'em find some silver money. That way they'll be less suspicious you hid it. I know truth is most of us don't have nothin' much to hide, but look around your house. If there's somethin' your lady don't want to part with, it's better to hide it. Sometimes a Murrellite will see something nice and just up and break it out of pure mean-ness. But if those skunks are in your house, be sure to let the women know to let 'em take what they want. If you've got any women who are good shots, tell 'em have no reservations about shootin' a Murrellite in the back, especially if he's walking out with her valuables.

"Eighth: Handle your own women how you think best, but they need to know today, and they need to know to keep our efforts quiet. Try to build confidence in all of us, 'specially the women and children.

"Ninth: Try to stay in your normal daily routine. If they see the whole town acting different, they're going to know something's up. Maybe it'll make 'em leave and we can take it as good news. But if they do, we're looking for about fifteen of our best hunters, shooters, riders and thinkers to give 'em chase because we don't want to just squeeze our problem on to the next town.

"Tenth: Aw, hell, nine's all the rules we need. I don't think we can remember any more, anyway. Remember what our Lord taught us, 'Greater love hath no man than this; that he lay down his life for his friend.' Let's all keep this in mind while we also remember what Ben Franklin said, 'If we don't all hang together, then we will surely all hang separately.' But I say if we stick together the only ones hangin' will be Murrell and his misfits."

Roux kept on. "There's only one more item of business. I guess I'm kind of in charge of this group, and my home here is the headquarters. It's up to you, but we need to vote a second in command, and a secretary, to help carry the load. I'm prepared to nominate John Lee for both jobs, but the floor's open. Roux's suggestion was all they needed to shout "Unanimous! Unanimous!" John found himself a soldier in an unauthorized army for the second time in his young life.

"Godspeed to us all, and may He lead us to victory over this evil enemy," Roux concluded.

He was then mobbed with three times the volunteers he needed for his traveling squadron.

Oh, and *D & L Meats* of White Springs sold out of every sliver of meat in its inventory that afternoon. I guess all the farmers intended to observe the second rule, the shooting ban!

Official history says not much came of the vigilante squad, drawing lots of folks to the conclusion Murrell's legend was a lot more fierce than his reality, or his bark was worse than his bite. Either way it leaves a whole lot of room for speculating whether Mr. Roux was a wily old swamp fox, or if he was just another frontier crackpot who had a brief moment of glory, only to be washed away by time's ever-rolling stream.

Was the real Murrell just a flea-bitten chicken thief who never lived anywhere close to his reputation? Or was he a threat at all? Did he, upon seeing how equipped and ready the Hamilton County farmers were, decide to move on to parts a little more ripe for the picking? As for the vigilantes, the record says they never got to take justice into their own hands, and they wanted it that way. This meant they never got public glory for saving the women and children from the dreaded public enemy. One thing is certain: none of the vigilantes took these risks for glory or notoriety. They simply had a job to do.

They were frequently hot on a trail but never bagged a prize, at least not so far as anyone knows, and anyone who would know never spoke a word. As for John Lee, as much of a friend and example as he was for me, he never spoke a word of his vigilante squad to me or any other family member. It wasn't because I never asked - I peppered him with questions about it since I was a young'un - but he and all his fellow soldiers took the whole truth about E. T. Roux's vigilante squad to their graves.

There are those who said the vigilantes were so silent because their "justice system" wasn't perfect and they made some real ugly mistakes, meaning innocent men paid big prices for crimes they didn't commit. It's known for fact there were several unsolved deaths and disappearances of some unsavory characters in the days of the vigilante gang, but the law was never able to connect any of them to the vigilantes. Maybe the law didn't try too hard in those cases. The vigilantes understood they were taking the law in their own hands and knew that wasn't the way it was supposed to be. For sure, though, they were going to protect their families and properties if the law couldn't . . . or wouldn't. If any evidence ever surfaced to prove vigilantism, there would have been serious trouble for some of the area's leading citizens. Among those, it was suspected John Lee might have had plenty to worry about.

The Second Seminole War

In rough and tumble early Florida, though, there never seemed to be a shortage of enemies. It could be the perceived threat of Murrell was replaced by another one like that of Indians. John Lee signed up for Capt. William Swilley's Mounted Company of the 2nd Regiment, 2nd Brigade, East Florida Military Company. Then later, about 1840, he enlisted in Capt. Duncan Buie's 1st Regiment, Florida Mounted Brigade. These campaigns later became known as the Second Seminole Indian War.

Not much is known about John's involvement in the Second Seminole War, but the point of the whole thing was to push the Indians ever further south, or better yet, get them to surrender for removal to life out west in the Oklahoma country.

We tried killing and catching them, but success was slow until our U.S. Army came up with the idea of offering them bounties. Sometimes a chief would take large lump sum to turn in his entire village, or individual Indians might be offered $200 each plus a rifle. Our soldiers were dying more of disease than of war wounds, and the Indians died more from starvation than battle injuries. The Army became more interested in practical solutions than the glories of war in the swamps, and thus offered the bribes, which turned out to be pretty effective in getting Indians out of our way for a second time.

You'll remember the War of 1812 and the subsequent First Seminole Indian War, the purpose of which was to route the Indians southward in order to make more land safe and available for settlers all the way down to and past the Georgia-Florida line. After forcing them to migrate not too far south of the state line, General Jackson and the powers of the day figured they'd pushed far enough and they'd opened up enough land for settlers of European descent than anyone could even dream.

Ever since territory-hood, the Northern part of Florida was steadily filling up with settlers. As more kept coming, more land was needed. The Second Seminole War was all about making all the farmable and livable land in Florida clear for civilizing. If it sounds to you as if we went about it in a pretty un-civilized way, well, you're not alone. But the land did get civilized.

Wiley Finds Love

With chasing bad guys and Indians added to all the other rigors of life in the wild, you'd think the last half of the 1830s would have been kinda slow in the Lee family growth area. However, if you did think so, you'd be thinking wrong. John and Ava saw fit to add three more to the Lee tribe in just a five year stretch. The newcomers were Jane (1835), Hettie Belle, nicknamed "Hattie" (1837) and Joshua Henry (1839). Now John had an even count with six children born to Lizzie, and six born to Ava. Later on, in 1842, baby Martha came along to break the tie.

Even Wiley finally got into the act. Through all his confusion about love when he was young, he managed to make it to the old age of twenty-two and reached the conclusion he'd better get on with his own family rather than just working all his life. He'd heard the stories of Jacob DeLoach and was real sure he didn't want to spend his life alone with his work.

Wiley remembered a lesson John taught him that John learned from DeLoach. One day ol' Jacob told John, "There's two kinds of young men; there's the ones who go to work chasing women, and others go to work chasing money. Well, the ones chasing the money end up with the women chasing them!" John probably used the story on Wiley to keep him working on the farm, but whatever the reason, it seemed to work, and here Wiley was, running the farm almost single-handedly while John was chasing Indians and marauders through the land. John was spending more time at his butcher shop and other ventures in town because *D & L* was beginning to prosper as supplier to the new White Springs Hotel and the new folks living in town. The area's timber business was coming into its own as the best road in the State of Florida was gradually getting improved and timbermen had better access to the coast and, therefore, the Northern markets. The booming timber business caused a booming business for the new boarding house, also a *D & L* customer.

Business was still a mere shadow of the ship provisioning trade *D & L* enjoyed back in St. Marys, and John felt like he surely left St. Marys and came to White Springs far too early to get the kind of booming growth he'd enjoyed with ol' Jacob. He never second-guessed his strategy to be first in town, though, and worked really hard to protect his premier position. Just as Jacob before him, he required his employees to look in the mirror by the door every time they left the shop, recite the Golden Rule, then ask themselves, "Did I follow this rule today?"

It was good morals. It was good business.

Wiley was pretty sure he fit the "young man chasing money" type. Despite his ripe age he didn't have much experience with the fairer sex and was still confused and afraid about how different they were. Ava tried to explain women to him, but she mostly just told him to relax, don't worry, and trust there'd be a perfect Mrs. Wiley Lee come along some fine day.

Alice McDonald was soon to come home from her women's college in Virginia, where she'd been doing post-graduate studies, for summer vacation. Wiley had no idea what post-graduate studies were but figured it was time to make the proper arrangements with Mr. McDonald. He'd always made a point to see Alice whenever she was home and paid attention to her at the Swift Creek church. They'd known each other for about ten years and called themselves good friends. She was gone so much of the time, though, with boarding school and college. He figured a girl smart enough to go to college would just have to be smart enough to want to settle down with the most industrious young man in her whole settlement. Surely she'd see he was going to make a lot of money so he'd be able to support her in the manner to which she'd become accustomed. Further, Wiley was certain Alice knew how attentive he was to her little sister during the times she was gone - the one with four names, you'll recall. Didn't all this show he'd be a fine family man and wouldn't this clinch Alice to run into his arms knowing he was just perfect for her?

It sounded like a deal to Wiley. Even though his heart didn't flutter when he thought of Alice, like it did with past brief romances, he figured it was a sign of the maturity and sophistication he and Alice had achieved together. She played better harpsichord than anyone within fifty miles and knew all those other languages. Surely she thought of Wiley back home while she was slaving away at her studies and couldn't wait to get back home to be with her one and only love.

Confidently, Wiley set out for old McDonald's farm, and asked for a meeting. Mr. James Hiram McDonald came into the parlor and asked Wiley to sit down. "What can I do for you today?" he inquired. Well, suddenly it happened again, the generational Lee curse, making it impossible for a Lee man to be able to talk sensibly whenever the topic revolved around a female.

Different from his father, though, Wiley didn't babble; he just said nothing. He said nothing because that's precisely what he could make come forth from his lips at the time. I guess he figured saying nothing was better than saying what he feared would spill out. He remembered Ava teaching him, "It's better to be silent and thought a fool than to speak and prove it."

Well this moment was undeniably awkward, but Mr. McDonald, kind gentleman he was, decided to try to make things easier as he watched Wiley twitching. "Wiley, are you here to talk to me about affairs of the heart?" Wiley turned flush, and nervously nodded. "Well, just relax. I want you to know I think the world of you, and I think you're going to be one fine catch for some girl. Is this what you wanted to hear?" Wiley produced another, more enthusiastic nod, but still no words. Maybe, he was beginning to think, he'd be able to get out of here without saying a word since McDonald was being so helpful.

"This guy's going to be the best father-in-law ever," Wiley thought to himself.

The old man continued, "You may be surprised to know Mrs. McDonald and I have talked a fair amount about this very subject. We're a little surprised you're so soon, but I'm glad to know you're thinking the same way. She is still very young, you know." This time Wiley was so relaxed he was able to eke out a "Yes sir," while really thinking, "Are you crazed, Mister, Alice is twenty-four; most women around here have been hitched and have two or three young'uns by now. Heck, most of us here in Genoa think twenty-four is middle aged!" The mere occurrence of said thought made him re-remember the wisdom of his non-speaking policy. From then forward, he was a committed silent-ist.

"We've admired your hard work since we first knew you ten years ago," McDonald added, "and now you're a grown man, and we know you're well on your way. What more could a man want for his daughter than a hard-working, faithful God-fearing man?"

Now this statement caused Wiley to well up not only with pride in himself, but in his love for his beautiful Alice. Now he knew he must suspend his silence policy and speak up, seal the deal and claim his prize like a real man!

"Thank you, Mr. McDonald, for those kind words, and today I make a solemn vow to you and to God above, I love your daughter more than the air I breathe. I will always be faithful to her, and will work every day to provide for her comfort and give her every happiness her heart desires. And so I am here to ask your blessing and permission to take the hand of . . ."

McDonald was so excited he blurted out, "And her Mother and I will be delighted to give you the hand of our beautiful young daughter, Mary Ann Elizabeth McDonald, in Holy Matrimony!"

Silence . . . dead silence filled the room.

Mr. McDonald just said "Holy Matrimony," but Wiley was thinking, "Holy crap!"

Wiley thought about what he'd just heard, and his mind raced as he wondered if he was really being offered the wrong girl by this confused man. Now he understood why he said she was so young; because the McDonald girl now in play *was* so young!

"I've got to think fast," he thought. "I really do like the younger girls, and Mary has always been a delight to me when I visited her, and her smile, and her giggle, and I can talk to her so easily, and I don't have to try to act all sophisticated, and I'm not always worried about her thinking me some kind of bumpkin, and she loves the land, and she was one hundred percent sure she did not want to go to boarding school because she loved her home in Hamilton County. She once told me all she wanted was to be a country momma in a place just like this one. The simple house we're building for me on the farm will be perfect for her, but would probably never do for Alice; not for long, anyway."

Now, strangely, Wiley felt his heart aflutter in a way he never experienced before. Suddenly it all made sense, and all seemed right.

"Thank you so much Mr. McDonald. You don't know how happy you've made me. I can't wait to ask, um, Mary for her hand!"

"Yes, Wiley, Alice said she never wanted to come back to Florida ever since she was sixteen. And this place is emptier to her each time she comes home. We feared Mary was going to go the same way, but she steadfastly says she loves it here and wants to build her life right here. I guess Mary must've told you - since Alice's letter arrived last week telling us she's going to marry some big city lawyer in Washington, DC. We've quietly and fervently prayed for some sign from above to tell us our Mary isn't going to catch the bug to follow her sister's footsteps. We so hoped she wouldn't leave us for the big city, too. We want our girls happy, but we just fear Alice isn't seeing some of the traps of metropolitan life which led us away from there and onto the farm."

Of course, no one had told Wiley any of the above. He wasn't even real sure what a "metropolitan" was!

"And here you are, right here in our house asking for Mary's hand in marriage! God has been so good to us!"

"To all of us, sir," Wiley said with all sincerity.

"And isn't it true God works in mysterious ways?"

"I'm more amazed by God's mysterious ways every day of my life," Wiley replied very slowly and almost silently. He was also amused by the fact after all the years of teasing Mary about her four names, she was gonna get a fifth, and it was gonna be Lee!

The Mary Ann Elizabeth McDonald and Wiley Lee betrothal occurred August 22, 1839. It featured the customary radiant (though scared) bride, proud Poppa, nervous and fidgety groom and fully supportive Genoa community. Alice, the maid of honor, couldn't wait to get back to her new life in DC, away from all the rural sights and smells. Equally, Mary couldn't wait to start her hard country life with her hardworking, no-nonsense husband on the Lee farm. She was beautiful, of course, in the tailored dress Mrs. McDonald had worn in her wedding back in Scotland. It was still in fine condition given what it'd been through with an ocean passage, a trip down Florida's finest road, and years of hanging around in a humid Florida closet. Wiley took on a whole new look, too, because McDonald loaned him one of his fine white wool suits, also from the wedding in the old country. The girls set to work tailoring it to Wiley; when done, it fit as much like a fine-tailored big-city suit as Genoa ever saw. Everyone but John noticed how much better Wiley's suit looked than his father's plain clothes in the wedding to Ava about a decade before, and they noted how things had changed in Genoa.

Swift Creek Church, on the other hand, hadn't changed a bit. It was the *Rock of Ages* for all Genoans. Like the Lord it served, it was the same yesterday, today, and tomorrow. Whether you needed christening, confirming, condemning, delivering, inspiring, praying, preaching, teaching, salvation, marrying or burying, it was the beacon on the hill for all who needed respite from the truly tough yet glorious lives these settlers lived.

Wiley and his young wife began their lives in the small house Wiley had been working on for over a year as he had time. It sat about two hundred feet from the big Lee house. He was building it for himself just because it was time for a young man to leave his home and make his own way, even though he wasn't even engaged when he started. He had been in no hurry 'til now because although he wanted a house of his own, he still greatly enjoyed life with the big family in the big house. After his engagement was made official, he decided being alone in his house with his young bride had a special appeal, and the house was finished in about two weeks. Every Lee old enough to hold a hammer was scrambling to do whatever job was there for the doing. More work was accomplished in the last stretch than in the previous six months. It was yet another new beginning in Hamilton County and just one of multitudes of new beginnings to occur on the Lee Farm.

The house was a fine start for a new couple. It was a cracker-style house with three rooms. The front half was an eating and sitting room, while the back half was divided into two rooms on either side, and a center hall ran straight through from front to back. To the left was a bedroom for Wiley and Mary, and on the right was a sleeping room for the young'uns when the need arose. It was framed by stout heart pine lumber cut from the farm. The walls were built of rough-hewn two-by-ten, overlapping upright planks. It was twenty-five feet across the front and thirty-five feet deep, allowing for big rooms and space for a family to grow; more house could be added out back, or on a second floor, any time they wanted. The front porch was a generous ten feet deep and stretched the entire length of the front, allowing for plenty of front-porch sittin' on Sundays and the rare day off. The porch roof was supported by four rough-hewn cabbage palm logs, as near-to-matching as possible. It was planned to have glass windows someday, but the shutters worked just fine for starters. The cook shed in back was a replica of John's cooking house, with lots of room to cook for two or twenty.

The McDonald girls joined in to decorate the inside as much as possible, adding lacy curtains and beautifully crafted, old world wooden chairs for Wiley's rough, homemade dining table. The table was made of the same crude planks which made up the inside walls of the house, then polished with turpentine varnish. It was nothing fancy, but it was ready to do some feedin'. The girls added silver candle holders and real oil paintings in real ornate frames from the McDonald house for the walls.

To brighten the room, they placed a stunning hand cut leaded crystal punchbowl on the table. When a roaring fire was in the fireplace, or you put the lantern near it, it would look like it caught fire itself as it reflected brilliantly through the room, with each facet letting loose an exclamation of color. It was a gift from Mary's Aunt Edna and Uncle William in Scotland. They sent it five years ago with instructions to Mrs. McDonald to give it to their first daughter to marry. It was likely the very finest article in any Hamilton County house at the time, and Mary treasured it. Sister Alice made known what a shame it was for such a beautiful thing to be staying in Hamilton County, when it could be used to light up her socialite parties in DC. Thus, any concern Wiley may have had that he was marrying the wrong McDonald girl was forever put to rest.

As a surprise for Mary, her parents brought in her harpsichord and placed it in the corner of the sitting room. Some thought it more a cruel joke than a nice gift because it didn't take a genius to know Mary would find little time for playing it.

John acted alarmed at how many things in the house were meant to be looked at but not used. The McDonalds, however, were concerned with how Spartan it was. "It's all fluff," huffed John as he looked grumpily around at the finished product, "wasteful fluff." He made sure none of his new in-laws were around to hear, though, because he didn't want to hurt them, and was secretly proud. Wiley's house, he thought, was decorated a lot like the house Lizzie would have wanted if he would've parted with the money to allow her to make a home of it.

Old unsentimental John gave them what turned out to be Mary's favorite piece, which was Lizzie's old rocking chair. Just a simple rocker, it traveled with them from St. Marys and was one of the few things John cared anything about besides work, his family and Swift Creek church.

Newlywed Bliss!

Following the Lee tradition, there was no honeymoon after Wiley's wedding. Wedding trips were very rare and only for the very wealthy, the idle rich, you might say. Wiley and Mary, figuring they fit into neither the idle nor rich category, spent their wedding night at their brand new house. The next day, they went to work, Wiley in the fields and Mary right there at the house. Her typical day might include drawing water, feeding animals, milking cows, churning butter, gathering eggs, tending the curing shed, cleaning a brand new but already dusty abode, working hours to fix breakfast, dinner (lunch), and supper for the two of them, patching the holes in Wiley's britches and shirt, tending a garden, carrying firewood, cleaning pots and dishes, spinning cotton, weaving cloth, cutting material and sewing a new shirt for Wiley, grinding corn for meal, harvesting the ripe summer vegetables, washing them for canning, cooking and canning them for winter consumption and other jobs. After these tasks, she would be excitedly ready for her new husband to come home. She would throw herself into his arms, feed him a big supper, and then they'd dream of the future together.

Well, that's not exactly how it happened. By mid-morning, Mary realized in her fourteen years she had barely experienced the aforementioned duties. In fact, all the above had been done for her every day of her tender young life. Sure, she'd helped out at all these jobs and was fully capable of doing them, but she felt more than a little overwhelmed at her new job as the Mistress of the Wiley Lee house.

Before marriage, she'd spent most of her days in studies and playing the family harpsichord and her own cello, filling the house with the likes of Bach, Beethoven, and Mozart. Since she wasn't sent to boarding school as Alice was, she was taught the finer things of life right there on the farm. She wasn't real sure how she would put her extensive Latin training to work there on the Lee farm, but her parents were darn sure she was going to have it.

Mary loved her life and never second-guessed her decision to stay on the farm when her sister would regale her with stories of playing a real piano in her new hometown of Washington, D.C. She'd gloat how it was so superior to the harpsichord in every way because you could milk so much more from it by increasing the volume simply by striking the keys harder or softer; and the damper peddle added a new dimension of sound, making the harpsichord dull by comparison. Some said the harpsichord was going to fade away, and the superior sound of the piano would make it obsolete.

Alice's account of playing piano sounded exciting to young Mary, who in her life on the farm had only once seen and played this fabulous new instrument on a trip to Fernandina with her father. The McDonalds could afford one, the church might even be able to pay for one, and certainly Mary would be able to play it superbly, but a piano didn't yet exist for miles around because it was wisely judged it couldn't survive the trip from port to White Springs on the finest road in all Florida. Besides, the church leaders, John Lee included, would probably never approve of such a frivolous expense. "Nothing wrong with our harpsichord and Mary's cello playing," they'd say.

Even though she was home-taught, Mary was educated well beyond your typical Genoan, except her own family. The McDonalds were never haughty or boastful about their education and social graces so lacking in Genoa society. They were going to be sure, though, their children would learn more than just the simple life on the farm. For this reason, the rest of Genoa never could understand why they chose to come to Hamilton County in the first place, but they seemed to mix just fine. It seemed on the farm all the neighbors were on level ground. They fought the same elements, took the same risks, and worked like dogs sunup to sundown six days a week.

On their first full day as newlyweds, Wiley was working on the forty acres he'd just acquired, he called it *Mary's Farm*. Since it was a little over a mile away, he took a lunch bucket with him and told Mary he wouldn't be home 'til supper. He kissed her, held her, and told her he couldn't wait for the day to be done so he could see her again. With that, he picked up his lunch pail, mounted his horse and was off to work.

Since he really couldn't wait, he came home a little early. He was expecting his supper would be near-ready, Mary would be anxious to run into his arms, and last night would replay itself for the lovebirds. He burst into the house, cheerfully calling, "Guess who's home?" Instead of the desired response, he found Mary splattered on the floor like a human puddle, crying uncontrollably and nervously shaking like a guilty pup.

"What's wrong with you?" He screamed indelicately as he ran to pick her up. To say the least, he was confused by her greeting. Now holding her tiny, still developing frame tight, he carried her to Lizzie's old rocking chair.

Wiley implored, "What's wrong, honey?" She responded by more sobbing. "Are you sick?"

After a pause, the reply came, pathetically. . ."NOoooooo."

"Did you fall and break your arm?" Same response with evermore sobbing.

"Did some renegade come in here and mistreat you? I will kill him." Her head shook violently.

"Did someone die? Your mother? Was it Ava? Tell me, who?" No answer, unless you count streams of tears and endless boo-hoos as an answer.

"Well, Mary, I'm all out of guesses. Please tell me what's wrong."

It seemed it took another hour of holding, and Wiley didn't mind that part, but needless to say he was about as confused as Adam on Mother's Day.

When she was finally able to talk, she looked up at Wiley and said, "I've been bleeding all day, and I'm afraid I'm dying, and you were out there the whole time," pointing to the farm.

Wiley pleaded, "What can I do?" Mary just started sobbing again. Luckily, Wiley had enough experience on the farm to know just what to do, so he told her, "Show me the cut, and I'll squeeze it hard enough so the pressure will make the bleeding stop. Quick, where is it?" to which Mary added still more tears.

"Mary, I don't want you to die, and if you've been bleeding for so long, you could be in big danger! Where is it? I don't see any blood!" He ran to the storage bin and grabbed for the wedding gift cleaning rags they'd been given by the slave women. Noticing most of the rags were gone, he ran back screaming, "Show me where you're cut! Did a knife slip? Did the no-good dog bite you?"

Now Wiley'd grown up in a house full of women, so he knew to lay low at certain times of the month. He didn't bother trying to understand it, and sure didn't expect his beautiful young bride to act like one of his sisters. To make things worse, John wasn't real good at explaining things about the fairer sex to his son. Thus, it's easy to see how Wiley wasn't putting two and two together very well on this, the sundown of his first full day of wedded bliss.

Finally, Mary gained enough composure to be real clear and express herself to her caring but very stupid new beau. She lifted her dress just a little bit hoping to indicate where she bled. Turning white as a ghost, Wiley screamed, "What do you want me to do? I can't squeeze that!" In the blink of an eye Mary transformed from a helpless, scared kitten on the floor to a fire-breathing lioness with raging eyes and a fearsome, gravelly voice bellering, "GET ME AVA, YOU IDIOT!"

Getting Ava seemed a real good idea. Not only would Ava be able to size up the situation, but just getting out of the house was welcome relief for Wiley.

Running for the door, he checked one more time, "Are you sure you'll be alright?"

"GET AVA!" She screamed at the top of her voice.

Wiley ran screaming all the way to the big house so the whole Lee clan heard and was running to him, meeting about at the big oak. Wiley shouted to Ava, "Go see Mary. She's bleeding and can't stop. She only wants to see you. You gotta run fast!"

Ava took off for Mary, turning back she hollered, "Josie, you come, too." Doing some quick figuring on what might be happening, she turned again to shout, "And bring some rags."

As Wiley turned back toward his house and his dying bride, he heard his father's voice saying firmly, "Wiley, come talk to me a minute, Ava can take care of this." When John and Wiley got alone, John didn't need to ask any details. "Son, looks like your second night together isn't going to turn out as you planned."

"OF COURSE it's not, my new wife's DYING!"

"Now settle down. She's gonna be just fine, but I guess there's a few things we forgot to tell you. Ava can handle this, and Mary'll be good as new in a few days, but you can expect this kind of thing to happen for a few days just about every month. It's nature's way of cleaning a woman out and getting her ready for another shot at being a Momma. It's all real normal, and you've just got to understand what's happening. Mind you, I can't tell you I'm any good at it myself, even after all my years of practice. If you can learn to recognize the warning signs, though, you'll be way ahead of any man I know. I guess we get busy or something, and we lose track of time, but every husband gets surprised by this every single month. We're not stupid, but we do seem to be pretty lame at understanding women, and that's not just us Lees, it's all men."

"I sure can't give you any advice as to why it's usually gonna be your fault, but it's gonna be, and you're a whole lot smarter to just accept the blame and remember you've got some chores to do on the back forty. Just keep tellin' yourself it'll blow over and you'll go back to being the best new husband in Hamilton County. And for God's sake, when it does blow over, don't bring it back up and try to set the record straight. By then, she'll have forgotten the whole thing so you should, too. Just be glad it's over. Best I can tell, it's God's punishment to us men for not having to bear the young'uns, and if you'll look at it thattaway it won't seem such a bad trade, 'specially after you watch your first young'un born."

"So good luck, and if you can find some special miracle cure, or you can learn the signs it's coming on, maybe you'll be able to get out of the way of the monthly tornado. If you can, you'll get rich by startin' a travelin' show just tellin' men how to figure women out.

"Why don't you and Mary take tomorrow off? Take her up to see her Momma, and let the two of them talk it over some. We can get everything done here on the farm. Better yet, why don't you two just go ahead and take a couple of days off. We're going to be real busy soon when we start cotton harvest. Now go on home and baby her a little, and don't expect anything in return. And again, good luck!"

Wiley did take those two days off as his Daddy suggested, but you couldn't really call it a honeymoon. It might be better termed boot camp for new husbands.

As they parted, John said to his son, "You take real good care of her, and be sure to tell her you love her, and tell her real often. It'll help a lot." As John listened to his own words, it dawned on him he might have been better off to have heeded his own advice over the years.

Mary and her Momma talked. And talked some more. Of course they'd talked about the woman things many times before. I guess when your first episode happens a day after your wedding, and you're in a new house with a brand new husband, away from your Momma, and you're only fourteen, it makes a lasting impression. The impression it made on Wiley was no more subtle than a two-by-four across the back of the head.

When the newlyweds got back home, Ava gave Josie over to work with Mary for a few weeks and teach her how to get everything done she needed to do as a new young frontier wife. It was decided Josie's eight year old daughter, Eliza, would help, too, and would stay on with Mary when time came for Josie to return to the big house. In a different kind of way, the new Lees were off to a good start as a family.

As suspected, Mary's beloved harpsichord didn't get much play, and there was no one at the Lee farm to talk Latin with, but she hardly noticed.

Wiley and Mary led a great young life. The farm prospered as John and Wiley regularly added new farmland and new farmhands.

As they felt they could handle more, John and Wiley added land to their original homesteaded farm. By 1864, John had a total of 600 acres to his name. There's no telling how many acres his land and his sons' and grandsons' lands eventually totaled. It was a time to prosper mightily for this family.

John had Ava pretty much full time in the baby business from their wedding until about 1860. They produced seventeen together, of which four (including little John Lee previously discussed) died in infancy. John had a total of thirteen grow to adulthood from Ava, and all six of Lizzie's young grew up and married.

Not to be outdone by his Daddy, Wiley and Mary had twelve children between 1842 and 1863. Remarkably, only one of those children did not grow to adulthood. The firstborn was Sophia Jane. She came just about a month short of Mary's sixteenth birthday. You could say

Mary grew up in a hurry, coming from a rigorous but relatively privileged life in the McDonald house to the Lee lifestyle where everyone did every job.

Well, Sophia was only a little more than a year old when Mary figured out she was pregnant again. She carried this baby in the normal way, but this time she had a one-year-old along with everything else under her charge. It was a very busy time in Wiley's household.

When the time was right, Mary had Eliza ring the farm bell as hard as she could so the girls at John's house would know to come a-runnin' and Wiley'd know to come a-gallopin' from wherever he was on the farm. Delivery went pretty smoothly, but of course there was plenty of grunting, groaning, pushing, breathing, timing, worrying and pacing with faithful Mamie by her side as the mid-wife. When the baby finally let out a cry, the whole house erupted. Wiley exuberantly proclaimed, "It's a BOY!"

The day was 24 March, 1844.

Wiley's Growing Family

Hi. Allow me to introduce myself. M' name's James Hiram Lee. That was me who was just birthed, and it's been me talking to you all along, but I just didn't feel it was fittin' to introduce myself until after I was born. I guess I've been introducing myself to you this whole time through my three generations of ancestors. You might've noticed I was named for my maternal grandfather, James Hiram McDonald. I am who these independent country people are, and everything they've been building and the land they've been taming around here is my home. It's going to be my job to take up where they leave off and to keep building the legacy they've started here in frontier Florida.

Though my name's James Hiram, the only name most folks know me by is "JH." I only have one other name and that'ns reserved only for my Momma; she calls me "Jimmy," and only at those times when she knows a boy needs his Momma.

I was three weeks shy of a year old when Florida achieved statehood, so I guess I'm one of the last natives born in the Territory of Florida.

Lee is not just my last name. It's who I am, and I'm proud of what my family has done and of the people the good Lord used to bring me into the world. There was nothing unusual about this family, just typical of so many who've risked everything to settle farther and farther south on this big spit of land called Florida. You already know I lived in Genoa settlement, near White Springs; and my parents, Wiley and Mary, and all four Grandparents, John and Ava Lee and James Hiram and Mary McDonald, lived here and worked real hard to provide and care for us, their many, many kids and grandkids.

My Granddaddy John was the second born but first son of his parents; Daddy was a second born first son, and so was I. At a very young age, I'd hear talk about me being the one to take over the farm someday. That made me feel real special because I lived in a sea of cousins. I even had a whole peck of uncles and aunts younger than me. We had a great time growing up together on the farm.

We knew not all of us could live on the farm or make our living from the farm, but since I was the oldest son of the oldest son, all things pointed toward my future being set. I guess it was all just fine for me. It gave me a special pride in the farm, and I think it helped me work a little harder when I had work time. John, Wiley, and all the Lees who grew up on this farm made it into a very fine place. It could easily feed the masses who'd lived on it, but every one of us had the importance of work drilled into us, and most had a drive to be independent

106

and to "Be fruitful and multiply," as the Good Book commands. To open new land was seen as high achievement, and this crop of Lees born from John or one of his twenty-three children (twenty lived to child-bearing age) poured into not only Hamilton, Columbia and Suwanee Counties, but also scattered throughout this budding young state all the way to Dade County.

As you know, I lived just a stone's throw from Granddaddy John Lee's house, and by time I was ten years old, I had eleven aunts and uncles living next door (not counting my Dad's older siblings), and my house had seven children and growing. Wiley and his siblings were busy running up the tally of grandkids for John and Ava. We always had a lot of activity between our two houses. By time my parents and all the aunts and uncles were done having their litters, I counted easily over a hundred of us grandkids, and I can guarantee I didn't count 'em all. When most of us were at home, we could overflow the Swift Creek Church with just the Lees. Several other Genoa families were getting really big too, but I think the Lee clan was the biggest.

Our family's story, like every family's, is unique. It's also pretty normal, though, because the people out here had very similar lives and had to do an awful lot just to survive. Daddy taught us those who work really, really hard and just a little bit smart were likely to do well.

The failure rate of the homestead farms was high in those early days for various reasons. Many of the settlers were never able to save enough money or food to get them through a crop failure. Many simply didn't know what they were doing and couldn't learn fast enough to make up for their early mis-steps. Some couldn't imagine how hard life was going to be. Most of them just greatly under-guessed how long it would take to get established.

The saddest cases, though, were when sickness or an accident either killed or disabled the head of the farm, and the farm work could no more get done.

You know Mom and Dad had different upbringings and different ideas about upbringing. The McDonalds taught their kids the classics, music, Latin, and higher mathematics. The Lees were readin', writin' and 'rithmetic, then go-to-work kind of folks. Once you got beyond the basics, a Lee was supposed to be in the field. He was to be sure to work harder than everyone else. McDonalds believed you never stopped learning, and thought you could teach a joy of learning.

Sometimes these ideas led to tension in my house. Since I was the oldest son, Daddy wanted me behind a mule just as young as I could stand it. He'd say he worked too hard when he was little, but he never seemed to let up on me because of it. Momma said I needed more time for studying.

One time I heard them getting into it because Daddy said there was "No way on God's green earth JH needs to know Latin. Ain't gonna do him no good out here."

"*Isn't* going to do him *any* good," Momma corrected.

"Glad we agree," said Wiley as he ducked out of the room laughing. She'd get furious when he tricked her onto his side of the argument. He knew he'd never beat her on facts, but she knew he was going to keep her on her toes with his quick mind and sharp, country wit.

Now I didn't like studying too terribly much, but neither did I care much for spending my days watching the south end of a northbound mule. So when I was studying, I'd sort of feel like Daddy was right that "All a boy needs to know out here is how to work." When I was sweating away in the fields, though, I'd hear Momma's wisdom, "If a child can learn, a child can earn." What I liked about hard work was being able to look at what I'd done and to know my effort went into causing something productive and good to happen, like looking at a freshly-plowed field with its nice, straight rows. Sometimes my studies didn't give the same feeling of satisfaction but Momma promised I'd be served well by my learnin', too.

I must confess I don't remember much of Momma's Latin lessons, except every time she thought I hadn't done my very best, she would scold me by writing on the top of my slate "Debes Cognoscere," meaning, "you ought to learn." I wish I didn't have to tell you how familiar this one little Latin phrase was to me, but I got to know it well. Momma kind of gave up on the Latin with the younger kids. It really did help me, though, when I'd be dealing with some fancy lawyer or high-on-himself politician trying to throw big words around. I could usually figure out what they'd be saying, and they'd get all flummoxed how some ol' bumpkin could keep up with their high intellects. I made some of my best deals that way. Thanks, Mom.

I guess it worked out well for me to have my Daddy pushing me hard to get more work done while Momma was pushing me to learn more. Between the two of them I learned I wanted to build and do things in my life and was pretty sure hard, smart work was the way to accomplish whatever I decided to go after.

The farm's population wasn't limited to just us Lees. Daniel and Josie, Robert and Mamie, though getting older, were still working hard. They had a total of twelve children who all worked with us, too. Without their labors, there was no way all the mouths could be fed and all the work done on this farm. Momma took up educating the slaves again, just like my real grandma Lizzie started to do before she passed on.

The farm also had help nearly year-round from various freemen. They might be white, Indian or free black men. Maroons, they were called. We didn't ask many questions because it was important to have a steady flow of migrants. They tended to come and go, but there was rough housing for them on the far side of the original farm. They usually didn't get paid anything except during high labor times like cotton harvest. Other times they seemed to be happy to work for food, shelter, and some worn out clothes for their families. They were free to go when they wanted, and sometimes the Lee men would give them a small amount of food or money to help them get to the next town.

Our farmland has developed a whole lot since we last spoke of it. We originally used horses and mules only for the heaviest work like plowing, stumping, and hauling logs, but we'd just use our own (or the slaves') backs to do most everything else. We were some of the first farmers to use horse-drawn implements to do things like sowing, tilling, cultivating and even harvesting the grain crops and hay. Our wagons got bigger and the horses stronger. Every decision we made was all about getting more done with less effort on our part, and the modern horse-drawn machinery led the way. If we could be convinced a horse-powered machine with one man could do the work of three or more men, we were convinced it was a good investment, and Wiley was likely to buy it. As much as Granddaddy John huffed about any kind of personal luxuries, he was all in when it came to investing to make the farm more efficient.

If only we could find a way to get all the things we grew to the cities before they spoiled. Those folks would've loved all the good stuff we grew, and we could grow something almost year-round! The road to Jacksonville was getting smoother and the ships were getting faster, but our perishables just couldn't make it to a distant city before too much of it went bad.

We had a small peach orchard and pecan grove for the family but were expanding them so we could sell more through the meat market in town. The wealthy Northerners at the hotels really liked the peaches. We were trying to teach them what pecans were and hoping we'd be able to ship them up North. We had a corn silo for feeding the dairy cows. We grew a patch or two of peanuts and cow peas for cow and horse feed every year. People didn't eat either one of those unless they were starving, but the cows and horses liked 'em, and they seemed to fatten the cows up real good. We also noticed if we planted our cotton and corn after peanuts or any kind of beans or alfalfa hay, we'd get a lot stronger plants and better yields than if we grew cotton one crop right after the other. We started doin' a lot of this new crop rotation thing, and it worked well.

My favorite project was the six or seven orange trees we had. They'd grow and produce a little, but we were too far north for them. We would really have to worry about freezes if we ever tried to grow enough of them to be meaningful. I believed citrus was a market waiting to open up for Florida growers. The nice, tough peel helped it have a good shelf life, and because ships and trains were getting faster and better, we thought we might someday put them on the streets of New York in the dead of winter!

We had a puny stand of lady-finger bananas in the low ground by the swimming hole. It was too cold here for them, too, but 'twas fun trying to grow 'em. We loved those things, the few we got.

Okra grew like a weed on our land, as it did on most southern land. We couldn't sell it for much, but we could sure eat a lot of it. We'd steam it, pickle it, bread and fry it, or stew it up with tomatoes and onions. Okra was a very versatile vegetable.

The wild blueberries and blackberries were a treat when they came in. The women preserved what we didn't eat fresh. We kept some and sold the rest to the hotels or at the butcher shop.

We never ate coontie anymore. We figured coontie was why the Indians were so skinny. It was hard to imagine living off something you didn't like, but we kept some of it growing untended in the turpentine plot so we'd have it for survival if we needed. If we ever had real hard times we knew we'd have enough coontie root to make flour for a good while. No drought could kill it, and pests and diseases just didn't seem to bother it.

The tobacco curing barn was a favorite place for all us young'uns to play in when we weren't studying Momma's lessons or doing chores. We had a gristmill for milling our own flour and grits. Our tiny hemp plot grew all the fiber we need for all the rope the farm could use.

Although there were a lot of mouths to feed on this farm, we were self-sufficient.

Several of the area farmers got together to build a cotton gin in White Springs. It helped us get better prices for our processed cotton lint, instead of selling it rough, and we got to keep our own seed. We kept learning to grow all these things better and cheaper, and the cheaper we could sell it, the more people could buy it. Our horse-drawn farm machines were making life ever-better. Some experts were saying someday we'd get a hundred pounds of cotton per acre! Seemed a stretch to me at the time, but it did happen, and we kept learning how to grow more, better and cheaper.

However, we remained deviled by the fact it just seemed there was no way to get a boll of cotton into the sack other than by a human hand.

Beyond the farm, life was improving in many ways, making it a magical time when I chose to be born. For instance, just a few years before my arrival, a Mr. Morse started producing his electrical telegraph. With this machine he developed his own special system called Morse code. It was nothing but a series of short (dots) or long (dashes) electrical pulses which could travel very long distances along wires to make news travel faster. By my birthday there was a telegraph office in Jacksonville. It became possible for an event to happen in New York and one hour later, it was known on the streets in Jacksonville. What an incredible new day I came into! In those days a ten-word telegram cost a bit more than $1.50. Now figurin' how hard a man had to work to earn $1.50 then, it was obvious the telegram wasn't just for sending silly messages, but what an aid to business it was!

It would still take the same message a couple of days to get from Jacksonville to White Springs, but news was getting around, and business was getting done over longer distances and shorter times than anyone could have dreamed just a few years back. The telegraph would make it into Middle Florida in a few years. American life was speeding up.

Another big improvement was the growth of railroads. A train line had been trying to come from Jacksonville to Alligator Town (which by the time of my youth was a thriving English settlement) since the 1830s. It would open Middle Florida up to better access to the Jacksonville port and the Northern and European markets. They tried but failed in 1834 due to an Indian attack. Afterward, it lay dormant until 1852, when an investor group led by a Dr. Baldwin bought the old right-of-way and got it up and running within a couple of years.

The train traveled slower than a good horse and buggy. It was smoother, though, and carried far heavier loads than our horses and wagons could. For passengers, it was said the train would deliver you a lot less beat up than travel by horse and buggy, but you'd be a whole lot more sooty!

There was growing need for more wood in the port towns because steam-driven boats were booming. Like the trains, they were only a little faster than a sailing ship but were much more reliable because they didn't have to depend on the wind to make headway. A steam-powered ship didn't have to tack to and fro against an unfriendly wind like a sailboat. It could just set its course and head a straight path to its object, compensating only for currents and just a little for winds. A lot of folks couldn't believe it then, but it wouldn't take long before steam power totally removed wind power from the seas and rivers.

The trains burned a lot of wood, too, and I thought us inland farmers and timbermen would be the ones to supply it, along with all the other things we were finding we could sell. All things pointed to more prosperity for years to come.

If my young days had only consisted of life on the farm and around Hamilton County, it would have been about as carefree and simple as any life anywhere, but dark clouds were looming in the bigger world.

Dark Clouds Looming

From my earliest memories of listening to the older men talk, I remember hearing of tensions with the North. I heard heated debates over Northern attempts to put big tariffs on our cotton bound for Europe, and on the machinery we liked to buy from Europe. I heard of fights breaking out between some of the locals and the winter guests in the hotels. They were getting accustomed to coming here just as regular as the black clouds of mallards we saw every fall, but they started saying they wouldn't be back if things didn't change. Daddy said, "We'll see. The winters are mighty cold where they come from. They'll keep looking down their noses as long as we let 'em, and we'll let 'em as long as they keep paying for our weather as well as they do."

Even worse, there were scary slave uprisings and political debates over disallowing slavery. Since I didn't know what slavery was, I asked Daddy. Wiley started, "Well, slavery is when one man owns another man."

"How can one man own another man, Pop?"

Wiley weighed his words carefully, saying, "Well, most of the darkies around here are owned by white folks."

"You mean black folks like Daniel and Robert?" I asked honestly.

"Well, yeah."

So I said, "We'd never let Daniel and Robert be owned by someone, would we?"

Wiley could see the questions were going to get more difficult, so he decided to come clean. "Of course we wouldn't, because we already own them."

"You mean they can't go wherever they want, whenever they want?"

"That's right, JH," said Wiley as he nervously lit his corncob pipe.

"And their families, what about them?"

Wiley followed through, even more directly this time. "They're all slaves, son, and you know they're important members of our family, too, don't you?"

"I guess so."

112

Wiley continued, "I grew up with Daniel and Robert, they were like big brothers to me. I think I was better friends with them than any of our white neighbors, but your Grandfather John bought them when he moved here from St. Marys. He knew he had a lot of work to do, and there just wasn't labor for hire out here then. He's given them a good life, but just like you, I had a real hard time knowing we owned them. Your Granddaddy would tell me I was making a big mistake becoming friends with them. He'd say I needed to treat them fairly and with respect, but should remember they're just property. It was hard for me, just like I see it's hard for you. Granddaddy did what he had to do to build this life for us, and if you take over the farms, you'll be a slave owner someday yourself. You'll have to get a lot of work out of them, but you'll also be responsible to protect them and care for them.

"There have been some real bad stories of slaves being treated real badly, even here in Hamilton County. Some men promised their slaves they'd set them free, but then they'd keep them 'til every drop of work was squeezed out of them. Once they were old and feeble, they'd tell them, 'You're free now. Now, get off my farm.' Those poor men and women were left to wander and had no money and no way to earn their livings. Since their younger families were still slaves on the farm, there was no way the younger ones could look after their elders.

"Even if they are 'just property,' only an idiot would treat his property in such a way. They're expensive to buy, and if they're healthy, they can produce more than one who's been beaten near to death. You see our cows? Those are property. And we take care of 'em. Your cotton plants take better care of you if you take care of them. If slaves are nothing but property, the same principle applies. Again, only an idiot would treat a slave poorly, but it happens. Son, I've seen a lot of idiots in my day. Some of them live real near us, and it's going to make trouble for all of us."

I just soaked it in, hoping not to have to answer any questions from my slave master father.

"You don't ever want something like that on your conscience. In fact, there's no way a man can do what I just told you and even have a conscience. It's complicated, JH. The slaves have every right to resent their circumstances, especially in this country we call the 'Land of the Free.' It's not free for them, and you sure can't blame them for wanting to have things for themselves. And there's folks goin' around stirrin' up trouble for them all over the South."

He concluded his lesson with, "Most European countries have outlawed slavery. It seems to be working alright for them, but they don't have a cotton crop to grow and harvest. They buy all their cotton from us, and their laborers mostly do higher-value jobs than farming. It's the same with the folks up North. Seems those people want to wear our cotton, and buy it real cheap, but they don't think we should be able to do what we have to do to grow it and get it to them."

There were slave rebellions, large and small, organized and disorganized, throughout the slave states. The biggest and most frightening of all was the 1791 uprising in Haiti. Between 1791 and 1804, it's reported more than 100,000 people were killed on that small island. The slaves took over, killed every white man, woman, child and soldier on the island. Then they destroyed all the means of production on one of the most productive places on earth.

Prior to the rebellion, Haiti produced almost half of the sugar and coffee for the entire world. After all the destruction, the island was left with huge amounts of self-freed slaves living in lawlessness and starvation.

The Haitian situation sent shivers throughout America because many feared a similar uprising would be the ruin of our country, too. At least in Haiti it was contained to the little island country. Here, would it have no limits?

Let's talk about the slavery situation now, man to man, and let's see if we can touch on all points of view. Here goes.

Among those who agreed slavery should end, there was much disagreement over how to best do it. There were those who said it should be done abruptly. All slaves should suddenly and all at once be granted their freedom. Obviously, there were complications with this strategy because many slaves, not all, were without question unequipped for life on their own.

Some argued the life skills necessary to cope with free life needed time to develop. These were often discounted as just wanting to prolong the institution and the bounty of free labor. There was obviously a point to this because many or most slaves had no experience managing money, time or personal affairs. Many had spent their lives doing nothing more than they were told and were used to being punished for doing anything else, even if it showed initiative.

Some were sure society-at-large owed compensation to the freed slaves, usually in the form of land and work animals. This view was just as controversial, because some felt there should be no public price to bear, because the public had nothing to do with slavery, while others argued society had turned its back on the problem for years and enjoyed the cheap food and clothing resulting from captive labor.

Some said the slaveholders should not only free their slaves, but also owed them compensation for their past captivity. To this the slaveholders argued what they'd done was legal for centuries. They couldn't see where they owed anything.

Of course, there was a considerable and powerful group who saw no need for change. To them, the slavery system had long been legal and should continue. By their way of thinking, a slave was property of the slave owner, and property should always be sacred in America.

Among the slaves themselves was just as much divergence of opinion. Some were happy (or at least content) with their lives as they were. Maybe they were under benevolent ownership, or maybe they were just afraid of the unknown and insecure with the idea of having self-responsibility.

Others, of course, yearned to breathe free air, to be able to use their labors as they saw fit, and to come and go as they pleased. They watched free men grow wealthy by owning property, yet the slaves didn't even have ownership of themselves. The ultimate property right is the ownership of one's own body, and the labor he can produce with it. Of course it's an un-natural, self-conflicted system which doesn't allow a person to even own his own body.

In addition to the above thoughts from the slave population, were the bondsmen who, filled with rage over their situations, wanted not only freedom but revenge. They were ready for revolt and retribution as their Haitian brethren had inflicted. These people wanted to stir up and foment mass, destructive uprising and inflict serious pain, even death upon their holders and families, not out of a righteous desire for freedom as much as for resentful, destructive, but understandable, revenge.

I think most can agree to some extent, or see some validity in each of the above, widely-differing positions. Add to this array of beliefs the emotional charge and passion surrounding the "Peculiar Institution" of American slavery, as Lincoln dubbed it, and it was easy to see it was a powder keg fixing to blow sky-high. America's slave predicament was extremely complex. While the church was the center of life in many ways, and the leader in so many areas of thought, it got stuck when it came to the issue of slavery.

We should have been able to rely on our churches to give guidance and leadership on the issue, but most would probably be disappointed by what we got.

The church's main weakness boiled down to one simple item . . . money. In the Southern churches, heavily supported by slaveholders and pro-slavery interests, the pulpits rang out with defense of bondage, and rationalization for keeping the system as it was. Didn't our

Savior himself several times address the master-slave relationship? Didn't he never once condemn the institution of slavery?

The Northern churches were much more likely to be supported by abolitionists. As you might guess, those pulpits echoed with fiery rhetoric about the evils of slavery and condemnation against any man who would own another man.

Just as the country was starting to split, so were the churches. Most notably, a very large group of Baptists, mostly from Georgia and Alabama, met in May 1845. They achieved their purpose of seceding from the national church and formed the Southern Baptist Convention. This new denomination spread quickly throughout the South with a fiery message of slave-owner rights and self-determination.

The Episcopal Church in Florida was influential despite its small size of only fourteen total parishes in 1860. It was mostly located in the larger, more settled towns of Florida and represented a lot of influential Northerners, Old South planters, and transplanted Englishmen. In spite of these widely conflicting influences, its Bishop, Francis Huger Rutledge, was a staunch and adamant secessionist and advocate for the Southern position, yet he was also a fervent advocate for black rights and education.

In 1836, the "Hopewell Presbytery" tried hard to come up with a unifying statement. It crafted a document to establish the Presbyterian Church's position, attempting to make a statement satisfactory to both North and South. It stated,

> "Slavery is a political issue, with which the church has nothing to do, except to inculcate the duties of Master and Slave, and to use lawful, spiritual means to have all, both bond and free, to become one in Christ by faith."

This document was a good try at getting the Presbyterian church above the fray by making a very strong, decisive statement neither condemning nor condoning the mostly Southern institution of slavery. Rather, it tried to establish the church's higher call was to win souls, not to struggle with the earthly and temporary problem of whether or not one man should own another. In my opinion it said a whole lot of nothin' and by trying to satisfy everyone, it served to make all its faithful members unhappy.

Southerners thought the North wanted the cheap cotton, tobacco and food it could get from the slaveholding South; but Northerners didn't mind looking down their self-righteous noses at us for doing what we had to do to develop the new land and supply their food and fiber needs a lot cheaper than they could do it themselves.

Many Southerners would implore, "We never told them they should be required to have slaves, so why did they think they had moral grounds to tell us we shouldn't?"

Slavery was a hot and tense issue of debate in the Constitutional Convention about seventy years before my time, and it was settled by our Constitution having exactly nothing to say about it. It was one of the many things our Founders purposely *left out* of the federal oversight and it was left to be dealt with by the states. Yes, it was an issue of states-rights, and the Southern man was pretty sure the Constitution settled it upon its signing.

Northerners, of course, felt they were only imposing a higher standard of morality on their wayward Southern brethren. Even though slavery had been around since civilization itself, it was obvious to them such a barbaric practice as ownership of men could never pass muster in a truly civilized and free society. Furthermore, by the mid-nineteenth century, *most* of the civilized countries had resolved the issue. It was settled. Slavery was abolished and those countries were moving on right smartly without having to operate a slave culture. England, our closest role model as a society, ended slavery in 1833.

The Northern man couldn't see why the Southern man couldn't see his enlightened view.

Florida, of course, was a burgeoning slave state. With its later start and shortage of workers for the heavy jobs, its demand for the real hard manual labor to clear and build farms, roads, bridges and all things necessary for a new civilization was very hard to fill. The slave population of the new state was growing by leaps and bounds, and no matter what a man thought of the practice, it was one way to get strong bodies to the state and to get work done.

Dark clouds loomed over the slave business, and I heard about it when I'd sit on the porch and listen to the older men talk. I didn't understand what it all meant, but I could feel a growing tension in the air.

Nowhere was the tension tenser than between two of the men I admired most: my grandfathers. Of course you know my Grandpa Lee owned slaves, but Grandpa McDonald did not. As you might imagine, when America's sentiment started to change, it was much easier for a non-slaveholder to change his thinking than for a man who owned slaves. None of us like to be told we're doing something wrong, much less immoral or evil, whether or not it's the truth. Slaveholders were no exception, and the South was no exception.

We had several Sunday afternoon get-togethers spoiled for us when my two grandfathers would decide to go another round about the slavery issue. It wasn't like ol' McDonald was an outright abolitionist, but it just didn't sit right with Grandpa Lee for him to be a neighboring farmer, not to mention kinfolk, and think maybe we needed to re-think the business of having humans as property.

Our Sunday get-togethers were usually at one of four places: the McDonalds' farmhouse, John Lee's, Wiley's house, or the swimming hole. After church we'd retire to one of our family places with the whole Lee clan and maybe one or two other families. If it was at John's, the slave families weren't invited. At Wiley's, they were invited but always stayed out back, and at the McDonald place, they were invited but knew better than to come, or big boss John would be out of sorts all week. It's just kinda the way it was.

That simple example of Sunday dinners might show you how the tension started between those two fine men. John might say something real soothing like, "Why don't you mind your own business and quit invitin' my farmhands to your house?" To which McDonald, being your typical Scottish peacemaker, might say, "Those black kids are some of *my* grandkids' best friends. Why don't you treat 'em like humans?" I just don't know a delicate way to say it, but when two grown and accomplished men get into a pissin' contest, then get their own mutual grandkids involved, you're probably gonna have quite a show on your hands. It reminded me of when you see two bulls stompin' and snortin' at each other, and neither one of those mostly-Godly and mostly-proper men cared who heard it.

The two loving granddaddies never came to blows, but they sure showed how high strung the nerves were in those days and how our country was struggling for a solution to a problem we got ourselves into many generations ago yet really couldn't figure how to solve.

Growing Up and Prosperity in Hamilton County

Now I don't mean to make you think I had a tough upbringing, because I didn't. Other than the aforementioned growing dark cloud, the Lee farm on Swift Creek, in the settlement of Genoa, near White Springs, in the new State of Florida was one terrific place to be a kid.

We worked hard, and I had to study hard, too, but I always felt like that farm was where I wanted to grow up, live a long life, and someday way off in the future pass on to the Sweet Bye and Bye.

The men of the farm put all us boys on a horse almost as soon as we could walk. First we'd be on an old, worn-out pony they kept around just for us to learn on, and so we wouldn't have so far to fall when we did fall. After a while, we'd graduate to the old, full-sized, gentle mares. By time we were, oh, about seven years old, we'd be on the most spirited ride on the farm, and we could handle it. The Lee kids were known for miles around as fine horsemen.

Don't think we were taught all this horsemanship just for fun, though. For the men, horses were about nothing but work, and we were trained to work those horses and get the most out of them as we possibly could. We loved our horses, and if this is what was called work, well, we said, "Let's go to work!"

The Lees were normally first in the county to take on almost any kind of machinery, and all the new farm machines were powered by horses. Those smart farm machine makers, like Deering, McCormick, and lots of others were working just as hard in their shops to create ever better ways to grow more with less effort. It was amazing how slow other farmers were to buy into the new machinery. "This here's the way we've always done it," they'd say, or "Look at the cost of those contraptions," or "I bet it spends all its time broke down." Maybe they were right, but when Daddy saw a horse-drawn machine tiller, or planter, or hay-cutter, or harrow, he knew that horse and machine could do the job of ten men every day. He knew enough "figgerin" to know it wouldn't take long for the new machine to pay for itself. Sometimes he'd even buy a new, improved machine even before the old one was worn out. He had horse-drawn (or mule-drawn) tools of all kinds.

It was really exciting for a young boy to see ever better things coming along to make our farms getting ever more productive. Everything we grew cost less to grow per pound every year because the fields were getting better yields with less labor; and we were doing it better.

Daddy taught me the fewer men we had to feed on the farm, the more cash crops we could grow. We had to first grow enough to feed the hands and the family, only after that could we worry about growing food to sell for money. You know my Daddy and Granddaddy John didn't mind growing the family, but they sure liked the idea of having fewer farmhands to feed.

Daddy studied hard to grow better crops. He learned from books and took the new farming magazines by mail so he could learn how farmers all around the country were becoming more efficient. Once the magazines and farm catalogues were read, he made sure they were removed to the outhouse, where they were put to their final use. "Waste not, want not," he'd say.

One of the things Daddy learned from his farming magazines was how the chaff of one crop might be used on other crops. For example, when we'd harvest the tobacco leaves and put them up in the curing barn, we'd keep the stems and stalks and put them through a horse-powered grinding machine. Once they were down to pieces an inch or shorter, they'd be piled in the open barnyard for storage until needed next growing season. They'd be covered with a layer of hay to create a thatch to protect the stems from getting too wet and souring before they were needed.

Then, the next season, when we'd get an outbreak of almost any kind of crop-eating insect, we'd put those tobacco stems to work. Horse and cart would go to the field and two men with pitchforks would take the fine cuttings and spread them as far and evenly as possible. We'd have no more insect problems there. Not, at least, until the next time we had insect problems. We were using tobacco stems to control pests for several years before we learned why it worked. It was a chemical inside the tobacco called nicotine. Nicotine was poisonous to insects and therefore good for yields. The stems also provided some nitrogen, phosphorous, potassium and other things plants need to grow.

Like the tobacco stems, we also saved manure from the livestock. We collected it by bucket and wagon and then dumped it in big stacks for storage. When ready, our brand new manure spreader and two horses and one man could do the work of five men with much more even distribution and less wear and tear on the men. The spreader had an adjustable chain-driven conveyor, powered by a big sprocket and chain on the axle. It scooped out measured amounts of manure and spread it behind the wagon according to the speed of the horses.

Here I am off subject again. I'm supposed to be talking about an ideal childhood on the farm, but I just seem to go back to telling about how excited I was to see improvement on the land and couldn't wait to be in charge and take my turn at making this land even better.

We had a lot of love for each other. There were lots of animals; some were pets, some nothing more than work tools, and some we knew were going to be food or cash someday, but we liked them all. There were lots of chores to do, but we knew there was honor in work, and the good Lord would someday reward our hard work.

We heard Daddy say, "It's good to come to the table hungry and to the bed sleepy." We didn't have to be too far along in our studies to understand fully what he meant. Work was glorified in our family, and we felt our best when we were productive.

The swimming hole was the jewel of the farm. It had grown from just a wide spot in the creek into a pond fully stocked with bass, panfish, catfish and bullfrogs. Over time, we built a cypress board dam to give it more depth and width, raising the level up to as much as four feet higher than the creek's natural level.

The near bank had a gradual, shallow shoreline so the youngest could play without the mommas fearing they'd drown. It had a couple of graceful live oaks with branches out over the water, and a rope swing was in service ready for all to enjoy. The far side, about two hundred feet across, was a small cypress head which produced a steady stream of shiner minnows and other critters supplying the hungry big-mouth bass and bream with all the food they needed to grow big enough to grace our dinner table.

The swimming hole was also the watering spot for the local wildlife. Deer, turkeys, fox-squirrels, foxes, raccoons, gators, all kinds of ducks and many more called the swimming hole home at various times and for various reasons. Many of them supplied our table abundantly.

Our favorite visitor was the family of otters who would entertain us with their antics. They were so favored by all that it was an unbendable rule no harm would come to them by any member of the Lee family, even though they had very nice hides and their meat would surely be tasty.

With all the small animal life there, the swimming hole was an ideal spot for cottonmouth moccasins, too. We had to be vigilant against them, but the animals and humans mostly seemed to get along just fine there. I think the people loved the swimming hole best. Whether it was for cooling off at the end of a scorcher of a workday on the farm, family gatherings, romance, or just a quiet place to get away from the noise and stress of overflowing houses, everybody loved the swimming hole. It was a respite, a source of peace, fun and food for all.

While I was busy growing up, Hamilton County was doing some pretty fancy growing of its own. The railroad finally came through when I was almost a teenager. The first leg was from

Jacksonville to Alligator Town, which had changed its name to Lake City. Eventually the train made its way through to Tallahassee and on to Pensacola. It was rough and slow, but a big improvement, over the horse-drawn carts on the best road in Florida. The improvement was not so much in speed, but in payload and number of people. The train could run night and day without stopping to camp, tend animals, rest, etc.

The locomotives were nothing but wood-burning steam engines with iron wheels, so they would need to stop every now and then to re-supply the water tanks and refill the woodbins. The lady passengers would need to make stops, too, and you know why. The first passenger cars were just platforms on wheels with a few chairs scattered around on them, so a man could just jump off the train, step off the tracks, do his business, and run to catch up. It was a point of pride for the men to never need to use an outhouse at a train stop.

The rails on the early railroads were made of wood. They were spiked into the cross-ties. They'd be made of the best heart pine or cypress possible, and would work pretty well for a few years. Eventually, though, they'd develop soft spots or rot from the heavy loads, sun exposure, or the extremely wet or dry conditions. When they did, the heavy steam engines would splinter the rails and sure enough, the train would run off the track.

Whenever they rode on one of these trains, the able-bodied men knew they were going to be enlisted several times per trip for various labors. They might be called on to replace rails (all trains carried a supply of replacements in the back of the firewood box), remove debris from the tracks, or shoo away animals. In later years, the wooden rails would have an iron cap put on top of them, improving the speed a little but mainly reducing wear and tear, buttressing the weak spots, and increasing the life of the wooden rails.

In summertime, the men might be issued machetes to go ahead of the train and chop and move the fast growing grasses over-growing the rails. If the vegetation got too thick, it could mat up on the rails and stop the train by making the rails too slippery, causing the drive wheels of the train to just sit there spinning. A team of men would have no trouble chopping the grass while boys removed it from the rails, normally while the train kept moving.

Every now and then a stubborn bull or ornery gator would be reluctant to yield to the locomotive. Again, several men would be deployed to scare off the critter, usually without incident. Later, as the trains picked up speed, cowcatchers were installed to scoop the animal off the tracks without the train having to stop, usually not a pleasant experience for the scoopee.

During this exciting new age of the locomotive, White Springs was booming with five fine hotels and prosperous timber, turpentine, sawmill, cotton ginning and farming businesses.

Of course, all these booming businesses caused lots of people to earn their livings away from the farm, finally making the second *D & L* a prosperous enterprise. As more people lived and worked in towns, more people relied on businesses to provide services most farmers did for themselves.

With the new population, especially the wealthy Northern winterers (we called them "snowbirds" for their migratory habits and the cold weather they were escaping), White Springs became quite a cultural center. Momma tried mightily to get the Lee boys and girls to partake in the big city delights of high culture concerts and plays by traveling acting troupes. These Lee young'uns, however, were born and bred in the country life of early Florida. They loathed high society and culture as much as they were thrilled by the daily concert of nature and the chorus of miracles of farm life they witnessed. To get even one of the girls off her horse and into her Sunday dress for a Saturday night of symphony at the hotel was a hard row-to-hoe for poor Mary McDonald Lee. Further, the Lee kids were normally far too tired from their days on the farm to be able to stay awake through even the most exciting performance of music or theatre. Wiley wasn't opposed to them having some culture, but they all knew he expected them up and ready to work before the sun came up every day but Sunday.

Just as John's Indian Momma taught, "Idle hands are the devil's workshop," Wiley was teaching his brood, "Early to bed and early to rise makes a man healthy, wealthy, and wise." Our part-Indian great-grandma would've been real proud of the way her grandson was raising her fourth generation because those hands were *never* idle if Wiley Lee had anything to do with it.

The farm prospered unabated. We learned how to produce more and better of everything we grew. Cotton was truly king, though. Because of better seed, better methods like crop rotation, and new or improved machines to let horses do more work while men did less, most farms' yields were improving. Because the yields improved, our costs per bushel (or pound, bale, etc.) went relentlessly lower. Those cotton yields over one hundred pounds per acre which Wiley used to dream of became routine by 1860. Experts said we'd be able to someday get it to three hundred pounds! I didn't know if we could or not, but I was willin' to try.

In those days I dreamed of the kind of cotton demand we'd have if every man could afford not just one, but two pairs of pants and two shirts. What if it wasn't just the wealthy women who could have two or more dresses? Was it possible someday everybody could afford a pair of underwear?

The cotton gin was getting better and faster, thus continuing to reduce our costs. A steam-driven gin was built. It ran about three times faster than the best one run by man and mule. Because we could deliver the cotton ever cheaper, the demand grew ever more. It was a phenomenal time in farming. Prices received by farmers were going relentlessly down, yet the farmers who adapted to new ways were making better profits with every price cut. Productivity was a wonderful thing!

The neighboring towns of Lake City, Live Oak and Jasper were all beginning to come into their own, but White Springs on the Suwanee was the crown jewel of them all. With the big hotels and the spring and its natural "healing waters" becoming known throughout the country, growth in White Springs seemed unstoppable. Middle Florida was really beginning to shape up.

The South benefitted from agricultural productivity while the North was reaping rewards of industrial improvements. We'd heard of the industrial revolution for almost a hundred years, but it had really only been changing life on the farm for the last twenty. There were many wonderful machines men were making to do man's work for him.

The raw cotton was shipped from farms to Southern gins. From the gins it went north where it was milled and woven into yarn or fabric. Much of the U.S. production was sent to England, which was having a mass change as the country transitioned from wool-based clothing to much cheaper, more versatile cotton. It's hard to describe the change brought about by being able to make new clothes available to even factory workers, not just royalty. As ever more material was made, ever more factory workers were needed. Additionally, steam power meant more factory workers were needed, and the factory workers were more productive. This meant fewer hands on the farm as city jobs became attractive, but horse-powered machines made men and women more productive at the farm. As we've been speaking of a mass migration from North to South, another migration was happening from farm to city. As it was taking fewer of us to feed all of us, we were in the midst of a real revolution and could see the change from day to day. As good jobs took folks off the farms into cities, more city folks needed ever more of what we farmers grew. It was an exciting time.

There were so many things happening at once, and all were wrapped up under the title of the Industrial Revolution. This revolution brought about the most notable and rapid change in human lifestyle since Adam and Eve, and it appeared to be setting us on a path of change which may never end.

A Call to Arms

With so much improvement in quality of life, you might think America would be at peace forever. After all, with so much opportunity and prosperity, shouldn't every American be busy working to build a better life for himself and his family? Shouldn't there be no time for war in times like these?

The tensions grew thick between the agrarian South and the industrial North. We don't have time to talk about all the differences, but we can hit the high points.

We had tensions because of our economic and social differences, just as Alexander Hamilton and Thomas Jefferson had their differences over their visions for America. Hamilton saw great cities and urban living, while Jefferson saw the potential of our land and envisioned a prosperous agrarian society with great farms and lots of space for everybody.

Well, it seems now both men were right. I'm guessing each was more right than they themselves could have imagined. The Industrial Revolution was building great cities beyond anything Hamilton could have foreseen, and same for Jefferson and his agricultural dream. Modern farms were providing so much more than the farms of his day, and Jefferson had only been dead a little over thirty years at this point.

Why couldn't this great nation live together with the fine cities and the beautiful sprawling farms co-existing? Those city folks needed to eat, didn't they? A farmer's gotta sell what he grows, doesn't he? What could be better than for America to become the greatest agricultural *and* urban society the world has ever known?

Well, I guess the unfortunate fact is the great cities and the great farms were separated. Maybe if they'd been commingled throughout the land they'd have gotten along better, but they were starkly divided between North and South. Could all the tension really be about nothing more than mutual jealousy?

Now let's throw in the states' rights issue, which was just an extension of the Jefferson and Hamilton quarrels. The agrarian model relied on self-determination for each of the states to run their lives as they saw fit. Further, it allowed for wide variety of differences from state to state, but required each state to respect the different choices made by its sister states.

In Hamilton's view, because great cities required lots of people living close together, a much stronger government was needed to keep the people all stacked up like cordwood and living civilly together.

Add to all the states' rights confusion the highly flammable topic of slavery. We'd been grappling with it since well before the Constitutional Convention and it's been festerin' like a snake bite on America's rump since our beginning. Every time we tried to quell the issue with another compromise, we would satisfy a few folks and outrage another group. Additionally, with the mass new purchases of land we were making as we moved west towards the Pacific and south to Florida, we had to fight about slavery every time we set policy for each new piece of land, whether it be Spanish Florida, the Louisiana Purchase or the Mexican territories. Each new expansion of our great country brought with it the dividing, rancorous decision of whether the new land would be slave or free. It was hard not to be on one side or the other of this issue. It sharply divided people who otherwise had the same values. As we've stated before, it divided the churches, families, states, territories - it just divided everybody.

Eventually the North got tired of all the compromising which only led to dissatisfaction on both sides. The predictable result was the Abolition Movement, which gained strength with those who didn't own slaves and left those who did clinging to their states' rights doctrine and striving to keep the lives they'd known for two hundred years.

The final nail in the young republic's coffin of peace was the 1860 election of Mr. Abraham Lincoln as President. Lincoln's debates of 1858 with Mr. Douglas were just too much for the South. Lincoln made a name for himself with eloquent and clever arguments against slavery, all the while proclaiming he was absolutely *not* an abolitionist. The record shows he was the best double-speaker ever to hit our national podium. In speech after speech, he would plant one foot firmly on each side of our most divisive issue. Then he had the nerve to call himself "Honest Abe."

The secession was probably inevitable no matter who was elected, but the South was particularly repulsed by Lincoln. This new Republican Party of his was just a new schism of the Whig Party with a strong abolition plank right smack in the middle of its platform. Yet Lincoln said he wasn't an abolitionist . . . us Southerners were pretty sure we couldn't trust ol' Honest Abe.

He was elected November 6, 1860.

The inauguration was March 4, 1861.

In his first inaugural address, he made a solemn pledge to the South to do nothing to interfere with its "Peculiar Institution" of slavery.

Sadly, the representatives of seven Southern states - South Carolina, Mississippi, Florida, Alabama, Georgia, Louisiana and Texas- weren't present to hear his conciliatory promise to the South. Those states had already seceded before he took office.

The attack on Fort Sumter, in Charleston Harbor, was about a month after inauguration.

Nobody from either side died in the attack on the Fort . . . but a whole lot were fixin' to.

News was travelin' fast and furious. Not all of it was true, of course, but most of it was very disturbing. There were rumors Union troops had taken over Charleston and were savaging innocent men, women and children. There were rumors about Lincoln and rumors about Jefferson Davis, the President of the Confederate States of America (CSA). Anything that could possibly cause panic was hitting the telegraph wires and instantly going to all parts of the country.

We did know Lincoln was mustering up troops, demanding specific numbers of regiments of militia from each of his remaining states to report to him and William Seward, his Secretary of State, all without Congress' approval. The Constitution required the President to call an emergency session in order to approve or disapprove such preparations for war, but the Constitution was ignored. Just as alarming, he was closing newspapers and jailing writers who were critical of his actions or supportive of the South's right to secede. He jailed many men and held them there without charges in direct defiance of the Constitutional right of *habeas corpus*.

Lincoln demanded each of his remaining states submit militia to his command, again without Congress' approval. It was clear he was positioning to invade. All the while, the North stood firmly, saying it was "in no way positioning for war" and only wanted to preserve the Union. If this was true, however, it might've been smart to release some of the forts to the rebelling states and leave peacefully. Then the Yanks could try to woo the South back into the fold with something a bit more inviting than blockades to harbors and seizing control of key cities. We guessed Lincoln didn't want to have to do without the tariff revenue he would lose from the Southern states if secession succeeded.

Of course the South would say it didn't want a war, it just wanted out of the Union, but it might have been smart to tell that to whoever it was who decided to open fire on Fort Sumter; and whoever it was who had enough of an arsenal to turn the mighty fort into a pile of rubble. It sure woulda felt like an act of war to those poor slobs on the receiving end of all those cannonballs.

While declaring innocence, the South maintained it didn't want war while it was issuing a call to arms for all its loyal sons to come to the glorious aid of their brand new country, the Confederate States of America. I'm sure you know it didn't take long for all to figure a big war was bound to happen.

To this day, people speculate and argue over what happened to make the states go to war. Maybe the words of some objective bystanders might help. The European press was fascinated with the goings-on in the new republic. While opinions varied, most agreed it boiled down to money. None wrote it better than Charles Dickens, Europe's premier political writer of the 19th century, who said in December, 1861,

> Union means so many millions a year lost to the South; secession means the loss of the same millions to the North. The love of money is the root of this as of many, many other evils . . . The quarrel between the North and South is, as it stands, solely a fiscal squabble.

The whole Genoa settlement made a pilgrimage to the Swift Creek Church for one bodacious special prayer meeting. Oh, how the preachers preached and the singers sang! With Aunt Nancy Lee Roberts playing powerfully on the church's new upright piano, we started off by singing,

> Stand up, stand up for Jesus, ye soldiers of the cross;
> Lift high his royal banner, it must not suffer loss:
> From victory unto victory His army shall He lead,
> 'Til every foe is vanquished, and Christ is Lord in-deed.
>
> Stand up, stand up for Jesus, stand in his strength alone;
> The arm of flesh will fail you, ye dare not trust your own:
> Put on the gospel armor, each piece put on with prayer;
> Where duty calls or danger, be never wanting there.
>
> Stand up, stand up for Jesus, the strife will not be long;
> This day the noise of battle, the next the victor's song:
> To him that overcometh, a crown of life shall be;
> He, with the King of Glory, shall reign eternally.

The little log church on the little hill was booming. With the end of verse three, all the men of the congregation, except John Lee, erupted into a big cheer, sounding more like a Seminole War rally than a Methodist church.

The guest preacher, the Rev. William Jabish Barnett, son of the Rev. T.R. Barnett, also a circuit rider from the town of Sanderson, gave an inspiring message on the call of duty and doing the Lord's work in our lives, no matter what the circumstances or the consequences may be. He made a special call on the gathered faithful to, "As the grand hymn states . . . 'Stand Up For Jeeeesus!'" Surely God himself was on our side. Just as He'd inspired the great Old Testament warriors, He was now here and calling us into service. It was our time to stand.

Just as the Founding Fathers pledged their "Lives, fortunes, and sacred honor," to the cause of independence from the crown, we were doing the same for the cause of states' rights and liberty from the tyranny of a big central government.

At the conclusion of the message, and after a long prayer for all the young men serving and yet to serve in the War against the evil Northern powers, Reverend Barnett asked for all the young men of soldiering age to come forward so the elders could lay hands on them and pray for God to grant them safety and victory; and for each of these Christian Soldiers to put on the "whole armor of God." He prayed for Almighty God to give them strength and courage to go forth and defend the righteous Southern way of life, which God ordained in the first place and with which the Yankee hordes were trying to disrupt. "May the God of Abraham, Isaac and Jacob be with us in the battle," he begged, "and may the peace of Christ which passeth all understanding be with us all on this night and for the duration of the conflict. And may His grace bring us all home to this place when the battle is done, and the victory won!"

"AMEN!" Shouted the congregation.

Some young men cried, overcome by the emotion and overwhelmed by the realization of their peaceful Genoan existence being stripped from them. Some just gave blank stares as their way of gripping their new lot in life. Most, though, were button-poppin' proud of themselves and the attention they were getting. They could only stand there and smile, hoping all would see how big they'd become. They wanted to catch the eye of that special girl in the crowd, really, really hoping to catch the glisten of a tear in her eye, that most tangible, most feminine sign she really cared and she knew what a dangerous and heroic stand her man was taking for the glorious cause of the South. Just as the soldier boys hoped, the younger girls saw something very exciting about the whole thing, and so the boys' minds were on not valor and danger, but the opportunity to escort the poor damsel home, the long way, that is, and console her fears over the great danger the brave young soldiers would confront.

The older women were far too choked up with fear of the future for their men and boys to do much of anything but wipe their faces with their hankies and pray, pray, pray. There was more appealing and beseeching coming from these women than this little church had ever seen. I think the women were mainly beseeching the Almighty to bring some sanity to these men with bloodlust running their minds. The soldiers were appealing for divine intervention to give them the glory of the best hero story in all the Southland. If God ever gets confused, I think he just might have been a little befuddled by the prayers coming out of Swift Creek Methodist that evening. For that matter, I reckon he was hearing similarly conflicting prayers out of every church across all of America in this particular season of our nation's story.

After the prayer, the congregation stood and sang "Amazing Grace" together. It wasn't lost on John Lee that this fine hymn was written by a reformed slave trader.

Aunt Nancy Lee remembered being a little girl and playing the same hymn at her mother's funeral so long ago. The congregation did as congregations do whenever they sing "Amazing Grace" at an emotional time; everyone cried. Although there are lots of ways of dealing with an impending war, times like these help everyone to see how important faith, family, friends and fellowship are for all of us all the time. What a shame we don't live as if each day is a crisis and our only way to handle it is to put our worries into those hands much greater than our own.

To end on an upbeat note, Reverend Barnett, turning to Nancy, said, "Let's sing together again that new hymn, 'Stand Up, Stand Up For Jesus!'" Then turning to the whole congregation, he boomed, "And as we leave this place, let's never forget our cause is God's cause, and He will be with us as we defend His cause to the ends of the earth!"

Early Glories of War

During the early part of the War, the Lees dealt with these emotion-charged issues by doing what they did best: farming.

Us Lee boys were were doing our part for the war effort by staying at the farm and making sure the Army was fed and clothed. We realized what an important role it was, but most of us wished to be on the battlefield. Many of the local boys went ahead and volunteered early in the conflict. Almost all the Florida Infantry and Artillery units were sent straight north to the aid of General Lee and the Army of Northern Virginia. Our state was well represented in all the big, early battles after Bull Run.

The young soldier boys were thrilled by the prospect of going to war and finally having their chance to show valor and courage. Each had already planned his homecoming to Genoa after a brief, glorious war against those Yankee bastards. They'd regale the girls with daring tales of whuppin' up on the Northern miscreants. They might even walk with a bit of a limp, and if they inherited a little limp from the glorious conflict, they might just make sure it became a big limp anytime the girls were watchin'. The really lucky ones would need just a single crutch, not two, and would, of course, be just fine with only a few months of recuperation and the appropriate amount of female attention. The local girls, in turn, would throw themselves at the soldier boys in fawning admiration and just wouldn't be able to get enough of the stories of heroism and derring-do. And didn't the young girls swoon and the mommas fret at the sight of their young men in uniform?

However, our patriarch, John Lee, who wore uniforms in the War of 1812, the First and Second Seminole Indian Wars, and had been a leader in the local vigilante group to fight off the Murrellites, was not amused. He got more gruff than we'd ever seen him, and told us youngsters to stop the nonsense and quit glorifying war. He went so far as to forbid us from volunteering. At first none of his sons or grandsons would brave a challenge to his forbidding.

John was about sixty-eight at the time, and to everyone's surprise, he was taking charge of his family again. For years he had just seemed to enjoy the bounty of the land and gloried in watching his children and grandchildren run the farm he sacrificed so much to develop.

"I want to be the next one planted in the Swift Creek cemetery," he said feistily, "and I don't want to go there for at least another twenty years. You're all talking foolishness and need to have some sense knocked into you. I'm telling you, you don't want to go to war!" Then, very somberly, "There will be no winners if America gets in a fight against itself."

Well, us younger Lees agreed, "There's no fool like an old fool," and maybe our poor dear old patriarch was just getting a little soft in his old age. Maybe he no longer understood how men had to stand up for honor and principle and all that's good and right.

Even Wiley, at forty-five years old, seemed to be itching for a fight. Maybe he thought it was his last and only chance to prove himself in battle. His only real effort at defending home and hearth to this point was his role in Roux's vigilantes, where he served in the shadow of his father. Maybe he thought time was running out for him to prove himself a warrior. Further, Wiley seemed impatient, maybe even disgusted with his father. He'd been the dutiful son all his life and worked himself like a slave, literally, to make this farm a success. Yet all he felt he got from ol' John was a look of "You're just doin' what you're s'posed to do, son."

Wiley began to show evermore disdain for John's child-siring habits. "I guess the old man thinks I will just keep on feeding however many pups he wants to sire," said my father about my grandfather. "Doesn't he know, every time you hang your britches on the bedpost, here comes another young'un? Is he going to kill Ava just like he killed Lizzie? Imagine this old man still having kids though he's pert near seventy years old, and poor Ava's into her fifties. He'd produced twenty-three in total. Wiley wondered how many was enough for that man."

I'd never seen my father like this, but there were a whole lot of things going on at the farm then, and nerves were running real high. I was afraid the tension of this American War with ourselves was causing lots of other tensions to boil to the surface. It almost looked like there was a war between the Lees brewing at the same time we had a War Between the States in the making.

I tried talking with Wiley calm and reasonable-like, but didn't get very far. I'd never seen him give anything but respect to his father. This time, though, it looked like he'd been a simmering cauldron his whole adult life. I just hoped the cauldron wouldn't blow.

Out of respect for the elder statesman of the Lee clan, we toned down our talk and excitement about going to war, but it was still high on the minds of all the younger Lee men. As the news stories flowed in with tales of Rebel victories, the boys would burn ever more to take part in the glories of war, and it didn't help when John would constantly see the young boys running around the yard with their wooden toy guns shouting things like, "POW! Just killed me another yeller-bellied Yank!"

My older sister Sophia's husband, Lewis Hogans, figured as an in-law he wasn't subject to John's rule and volunteered as soon as he could. He left his two young sons and pregnant wife in early '62 to join the 1ˢᵗ Florida Cavalry. He was captured when his horse was shot out from under him in a skirmish in Northern Alabama. Later released in a prisoner trade, he went back into battle, fell ill and died in a hospital in Knoxville in December of '62. His daughter, Mary Catharine, was six months old when her Daddy died. They never had the pleasure of meeting.

As the War heated up, we Lees just kept on farming. Demand for everything we could grow was higher than ever. Both armies were in constant demand for every thread of cotton the South could grow, with the North buying our cotton through circuitous channels of European brokers. We found the old saying, "An army marches on its stomach," was true, but armies also needed lots of cotton and were financed by the sale of cotton fiber to Europe. Florida provided it all, food and fiber. Everything we grew was sold before we planted it. The War started out as a great time to be in farming, but all the young Lees had Johnny Reb dreams running wild in their heads.

In the early days the military buyers were happy to take whatever we grew, but as early as fall of 1861, they were "suggesting" we not plant as much cotton, but grow more food items, particularly corn and beans. Before the New Year, it was clear this was not a suggestion. It felt like maybe a bit of the oppressiveness we thought we seceded from was coming out in the new CSA.

The new Confederate currency was good and strong. At first there was no problem exchanging it for United States currency or state or private bank notes. John, though, didn't trust it. Whenever he accumulated a good batch of Confederate currency, he'd load it up in his saddlebags, take it in to Fernandina, trade it for gold, and bring it home. We were never real sure why he didn't do his gold trading at the White Springs or Lake City banks. Maybe he didn't trust the bank or its bankers, or maybe he knew local tongues would wag a little too freely. Maybe he still feared the return of John Murrell and his Murrellites. Whatever the reason, he did his gold trading out of town. He would slip away with little fanfare, be gone six or seven days, and returned just as secretly as he left. The saddlebags he left with were crammed full of paper bills, but the return saddlebags sported gold coins.

John had his gold buried in places only he, Wiley or Ava knew, and Wiley and Ava were pretty sure there were some only John knew. They strongly suggested he leave some maps somewhere in case he met his demise before he planned. He stubbornly kept all his hiding places in his memory.

The South was doing very well in the War and routinely out-killed the Yanks in the early battles. We knew they had more men to pull from than we did, but most battles were decisive victories for the CSA. We normally reported to battle with fewer troops and guns but extracted more blood than our opponents.

We could argue a lot about why this was, but it seemed the main advantage for the South was that our fighters mostly came off the farm, theirs from the city. They had plenty of big, strong, well-fed boys, but our skinny, wiry lads knew the woods, were used to improvising, and knew how to work long, hard hours. They had some very good fighters. We liked to think we had better instincts for this game by being born and raised with hard work, tracking animals and shooting our food. Heck, if you wanted a Reb to shoot a Yank, all you had to do was tell him it was venison dressed in blue, he'd get it!

It was well known Mr. Lincoln was expecting the whole secession affair to be over in just a few months. Us Rebs were beginning to think we might just agree with ol' Honest Abe on his timing, but we didn't see eye-to-eye on who we thought the victor might be.

D & L Meats of White Springs never sold more meat at higher prices than the early years of the War. The War effort was taking every piece of cured meat just as fast as it could be cured. The hotel business had gone away because Northerners were no longer free to travel to White Springs for the winter. John Lee found the CSA a lot less demanding a customer than the local hoteliers. The meat market was adding to his wealth and giving him still more money to exchange for gold.

However, John got no sense of joy from the success he was experiencing after so many years of very hard work. All these generous profits felt more like ill-gotten gains to him than the free-trade capitalism he'd enjoyed his whole life. He'd look at the huge quantities leaving his farm and butcher shop and sullenly wonder how much of it was going to end up in a dead boy's belly.

As long as *D & L* was buying its meat with Confederate Dollars and selling in the same currency, it was making a good spread on ever-increasing volume. John relentlessly continued trading his Confederate money just as fast as he could for things of durable value, preferably gold.

As the shortage of fighting men became more severe, the Confederate leadership knew it would have to take desperate measures. In early '62, President Davis issued a proclamation which had the effect of eliminating our Florida state militia. Its intent was to move those soldiers on into the main War, and it did so, at least a little bit. The state militia, though, consisted of a lot of men too old, too young or too disabled to face the rigors of the main war. A lot of them were also the farmers doing the crucial work of feeding the rest of the Confederacy. They were valuable in defending the home front and supplying our troops, but might be sitting ducks on a battlefield.

The Second Florida Cavalry was to stay in the state in place of the militia as the bulk of the remaining Home Guard for our strategically-valuable farmland and vast cattle herds.

The disbanding of the militia sent many of the volunteers back to the farm, not into the bigger theatre to the North as intended. It also left the state much less defended than it was previously. Even worse, the entire state was evacuated of regular Confederate forces except for a regiment to guard from Jacksonville to St. Augustine and one to protect Apalachicola. The Second Cavalry was left in Florida to cover as much of the remaining ground with as few men as possible. This stretch from Jacksonville to Tallahassee was fast becoming the main source of food supply, including salt, corn, cattle and hogs, for the South.

In August of '62, I got my notice from the Confederate Army; so much for the policy of leaving the plowboys and cowboys home to farm and provide food for our fighting men. I was drafted, but was told I'd be free to go back to the farm and finish the fall harvest. The War was still young, but the Confederacy was already getting drained of volunteer soldiers to the point of having to draft its fighting-age men, even the ones it earlier intended to leave on the farm. Neither we nor the CSA were real sure how the CSA would feed itself with all its fine farms being run by old men, women, children and slaves, but the most immediate problem was to get warm bodies on the battlefield. Sadly, conscription in Florida yielded extremely few soldiers because so many of the draft-able men had already volunteered.

Daddy Wiley, well over forty, my younger brother John Harley, a lad of sixteen, and I rode into Lake City to the Army office to report for duty, John Harley and Dad as volunteers, I as a draftee. The Rebel cause needed lots of men. The army was telling us Florida boys it not only needed our produce but also our bodies. It should have been an ominous sign to us, but we weren't too smart at the time. Even though we were still winning most battles, the cold fact was we just didn't have as many men to throw at them as they had to throw at us. Our numbers were dwindling fast.

I was put into Company C, Second Battalion, Florida Infantry, CSA, under Captain Walter Moore. We were named the "Columbia Rifles." My home company should've been the "Hamilton Blues" under Captain Henry Stewart. I was joined with the Columbia County boys, though, because they had been decimated at the Beaver Dam, Gaines Mill and Frayser Farm battles in Virginia. Wiley and John Harley were put into Company K of the Second Florida Cavalry volunteers. Wiley was madder than a mule chewin' on a bumblebee that I wasn't also in a cavalry. It was well known the Lees were fine horsemen with fine horses.

Why would Wiley's son be put in an infantry? Could the CSA possibly be any more stupid? All we could figure was I was the one of drafting age, so the Army put me where it wanted. Daddy was too old for foot soldiering and John Harley was too young for drafting, so they got better assignments.

Even though he had no military experience, Wiley was made a Lieutenant due to his age and success in farming. John Harley and I were mere Privates.

While Wiley fumed I resigned myself to my new lot in life as an infantryman. I rode my horse home and would have to get a wagon ride back to Lake City when it was time to report for duty. Not only did infantrymen have to wear out their feet marching everywhere they went, but they were the ones who were lined up and told to take direct enemy fire. They charged the hills. In other words, it was the infantrymen who did the most dyin'.

I had to feel good about one thing, though: at least I finally knew my ol' man cared. He'd have pulled all of us out over my mis-assignment if he could, but even he understood the CSA owned us now and he didn't have a whole lot of say in the matter.

Not only was I thrown into infantry, but I also wasn't free to go back to finish harvest. Due to the heavy losses up North, foot soldiers were becoming in critically short supply. I had three days to return my horse and be back reporting to Lake City headquarters. I was a-gonna be a foot soldier, the lowest rung on the military ladder. Well, I was taught to believe if I worked as hard as I could and prayed as hard as I could for God's divine guidance, mercy and providence, He would watch over me and all would be well. I really believed it, but I'd never had to put it to the test like I was going to as a foot soldier.

Us Lees believed we were here for a purpose, and God would watch over us and make our purpose clear to us in time.

Was my purpose on this earth going to be to march with my rifle and possessions, about forty pounds of it, for hundreds of miles per year? Was it to then line up in front of another bunch of scared eighteen-year-olds, just like me except they wear blue and I wear gray? We'd exchange fire, and once the first volley was fired, the survivors would be frantically reloading to take another shot at our brethren-enemy just a few yards away. Would the Yankee cavalry come in with sabers drawn to mutilate us while we were defenselessly striving to get another pack of powder and another round of lead tamped into our rifles? Was this my high calling in life? It wasn't unusual, we were told, for a quarter to a third of the soldiers, most of them infantry, to be killed, maimed or wounded in any given battle.

I was told to come back with my best shooting piece, so I armed myself with my Kentucky Long rifle and loaded up my Colt 1851 six-shooter. The Kentucky Long was a reliable old cuss and had been in service for hunters and soldiers since before the Revolutionary War. With practice I could peel off between two and three rounds a minute and be accurate up to a hundred yards. It was long, heavy and cumbersome, but tried and true. This baby had been my Daddy's hunting rifle when he was a teenager, and he gave it to me when I turned ten. At that age it knocked me backwards when I shot it, but I loved the thing and learned to prop it against a fence or a stump when I could to have something other than my shoulder absorb most of the kick. Having my Kentucky Long with me would be sort of like having an old friend from home on whatever trail this War adventure led me.

Training was not so hard it involved doing lots of the things we normally did on the farm. It was hard work, but I was used to it. I was already a sharpshooter, and because of Mom's insistence on us getting a good education, I was at the head of the class on what little book training we had. In the infantry, the academic competition was not real tough.

Fortunately, I was notified on October 17 of a re-assignment. By some miracle I was moved over to the Second Cavalry where I'd wanted to be all along. I was somehow made to trade places with some other poor chap who had to give up his horse and take over my place as a foot soldier. Now serving with Dad and John Harley, and with my horse, Charlie, under me, I was ready to go to war. The Army actually paid me rent for my horse, too.

Charlie was a prize on the drill field. He was not overly impressive to look at, just a regular brown horse, medium build, with a white blaze on his forehead, but he was without doubt the best cutting horse for miles around. He wasn't real fast on the run but very smart, quick and agile. When he worked cows, he thought like a cow and seemed to know what the cow was going to do before the cow did. Our joke was, "If ol' Charlie's smarter'n a cow, he otta be able to out-figger any Yankee infantryman!"

When I got back to the farm to pick up Charlie, I loaded up four of the Colt 1851 six-shooter pistols. The pistol is a muzzle loader, but you load six shots at a time. They're real time consuming to load, but with four of them loaded and ready to go on the battle field, a horseman can run into the fray, peel off twenty-four shots, then make a fast retreat to cover for reloading. I wore a double-holster belt with one pistol on each hip and the other two holstered to my saddle where I could get to them real fast.

I traded my Kentucky Long rifle for John's new Sharps Carbine. It was not as accurate as the Kentucky Long, but it was shorter, lighter and had a cartridge load for much faster firing. It could fire eight to ten rounds a minute, about three times faster than any muzzle loader.

The Yankee cavalrymen were still carrying sabers along with rifles and six-shooters. Those sabers could do an awful lot of damage, but they got awfully cumbersome in close combat.

The Yanks lost a lot more cavalry men and horses than we did for fighting this way. They still thought it was the gallant and noble way to fight a war, and we were happy to let them keep on thinking so. I loaded my Bowie knife in a sheath on the saddle. In case I got into close combat, I could swing the Bowie a lot faster and more deadly than a saber, and it didn't take so much room in the saddle as the outdated saber did.

Not only was I going to be the fastest mover on the battlefield, but I would be as well armed as any on the field, and a much better shot than most. The cavalryman was one of the most powerful men on the field because of his speed and firepower. He was also the most desirable target because he sat up high above the foot soldiers and the enemy knew how well armed he was. It was said eliminating one horse soldier was as good as killing ten infantrymen.

For Florida, by early 1862, civilian life was getting tougher by the month. We had little of the horrors of war yet, just a few skirmishes here and there but no mass destruction of property and taking of goods (by both sides) suffered by the farmers and town folks in, say, Virginia, where the hottest battles were.

In December of 1861, the Union passed a law suspending "Specie payments." This law meant a bearer of U.S. currency notes could no longer trade his currency at the bank for gold or silver coin. Therefore the official Union currency was officially just paper. The value of bank notes was vanishing on a daily basis. Counterfeiters were having a heyday. Of course, the Confederate Dollar was nothing but a paper promise from the day the very first one rolled off the press.

Farmers found they were getting paid even more for their crops than last year. Problem was, they were finding fewer and fewer places they could spend their Confederate Dollars. Because of the state's rising debt load, it was also getting harder to use Florida's state notes. Seems we could trade them around among ourselves, but they were no longer convertible with U.S. dollars, and anyone with gold would laugh at the man who offered to trade Confederate Notes for gold at par value. There was the official value of the two countries' currencies, which was one hundred dollars for approximately 4.8 ounces, then there was the real value. In the real world the same hundred was buying the bearer less and less gold by the week.

We knew something was going on with our money, but we didn't know exactly what. Well, I guess John Lee and some of the other cagey old farmers did. Even though John could no longer trade his currency for gold at par, the gold he did get over the last year and a half would serve his family very well in the years to come. In fact, he continued trading for gold well into the War. Even though he was paying a huge premium for it, he was all too convinced the paper of his state and his new country would soon be worth little or nothing. Those gold coins he was trading for would always have value.

Even worse, the death rate was mounting among the boys who'd gone North to fight for the cause. Along with the glowing news of glorious victory on the battlefields, it seemed daily another set of Hamilton County parents was getting the grim news their son was dead, missing in action, or severely wounded. If he was killed on the battleground, he and his fellow dead soldiers were packed into a long shallow trench like bacon strips in a very long skillet. If there was time, a few words were said by some unknown preacher. Then some soldiers or local slaves would go to work throwing just enough dirt on top of him to cover him up and hold down the stench. Then the diggers would go to the next line of bodies to do the same. When the burying team had oh, say, twelve thousand troops to bury in an afternoon, there wasn't a lot of time for individual attention. My friend Charles Gerry was one of the few shipped home in a box. He died of battle wounds in Virginia. Since he was the son of the late Reverend Gerry, the church members took up a collection for him. He was exhumed from his mass grave at the battle site near Richmond and shipped home to lie at rest in the Swift Creek cemetery next to his father. We thought it was good the Reverend had passed on in 1859, shortly before all this War pain began. No one was ever sure it was Charles's remains in the box sent home, but the CSA said it was, so I guess it was.

If your son was shot but not killed, he'd get a ride to a local house commandeered as a field hospital. If he survived the ride, he'd be laid outside the hospital to wait his turn, which could be hours or days. If he needed an amputation, he'd probably get pretty good service because the field surgeons were getting real good at sawing off limbs. He'd give your son a big chug of whiskey, then likely take one for himself, give him a lead bullet to bite down on to keep him from biting off his tongue, then go to cuttin', just like pruning a limb off a tree. The Doc had to make sure to cut into the live wood 'cause if you left any wounded flesh on him, it would surely fester and grow and your little boy would be dead of gangrene in a matter of days; very painful, miserable, days.

The maggots arising from the waste piles of human body parts would be collected and applied to infections to eat out the impurities. It was believed maggots saved many lives in those days.

If the apple of his momma's eye was shot and dyin', but not quite dead yet, the buryin' troops would just leave him where he sat. By time they finished buryin' the field full of sure enough dead folks, and if the ambulance wagon hadn't gotten to him yet, he'd probably be a candidate for the next trench. The burying team wished he could just make up his mind to live or die.

Most likely, the momma and daddy would go on to their own graves without ever seeing the spot where their son had breathed his last; where his youthful dreams for a full life were suddenly cut short; where all his plans changed in an instant.

If your li'l dumplin' was just wounded, maybe crippled or maimed, he might just live out a long life. Mind you, I didn't say a *good* long life, just a long life. In the frontier days of the American South, what good was a returning veteran, even a hero, with one leg, or one arm, or his face disfigured, or burns on half his body? When we saw the survivors, we had to wonder if maybe the dead ones were luckier.

The pain of all this made it hard to remember when so many of us were so excited to be taking up arms and taking on those Yankees. We just knew this thing was going to be over in a matter of months, and the new and glorious Republic of the Confederate States of America would last forever.

Those jubilant sentiments were quickly giving in to a sense this situation was going to get worse before it got better.

Emancipation Proclamation, Impressment & War Economy

On January 1, 1863, Mr. Lincoln signed the Emancipation Proclamation, thus immediately freeing all slaves in the "rebellion states." Never mind the fact there were slave states in the Union. He wasn't going to touch them whom he did have some jurisdiction over. His act declared the states no longer under his presidency must free their slaves. As you might imagine, this proclamation had a very low degree of compliance among Confederate citizens.

In March of 1863, Confederate President Davis signed into law the Impressment Act, which codified and made legal what the CSA procurement officers and soldiers had been doing since the War began. Impressment meant soldiers could take supplies and slaves from private citizens upon payment of a "fair price." Of course, as the Confederacy became financially strapped, and supplies became scarcer, Confederate procurement officers became more aggressive in their dealings with the civilian suppliers. All the Florida farmers learned a fair price was almost always more fair for the negotiator with an army behind him than for the individual farmer looking to sell his goods.

Most Southerners, especially the farmers, wanted to see the South do well and were inclined to help the CSA. Eventually, though, the currency became so worthless they couldn't see it being worth anywhere near the face value. As the farmers and producers of goods became demoralized, yields went down. As supplies of all types became scarce, everybody got hungry.

In midsummer 1863, the two great armies faced each other at a heretofore unheard of place called Gettysburg, Pennsylvania, with Florida troops in the middle of the battle, including our Hamilton and Columbia County boys. This battle became the first big loss for the Rebs and spelled the beginning of the end for the dreams of the Confederate cause of self-rule and states' rights. Even while we were winning all the battles, we were losing the War because the North just had so much more depth in men, machines, money and ammunition. Also in mid-'63, the Yanks got full control of the Mississippi river, cutting off the single major supply line to the Rebel forces. The Southern forces lost at least half of their supplies of munitions, food and clothing, leaving Florida as almost the sole source of supply.

In September of the same year, Fort Wagner, which protected Charleston Harbor, fell. It was the last of the major Southern ports held by Rebel forces. With it gone, any hope for supplies to come into or products to go out of the Southern seaports also vanished. Thus, Florida goods had to travel a complicated and uncertain combination of train and wagon trails through Georgia and South Carolina to reach the troops at the front lines. Our goods could easily be found and confiscated or destroyed in transit. Even if we could supply enough to keep the War effort going, the chances of our goods getting to their destinations were becoming very dicey.

With the Mississippi River firmly in Yankee hands, Louisiana was no longer able to supply salt to the Rebel troops. We noticed a big increase in the number of salt wagons heading north on Florida's interior roads. Settlers on both coasts of South Florida had been recruited to increase their production of salt. Salt was made by filling large iron kettles with sea water and simply boiling the water out. The salt remaining in the kettle was bagged into croaker sacks and sent north to the Rebels for preserving meat or adding a little flavor to the hardtack each soldier was issued. If any was left over, it was for the horses to lick. Union patrol boats were commissioned to search the brackish inland rivers and the Atlantic and Gulf Coasts looking for saltworks. When they found one, the Yanks would destroy all the equipment and arrest or kill the operators.

Of course we didn't yet believe we were losing not only the War, but all hope for the South. We had to go on believing our righteous and glorious cause would surely prevail in the end, even as the Yanks tightened their chokehold on our supply lines and continued sending their seeming endless supply of boys to the front lines for us to mow down.

Olustee

As the sun came up on 1864, we in the 2nd Florida Cavalry were on constant alert and stretched as thin as possible to patrol the huge area under our charge. We knew how important Florida was as the sole remaining supplier to the Confederate troops. And we knew the enemy knew, too.

Our Company K was in charge of a strip of land from Baldwin on the east, down to Gainesville, then on past Live Oak to the west. Our northern boundary was the Georgia state line. The most important assets we protected were the main highway and the east-west railroad line. Sometimes we'd patrol in pairs and sometimes in squadrons of about ten.

Brother John Harley landed a job as a messenger to General Finegan, who was over all Florida forces. He was based in Baldwin, about twenty miles east of Jacksonville. Whenever my patrolling took me toward Baldwin, I'd be sure to stay in Sanderson, a little turpentine settlement, with our family friends, the Barnetts. You've earlier met the Rev. Thomas Robinson Barnett at the vigilante meeting at Mr. Roux's house. Later, you met his son, the Rev. William Jabish Barnett at the War rally, I mean prayer meeting, at Swift Creek Methodist. Sanderson had been the base camp for this father-son Methodist circuit riding team since territorial days. There's no telling how many churches these two men established in early Florida.

Jabish's only child was a girl of twelve named Laura, a good friend of my sister Sadie. Laura would often stay with us when traveling the circuit with her father. So when I stayed with them it was the closest feeling to home I got as a cavalryman. I teased her the same way I did Sadie. I called her my little sister-away-from-home.

Thus far my job as a Cavalryman has been my best job ever. I was paid, although Confederate money was fast losing value by the time I joined, to ride around on my faithful Charlie, see our beautiful state, and help assure the good but nervous folks of Middle Florida we were going to be alright. I'd ask if they'd seen or heard of any Yanks. If so, how many, what direction, what firepower did they have? The settlers were usually kind to us, and even though everybody was hungry, they'd often offer us a serving of whatever meager portions they had. Sometimes they believed in our cause, sometimes they wanted us to remember them so we might protect their property if the need arose. Other times they were hoping we wouldn't raid their stores of food. Under the Impressment Act, and also because of our firepower, we had a lot of latitude. We could take just about anything we wanted with little more than a promise Mr. Davis would pay them back. Most of us home guard soldiers were pretty careful not to abuse this power because these were our people, but throughout the War, many soldiers on both sides took advantage just because they could.

Thomas Jefferson is credited with saying, "The price of Freedom is eternal vigilance." I felt like my job was to be eternally vigilant against the threat to our Confederate States by the barbarians from the North. My instructions were to get the message of anything unusual to the headquarters absolutely as quickly as possible. So far I'd been able to track and spot a few small teams of Yank scouts. I hadn't yet had to take 'em on, but once I got their location and direction firm, I would get the information to Baldwin. I might then join a team to find and handle them the best way we could. We always hoped for a capture, because these mounted scouts usually knew at least a little bit of what their commanding officers were up to, and our interrogators had their ways of getting the information out of them. A prisoner was worth a lot more to us than a dead Yank.

I'd been in a couple of little engagements thus far, but each time the Union soldiers quickly surrendered and we'd take our prisoners to the nearest POW station.

By late January 1864, we noticed a big increase in Union traffic into Middle Florida.

The tension built.

February 4: Union Major General Quincy Gilmore, Federal Commander of Southern operations, ordered Brigadier General Truman Seymour to march west from Jacksonville.

February 5: Somehow we knew of the order. And we knew Union General Seymour had about five thousand troops at his disposal. With our troop count of fewer than two thousand, we knew we were badly outnumbered. Frantic calls went out for reinforcements to Georgia, Alabama and South Carolina. Because of modern telegraphy, we were able to make our dire situation known in just a few hours.

In just a few more hours, we got back responses telling us help was on the way from Savannah in the form of General Colquitt's Georgia Regulars, a bunch of battle-hardened veterans. At this point we could only hope and pray they'd get here before it was too late. They were quickly put on the train to Valdosta from where they would march south to Lake City then to Olustee.

February 7: Yankee General Seymour had Jacksonville fully secured. The North controlled Jacksonville on and off several times during the War. We were still hopeful that's all Seymour wanted, but our intelligence told us something bigger was up. We could only guess it had to do with the supply lines. But if it was just a way to draw us off balance by bringing the Georgia troops down, we were playing right into General Gilmore's hands.

144

We just couldn't imagine what was left in middle Georgia for them to come after, so we assumed Seymour was out to do his evil to our supply lines. If he could destroy our railroad and control our road, the last remaining supply line for the CSA Army would be choked off. Both our soldiers and civilians would quickly starve and this War would be over.

February 8: Seymour's army began to move. Hard to tell, but it looked to us he was sending all he could muster our way. He was wasting no time. Florida's General Joseph Finegan quickly abandoned Baldwin. Seymour's men marched twenty miles with full loads to get to Baldwin in one day. They picked up a big supply of food and ammunition we left behind in our hasty retreat.

Then they kept marching.

Finegan was conducting an orderly retreat. He was using us cavalrymen to run in close to the Union formation, trying to slow their march down as much as possible. One of our jobs was to size up what we saw. How many men? What kind of guns? Our main duty, though, was just to slow the enemy down as much as we could. Any time we could make the front line stop marching and move into formation for battle, we were winning one very small battle without firing a shot. I assigned myself my most important job of this mission: *not* to get shot.

February 9: Just after sunrise, the first wave of the Union invasion arrived at Sanderson. Those poor devils marched another twenty miles all night long! If we had our reinforcements, they would be easy pickin's for us. Seymour must've known we were short on forces or he wouldn't take the risk of fatiguing his men so badly. He was expecting an easy march to wherever he was going. And if Colquitt didn't get here real soon, we knew it was just what he was going to get.

We made sure all our remaining provisions were out of Sanderson before we left. The only thing we couldn't get moved in time was about 1500 bushels of corn. General Finegan himself ordered it all burned. We were heart-broken to see such a good pile of food destroyed. It was still smoldering when Mr. Lincoln's troops arrived. They set up camp there. It took at least five hours for the whole Yankee parade to arrive. The Barnett home became an officer's quarters. I couldn't bear the thought of those filthy barbarians in my friends' house.

It was especially hard knowing one of those blood sucking varmints was sleeping in sweet Laura's bed. She was only twelve, but she was sweet as sugar. She tried so hard to act unimpressed by me in my uniform, but I liked to think I knew better. She was no bigger'n a minute, but her smile and her voice could charm a squirrel off a nut wagon. Her flowing dark hair went halfway down her back when she'd let it, but she usually had it all bundled up on top with a clip somehow. She made all her own dresses, but even though homemade, they still had all the frilly stuff like you see on the fancy store-bought dresses. I guess since she made her own, they oughta fit her perfectly. She knew just how to cover herself with her clothes without wasting one square inch of cloth. And when she sang, you'da thought the heavens were opening up and the angels were coming after you.

I thought briefly of doing something heroic to defend her honor and purge her bed of the swine occupying it; but I kept my thought to myself. I was real sure I wanted to get through this War and come out of it a live young man, not a dead hero.

The Barnetts moved to the Lee farm for the duration of this confrontation. We figured they'd be safe there.

From their new base in Sanderson, the Federals were camped for a few days, sending out horsemen on regular, brief forays either to get the lay of the land or to draw us in to some sort of a surprise. We couldn't know for sure what they were doing, nor could they know for sure about us.

We reset our headquarters at Olustee Station. It wasn't much more than a whistle stop and a few houses to support the railroad operation. At only ten miles away, some of us thought it was awful close to the enemy camp for our General and his top aides. General Finegan was real brave to camp so close, but we were to stay ready to move at a moment's notice if we saw movement from Seymour's troops.

Battle of Olustee Florida

On February 14, Captain Dickison of Company C, 2nd Cavalry, had a brush with the 40th Massachusetts Cavalry in Gainesville. It was about fifty Yank horsemen and 130 Reb horsemen. Dickison took care of this one in stride. But we knew those 5,000 union troops at Sanderson were there for more than just the little Gainesville skirmish.

About February 16, General Colquitt arrived with his Georgia troops. We were told some South Carolina troops were just a couple days behind. Finegan put our 2nd Cavalry under him for this battle. We had no way of knowing if Seymour had knowledge of the arrival of this strong new reinforcement.

All we knew for sure is the longer they tarried, the more ready we were sure to be.

On the afternoon of the 19th, Seymour's forces started to stir. It looked like they were beginning to break camp. Would they be marching today? Was a big showdown about to happen?

It was decided where we would confront our unwelcome visitors. We would no longer do our orderly and timid retreat as we had all the way since Seymour's troops left Sanderson. Finegan's command post would remain at Olustee Station, and the enemy would hit our front line about three miles east from the station. The battlefield was an area of scattered piney woods well under-brushed by grazing cattle and turpentine operations. We could move freely around in there and our visibility was good. Only problem was this meant their visibility would also be good. We had trees, stumps and bushes to hide behind, but neither side had time to dig any trenches or build fortifications. The substantial trenches we dug in anticipation were well behind us and would be of no value unless we had to retreat that far.

What we liked about this spot was it's a piece of high ground constrained by Ocean Pond on the north and a big swamp on the south. The lake and the swamp were a little over a mile apart at this point. If we could hold this line, they couldn't flank us, but we could possiblyflank them. If they tried, they'd be cornered at the lake or swamp and we should be able to take care of those troops pretty easily. Flanking meant to get around and past the front line of the enemy. Once you've flanked the enemy, he suddenly has battle going on several sides of him rather than only straight ahead. You don't want to be flanked, and we chose ourselves a pretty unflankable position.

We would also have an advantage because a lot of us grew up in these woods. It was disturbing, though, to find out just how many on Seymour's roster also grew up here. For various reasons, mostly hunger and the realization of the futility of the Southern cause, we'd had many defections lately. Seymour would be sure to use those defectors in this battle.

We knew there was a good chance some of us would come muzzle-to-muzzle with one of our neighbors or a schoolmate; some would even see a cousin or brother on the enemy side today. No amount of training in this world could prepare a man for that. As long as my job was just to hate and kill a man because he was wearing blue, I could do it. But if I happened to see his face and could instantly put a name to it, I wasn't real sure what my reaction might be. And it scared me even more because I didn't know what his reaction might be either. For a warrior to personally know the enemy was not unheard of in the history of war, but it was rare. Usually one army against another was stranger against stranger. Typically, the men involved looked different, had different weapons, different tactics and different languages. None of this applied to the American Civil War. Quite the contrary, many of the Generals and officers on both sides were classmates and best friends at West Point.

I knew I had no relatives fighting for the North, but I'm pretty sure I knew some recent defectors. As we got hungrier and our cause got more hopeless, there had been frequent stories of fellas slipping over to Jacksonville and turning themselves in for some rations and a little forgiveness. Every so often we heard of another of our fellow soldiers disappearing. We knew it could mean he was captured, but we knew it usually meant another defection. When, er, I mean *if* it came time to surrender, defecting may seem to have been the smart thing to do.

My best training for this situation of confronting a friend was simply to avoid eye contact. My Captain taught us to make sure we were sighting on the enemy. We chanted, "If it's grey, don't shoot; if it's blue, let him have it 'fore he does same to you."

Sort of the opposite of the Golden Rule, huh?

The old warrior John Lee taught me to never look an enemy in the face, even after I'd shot him, for two reasons: "First, it will slow you down. If you waste even a split second looking at the man you're gonna engage, or already dispatched, you're giving some other man an opportunity to hurt you, and, second, if it was somebody you knew, for God's sakes, you *never . . . and I mean never,* want to know it."

Another important thing was to be sure to not think too much about any of this stuff before a battle, and you were on your own to forget it after the battle.

Our hope was Seymour wouldn't find out about our Georgia reinforcements until after the battle began, so Colquitt stayed back about three miles when he arrived, then closed about half the gap the next day. With the latest stirring, Colquitt was summoned to close the gap and join forces with us.

The orders were given to begin the march east along the main road as soon as we knew the Federals were moving west. We were to continue forward until we engaged in battle. At this point, our infantry was to spread out roughly evenly across the 1 1/2 mile stretch between the lake and the swamp. Our big guns were horse-drawn behind the infantry and would be set up for firing as soon as we could reasonably determine where the initial clash would be. We had three groups of twelve cannon.

Just before we went into action, my Daddy rode up to me, tossed me a half-full pint bottle, and said, "Have just a little of this. It'll calm your nerves . . . and good luck, son."

Now, I tried to stay away from the whiskey. I'd had some fun with it a time or two but tried hard to do as the preachers said. Today, though, Daddy's advice seemed to make sense. "Thanks, Dad," I said after taking a swig. I looked over to him and he was gone. I had to wonder if that was going to be my last conversation with my Father. I took another swig and put the rest of the pint in my saddlebag.

The 2nd Cavalry's job was to continue harassing the Union front line just as we'd done on the previous days. We wanted them to think that day's march was going to meet the same weak resistance they had coming into Baldwin and Sanderson. It was a very dangerous game of cat and mouse we played. We rode in within rifle distance, emptied our carbines, then charged in just a little more, keeping the horses on a hard run while we unloaded our pistols. We might hit some targets with our rifles, but you gotta remember our objective was more to delay than to kill. While we were shooting pistols on the gallop, the fellow we aimed at wasn't in so much danger, but the poor man next to him surely was!

I think we were effective at catching them off their guard. We wanted them a little too confident this was going to be an easy mission.

When the time came for the two front lines to clash, the Georgia and Florida Cavalries split, with the Florida 2nd taking to the right flank, Georgia to the left. Our job was to be real sure none of the union forces were able to flank our lines. If they could get a few dozen men around and behind our lines, they could fire on us from two sides and make us break our line to defend two directions. With the help of the swamp to the south of us, the attempting flankers pretty well corralled themselves for us to arrest or kill. It was very much their choice. We did take some fire, but I'm proud to say our Company didn't lose a man in the whole exercise.

This major Civil War battle started roaring a little before two o'clock in the afternoon of February 20. As the battle began, it was a head-on clash between Seymour's 5,500 Yankee troops against Finegan's and Colquitt's 5,000. We took early control of the field and it seemed we gained ground with every volley.

A little after three o'clock, the tables turned. We were running real low on ammunition at the front. We knew there was plenty of supply behind us, but the Georgia supplies didn't arrive as quickly as the soldiers did. There was about a twenty-minute period when the 6th and 23rd

Georgia Infantries were both slap out of ammunition. They stood their ground and did what they could with their bayonets and Bowie knives. Those poor chaps were so brave — as they were relentlessly mown down.

We Cavalrymen would sweep in to help them as much as we could, but our main responsibility was to guard the right flank. If we allowed the Yanks to flank us, we would stand a very good chance of being routed.

About then, three colored Yankee regiments moved onto the field. Two of them were inexperienced and seeing battle for the very first time. They fell into disarray quickly, and none could blame them because the field they came onto was already a gruesome scene. The third colored regiment to enter was the famed 54th Massachusetts, which had made such a name for itself last summer in the taking of Fort Wagner. They were decimated there but were back in full fighting force now. They fought fiercely yet again. Later, we agreed they were well-deserving of their fierce reputation.

During the battle I heard several rounds pass right by my head or thwack into a tree within a few feet of me. It's been said since ancient times, only about twenty to twenty-five percent of soldiers in a battle will actually aim to kill. The rest are subject to some inner aversion to shooting a fellow man, even a fellow man who's aiming to kill him. Maybe my hunting experience made it easier for me to draw blood. Or maybe I could shoot because I had a father, brother and a bunch of cousins on the field. All I knew was I really wanted all of us to come out of this chaos alive. Now I'm not trying to say it was easy, but shooting the other guy before he could shoot me just seemed the very best way I could figure to help my chances of surviving this hellish day.

The entire Rebel front line was getting dangerously short of ammunition when the new ammo supplies finally arrived. With the new supplies, the Rebel forces were all in and fighting as fiercely as if they'd just begun. With this final turn of the tide, the battle was quickly brought to conclusion. By about four-thirty, Seymour's army was shifting into full retreat. By sundown, any Yankee who could still walk was off the field and on his way back to Sanderson, then Baldwin, then Jacksonville.

As they went into full retreat, we began full pursuit. While Charlie and I raced around the field, it was sickening to see how thick the bodies were piling up. When we drove into the ruckus, Charlie couldn't help trampling those poor men, dead and alive. All around I was hearing not only the screams of soldiers who'd been hit by hot lead, but also the screams of wounded soldiers getting trampled by heavy hooves. It will never be known how many soldiers might have survived their bullet wounds if their skulls hadn't been crushed, or necks broken, or guts instantly scrambled by a swift stomp from Charlie or one of his buddies. It wouldn't have been so bad if we could stomp only Yankees, but we had another job to do - to protect our soldiers who were still on their feet. We couldn't pick our way over the ground, and we knew we were just one lead slug away from joining those poor souls down there ourselves.

It was terrifying.

As the retreat reached full throttle, many of the Yanks dropped their weapons and ammunition so they could get out of there as fast as possible. I believe they'da stripped naked if they thought it would speed 'em up any! Our orders were to follow and finish off the stragglers who were still running, but to first shout out an offer to surrender. Us horsemen corralled up the surrendering men about ten to twenty-five in a group. We held 'em at gunpoint until foot soldiers could catch up and take charge of them. Then we'd go find another group and do the same thing over again. Ol' Charlie proved to be just as good at rounding up Yankees as he was at rounding up cows!

I saw the taking of these prisoners, not "dispatching" them, as a sort of act of kindness by General Finegan. He well knew these foot soldiers had no information we could use, unlike the scouts we'd captured before. It was cheaper, more efficient and maybe even more humane to give them a bullet to the head right there than to have to support them in a camp for the duration of the War. The CSA could no longer feed these men, just like it couldn't properly feed its own soldiers. Indeed, some of the prisoners-of-war would starve to death at the prison camps, not because of cruelty and inhumane treatment, but purely due to lack of food.

I was real glad I had *not* been ordered to shoot a man who had his unarmed hands up in surrender.

Every now and then some hothead would take a potshot at us, but none hit their mark. Those fleeing soldiers were so fatigued and frightened they couldn't hold a rifle steady, much less sight it in, if their lives depended on it. And their lives would depend on it if they tried. Thus, not many shots were fired after the Yanks went into full retreat. When they took those wild shots, they were pretty much signing their own death warrants; and we had to do what we had to do.

Several of the 2nd Cavalry companies followed at a safe distance to help make sure the Union troops found their way back to Jacksonville. A few miles before we got to Sanderson, our Company K was turned back to Olustee. Upon their return, the other companies informed us the entire settlement of Baldwin had been burned to the ground as those Yankees passed through; civilian houses, barns, churches, all of it. The news made us wonder if maybe we should've slaughtered the fleeing bastards after all. Fortunately, they were still running too fast to stop and burn when they passed through Sanderson. The Barnett house was just fine and was left pretty much as it was when the Barnetts fled.

General Finegan was later criticized for not putting up a harder pursuit and fully vanquishing Seymour's forces. Why he didn't is still not clear.

In his official final report to President Davis, General Finegan cited a combination of fatigue of his men, lack of rations and a report stating the fleeing Union troops had established a position west of Sanderson, from which they could easily pick off their Rebel pursuers in the dark. For these reasons, Finegan's report claims, the pursuit of the fleeing Yanks was called off. That was good enough for me.

Mr. Lincoln himself received strong criticism from the Northern press because of the Olustee debacle and the unnecessary loss of life and equipment suffered by the North.

We got back to the camp at Olustee Station well after midnight on the morning of February 21. It had been a very long day. A group of us sat up 'til near sunrise talking about what we'd been through. We cried, shouted, swore, pumped our fists at the air in frustration, puked and displayed just about every emotion a man can conjure up. There were still reports coming in of various deaths, injuries, amputations, etc. Occasionally, there'd be happy news of a soldier whom we thought was dead showing up at camp. It was a strange night. After just a quick, two-hour nap, I got up to look at the aftermath of yesterday's big event.

Olustee's Aftermath

The next morning, the other local farm boys and I were free to go home for spring planting. We had to stay overnight just in case General Seymour decided he wanted another bite at the Olustee apple, which we all thought highly unlikely. Finegan's forces received orders to head back North all the way to Virginia. I imagined they'd have a real good time up there.

As Wiley, John Harley and I rode one last time over the battle site, we could see the local slaves still burying the nearly three hundred dead on the field. Of the two thousand wounded, a large portion died during the night, and another large group would die in the course of the next month. Of the remaining wounded, many would live out non-useful lives because of their wounds. Only a relatively small number would heal up and have potential for productive lives. Many of the unscathed soldiers suffered early hearing loss as a result of our day at battle. I was one of those.

The dead would all be buried right here, except for a few important ones, like high officers or sons of wealthy or important folks. They'd be identified by their superiors and the field morticians, who always showed up after a battle. They'd drain the blood from the corpse, inject a little alcohol and arsenic salt, provide a nice box and send him COD on his way to his nice family plot, all for a modest fee.

I was told it cost about five dollars to go home in a box, or you could just stay there in the warm, invitin' ground of Olustee, Florida for free! That was courtesy of the CSA, of course. Most of the bodies chose the free route.

It was a good thing for us the battle happened right by Ocean Pond - it made it very convenient for the several hundred of us whose only wound was the one we got to our pride after we'd soiled our britches in the heat of the battle. The big lake offered us a real convenient clean-up, while the poor Yanks had to run all the way to Jacksonville in such condition. Diaper rash was a very big problem in the great American Civil War.

Olustee was a large battle, not a major one by Civil War standards, but the pain from the casualties spread throughout the land at least as far as Connecticut, Massachusetts, New Hampshire and New York. The tears would also flow as near as Lake City, Live Oak, White Springs, Jasper and Jacksonville as news went out to families.

We later learned General Seymour had four objectives for his foray into Columbia County which culminated in the battle of Olustee. He was to: Begin a campaign to overturn the

Florida State Confederate Government by getting locals to sign loyalty oaths to the Union, Take or destroy supplies from Florida's army and people, Steal slaves from farmers for the Union black forces, and blow up the railroad bridge over the Suwannee River to finally and totally disrupt the Confederate supply lines

Of these four, the last was most important. Seymour failed on every count. Even though they did take and destroy some supplies according to mandate number two, we got back more weaponry and ammunition than we lost to them.

My mind couldn't quit reviewing what I lived through. I spent a lot of time thinking through some of the sights, sounds and smells of the battle. By twelve hours after the battle ended, the surrounding atmosphere seemed eerily peaceful. The only activity was the poor slaves, the buzzards, the wild hogs and dogs. There were a few infantry privates tasked with taking ammunition, guns, knives, money, buttons and any still-serviceable clothes off the corpses. They also recorded any identification found on the dead for notification of next-of-kin. The most pitiful sight, though, was the women, several of them real pregnant, dashing from corpse to corpse to see if they could identify their husbands, sons or brothers.

The slaves, who'd been impressed away from their owners by the CSA to take care of the grim task of burying the bodies, were scared out of their skins by the grizzly sights they were witnessing. The hogs, dogs and buzzards, of course, were just there for a meal. The slaves didn't even get a meal, though. They were told they'd be done in just a couple of days, and their masters could feed 'em up real good once they walked home with a mounted and armed escort in front of and behind them. Some of them were from several miles away, and of course, the escorts had a few sets of manacles just in case a slave or two acted unappreciative of the work opportunity the CSA had afforded them. Here we were in one of the richest farming areas in America, and our new Army couldn't even afford to thank its slave labor with a little food. It was said we needed all of it for the soldiers. Besides, the slaves could eat any hardtack they might find in the dead men's pockets, and some of the Yanks were considerate enough to leave a little water in their canteens. God knows they didn't need it anymore.

We three Lees emptied our saddlebags of anything edible we had left for those poor slaves doing their gruesome task.

The Rebs would be laid side-by-side in a trench. Strips of ground were deep-plowed using the heaviest two-horse plow we could find from a nearby farm to start the trench. The slaves then finished digging the trench to accommodate the ninety-three Rebel soldiers dead on the field. They needed to be at least two feet underground to be deeper than the hogs could dig, that was a lot of digging, and there was surely parts of those ditches weren't deep enough.

Where a body was protruding, the slaves were told to just mound the dirt up a little higher over that fellow. The hogs were likely to be there digging in as soon as the last man moved away. A hungry hog is a pretty determined rascal.

A chaplain would say a few words and they'd be covered up for good.

The Yanks abandoned their dead in the field, so it was left to the slaves to bury them, too. Yanks got buried last, of course. For the 203 Northern soldiers dead in the field, the slaves were told to dig one huge hole, dump 'em in and cover it up. If they stack up a little higher than ground level, they'd just have to be sure to pile enough dirt on them to keep them covered for a while. They'd rot and compress down over time anyway. As they got tossed into the hole, some of them, upon impact with the ground or another dead man, would let out one final groan or maybe a gurgle. It sounded for all the world like they were still alive, but it was just the noise dead lungs make when the air is pushed out of them one last time. That took a little getting used to.

The official count of killed on the field was 203 Yanks and 93 Rebs, but total killed, wounded or missing was 1861 Yankees, and 946 Rebs. After the War we learned Olustee was the second worst casualty percentage of the whole War for the Yankees. What a great victory! What a special day! What a hollow, sickening feeling.

I thought again about my training to make sure not to look the enemy in the eye, just in case the enemy was a friend. Now I wondered, because I know I hit some of my targets, if maybe I did hit a friend or two. I thought of all the poor wretches writhing on the field, some of them still moaning come morning, but most already expired. The field hospital was about caught up with yesterday's amputations, so maybe the doctors could start to pay attention to those ones with holes in their chests. Some whiskey might help, but not much else would.

Since I was such a good soldier by not lookin' anyone in the eye, not even my own teammates, I got my first look at the Georgia and South Carolina boys this morning. At first I told myself it was the long march they just took, but it finally sank in to me, these men were just plain hungry! Every one of them had his pants bunched up at the waist. Each one looked like a fat man who just lost fifty pounds but hadn't had his britches adjusted yet. You could, however, easily see these weren't men who ever needed to lose fifty pounds. In fact most of them were pretty desperate to *gain* about as much. The sunken eyes and gaunt cheeks were a sure sign of malnourishment. If our soldiers were this desperate, our cause couldn't have long to live. I was amazed these poor mongrels could fight at all, but they put on an impressive show yesterday, and it could well be I owe my life to their coming along when they did.

I realized us skinny Florida boys were probably the fattest soldiers in the whole CSA. Not only were we posted right at the source of the food, but we'd also had the least fighting and marching of any of our brethren. I couldn't imagine being in the thick of all the fighting and dying, then adding near freezing in the winter and near starving every day in this time of severe shortage. We'd been on strict discipline to not waste any food, and our rations had been a little skinny, but until now, we had no idea how good we had it here protecting Florida against the Northern threat.

I saw strewn in the field the grossly disfigured bodies, you know, the ones who took a cannonball to the gut or caught a carbine round square in the face. I thought maybe they were the lucky ones because they were certainly dead on impact. No suffering for them, just dyin' real quick-like. If you looked at those faces, or those torsos, it was real hard to tell Yankee from Rebel. I observed when soaked with dried blood, grey and blue looked pretty much alike.

Many of the bodies had begun to swell, but not as bad yet as it was going to get if they weren't punctured and buried real soon.

Then there were the random body parts strewn around the field like broken, discarded toys of a spoiled child. They were all black now, with soured blood oozing out where it could, sinews and muscle protruding, and ants, roaches and flies crawling all over them. Come the next day, maggots would likely be joining the feast.

What a shame the mothers, fathers, sisters, brothers, wives, children and friends back home would have to wait, maybe for months, before getting the news of how their special young man died valiantly and valorously on the field of glorious battle bravely defending his cause. Wouldn't they be proud?

What I saw that morning after didn't look so valorous, but it for dern sure smelled malodorous! Hope you like that word. See, I just put a little of my Latin training to work for you, right here on the battlefield.

And the horses, all the dead horse flesh littering the field. I was thankful Charlie was still healthy. What must he have thought in the middle of all the mayhem and carnage?

I'm not near tellin' you everything I saw during or after the battle. Some sights and experiences will go with me to my grave, because that's right where they belong.

None of us three Lees, nor our cousins or various in-laws were killed or injured in the battle, for which I'm very thankful.

Why did General Seymour wait so long at Sanderson? If he'd pushed right through, he'd have over-powered Finegan's forces. The railroad bridge and the wagon bridge would both be blown up and Florida's supply lines severed. He could certainly have been back to Jacksonville before Colquitt's Brigade arrived from Georgia if he hadn't delayed.

As I readied to leave this horrible scene, I couldn't help but have the thought maybe it would have been best if the CSA had *lost* Olustee. If the Suwannee railroad bridge had been blown up, it's almost certain the already-starving Rebel troops would be forced to give up sooner instead of later. The killing would stop and we could go back to healing our land. I kept that thought to myself for obvious reasons, but I figured I wasn't the only one figuring the same way.

We had to continue fighting for our already lost cause, acting as if there was a chance we'd prevail, and states' rights would rule the land. I was still getting paid the fine CSA Private's salary of eleven dollars of those "Greybacks" per month plus my horse rent for Charlie. This was the same pay a private got before the War started, but at this point it bought me about as much as two dollars did then. We joked that soon we'd be working two months just to buy a bar of soap.

Most married soldiers had their pay shipped home, and the wives would send back a little spending money. When we got paid our precious eleven dollars, and wherever we were, we could always count on some under-fed local girls to come out to see if they could give us some . . . "company". For their company they usually got about $2.00 to $3.50 of the soldier's hard earned pay, depending on how much company they gave. The rest of the pay was often wasted on booze. After two days at most, many of the soldiers were penniless until the next month rolled around. I understood all the temptations, certainly I did, but every month I saw what I thought was the world's best re-enactment of the age-old saying, "A fool and his money are soon parted."

"Come on, JH," Wiley said, "we got ridin' to do." We needed to make about thirty miles, and we definitely wanted to be home before sundown and didn't want to push the horses too much after the day they had yesterday.

"I'm ready, Dad, let's go," I said as we turned the horses and left the scene of so much death and pain. John Harley seemed to be about as shaken over all this as I was. He'd spent his day racing back and forth from Gerneral Finegan's temporary Headquarters at Olustee Station to the officers in the rear of the CSA formation. Even there, he'd seen plenty. We rode silently for long stretches.

Our senses seemed to be on high alert, so we were each very aware of what a beautiful day and time of year we were in. As we made distance between us and the battlefield, we noticed the stench of rigor mortis quickly left and we got the occasional sweet smell of the very first wild orange blossoms. They reminded us our own scrawny trees would be trying to bloom when we got home. Our farm should be primed and ready to go into that glorious life re-creating springtime.

We also noticed the ear-ringing from the deafening thunder of yesterday's festivities was abating. As our ears slowly settled into normal, we could start to hear various birds chirping. We'd get amused by the tied up dog barking ferociously as we passed another farmhouse. We chuckled when John Harley said "Hey, mutt, if you had any idea how much firepower we're totin', you'd keep your mouth shut."

Just the mundane sound of the horses clopping along was somehow beautiful to us. The squeak of the saddle leather and an occasional horse-snort were all little reminders we survived. The three of us were still alive and healthy, and between us we still had all six arms and six legs issued us by the good Lord in the beginning. So far as we knew, our cousins by marriage, the Cone Brothers, all seven of them, came through just fine, too.

Further, I became keenly aware I was a farmer, not a soldier, and farming was what the Almighty intended me to do. As a farmer, I had no interest in killing people. I wanted to feed them, and dead people couldn't eat what I was trying to feed 'em. I proved I could be a soldier if I had to, but I sure hoped I never got an opportunity like it again.

This experience made me know I was attached to the land, and until they put me in the ground, I wanted to work the ground. I felt so blessed to be the next in line to run the Lee Farm in Genoa, Hamilton County, Florida. I couldn't think of anything else I could ever want to do.

I never felt closer to my Daddy or John Harley as I did on that long ride home. We talked about everything, acted like silly boys (even Dad), and laughed at ourselves. We even cried a bit when we re-hashed some of the things we saw and some of our friends we knew we'd never see again. We planned. We fretted. We dreamed of what we might build together in our little corner of the world.

And soon we were home.

Home for Spring Planting

Granny Ava made sure one of the girls kept watch in the front yard so she could run back to ring the farm bell at first sighting of us.

"There's three of them!!!!!" Mary Elizabeth shouted as it seemed she was trying to crack that bell in her jubilation. Everyone came running to the old live oak, the official meeting place of the Lees.

When we heard the bell, we gave the horses a little spur to see if they had any speed left in them for this final stretch of the journey. To our surprise, you'da thought they were fresh race horses by the way they sprinted. Of course, they knew they were home, too, and were just as happy as we were.

While the family tried to act reserved and stay at the tree for our arrival, little Laura Barnett raced out to meet us. As she approached, I reached down and she grabbed my arm with both of her tiny spindles. She held on tight, and her momentum and my lift launched her up and flipped her right behind me to straddle ol' Charlie. She grabbed my waist from behind and said "Welcome home, Mr. JH Lee! We could hear the bombs from here all day yesterday, and every time I heard one I prayed you were safe. I see my prayers worked!"

"They sure did, my little-sister-away-from-home, they surely did. And I made sure they didn't hurt your house back in Sanderson, too."

It was quite a welcome home.

The feast was over quickly, but the party went on 'til past dark. We set a big bonfire and splurged by lighting up a few candles for the parlor. After Reverend Barnett led us in a fitting invocation and Momma gave all the children her famous admonition, "Now don't let your eyes get bigger than your stomach," we lit in. The food was fine and made a nice spread, and all insisted us soldiers go first. We did. And we loaded our plates. We thought we'd just struck gold with such good looking, home-cooked food. We noticed everything was made of corn, except a nice big bowl of swamp cabbage and just a couple of roasted chickens for this whole big clan. I wasn't worried, though, I knew there'd be a whole 'nother potfull of birds in the cook shed ready to come out steamin' hot as soon as the first ones were picked over.

159

The homecoming celebration took a somber turn when I saw everyone behind me taking tiny portions and treating each spoonful as if it were gold. Portions were carefully metered so there would be no waste. The girls were all looking too thin, some even like walking skeletons. I was amazed we were in such a rich area on such a fine farm and were all so skinny. John Harley and I were quickly putting two and two together and shuddered at what we saw. We were witnessing a whole different kind of tragedy than on the Olustee battlefield. We were seeing the ravages of war in the faces of our sisters, brothers, aunts and uncles, parents and grandparents, right here in our own home.

John Harley and I ate about half of our bounteous platefuls. Then we called over the younger kids and asked if they'd please finish for us, because we musta' let our eyes get bigger than our stomachs. They had no problem helping us out this way, and we regretfully gave up the only decent meal we'd had in months.

Momma was one of the first to retire to bed, which was unusual for her. She didn't look so good. I'd heard worrying about a son at war can take a toll on a momma. Since she had two sons and a husband there, I figured she had an extra load. She should shake this in no time with all of us here for a while to get the planting done.

The girls, the young boys and the old men were ready to call it a day, and they slept like logs, hollow logs, I guess. So relieved were they that their men made it through the Battle of Olustee. Us three soldiers were dead tired, too, but we couldn't sleep because our minds were still racing from the traumas we witnessed, both in war and at home. Wiley suggested we adjourn to meet at the turpentine still to make sure the folks at home had "kept it in good order," meaning we needed to make sure they hadn't found the hiding place.

On my way out of the yard heading to the still, I took a look into the curing shed. I was heartbroken to see there was not one single piece of meat hanging in the whole, great big shed. While still retaining the rich smell of the meaty, smoky bounty of the past, today it was bare. I noticed the chicken coop had only four live chickens left. I got sick when I realized tonight's feast featured a big portion of the farm's egg-laying stock.

The women had kept the turpentine still in very good order. The special hiding place must've not been found, because it was just as we'd left it with about six cases of the beautiful liquid gold. Seeing my gaunt family, I felt ashamed we wasted good corn for evil indulgence, yet I was enticed by its crystal clear, shimmering elegance in this time of such extreme want. And Lord knows my shot nerves could use a little calming. We each took a jar, then Daddy said "Let's take it to the swimmin' hole and clean some of the battle off ourselves."

With just a couple of sips along the way, we arrived, dismounted, disrobed and carefully waded in. Since it was February, none of us was gonna be diving in. We just splashed a little of the too-cold Swift Creek water on ourselves and tried to get as clean as we could while staying as dry as we could. But did it ever feel wonderful to be home! No matter what this War did to family and farm, the swimmin' hole didn't change. We led the horses into the water and let them clean up some, too. When we thought we might be about half-clean, we dried ourselves by using our filthy clothes as towels. After re-dressing, we just sat with our jars on the bank and had another session of talkin' and sippin'.

I wanted to sip just enough to help me sleep and planned to not drink enough to have a headache in the morning, but my plan didn't go too well. All I can say is by time my jar was empty, I wasn't so sure the world wasn't spinnin' a little faster or something. All of a sudden everything was funny, and John Harley and I didn't seem to have a care anymore about much anything. We figured we might better walk the horses home because we figured they mighta had too much, too, on account of they'd gotten really hard to mount.

We got home and were pretty sure we were the proverbial church mice. Surely no one would be disturbed by our silent arrival, or at least 'til John Harley accidentally kicked a chair, stubbed his toe and went to howlin'. . . and I went to laughin'. . . and Daddy went to tryin' to shut us up. Well, nobody stirred, so we were real sure we'd made it home without detection. We said 'night to Daddy and he went to his bedroom. John Harley and I went to our cots in the boys' sleeping porch where the younger boys were all sound asleep.

The morning sun was cruel, and those annoying chirping birds outside the house wouldn't shut up. Why is it they normally help me get up and start a day, but today they just made my head explode? I heard the women shushing the kids and telling them to let me sleep. They said I was "tired from the battle and needed some rest."

I heard William Henry, my ten-year-old brother, nicknamed Willie, protesting to Mom, "But JH loves to get up early and told me we'd go fishin' together this morning." I felt like a heel for over-drinking last night, but also remembered how badly I wanted to escape the whole situation of the South's losing cause and my starving family. It sure was easy to drink too much of the devil's brew. I promised myself and my God I'd never do it again.

It must've been about ten o'clock. I would normally pride myself on having three quarters of a day's work, by any other man's standards, done by now. Instead I just lay in my cot frozen by my head pain and fear of my condition being found out by those I cared about most.

With the Barnetts still at the big house, I didn't want the Reverend to see me because he would think so much less of me. I had in mind a very serious talk with him very soon, and figured I was better to stay in bed. Since Laura stayed here with Sadie, I knew the Reverend and Missus Barnett would be by to pick her up soon on their way home. Maybe he could understand my sleeping off battle stress, but there was no chance he'd understand my sleeping off the demon alcohol.

Besides, I didn't want my Momma to find out. She'd be crushed.

When I heard the Barnetts come for Laura, I listened to hear her voice. How I wished I could be presentable so I could say good-bye and maybe get a smile and a little hug from my sister-away-from-home for whom I had designs of becoming much more than just a brother. I heard everyone speaking in hushed tones to not wake our War heroes. Reverend Barnett said how proud he was of John Harley and me, and how deserving of rest we were because of our selfless devotion to the Southern cause.

Immediately after they left, Momma walked in and said, "They're gone. You can get up now. I can't imagine what you've been through, but I can promise you the bottle is not what you need to help you through it. Only weak men reach for booze to help them through life's troubles, and I know you two are not weak men. Your father's not either, but he's letting it all get to him. You came home last night about as quiet as three bulls in a china shop, so don't think you're (sob) fooling (sob) me." Then she left.

"Well," I congratulated myself, "I've really done it now. I didn't get to see Laura, made a fool out of a man of the cloth for believing in me, and crushed my dear mother all at once." And on top of it all, I felt like Charlie must've kicked me in the head sometime last night.

I forced myself up. My pounding head needed water, and if only my stomach had anything other than sour booze in it I thought I'd be greatly relieved by spewing it, but no such luck. Sweet sister Sadie brought me a glass of water. She said I didn't look too well. I thanked her. "Laura cried when she left because she wanted to see you," she said so sweetly. I didn't need to hear that, either.

I made another silent but solemn vow to my God and to my family never to drink alcohol again.

Once I got moving I thought it would be the responsible thing to take a look around the farm and see how things were looking for spring planting. For several seasons we'd been told what to plant and where to plant it. In fact, we were just rotating corn, beans, a little bit of sugar and not much else on what we called the "Lee Family CSA Government Farm." We were allowed a little family food plot, but it wasn't close to big enough to feed us Lees, the farmhands and the slaves well. We had our ways of "enhancing" our yields on the family plot. We were learning the painful lesson, and we did what we had to do when we had to do it. The family plot was on the best ground. We dug a little hand-pumped well in the middle of the family plot. Whenever we had drought, an army of us would go out there and water those family vegetables one bucketful at a time. It was no substitute for rain, but it'd keep those plants goin' through most any kind of drought. The manure from the farm animals was spread, you guessed it, on the family plot before it ever went anywhere else. Every squash, tomato, carrot, okra or melon that came from our hallowed family plot must have felt well-loved.

We knew we'd get paid as agreed for everything we grew for the Rebel cause on the government farm. Those Confederate dollars just flowed like clockwork, but they bought less with every passing month. We called it pretend money. Our joke was, "As long as the CSA continues to pretend to pay us, we'll continue to pretend to grow the crops." It wasn't like we didn't believe in the cause of the South, particularly states' rights, but it was just real difficult to work hard to produce something we knew would be paid for by valueless money. Kind of put us in the same position as the slave, didn't it?

Sometime mid-War our government began quietly posting on the greybacks, "Two years after the ratification of a treaty of peace between the Confederate States and the United States of America, the Confederate States of America will pay (the amount of the bill) to Bearer." We weren't sure what it meant but had a suspicion it didn't bode well for the trading value of our greybacks.

We were real thankful Granddaddy John traded Confederate money for gold while he could, and later he bought some land with his withering Rebel money. He wasn't letting go of his gold very easy, either. He told us there was no telling how long the suffering would last, even once the foolish War was over.

I was only on the farm about two weeks. It was determined we had enough men to get the planting done, so John Harley and I packed up our horses and rode off to report back to K Company at Baldwin. Daddy stayed and supervised a few more weeks. A lot of the farms around White Springs were desperately short of men, mules and horses. The farms with enough men were helping the others when they could, but there was fully too much work to get done and too few men to plant and grow the crops on all the farms of middle-Florida.

Cotton planting had been all but halted. The world market for it had plummeted due to massive stockpiles in Europe and Egypt. Even though the worldwide need for it was soaring, we figured governments and speculators all over had hoarded it in huge amounts so they could sell it at higher prices as the War played out. The result was the market dropped because the hoarding was so great all the warehouses were full and buyers wouldn't buy any more. Besides that, the CSA wanted only food crops. It figured we could stretch our clothing supplies but couldn't stretch our food any more than we'd already done. All of us, even soldiers, had to get by with what we had for clothes, because no one got any new cotton material. We'd all gotten ragged and threadbare - a very sad sight to see. Everything we grew was for eating. Ironically, our best export customer, Great Britain, had warehoused so much of our cotton at the onset of the War that it still had bulging supplies in the warehouses. This may explain why our friends, the Brits, hadn't yet come to the aid of the CSA as we kept hearing they would.

I still couldn't quite understand why the Lees were so hungry. I asked Willy, and I got an earful. "You know John Lee's about the finest farmer in this state, but you see that tiny little plot we're given for our own. Now we snitch from the Government farm some, too, but they tell us we can be shot for doing it. The government buyers see our family plot looking so much better than the rest of the land, and they say if we don't start working *their* land harder, and that's what they call it, they will start sending in harvesters to take the family plot, too. And you know the women in this family; every time someone comes along with a story about a hungry baby, or a sick man on their farm who can't work, or a crop failure, those folks are going to leave here with food. I'm not saying it's the wrong thing to do, and maybe it's our Christian duty, but we can't feed ourselves anymore, much less the rest of the world."

Stunned, I asked, "Well I know you're a real good shot now, can't you get wild meat for the family? We always helped out the food supply with our hunting and trapping."

Willy looked me straight in the eye and said, "JH, the lead's all gone, and if we had lead, the powder's all gone. You know I know how to trap, too, but the critters are all gone." I sat down. "There's not a deer in these woods anymore. You know the wild hogs we couldn't keep out of the fields?" I nodded. "No problem anymore. If they were here we could trap 'em. You seen any squirrels in the trees?" I shook my head. "Any stray dogs, or wild cats?" My head shook again. "There ain't a 'coon or 'possum left for miles 'round anymore. Did you see any rats in the barn or corn cribs while you've been home?" Again I shook my head no. "Well we left all the rats to the slaves, and you've seen how starvin' they are. We're desperate here, and we know we've got it better than most of the South.

"After we killed and ate most of the livestock," Willy continued, "we took to eating their peanuts and cowpeas. We found they wasn't all bad. We can boil the peanuts or just eat 'em raw; and the cowpeas, if ya cook 'em with just a little grease, a little meat and salt, if you got any, they're not so bad either. And we've gone to callin' 'em black-eyed peas instead of cow peas so we don't feel like we're eatin' the food of our dead cows. Momma's all brokenhearted at havin' to feed that stuff to her young'uns, but honestly, we didn't mind it at all. We've really kinda grown a taste for 'em, especially the peanuts. Y' oughta try 'em.

164

"We're s'posed to not say anything to you and John Harley because you're fightin' the War and we don't want you worried about us, but I know you're seeing it, and that's the plain truth, JH."

I shuddered to think of the difference between my young brother at ten and me at the same age on this same land. How could this be happening? This glorious War was about to kill all its civilians even before it got the last of the soldiers! How quickly Willy grew up. I thought of him as a boy version of Laura, so wizened and grown-up by life's tough blows at such a young age.

I was sorely needed here, but I was also another mouth to feed. There was nothing anyone could do until the awful War was over and life could get back to some sort of normal. I prayed as earnestly as I knew for a quick end to all the evil wrecking our country.

As it became time to leave the farm and the family after two weeks of planting, I didn't want to go. This was my place, my people, my life. I was yearning for the day I could come back and build my life right here and begin refilling our bare pantries and smokehouse. I felt sorry for the local boys who had to leave Florida to fight for the CSA. Not only must they have been very homesick, but they were doing a whole lot more dyin' up there than we were down here. The little Olustee battle made such a mess of my head I didn't know how a Hamilton County farm boy could handle Bull Run, or Gettysburg, or Shiloh or all those other battles the Florida Infantry was flung into, but plenty of 'em had to.

I did my duty and went back to serving the South. My rounds were pretty normal. The Yanks led us to believe they weren't going to fool with us anymore. As long as we stayed out of Jacksonville, St. Augustine and Pensacola, we figured we wouldn't have too many problems. This suited me just fine. I guess Seymour and his officers weren't anxious to mess with us anymore either. They must not've been aware how many of our fighters had been pulled too far away to be of any assistance to us. We knew how vulnerable we were to a renewed Yankee attempt at breaking up our supply lines.

Late afternoon of May 15, I was on patrol around Lake City, heading toward the charred remains of Baldwin with a small group of cavalrymen. We headed slowly eastward on the highway. Coming onto the site of the Olustee battle, each of us got a sick feeling. We'd been by here a few times since the battle, but we still couldn't believe this quiet little place had been the scene of so much horror and destruction. The ground was pocked with ruins of wagons, crater holes and clean-picked horse carcasses. Dozens of mature pines were snapped in half by cannonballs. Their lower halves were standing upright and at attention as if nothing changed, but the top halves were lying next to their own trunks, sitting upside down like giant dead broccolis. There the decapitated pines would remain until nature slowly incorporated both halves into the ground. Once in the ground, they would stay forever just like all the dead soldiers, each a victim of the ruckus of February 20, 1864.

In the aftermath of death and destruction, the grass was beginning to sprout, adding a beautiful spring-green hue to the painful scene. The low palmettos were quickly recovering from their day of abuse and adding their own shade of green to the recovering land.

Suddenly we heard a galloping horseman gaining on us quickly from behind. Not knowing who it was, we each drew one of our six-shooters so we'd be able to offer him whatever greeting we deemed appropriate. At a hundred fifty yards we could tell it looked like one of us. At one hundred yards we were sure, so we re-holstered our Colts. It was a messenger from the telegraph office in Lake City. "Message for Lee," he shouted as he got in earshot. I waved my hand.

"Message isn't for you, it's for your Pa, but Captain Anderson said I should show it to you, though."

The telegram, addressed to Wiley Lee, said "Come home if can. Mother sick." It was sent by my brother Willy. I was confused.

The messenger told me Wiley had gotten released for as long as he needed. There was no other information. I thanked him. I wasn't released, but they thought it better for me to know. We continued our route toward Sanderson then on to Baldwin.

Of Death and Love

I stopped, as usual, at the Barnett house in Sanderson. First I had to make a joke to Mrs. Barnett. "Hope y'all've gotten all the Yankee scrubbed out of this poor old house," I said to Mrs. Julia Barnett.

She laughed, "We got the Yankee dirt gone right away, but took us a couple weeks to have done with that darned ol' smell!"

I told 'em I had to be going but wanted them to know about my message and how I was confused because I didn't know if the "Mother" in the message was my Mom or Wiley's Step-Mom, Ava. Mrs. Barnett told me from what she knew she was real sure it would be my Mom, Mary McDonald Lee. "I'm sorry to bear bad news, JH. All I know is she's not doing well, but I figure you'd rather know than not."

"Yes, ma'am. You figured right, and I thank you." I turned and left in a fog.

On the morning of May 19, a messenger rode into our camp at Baldwin with another telegram, this one for me. It was dated May 18, and said simply, "Mom died AM. Come if can."

My Captain gave me leave. "Report back at Lake City in three days, and sorry 'bout your Ma, son."

On my way through Sanderson, I stopped again at Barnett's. Laura answered the door. When she saw me she suddenly looked like she'd seen a ghost. Assuming she was afraid because she didn't know what to say to a man whose mother had died, I made my big mean face and lunged at her. She squealed with laughter and turned to run. I grabbed her from behind and tickled her just as if she was my sister Sadie. It was the most at home I'd felt since that awful battle.

"You let go of me, you Johnny Rebel trash," she teased, having never enjoyed my attention so much.

I remembered my Dad teaching me "Often when a woman tells you one thing, what she really means is she wants the opposite." I kinda thought that lesson might apply here but wasn't sure, and I've never been sure when it applies and when it doesn't.

I thought to myself, "This woman's only twelve, so it may not apply in this case, but why not give it a try?" So I said, "I'm so sorry, I can't let go, it's something I got in the War. Sometimes my arms just lock and I can't move 'em for about an hour." With that little made-up line my arms squeezed even tighter.

Laura quit her pretend struggle, going kind of limp for a split second, then just melted into tears, turning around as the words blurped out of her. She wrapped her arms around me and said "I'm so sorry about Mrs. Lee. I wish I could do something to make things better for you."

"Thanks. It's okay," I said, "with all I've been seein' lately, I kinda wonder if the people dyin' aren't the lucky ones. There's so much pain out there, and it never stops."

Being of the stern pioneer stock, Laura wasn't about to carry on her crying for very long. I watched, and I could feel, as she composed herself. She straightened up to her full four-foot-something stature, looking straight forward into my chest. Still in my embrace, she took her right index finger and so delicately wiped beneath her right, then left eye, then slowly looked up at me. Those eyes, as dark as her hair, were the biggest two things about her, and she could cut right through a wall with 'em. They still glistened from the tears, but she was clearly ready to move on.

She kinda half pushed, half guided me to take one step backwards. Loosening my grip on her, I found myself easily sinking back into a creaky bowback chair by the front door. Next thing I knew, she somehow, and so gracefully spun herself around and ended up sitting sidesaddle on my knee.

With her sassy but soft, slightly twangy yet sophisticated voice, she said spunkily, "You know you're just a momma's boy don't you? Your Momma never once said a sentence in her life that didn't have 'JH' somewhere in it. She thought you hung the moon, but I know better."

You well know this was not the first time a female befuddled a Lee man, but I couldn't see for the life of me where she was leading. Lacking any better response to my pre-teen midget friend, I said something real wise like, "I beg your pardon." I was hoping to buy just enough time to catch up with her, but it was no use.

"Yeah, your Ma might have had twelve young'uns but you're *the one*. And you are going to be the head of your big old clan whether you like it or not. It's been *ordained*," she said, reflecting a bit of her upbringing in the house of two preachers.

"I am the oldest son of the oldest son. Is that what you mean?"

"Oh, you wouldn't understand. I guess you're just too young," she had the nerve to say at barely over half my age, "and men are just plain stupid anyway."

Startled, I responded, "I just came off a field where I'd kill a man for a lesser slight than this."

"Then I guess it's a good thing I'm not a man, huh?"

"Yes . . . it's a real good thing." Suddenly I found myself thinking it a real good thing for more than one reason.

This fascinating woman in a little girl's body continued, "What I mean is, Mrs. Mary Lee was a real smart and special lady, and I learned a lot from her in the time I was around your house. I got to see her in a way you didn't because you were so busy workin' your farm. I was in the house with her and I might just have learned what made her tick. She showed me how to be strong and yet be a lady at the same time. And it's just what I'm doin' right now," she said as her voice cracked just a little bit with emotion, but continued on with the strength of a locomotive as she talked about someone she clearly revered in ways I never knew. "She'd want you to be strong, too, because you're the leader of her pack o' young'uns. So what good would I be to you if I just sat here and made my face all wet?" She continued talking, and I continued to be in awe of the strength oozing from this . . . child. "One of the good things of being a circuit-rider's daughter is I get to meet a lot of folks all over these three counties, and my Daddy taught me to find the good in everybody and just ignore the rest. With Mrs. Mary Lee, I didn't have to look, the good just oozed right out of her. And no jokin', your Momma believed in all her kids, but she really believed in you, JH Lee.

"You know you're her 'Jimmy,' and everybody knows she's the only one calls you that because of your special bond. She believed you could do whatever you set your mind to, and she sure wouldn't want you to give that up now just because she's gone. She left this earth praying you and all her brood'll end up wanting the same thing God wants for you here on earth. And I know she's up there watchin' and pullin' for you already."

Then she concluded her master oration with, "That's all." Somehow I felt stronger.

We found ourselves in an eye-lock, and it was then I learned why I'd been trained to avoid eye contact with the enemy. This near-baby of a person wasn't the enemy, but she had just conquered my heart. I have no idea how long we stared at each other, but I didn't care if I did nothing else the rest of my life.

Then it dawned on me I had a funeral to go to, and I'd better get going if I wanted any chance to make it in time.

"Can I go?" Laura asked.

"We better ask Mrs. Barnett. I'm not sure, we'll be late getting in, and it mightn't look too good to the folks at home. Let's ask your Ma to go with us.

"That would be just fine. My Daddy's already there. He got the same telegram you did," Laura informed.

The arrangements were made and we hit the trail in the Barnetts' two-horse wagon. It was a four-seater, built strong but light so the horses could carry on at a good clip. The horses, Martin and Luther, could make good time. It should be noted their jackass was named Charles V, after the German emporer who tried to make the real Martin Luther's life so miserable. We loaded up, I whistled for my horse Charlie and he followed us the whole way home. Charlie was such a good horse.

Mrs. Barnett sat on the back bench, and she seemed to be acting out a nap most of the way. I didn't believe she was really napping, but I did know with her stiff constitution, if I even thought a bad thought, I would have her hand upside the back of my head before I could think it a second time it. I liked knowing Laura had such a strong woman in her background, but I did stay ready to duck, for fear of a bad thought being sensed. That kind of strength would be good for our kids, I thought. Then suddenly my head was spinning at such thoughts. Did I really just think about "our kids"? Mrs. Barnett told me years later she was never asleep but was listening to every word, not because she mistrusted us, but because she was fascinated with the sparks she thought she was seeing between her very young daughter and this CSA soldier man.

As we passed through the Olustee battlefield, Laura seemed to get cold even though it was a hot, dry May afternoon. She asked innocently, "Why does this kind of thing happen?" Of course I had no answer for such a question, but sure didn't mind when she moved closer to me and linked her arm real tight in mine until we were well past the killing field. "I've been through here before," she said, "but it never gets any less scary."

"You don't have to worry this time. I'd never let anything happen to you, Laura."

We got to the Lee farm well after sundown. The house was full of mourners who turned briefly into rejoicers when I came in. No one knew if I'd be able to make it in time for the funeral or if I could come at all. John Harley arrived earlier in the day. It was good to be home again.

The casket was dead center in the parlor of the big house. It was already closed and well-sealed with Lee Farm rosin for the obvious reasons. Momma was the first Lee to be embalmed, but on these warm days, embalming only bought a little time. Since John Harley and I were here, the funeral would be next morning at 9:00.

All eleven of Wiley's and Mary's surviving children were present and presentable for her funeral. We lost little Louisa Catherine at just over one-year-old to the whooping cough back in '58. Otherwise, we were a very healthy lot, other than nowadays each of us was a little too skinny.

I pulled my father aside to talk to him. He seemed to be a little in his shell, which I easily understood. We walked outside to the front porch, just to get away from all the noise. "JH, you've been through a lot lately. I'm worried about you," Wiley said before I had a chance to ask him about himself.

"Well, you just lost your wife after going through a horrible War. I'm worried for you, too. But don't worry about me, all I care to do in this world now is to get this War over and see all my family back safe, fat and healthy on this farm. I plan on coming home and making your life a little easier because you deserve it. I know it must be hard to be in your shoes now. I just want you knowin' we're gonna get through this War and prosperity is coming back to middle Florida.

Wiley said, "I asked for a release from the CSA, and I got it. Told 'em I had a house full of young'uns and no momma to care for 'em. I was told I'd 'served nobly the cause of the CSA,' and I got my discharge." Now I guess I know what your Granddaddy felt like when he lost my Momma, Lizzie. I wanted to blame him because he'd sired so many kids with her in such a short time. Well, I doubled the six Daddy had with Lizzie and seems I'm in the same spot now. Of course, I will never catch up with what he and Ava did. Seventeen kids! Can you believe it? Don't know what I'm going to do. Don't know why I should go on. But I guess I will. Just like ol' John, I'm probably going to just go to work. It's what us Lees do. If I'm always looking forward to one more harvest, I can go on a long time here. I'm startin' to think your Granddaddy John is right about this war being a really stupid thing," he opined while wiping his brow. "I didn't believe it for a long time and thought maybe he'd just gotten soft or something, but the ol' fox has proven to me many times over he knows what he talks about."

None of us wanted the next morning to come, but it came just as predictably as every other morning since time began.

Since Momma was a McDonald, we had to have those Scottish bagpipes play "Amazing Grace" at her funeral service. They played as we processed from the Swift Creek Church across the little wagon trail and into the cemetery. Some folks say bagpipes are beautiful, but

171

they sound like dying geese to me, and always remind me of funerals. We followed the Barnett wagon, with its precious payload of one well-used body of one fine country woman, to the Lee plot. Not yet forty years old, Mary McDonald Lee had made a mark on her world. Martin and Luther seemed to know the solemn nature of their task and carried just the right pace with their heads hanging low. As we began our short march I felt Sister Sadie slip her hand in my left hand. My heart broke for her because she was so attached to her Momma. As I almost got overwhelmed and almost broke down myself, I felt Laura's hand slide into my right hand. Knowing the strong constitution of this young woman, I seemed to draw strength from her. I was amazed.

I thought a bit about Lizzie, the grandmother I never knew, and how sure I was she'd have really liked her daughter-in-law whom we were committing to the earth this day, and she'da sure been proud to see what came of her family out here in the middle of nowhere.

The Rev. William Jabish Barnett led a marvelous tribute to a marvelous woman. As he concluded with "Ashes to ashes and dust to dust" and we recited the Lord's Prayer together, we said good-bye to Momma in the best way we here on earth knew how.

Old Doctor Curlee from White Springs watched over her while she was sick. After the service, I asked him what he thought killed her. "I believe it was pure and simple starvation, son. Your Ma would always wait to help her own plate last of all, and maybe y'all didn't notice, but she was far too often just going without. When you do without for too long, it gets to the point you can't eat, and of course, you don't really starve to death, but you get to where you can't take any kind of little ailment. It's not unheard of out here nowadays." His words broke my heart. To think of this dear poor woman who'd worked so hard all her life to feed the family she loved, starving in this land of plenty, was unbearable to me. I knew if she could've held on just a little longer, the damnable War would be over and I would see to it this farm produced all she ever again wanted . . . but it just wasn't meant to be.

As I was about to leave to go back to war, Wiley pulled me aside, saying, "JH, we can see your heart's goin' all aflutter for Laura Barnett. Just make real sure your heart's the *only* thing goin' aflutter for her. I think you know what I mean. The Barnetts are as fine a folks as there are out here, but they are fire-breathin' preachers. I don't believe you want any reason for any of them to be crossways with you. I married a young one, too, and I wouldn't do any different if I was doing it again. You gotta remember, though, she's not even thirteen yet."

I didn't know whether to be furious at the old man for this un-asked for, but probably wise, advice, or should I just say "Thanks" and ride away?

"Thanks," I said as I rode away.

Charlie and I passed through the Swift Creek Cemetery to say good-bye to Momma one last time before I resumed my futile service to the lost cause. I can't tell you how many times I repeated my one last good-bye over the course of my life.

On the ride I thought a lot of Momma and how much I was going to miss her, but I found myself thinking even more of the young Barnett girl. I marveled how she stepped in and helped me through my loss, and even how she seemed to admire and would miss Momma as much as I would. How could someone so little, so young, be so capable and so wise beyond her years? And so darn cute, to boot?

It wasn't lost on me how strong she was for me when I needed strength to get through the loss of Momma. Then wee she wanted to see me, I couldn't get out of bed for her on account of my vicious hangover. I re-made my vow to never drink demon alcohol again. I imagined it woulda pleased Momma, or it woulda if she believed it.

Maybe Laura was placed in my life to be nothing more than an innocent refuge in a horribly tumultuous time, I thought. Whether this was all it was or she was the one for me to build my life around, I couldn't say, but this little slip of a girl absolutely gave me strength to go on in a world which seemed to be crumbling all around me.

I smiled to myself and said, "Self, I think I'm in love!" I gave Charlie a quick kick and we galloped down the road for what seemed five miles. Charlie seemed to know my every mood and his spirit reflected my state of mind when we rode together.

War Winds Down

The remainder of 1864 was quiet and slow for a Florida horse soldier. The typical day in a soldier's life was far from exciting, but if all days were like February 20, there would quickly be no soldiers left. Reflecting on Olustee, as I did too often, made me appreciate drudgery and boredom over its extreme opposite of sheer terror.

I found my rounds took me frequently into Sanderson, where I would make an official call on the Barnett household. Lookin' for Yankees, y' know. I felt like I spent most of my time doing what I had to do, but time moved along real slow during those days. My daydreamin' time was maybe too plentiful, and in every dream I found myself on the Lee Farm with Laura by my side.

Up in Virginia, 1864's second half was anything but quiet and slow as the War raged on. The news continued getting worse. More and more of the young men of Hamilton County were not coming home. It was the same throughout the South. Our food, our currency, our lives and our male population were all being depleted. The War was not turning out the way we imagined at those early prayer meetings, back when secession seemed such a good idea.

The news of Sherman's March struck fear in our hearts. By September he was in full control of Atlanta, the Deep South's single most important inland city. He stayed there for a while, but we assumed he was going to march from there to somewhere. Was it Tallahassee? Jacksonville? Savannah? Was he sending an overwhelming force to avenge the loss at Olustee and finally break up the Florida railroad system?

The most disheartening thing to hear was how Sherman could have battle after battle of worse casualties than we had, but he only had to send a message and he would be full again of fresh young fighting men. The same way we might reload a rifle, Sherman was reloading his troops. At the same time, we were fast running out of human ammunition, and the ones we had were running mighty hungry and real tired.

We no longer took joy in dealing ol' Abe Lincoln bigger losses than we suffered. Because of his endless supply, we knew Lincoln was going to last longer than we were.

When Sherman finally moved on from Atlanta, he had to add the insult of burning it to the ground. From there, he conducted a campaign of burning and destroying whole towns, houses, barns, sawmills and anything in his path as he made his way to the East Coast. He arrived at Savannah on December 22, just in time to arrogantly announce Savannah was his

Christmas gift to Mr. Lincoln. We couldn't have been more insulted, furious or devastated by his hatefulness. Of all the emotions Sherman brought out in us, the worst was just how impotent we were to change a thing about it. His fellow General Philip Sheridan was committing the same destruction throughout the Shenandoah Valley, and we saw a small dose of it during the Battle of Olustee when Seymour burned Baldwin to the ground during his hasty retreat.

The South knew the barbaric acts were approved by General Grant, and could only assume they were condoned by President Lincoln himself. The Generals certainly would have learned civilized conduct of War at West Point, but it was consciously and blatantly ignored in this War of brother against brother.

In early 1865 there was a rumbling of Union activity moving toward Tallahassee. My Company K, now under Captain Jesse Jones, was called in. We were ordered to protect the Capitol city from the invading troops. The result was the Battle of Natural Bridge, one of the very last battles of any consequence of the entire War.

The Southern defenders had some seasoned veterans, but a remarkably large part of our force was the Cadets of the West Florida Seminary. They were a sorry excuse for an army but we defended our Capitol and the Rebels were able to declare one last victory. The day was March 6, 1865. I took no joy in our victory because I knew it was just a token. And I felt guilty thinking of how easy my War-life had been here in Florida while so many of my friends, the ones who survived, in the infantry were living the hell of war day in and day out.

It should be noted Tallahassee was the only Confederate State Capitol east of the Mississippi to not fall to Union forces during the entire War; yet another hollow, futile, vain victory for Florida's 2nd Cavalry.

Even so, Florida's Governor John Milton was so distraught over the inevitable prospect of reunion with the Yankees that he took his own life with his own pistol on April 1, 1865.

Just over a week later, on Sunday, April 9, 1865, General Lee surrendered his sword and his Army of Northern Virginia to General Grant at Appomattox Courthouse. The rest of the states surrendered during the next two months.

At the end of the same week, on Good Friday, April 14, President Lincoln was assassinated.

On May 10 I was ordered to be in Baldwin to surrender and receive my parole.

I turned in my rifle, even though it was my own and not issued by the CSA. I was allowed to keep my revolvers and horse. I was forced to pledge an oath to never again take up arms against the United States of America. I then received my official parole, and was free to go home. The Union officers and soldiers were almost cordial to us and seemed to embody Mr. Lincoln's admonition in his second Inaugural address to try to re-make our country:

> With malice toward none; with charity for all; with firmness in the right, as God gives us to see the right, let us strive on to finish the work we are in; to bind up the nation's wounds; to care for him who shall have borne the battle, and for his widow and his orphan . . . to do all which may achieve and cherish a just and lasting peace among ourselves and with all nations.

We Southerners had lots of different feelings about Lincoln, but most of us believed he offered us an olive branch in this speech just weeks before his assassination. After he was killed, though, we feared there might be a big revenge for both the War and the assassination.

As soon as my buddies and I could, we left for home, about a day and a half ride. I was finally going to get to begin my adult life at the Lee Farm. The whole trip home I planned and figured and schemed all kinds of ways I could make the farm a better place and it could go back to supporting the large families which drew from it.

Of course, all my plans revolved around having Laura by my side. I knew she was too young and I would have to wait because her very proper parents weren't going to allow their little girl to get hitched until she was at least fifteen. I was sure of it and was very happy and willing to make the sacrifice, and would spend those next two years of precious time building a house and savings for us to get off to a strong start.

That short trip home seemed to never end. I never felt so frustrated with Charlie in all his life. Here this animal had been my friend and protector through the horrible War, yet now he couldn't get me home fast enough. I couldn't ride him too hard, but I wanted to make this trip fast. Why couldn't we be there already? I must get to the farm, my home soil, so I could start my life, my real life, as the best darn farmer Hamilton County ever saw. That is, after a quick stop in Sanderson, just a little bit out of my way home.

Since we got a late start, we figured we'd get almost to Darbyville before making camp. Once we got close, all the other fellows were ready to stop. It was getting' almost dark and we were all worn out. Suddenly, though, what made sense to them made no sense to me. I was going to go on. I said, "I'm gonna make Sanderson tonight if any of you wanna go."

"You're a fool for going on alone, JH. What am I gonna tell Daddy if you made it through the whole War but get ambushed by some wild no-count thieves on your way home?" John Harley asked good questions.

176

"Dunno John, but I'm goin'. Wanna join me? It's a big moon tonight so seeing won't be a problem."

"Sure," he said with disgust as we left the other ten former-CSA fighting men. They had already uncorked their special canteens to start the first no-more-War celebration. But I could only think of one thing, and I bet she only weighed seventy-five pounds soakin' wet!

"Thanks, John. You've been a great brother to me, and I will pay you back someday for riding with me tonight. But I've just gotta get home. There's something I've gotta do first, though."

"Barnett?"

"How'd you know?"

"'Cause it's written all over your face. You've been waitin' and hopin' to get out of this War alive so you can tell the old Rev you're ready and fittin' for marryin', haven't you?"

"John Harley, you old skunk! I'm not gonna pretend any different 'cause it's just what I have in mind. Laura's the one for me, and I don't understand it. I know she's just a baby. And you don't have to be any genius with numbers to know us soldiers still a-livin' are gonna have ourselves the pick of the litter. All our competition is buried in some mass grave in Virginia or Pennsylvania or somewhere. My best brotherly advice to you is don't be in any hurry because those women are gonna start gettin' lonely and we're gonna be prime pickin's! I can't tell you why I'm so crazy over Laura, but I am, and I think that's the way it's gotta be. If I wasn't, though, I think I'd just be real sweet to all the girls and let the biddin' begin and then I'd take my pick of the whole bunch. My heart won't let me do it, though, but it's sure what I recommend for you."

We sipped our canteens as we plodded along. We wondered why the South was all out of corn but we could still get the whiskey we wanted. Ain't it funny how things are?

We sipped some more, and decided we probably weren't going to make it to Sanderson if the road kept wobbling as much as it was. In fact, why not stop right here? We had no idea where "here" was, but it looked like a dandy spot for two hard-ridin' young men. "Hon Jarley . . . let'sh . . . shtop . . . right . . . here. Thish looksh like a good place," I said at my height of eloquence while sliding off the saddle.

"Okay, HJ," said Hon Jarley as he wondered why he was lying in the sand, having never dismounted his horse, at least not to his knowledge. "Let's shleep . . . heeere." I believe we both began to sleep right there on the edge of the busiest and most highly improved road in all of Florida. Somehow we forgot that when you're sleeping on the roadside, you always go off the road at least thirty paces because there could be unsavory characters on the highways at night. Hon Jarley had his left boot, complete with foot, still stuck in the stirrup, but it didn't seem to bother his slumber. Good thing his horse didn't spook easy or he mighta found his butt bumpin' down the road all night and never known it. As for me, it's a good thing I had the presence of mind to tell Charlie to "Stay," because that's just what he did. My horse stayed right there with me as I had sweet, lubricated dreams of home and, of course, Laura.

Morning came real early and real hard. I was somehow able to get up but wasn't real sure if I was alive. John Harley, his left boot still dangling in the stirrup, but his foot somehow free, stirred and said, "What's goin' on here? Why'd you stuff my boot in the stirrup?"

I laughed (and laughing hurt) and said, "I think you did that'n all on your own. You were pretty good at fallin' out of the saddle last night, you just weren't up to your best military dismount."

"Maybe it's cuz I'm not military anymore," he retorted.

John Harley started looking around for firewood and some wild leaves to make some tea to call breakfast. He knew I was already itchin' to get on the trail, but he knew also we wouldn't be able to travel in our current condition. He also was sure Reverend Barnett didn't want to see me in my current state. It was just after sun-up, still cool and invigorating, but we felt like we'd just been victims of a Yankee firing squad.

"JH, this drinking stuff is for the birds, ain't it?"

"Naw," I said, "the birds are too smart for it. Always seems a good idea at the time, but doesn't seem so brilliant in the morning." The birds were chirping their annoying morning songs, the same ones I usually enjoyed so much. "I think this is what Daddy means when he says, 'You can't soar with the eagles by day if you're a-gonna hoot with the owls by night.'"

I again made my vow to God and my family to never, ever touch alcohol again. It started seeming like every time I woke up with a bad headache, I'd renew my vow; and every time I meant it.

When we got to a creek crossing just outside Sanderson in the late morning, we were starting to feel a little better. We had nothing but a few worthless ol' Confederate dollars between us, and no place would take them for anything anymore, but we kept 'em anyway.

We'd gotten real used to riding trails hungry over the last year, but trail-riding hungover and hungry was a very special kind of hungry. We ate the last crumbs of the stale cornbread in our saddlebags, and we were plum out of food 'til we got home unless we could find some wild blackberries, which would be just about ready to turn ripe. Blackberries used to be plentiful in the woods along the roads, but in those times it seemed nothing the least bit edible ever made it quite to ripe before someone picked and ate it.

I told John Harley he could head on to White Springs if he wanted, or he could go with me on my mission. "I'll just be an extra day, but there's something I've just gotta do."

"If you need me for some reason, I'm with you, brother. But seems to me this is your deal. If it's alright with you, I'm gonna head on home and wish you all the best. I was honored to fight one War with you, and I'll do it again if you need me to. But absent you beggin' me, I'm plannin' to ride straight through Sanderson."

"Good-bye John Harley, thanks for being my brother. See you at the farm."

Waving good-bye, I walked with Charlie toward the creek. I decided I should take the time to pretty myself up as much as possible. Having had no bath or grooming of any kind for about two weeks, I might not have been at my peak of presentability. I found a suitable bathing spot where I had good visibility in all directions and figured it would be about as good as any. It was important to see all 'round me nowadays because folks throughout the South were desperate to steal anything they could get their hands on. My boots, weapons, even my worn-out soldier pants were very attractive to lots of folks in this now-desperately poor area. My most valuable possession, though, was Charlie himself. Folks could use him for all kinds of things, including feeding the family; that's just how desperate things were. I dismounted then tied him firmly to a cypress knee protruding from the dark brown water of the creek.

My boots were already tied to my saddle because I'd been riding mostly barefoot for months to save boot leather. Unloading my sidearms and parole papers, I slid off my shirt and pants, which made me stark, buck naked. Now, one little-known secret is there hadn't been a Confederate ass covered by underwear for at least a year, at least not a Confederate ass below the rank of Major. Every piece of underwear material had been used up as field bandages, rifle wadding, gun-barrel cleaning or patches for outer clothes. The miles we logged in the saddle were really hard on the crotches and backsides of a cavalryman's pants. Lucky for me, I inherited a pair of CSA gray britches from one of my fallen brethren who, shall we say, didn't need them anymore after Olustee. Since he was an infantryman, his seat was pretty good, but his pants legs were nothing but tangled threads from just below the knee all the way down due to all the marching through underbrush and palmetto woods.

Sadie cut out the seat and added it to my britches when I was home for Momma's funeral. Those pants were real close to lettin' go when I made the trip with Laura and Mrs. Barnett from Sanderson to the farm. Now wouldn't I have had some explaining to do to Mrs. Barnett if I'da gotten a big rip with her little girl riding next to me? At any given time, most of the Cavalry boys were just one bendover, one mount or dismount from total indecent exposure. With the current rampant poverty, most folks understood, but I still needed to avoid this embarrassment at my next meeting with Laura Barnett.

So, I took my rags, er, uniform, my straight razor and my skinny self and started my bath right next to Charlie. I had no soap, and my razor was pitifully pitted. This shave would be one I'd remember for life. It hurt. I found under my toes, there was just a bit of light clay content below the top mud layer of the creek bottom. I could rub the clay on my face and it made my shave a little less painful. I pulled out my cow bone and pig whisker toothbrush, reached down and got some more of the fine clay, and called it toothpaste. My teeth weren't clean, but maybe they were a little more presentable than before. So in this shin-deep water with a three-inch layer of silty mud on the bottom, every time I moved, or dunked myself, I was stirring up more mud. I was getting nothing more than a mud bath.

I dunked my clothes very carefully, so as not to cause a tear, then wrung 'em out and repeated three or four times. Knowing they weren't clean, but sure they were cleaner, I draped them over Charlie and dunked myself a few more times. Declaring myself clean and no longer hungover, I figured it was time to go and claim the love of my life. After, of course, putting back on my shirt, pants and revolvers, I mounted Charlie and we headed to Sanderson, hoping to be dry by time we got there.

The Talk

At the outskirts of Sanderson, I stopped Charlie to put on my boots and belt so I would look my military best, or at least as best as I could with the seat of my pants sporting a twelve-inch by twelve-inch homemade patch from a dead soldier's britches. As I dismounted in front of the Barnett house, I was astonished by how calm I was on this unusual mission to claim my now thirteen-and-one-half year old prize.

Since May 18 was a Thursday, I had a good chance of seeing the Reverend before he packed up to go wherever his appointed rounds took him that weekend.

I was in luck. At the door, Mrs. Barnett and Laura were very pleased but confused to see me. They thought I would already be home. After telling of the surrender, we spoke politely for a few more minutes. I then told them I wished to speak with the Reverend on some spiritual matters regarding the War. I felt it important to talk with him before I went home. Did they know where I might find him?

I was informed he was in the family farm next to the house and would be plenty happy to see me. I sure hoped so.

"Good afternoon," I shouted across the farm. He knew he recognized the voice but I was the last one he expected in his garden on this day. The Barnett farm was about ten acres and was planned to feed the family with the excess used to help those in need. However, it was nowhere near big enough for the needs of the day. Also, since it was so close to town, it was frequently robbed by dark of night by those who thought they were in need but didn't see the need to ask the clergyman and his family. He showed me where some radishes and early beans had been stolen just the night before. "I know I'm supposed to give freely, but I fear I'm going to have to start guarding the field at night if I want to have anything for my family's table. They are robbing us blind. They don't want to come help me grow it, but they sure don't mind stealing it."

I told him how farmers all over were assigning family members and farmhands to take turns guarding their fields. Even in Genoa, where there were no strangers, folks were so hungry for the first produce that it had gotten to neighbor stealing from neighbor. Good people, who would never consider taking the slightest thing, were pilfering food from their neighbors' farms.

Seizing opportunity, I volunteered to take the first night shift so he could rest up for his weekend of doing God's work on the circuit. I recommended he ask his local Methodist churchmen to take turns at guard. If the thieves saw it was only the preacher doing the guarding, they'd know to just wait 'til the weekends when he was away to clean him out. So far, once word spread that a farm was guarded the thieves seemed to stay away. We were pretty sure it was neighbor robbing neighbor with no ill intent, it's just what hunger will cause a man to do.

He liked my idea so much he expressed his appreciation by asking me to call him Jabish instead of all the formal names I'd addressed him in my younger days. He said after all I'd been through and because I was finally a full adult, he'd like for us to have an adult relationship.

I said, "Of course I appreciate this thought . . . Jabish," just trying it out, since we *were* both adults, "but I was hoping someday soon to call you by a name you'd think might be more fitting to call a father-in-law." Now I gulped at the thought of being so bold, but the cat was out of the bag and I had nothing left but to hope my delivery wasn't too direct.

I figured I'd better keep talking, "You know I'm the one who's going to take over the Lee Farm, and I've prepared myself to take on this responsibility all my life. I've now got my War obligation out of the way and want nothing more than to see your beautiful daughter at my side every step of the way. Of course, I mean when she is old enough. And I am fully prepared to wait 'til that day." I thought I'd better shut up at that point.

Jabish took his time to respond. He seemed to be torturing me just like when he was preaching and using the power of the pause to hold his audience in his hand. He was so good at controlling his human flock with his superb sermon delivery, and at that moment he had total domination of his flock of one.

The only way I could fight back against this master was to control myself and not engage in nervous blather, of which I was well accomplished. I waited . . . and waited some more.

Jabish stayed quiet, and I continued in full eye contact, again breaking my battle training, but this was a different kind of battle. It was verbal man-to-man combat, and I had to have eye contact. More importantly, I must never flinch, I had to wait for him to speak next. I could tell his mind was running fast at what he just heard.

Finally, he drew a deep breath and said,

"Will you always love and honor Laura with all your heart, soul and mind?"

"I will."

"Will you provide a peaceful home for my grandchildren?"

"I will with God's help."

"Will you raise your children, my grandchildren, in the knowledge and love of Christ?"

"By God's grace I will raise them in the faith." I was saying all the right words, passing the test and feeling real good about then.

"Do you promise never, NEVER, to raise your hand against Laura, whether in good times or bad?"

"Through the power of the Holy Spirit I shall never so much as speak an angry word to your daughter, my wife-to-be. She is too precious a jewel to defile in such a way." I meant all these things from the bottom of my heart because my love was pure. But I also felt I was beating the old lion at his own game, the game of words. Boy, was I good!

"Will you today and forevermore pledge to not let the demon alcohol have any part of you or your family."

"I, (cough) will."

"You're not a good liar, are you?"

"I'm a horrible liar, but I'm not lying because I made a solemn pledge to the Almighty to never touch the evil drink again. I've sinned by trying it when I cracked under stress of battle, but I feel I'm better for it because I know firsthand of the pain it can cause me and my family."

"Son, beating alcohol is a daily thing. The promise to never, ever, touch it again is hollow. But the pledge each morning to stay away and not let it get in the way of a productive day's work is very powerful. I don't condemn you for using it under the horrible stress of war. But you must now dominate it daily, or it will dominate you for life, make Laura miserable, and ruin your family. Period."

He went on, "You have my blessing, and I'm sure you will have Mrs. Barnett's blessing to marry my daughter when she reaches the right age, which is twenty-five."

"But sir!" I exclaimed.

Then the old preacher started laughing. He let out a belly laugh liked I'd never seen from him. Not being a big one for jokes, and so seldom seen out of his stiffly starched Methodist aplomb, he knew he'd just delivered the best joke ever. And I think he was right.

As I picked my heart up off the ground, we laughed and I thanked him for the father he'd been to his little girl, and I promised we would be there for him and the Missus when they needed us in their old age.

But I was afraid to ask exactly what the right marryin' age was.

I didn't tell Laura of our real conversation, but just how I'd had a fine talk between a man returning home from war and his favorite clergyman. She was happy it went well.

Being anxious to return to the farm, yet not wanting to leave the Barnett household, I was invited to spend the night, and I did so by fulfilling my commitment to protect the Lord's garden on its first night of the new guard duty program.

Laura was allowed to patrol with me 'til sundown. I had secretly flirted and courted this young lady for over a year now, but never kissed her lips - until that one very special twilight. I will never again see an okra plant without remembering the night in Sanderson, Florida, when the okra plants were the only thing tall enough for cover on that wide-open farm. Only a shade over waist-high at the time, those wonderful okra plants afforded us our first, second, third and more kisses without risk of being found out. Crouched low and seated on two bushel baskets we found, sometimes side-by-side, sometimes face-to-face, sometimes her on my knee, but always embraced and always with lips locked tight. That little vegetable plot coulda been robbed blind and us two vigilant guardsmen woulda never known. There mighta not been a rutabaga left in the ground if we were the only things standing in the way.

As sundown approached, and then some, and both of us with fiercely chapped lips, I mounted Charlie and gave Laura a hoist up into my saddle in front of me. She rode side-saddle and hung onto me like she would never let me go, and I hoped she wouldn't. Charlie and I took her to the house, she dismounted, I followed, and we had one more embrace, but no kisses, just in case we were being watched. I opened the door and said goodnight.

The rest of the night I spent on that crate, defending the cabbages and 'maters, painfully lonely but crazy in love.

Coming in about an hour before sun-up, I was happy Mrs. Barnett was already up and had a breakfast of cornbread and grits almost ready for me. When Laura came down the stairs I thought I was having a vision. She must've stayed up all night primping herself. She looked so calm and beautiful in her simple and radiantly clean Sunday dress and her hair with curls,

I think they're called ringlets. I learned girls have been curling hair since the ancient Greeks, but none ever achieved a more angelic result than Laura Barnett on that morning. How do they do it? And why? And why does it make us men-folk so crazy? Everything about her looked more grown up than I'd ever seen, especially her wide smile and those flashing eyes. She was as near perfect as any human female can be.

After breakfast we visited for just a little while on the front porch swing. I told her what a big step I was taking with this trip home, and how I was going home to settle in to my life's work. I aimed to be as hard a worker as my Daddy, and wise and cagey like my Grandfather John. But it was time for me to go and get started. I let Laura know I couldn't wait to see her again. "Daddy's preaching at Swift Creek in two Sundays," she said. My heart skipped at the news.

Again I told her how I couldn't wait to see her, and if she didn't mind too terribly, could she be sure to wear the same dress? She laughed and asked what else might she wear on Sunday than her only Sunday dress? I guess I never noticed it before. Then I leaned over and whispered, with the most timid and trembling voice, "I love you." Suddenly her arms locked around my neck, and our lips locked in the most passionate kiss ever by a young man and his woman. The fear of Jabish discovering us made it even more exciting, and we stayed in our embrace as long as we dared.

Then I left.

On the way home I couldn't help but notice how much better the morning feels when you're riding drunk on love rather than ridin' hungover!

Civil War Recap

On the ride home I thought about only two things. One was the big War we just fought. The other was Laura. The thought of Laura made me happy and overjoyed about our future. The War was downright perplexing.

What was it we just did to ourselves in the American War Between the States? What was it about?

If it was nothing but a War over slavery, then America is the biggest nation of fools on earth. All civilized countries had to grapple with the slave problem, and all of them except the U.S. settled peaceably. If our War was about slavery, then we were the only nation to resolve the issue with a war, especially such a bloody one. Shame on us.

The other civilized nations mostly treated slavery as a property rights issue. Those societies' thinking evolved to see slavery was a wrong and unworkable system, which it surely was. But they recognized, whether slavery was wrong or not, the slaveholder was holding legal property. Since those governments were taking the property away, the slaveholders were paid for them, and the "property" was freed. Again I say shame on us. Even if full compensation was paid to slaveholders, and some restitution paid to the freed slaves, it would be far less costly than the ghastly cost in money and lives of the War we just suffered.

Doesn't even the slaveholder have the protection of the Fifth Amendment to our Constitution? Passed in 1791, it clearly states, "No person shall be . . . deprived of life, liberty, or property, without due process of law; nor shall private property be taken for public use without just compensation." Even if slaveholding was made illegal by an act of law, isn't it still a taking of legal property to take away a right which was perfectly legal just prior to passage of the law?

Was it states' rights? Here's another common argument. Of course the burningest issue revolving around states' rights was, you guessed, slavery. The South said the federal government was getting too bloated and intrusive. And the more local our government systems could be, the more responsive government would be to the people's mandate. It would allow all states to be different in many ways with the federal government not involved in such decisions as slavery. The federal government would, as the Constitution says, "Establish Justice, insure domestic tranquility, provide for the common defense, promote the general welfare, and secure the blessings of liberty to ourselves and our posterity."

Those who wanted bigger, more powerful federal government (mostly in the North) wanted central controls, one set of rules for everyone everywhere in our nation. They would argue the same standards for everyone. They thought a strong central government was the best and only way to preserve the Union. The South wanted maximum personal liberty. And to achieve this goal, government needed to be as local as possible with Federal government as minimal as possible.

If that's all it was, was it worth such a War?

If not, who started it?

Was it the North, when it blockaded the harbors of the rebellion states?

Was it the South, when it chose to attack Fort Sumter?

If so, what foolish decisions both sides made. Why did so much blood have to spill when reasonable men could still have negotiated? And after those first, horrific battles, why didn't the powers come to the table and discuss solutions other than prolonged mutual destruction?

Didn't our Declaration of Independence from King George, written a mere eighty five years prior, assert

> When in the course of human events it becomes necessary for one people to dissolve the political bands which have connected them with another and to assume among the powers of the earth, the separate and equal station to which the Laws of Nature and of Nature's God entitle them, a decent respect to the opinions of mankind requires that they should declare the causes which impel them to the separation?

If this was valid enough as a reason to bid adieu to King George, why wouldn't it serve as divorce papers for the United States? We could have still had a loose confederation, and fight common enemies and trade freely, but had more sovereignty at a more local level. We're a nation founded on secession. Why isn't our Declaration of Independence a prescription for us to resume our secessionary ways?

Maybe I'm jaded by my War experience, but I'm convinced the whole reason is much simpler than any of the above arguments. The reason North and South went at it in the great American Civil War was simple: they wanted to.

That's right. They wanted to. No other reason is as complete and sufficient as this one.

We've all seen examples of two young boys, or two grown men for that matter. They're a lot alike, but they have some differences. Anyone can see these boys are going to come to blows. First comes a rivalry, then comes fists. Each believes he can whup the other. They may even be best of friends, and when it's over they may remain best of friends, but they're gonna find a reason to mix it up. North and South were just the same way. Call it "boys will be boys," but I called it a sorry excuse for the destruction of life, property and wealth we just witnessed. I hope and pray mankind could learn and grow from this, and maybe we'll never do anything this crazy again.

The mostly-urban North, living out Alexander Hamilton's dream of a country of great cities, and the rural South of Thomas Jefferson's agrarian dream, were together building one mighty fine country. But mutual jealousies, rivalries, power grabs and misunderstandings made war inevitable. It was like a nationwide re-enactment of Hamilton's and Jefferson's childish rivalry resulting in the Civil War.

Did Lincoln cause it, or could he have stopped it? Yes, no and maybe are all defensible answers to this question.

Did Jeff Davis instigate it or could he have nipped it in the bud? Yes, no and maybe would apply here also.

The issues are so complex there's room for everyone to be very right and very wrong all at once, but the bare facts are America suffered over 625,000 total dead from combat and other causes. The entire country was financially busted as a result. We survivors could go to work rebuilding, but the lost lives and families shattered could never be regained. Good men must always make sacrifices for causes greater than self, but this sacrifice was ridiculously out-of-proportion to any possible benefit, and I feared it would be a blight on America for years to come.

What happened was the worst of all possible outcomes, but with God's blessing, maybe the result would be a stronger America, and maybe we learned enough from this mass folly to never do anything like it again. Or maybe mankind is doomed, as we're taught in the book of Proverbs (26:11), "As a dog returneth to his vomit, so a fool returneth to his folly." Maybe we're condemned to repeat these self-destructive and mutually destructive follies forevermore.

I hope not.

I pray not.

Homecoming and Big Change on the Farm

Once the farm was in sight, I knew it was my turn to grow up. I was sure I couldn't be more ready for what awaited me. I was going to bring this farm back to life. We were all going to get healthy again together, and life would be good. My life was set. Just a lifetime of hard, honest work on the land I loved with the people I loved. It was simple, but all I ever wanted.

The men were in the field, but the women and girls were anxious for my arrival. They came a-runnin': Ava, aunts, cousins, and sisters. They were very happy to see me, even Martha Pennington.

"Martha Pennington!" I exclaimed while wondering what was going on. Martha was about a year younger than me. I'd known her all my life. Nobody disliked her but she was no particular friend of any of our girls. "How are you?" I asked. "I'm so sorry about your two brothers; I know it's been a blow to all of you. They really served the cause up there in those Virginia battles."

"Thanks, JH. It destroyed my parents. Momma died of a broken heart, and Daddy doesn't farm enough to even feed us anymore. He just wants to grow enough corn to make his whiskey, and then he mainly just drinks. Your father was very kind to let me move in." Well, it was known Mr. Pennington drank more than he farmed, but I wasn't in a mood for an argument. I was focused on her comment about moving in.

Moved in? Martha Pennington has moved in to the family house? Searching for those non-existent right words, I said, "Daddy's a really kind fellow," while thinking about my worries about the farm feeding John Harley and me. Even though we were going to be working for our food, we were still just two more mouths to feed until we got the store room re-stocked. Martha made yet another mouth. I knew charity was not something to do just in times of plenty. I thought of the parable of the widow's mite, and for the first time in my life, I felt like the poor widow, and it was real hard for me to let go of those two pennies.

The spring vegetables were just beginning to come in. It looked like the Civil War famine was finally getting over with, and since the family wasn't limited to eating only from the family plot anymore, we had both better portions and better variety. We were getting our energy back.

There's an old farmer saying goes, "Don't eat your seed corn." The farms of the South for a while now had been faced with eating the seed corn or starving. And it wasn't only the seed corn, but the breeding cattle, chickens and pigs the family had to eat. In order to not eat our seed corn, we had to eat our feed corn instead of feeding it to the animals, so we had to eat up most of our breeding and milking animals. And that's a lot like eating your seed corn. We hoped those times were over for good, and signs were good they would be. No matter how crazy the political world got, at least we knew we could make the land produce again.

It wouldn't be long before we would no longer had to stretch our cornbread with that sorry old coontie flour; a good thing, too, because even the coontie plants were beginning to get scarce around here. There wasn't even a cabbage palm with its heart left in it. The landscape was splattered with heart palms standing upright and dead with their tops cut out for that edible center core of it. There were young ones sprouting, though, and we'd have plenty of it again soon.

We were still very short on meat. Our edible animals were long gone, and nobody knew how long it would be 'til the wildlife came back. Some of the boys took a trip deep into the swamp south of Ocean Pond in hopes of trapping some piglets to re-stock our herd, and they bagged six of them. We concentrated on rebuilding the pig stock because they could throw off three or four piglets twice a year. Same goes for chickens. Real soon we'd be able to eat some and keep some for reproducing.

With cows, you get no more than one birthing a year, and they take a lot of feeding and a lot of time to grow out. Pigs grow real fast, and they eat anything. Once we got a hog population built and had plenty of corn in the bins again, we'd start to rebuild our cattle. For the time, though, we needed meat, and we needed it fast. That meant rebuilding our farm was all about pigs and chicken; pigs and chicken.

Once most of the boys who were coming home came home, we had a homecoming service at Swift Creek for the returning veterans and to remember those who didn't return.

Most of us farm boys left home for the War with visions of a festive homecoming. We were certain we'd be marching into the church in triumphal glory to a hymn such as this old, but newly translated into English, victory song:

> The strife is o'er, the battle done;
> The victory of life is won;
> The song of triumph has begun:
> Al-le-lu-ia, Al-le-lu-ia!
>
> The powers of death have done their worst,
> But Christ their legions hath dispersed;

Let shouts of holy joy outburst:
Al-le-lu-ia, Al-le-lu-ia.

We just knew the girls would be swooning and we'd be ever-more dashing in our splendid gray CSA uniforms, spit-shined boots and clanking dress swords. Our parents would smile approvingly as their hearts welled with pride, and the young boys would stare with envy and beg to hear story after story about our convincing victory over the Yanks for our just cause.

Instead, those of us valiant soldiers still barely alive hobbled in together sunken eyed, hollowed cheeked and with skin-and-bone frames. Our impoverished and malnourished families looked on dully, still with love for us and our cause, but with the demoralized blank stare of defeat and famishment. Instead of a victory march, we pitifully sang that beautiful funeral hymn *Abide With Me*, written almost twenty years before by a dying Scotsman:

Abide with me; fast falls the eventide;
The darkness deepens; Lord with me abide;
When other helpers fail and comforts flee,
Help of the helpless, O abide with me.

The wailing in that little church was enough to cover fifty funerals. And it really was a funeral, not just for the men who didn't return, but for our wealth, our health, our hopes and our pride in ourselves and everything our Southern cause stood for. We all knew we had to go back to work to rebuild what we'd lost, but we were so spent, broke and broken-spirited that we didn't see how. All we knew was we had to do it and we set out to do it.

I don't remember who the preacher was 'cause it wasn't Barnett and Laura wasn't sitting by my side, but something happened as he delivered the Word to stirred us all. As we left there singing *Amazing Grace* we had our raggedy hearts full of hope once again, and we were set right for our mission to rebuild our weary land. With no idea just how hard it was going to be, we left with a purpose to put behind us the unspeakable tragedy we'd just suffered and to look ahead to what could be.

Soon after, John and Wiley came to see me, saying, "We three need to talk to the slaves." So we went to the farm and told Daniel and Robert to have all the males gather for a meeting a half hour before sundown. Daniel and Robert were patriarchs of a growing family, and we hoped they would be able to give good advice to their younger members, and we hoped the youngers would be able to take good advice. These people, who'd never in their lives had the privilege or responsibility of making decisions, were about to have some very big decisions to make.

John took the floor first. "I guess you're all free to go. I'm here to tell you though, you're also free to stay. It may have been unfair, and it may have even been wrong (we all knew what "it" was), but we've all had a pretty good life here together on this farm. You can each make your own decisions; you don't have to go or stay as a group. If you stay, you will have housing and food, and I will have to start paying you something, I don't know what it'll be yet, but I will make it fair. If you stay in Lee housing, you will be expected to work on the Lee farm. But again, you are free to go. If you leave, then decide you want to come back, I cannot guarantee you a place here. Nobody knows what the future holds for the Southern farms now. Congratulations, and God bless us all."

With that, Wiley said, "All I can add to what Mr. John just said is I hope you will all talk this over with Robert and Daniel before you make your decisions. They are wise men, and they care for each of you. Robert and Daniel will report to me what each of you intends to do. You don't need to make quick decisions, but we need to know as soon as we can."

Wiley asked me to speak, but I only said I had nothing to say and we respected their decisions. I guess that was my first "management" meeting.

We left quietly and wondered what we were going to be facing and how each of the newly freed slaves would decide. The men, women and children numbered twenty and growing. The farm didn't need this number except at harvest time. It had to be a frightful time to be newly freed, just as much as it was a tough time for us staring at the possibility of losing all our farm labor. They finally had the freedom their hearts so yearned for, but they found themselves free men and women in a busted land.

Soon after, we learned the federal government passed a law requiring us Southern farmers to not only free our slaves, but offer them crop share, tenant farming, or daily-wage-type work. Of course, this mandate was bitter for the farmers to swallow, to have the federal government run our lives in a way King George himself wouldn't have dreamed of. Additionally, armies of federal agents were soon to be scattered throughout the South going from farm to farm making sure all the farmers were complying with these laws. It was our first taste of Reconstruction, and we were real sure we didn't like it.

Throughout the land, millions of decisions had to be made. As is often the case, those who acted hastily often made big mistakes. The most common was for younger freed men to grab instantly for their liberty. Of course this choice was understandable, but the men were setting themselves loose in a land where they had no idea how to survive at a time when survival wasn't easy. They'd lived in a world where all decisions were made for them. Most of them couldn't read, write or figure, and they had no idea of the value of their labor, which was their only marketable possession.

Some farmers and freedmen worked out sharecropping arrangements. If the farmer feared he wouldn't have enough labor to run all his land, he might rent out parcels of his farm in exchange for a set share, usually 50/50, of the crop. This agreement worked real well for a few tenants, but in general allowed only for a subsistence living. Since the sharecropper generally had no money, his first crop was all-important because he had no reserves to handle a crop failure or a market failure. The tenants also had to cope with lack of experience and self-discipline. I had to ask myself, "How would I be at handlin' money if I'd never had a quarter in my hand? How would I know I needed to save the money I earned so I could have it for the rainy day?"

Of course, the older slaves and weaker workers would mostly stay on their old farms if they could, but many masters, whether out of frustration, vengeance or because they were broke themselves, would turn loose the older and weaker ones, forcing them out into freedom whether they wanted it or not.

John and Ava together spoke with the women slaves in the same way we spoke with the men. We hoped the women could help the men make good choices.

Speaking of women and choices, the Lee women were hitting their own little rough patch and came to me for help. After a few weeks of listening to the frustrations the girls were having with Martha Pennington I went to Wiley and asked, "What are we going to do with her?" I was still baffled that he'd invited her to live with us on the Lee Farm.

Wiley quietly said, "What was I supposed to do, let her starve with that sot of a father of hers?"

"No, but we've given plenty of people food without taking them into the house," I said logically.

"This one's different. I felt sorry for her because of her mother and brothers dying the way they did. What else can I say?"

My only response as I left was to mutter something I can't even remember. Martha Pennington was certainly a sad case, and I didn't mind giving her some of our scarce food, but she didn't work well or get along well with the other girls. It sure seemed she wasn't trying too hard, either. I watched closely to see if the Lee girls were giving her a cold shoulder or trying to squeeze her out, but for the life of me, Martha seemed to be rejecting their outreach, not the other way around.

I tried talking to Martha and encouraging her to join in with the others and be a part of the family. It certainly took teamwork on the farm and at the house to feed everybody who needed to eat three times, hopefully, every day. We could use more willing hands, but we couldn't handle someone who wouldn't pull her own weight. When Laura was with us, even at her young age, she jumped right in. The girls said they hadn't yet found the job Laura couldn't or wouldn't do, and she was a guest.

When I approached Martha about it, she just told me Wiley said she was welcome here and she needed no other approval. It was my first "management headache" because it was really causing trouble among the other girls.

It was a mystery, but it didn't remain a mystery for long.

After supper one August evening, I took a ride on the farm just after sundown. Charlie and I liked our ride so we could clear our minds and get ready for the next day. I got my best thinking done then, too.

I was real proud of the way our summer crops were coming along. I'd been real grateful, too, for the War famine being over. The CSA gave us its planting order last winter, and it was mostly planted when the CSA suddenly went out of business. We continued to grow most of the fields as commanded, but we took a little of the land and planted some more of the summer vegetables, and we barely had time to plant a small patch of cotton, using some seed we'd stored for the last three years. Life would seem pretty normal again if only I could just shake my soldier's nightmares; they still visited me more nights than not.

On all my nightly rides during the growing season, I made a point of riding by the okra patch. What sweet memories a healthy stand of okra brought to me!

With a steady rotation of vegetables coming in, we were able to again eat our fill each night and some variety came back into our diet. The girls had each added back a pound or two, though most of 'em still needed a little more meat on their bones. The young boys were gaining again, too. Us older boys weren't gaining much yet because we were working so hard, but we'd lost the gaunt look and were finding we had the energy to do our daily work again. They told me what a big change it was from the previous summer. We figured we'd be able to gain some weight after harvest when the workload settled down a bit. We laughed that every one of us still needed a belt, suspenders or both, 'cause nary a one of us had enough ass to hold up a pair o' britches anymore! After the poundin' my poor hiney took from being on horseback for three and a half solid years, I wondered if I'd ever re-grow a backside.

For me, life was a constant daydream of how perfect this farm would be when Laura moved in. Back then I was hopin' it'd only be a little more'n a year, but every five minutes of waiting on my bride to get old enough seemed an eternity to me.

After a thorough ride, I was coming back by the swimming hole 'round about ten o'clock, when I heard laughter. Normally at this hour, it would be the teenage boys, who were known to sneak out for some skinny dipping and horsin' around after a hard day's work. They'd see me and keep on playing; I might even join them. It might be the teenage girls, but you normally heard them giggling clear across the farm. If it was them, they'd squeal and quickly dip into the water deep enough to cover anything they didn't want to show. The giggling would continue and I'd tease 'em about gainin' a little weight on the backside, or some similar foolishness. Then I'd go on.

Expecting a little innocent fun, I quietly dismounted and walked Charlie up behind a large, bushy mulberry tree on the bank. The half-moon had just gone behind a cloud, so it was pitch dark. I shouted out, "Who goes there?"

"JH, it's your Daddy," which I knew instantly by the sound of his deep voice. I quickly stripped jay-bird naked to join Daddy and whoever of my brothers, cousins or uncles it might be with him.

Just as I emerged from behind the mulberry tree, the moon re-emerged from its cloud cover to expose two heads, but I still couldn't make out Daddy's guest.

"Who else? Izzat you, John Harley?" I thought maybe they had some business to talk and did it while cooling off before retiring to the house on this hot, sticky night.

I was casually strolling in and had gotten about knee deep, just when Daddy's guest stood up facing me in the waste-deep water, took a turn, and with a giggle dived toward the middle of the swimmin' hole.

MARTHA!!!

It was my Daddy and a girl younger than two of his own kids!

Best I could tell, they were both naked as the day they were born, 'cause when I darted back to dry land, I looked to my right and saw two complete sets of clothes. They were splayed out in two straight parallel lines about thirty feet long, suggesting the disrobe was done on the run.

"Don't let me interrupt . . . uh, y'all have fun," I shouted, sprinting toward Charlie while scooping up my ownclothes. Charlie and I got out of there just as fast as we could. I gotta admit I was real disturbed by the sight.

My mind was crammed-full with questions about what this meant. But I still had a little room for some other thoughts, like, "I wish it was Laura and me!" But if it was, wouldn't my

195

skinny-dipper father give me the tongue-lashing of a lifetime about the Barnetts being straight-laced and all?

Next day, mid-morning, I saw ol' Dad on the front porch finishing up a meeting with a corn buyer. It was real good to see the private buyers coming around again. Last few years they mostly went to work as CSA Commissars or starved.

"Dad, I thought we oughta talk after last night's swimmin' hole surprise."

He had a kinda sheepish look. "Sit down," he said. "Guess you're wonderin' 'bout it some, huh?"

"A little," I said trying to not act too interested, but my mind was racing.

"Well, I think Martha and I are gettin' kinda' serious. She's turning out to be more than just a stray around here."

"You thinking of marrying her?" No sense beating around the bushes, I thought.

"Yes." No bush-beatin' from him either.

"Have you seen how she works, or doesn't work, with the other girls?"

"Yeah, but it'll work itself out. You know how women are. She says they're cold to her, but I tell her to give 'em a chance and they'll welcome her. She says she's anxious to pitch in and do more but the girls won't let her. She feels real honored and all, but she'd really rather carry her weight. You know she worked like a dog at the Pennington place. Maybe you can help them open up to her a little more."

It just came real clear to me, this poor man has been snowed worse than the whole "Donner Party" we'd been reading about out West. I wondered if I needed to worry about Wiley eating the kids. "Dad, I worry you're lonely since Mom died, and I'm afraid you're jumping at the first offer. You gotta know, if you'll just wait, there's a great supply of fine widows available now on account of the War. Some of them will be more of Mom's caliber. Can't you just wait a while? I know the Barnetts know lots of newly available women, and they'd love to help you get set up with another one like Momma. They miss her a lot, too. And I don't blame you for wanting a young one, but Martha's younger than me!"

Wiley said, "Thanks for your concern, son, but I might wanna do a little different this time around."

I asked just what he might want to do different.

196

"I loved your Momma, you don't ever need to worry about that, and I'd do anything in this world to bring her back to us. I always felt like those McDonalds liked me just fine, too. But ever since we got married, it was plain to me they thought I coulda been a little more refined; polished, they might say. With Martha, I'm real sure she ain't a-gonna be correctin' m' grammar no more. I think she's a real decent gal. She likes me just fine for who I am, and she ain't feelin' no need to be polishin' me none." He knew exactly what he was saying, and if Mary Lee had heard him talk such a way, she'd have let him have it. He could talk sloppy on the farm, but I never heard such plain talk from him around Mary's house. I figured the poor ol' boy was just real lonely and was falling for the first feminine company he could get.

And the figure Martha showed me last night at the swimmin' hole sure was feminine.

"So you love her because she doesn't speak well?" Wiley's look told me I hit a nerve, so I quickly excused myself to go check on the melon picking crew. I hoped my question might make him think, but solid logic isn't usually too influential when it's stacked up against a nightly trip to the swimmin' hole.

On the way to the farm, I thought a lot about Momma's education of all her kids. Even though I was just a farmboy, I had enough learnin' to be able to talk to the most educated lawyer or professor in Florida. I could also speak on the level of the simplest farmhand in a way the high-falutin' lawyer couldn't. I fancied myself sort of bi-lingual that way.

I felt bad for the younger kids. Under the future Martha Lee, they were sure to get none of the solid education us older ones did, and my guess was Martha wasn't going to be too worried about even the basics for them. I wished I could tell Momma thanks for all she made me learn, even though I didn't much appreciate it at the time.

Later in the afternoon, while the girls were busy cleaning the house, dishes and clothes and weeding the garden plot, I saw Martha idly swinging in the bench-swing under the big oak. I thought I might use this opportunity to get to know my year-younger-soon-to-be-step-mother a bit better.

"Hi, Martha, sorry to happen up on you two last night. I hope you weren't too embarrassed."

"Oh, not at all," she said. "We was just havin' a little fun. You know, ah'm shore. I figger you and yer li'l Miss Laura probley slip down there, too, when ya can. Ya coulda joined us if ya wanted. After all, looked to me like you was dressed just right fer it," she teased.

"Thanks for the invitation, and you made it mighty attractive, but it looked like a private party to me." I thought a little flattery might grease these wheels a little before I got to the point. Ignoring her dig about Laura, I got to the point. "So, you and Dad are kinda serious?"

"Oh, yes, it's been love ever since y'all first took me in."

"Well, congratulations, I guess. Aren't you worried about the age difference?"

"Not at all. He swears I make him feel yours and my age again, and it sure seems it to me!"

"Well, can I suggest if you're going to be permanent with us, you might help yourself a little if you'd pitch in with the girls a little more, y'know, work with them and get to know 'em a little better. They work hard and laugh hard and pray hard, and they'd welcome you to join 'em. And they are each other's best friends. You know how lonely it can be out here, but not a one of the Lee Farm girls would trade the life she lives out here because of the way they all get along. They can always use the extra hands, but even more, they love to see their circle grow. They're a big part of the success of this farm."

"Oh, JH, I don't think that'll be necessary, cuz I'm gonna be Mizz Wiley Lee, and I won't really need to be workin' *with* them, 'cause they're a-gonna be working *for* me. They don't know it yet, but they will soon."

"Martha, you're talking about your future family here. And the black ladies, they're family here, too." Then I added, "So, when Laura and I get married, will she be working for you, too?"

Martha smiled a huge confident smile, "Of course not, silly. She's just a baby, but since she's a-gonna be Mizz JH Lee, I can teach her how to run a house like a fittin' an' proper lady. Them others'll be working for her, too. JH, I've had my share of workin' my bloomin' ass off, and you see where it got me. You know I'm twenty years old now, and I done been a-strugglin' on my family's farm since I was born'd. An' I ain't never seen a nickel for my labors there. This is my chance to be somebody. I love yore Daddy an' he loves me, an' that there's the way hitsa gonna be. Me and him are gonna get married, and none of them mules o' your'n on that there farm o' your'n can stop us."

I had some thoughts I won't share here, but if you let your imagination run wild, you'll probably come pretty close.

Well, by now you know the Lee women well enough to know this was a disaster in the makin'. Lees were pioneer, hard-working women, and they were not going to spend their lives working for some young backwoods matriarch. Our farm was about work and teamwork, and it's been running smoothly for a long time just that way. We had no room for make-believe royalty. If given enough time, surely Dad would see and back away, but Miss Martha was clearly on a sprint for a wedding date, and yesterday woulda been just fine for her. She had one thing on her mind, and Dad, I'm afraid, had one thing on his. They weren't the same things, but they both led straight up to a wedding.

We began to notice most evenings Martha and dear ol' Dad would kinda disappear shortly after supper. First one of them was missing, then the other. I just made sure to stay away from the swimmin' hole when I made my nightly rounds. In those days of farmhouses loaded with sometimes more than twenty souls, you'd find mommas and daddies had to do lots of disappearing, because they sure weren't gonna get any peace and quiet at the house. Our house was no different.

I felt powerless to do anything about the Wiley and Martha situation, and it wasn't getting any better. I couldn't talk to Dad about it and the girls couldn't get Martha to budge from her throne.

In mid-September, they made the announcement. Wiley and Martha were going to marry in a month. I tried a few more times to throw some cold water on them and get them to at least slow down, but it was no use.

It became clear my role in the life of the farm had changed. I was not going to be the one to someday take over this farm. I saw no way in tarnation I could live and work under a step-mother who was a year my junior, and I wasn't about to subject Laura to her kind of leadership and domination. Maybe it's my own fault, call it pride or jealousy, but I was just real sure my father was making a big mistake. Not that the farm couldn't keep on supporting lots of folks, but something was just not right.

After knowing since birth this farm was my lot in life, I just didn't fit there anymore.

And it was alright with me. 'Twas just a change of plans; a very major change of plans. I was just going to have to try again. I would chart a new course. The old life-map I'd followed since I was born just got ripped to shreds like the seat of my old CSA britches.

I had to talk to Laura. And Jabish. And Granddaddy John.

First, I went to John. I had no idea what he would think or say. But after laying out for him the difficulty I thought I'd have working around Martha, I think he understood. I said I didn't know if he was aware of the silent rift between all the girls and Martha. Usually the old wolf is the smartest one in the pack, so as you might expect, John had this whole thing sized up just about the minute Martha moved in.

In his usual way, he broke it down to the very simplest logic. "You remember what I taught all you boys, from before you were old enough to understand what it meant?"

Well, John taught us lots of things, and most of them included a very colorful, and oh so memorable, punchline. "I'm not sure, which lesson do you mean?" I asked inquisitively.

"You think about it a minute and let me know."

My mind ran wild as it searched through all the wisdom this old man had imparted me in my young years:

"Is it: 'It's OK to rest on the Sabbath, but first you should work the first six days'?"

"Nope"

"How 'bout 'A nickel saved is worth more than a nickel earned'?"

"Wrong again."

"To train a dog, you should first be smarter than the dog?"

"Not even close," he laughed.

Trying again, I said, "Maybe it's, 'Be kind to folks on your way up, because those are the same ones you'll see on the way down.'"

John smirked and said, "I coulda benefited from that one a time or two myself, but it's not the one I'm lookin' for."

"What can't be cured must be endured?"

"You might apply it to this case, but it's not the one I'm thinking of." Here came my first hint when he asked, "Which one did you boys never understand until you became teenagers?"

"Oooohhh!" Suddenly it was very obvious what he wanted me to recite: "Nothin' good happens when a man lets his brain go down to his britches."

John Lee reared back and his laugh shook the walls. "Now your thinkin'! I knew you'd come up with it sooner or later. You know there's an adult version of it, too, don't you?"

"Yes, sir, you taught me that'n, too, when I was a little older."

"Well I used the grown-up version on your Daddy, and he got all bent out of shape. But it's exactly what he's done. You'd always expect to need this kind of advice to get into young heads, but looks like your Daddy is an old dog itchin' to learn some new tricks, and ain't much we can do about it." Changing the mood he said, "JH, it looks like he's got his feet firmly set in quicksand. None of us can understand it, and nobody'd a-thought it would be old reliable Wiley goin' off this way. At this point I think all we can do is pray for him, and pray for the best, and try to help the other girls have a sense of humor about it 'cause I hear they're about ready to string her up."

Then he added, "And I'm about half-ready to lend 'em the rope."

I told John I was thinking my place might not be at the farm after all. I was starting to feel the call of making it on my own and heard of very good prospects for lumbermen, since we had so many of the Shermanized cities to rebuild. Re-building Atlanta alone was going to have every sawmill for miles around buzzing for years to come.

I told him I was on my way to tell Laura and Jabish and wasn't real sure how it was going to go. I said if Laura rejected me, I didn't know if I'd want to live any longer. He told me if she couldn't accept the change, maybe it was a gift to both of us and we weren't meant to be anyway. I should be thankful for the good she showed me and trust there'd be a perfect little Mrs. Lee for me someday.

"Just don't worry and it'll all work out somehow. Ours isn't to pick our journey but to do our very best on the path we're placed, trust God for the rest, then work like hell!" We both got a good laugh. He never failed to lighten the mood when I got too serious.

Granddaddy John's advice was good as always, but it was real hard to hear him say Laura and I might not be right for each other when the feelings were so strong.

I made the trip to Sanderson. I never minded having a reason to go to Sanderson, but I feared this trip might be my last. Laura or her parents might think differently of me if I wasn't going to be the head of the Lee Farm anymore. But they needed to know and I sure needed to know how they'd take it.

I spoke with Laura first, then told her I'd like to talk with the parents right after dinner with all four of us, as if I was asking pastoral advice. I hadn't yet told her I'd had "the talk" with her father a few months before, and I was sure Jabish hadn't told her. I really thought I needed Laura beside me that day. I thought if she was, Jabish wouldn't do anything too rash, like kicking me out of the house and telling me never to come back again. He was a stern fellow, but Laura was the apple of his eye, and he'd have a real hard time being too hard on me in front of her. So went my theory.

After a nice supper with the whole family, I asked Reverend and Mrs. Barnett if we could meet on the front porch. Laura and I found ourselves sitting on the porch swing while her parents sat in separate wooden rockers. At the conclusion of my presentation, ol' Jabish took a long draw on his corncob pipe, and said, "Well, JH, I reckon this doesn't change much as far as I can tell. Laura's still too young, anyway, so it gives you a little time to get yourself established and prove to her and us and yourself you can support her. Let's say if you have $200 in the bank, and a respectable place for you both to live, and you're supporting yourself in your new endeavor, then I will give my blessing." Then he paused, and added, "And I mean it's to be earned money. You're not going to go to your family, and you can't get a loan from one of your friends. You've got to show me you earned it all."

"Thank you, sir," I said. "But there's one thing we never made clear. Exactly what age is old enough?"

"Eighteen."

"BUT, SIR! That's almost four years from now. There's no way I can wait so long to marry Laura."

"Why?" He demanded.

Oooops. The complete answer to this one woulda been, "Because we want to set up housekeeping together," but I didn't think that'n would sail too well, so I tried, "Because Laura and I are meant to be together. We're better together than apart. We all know she's young, but there's no doubt she's wiser and more mature than any woman I know of, at even twenty-two! She's surely more mature than my future step-mother."

"Martha ain't my daughter either, is she?"

"Well, no sir, she's not, and I'm real glad of it, because your daughter is the one I love. And I want to be married to her, and I want to marry her on her sixteenth birthday, and it's just two years and a month away. You know it's the legal age. She can make her own decisions then."

Jabish sat up real straight and sucked on his pipe so hard, the little ball of tobacco in it looked like it was going to ignite, "Are you threatening me, boy?"

"No sir, I'm not threatening; I'm appealing. You know I've never had a shine for anyone but Laura, and I want you to know I will protect and support her 'til my dying breath. And when I die I'm going to leave her comfortable. And there's just no use in making her wait 'til she's eighteen. You know me as well as you know any of the young men in your whole circuit, and

I hope you think I'm as good as any of 'em. You know my family stresses education like you do, and you know how rare that is out here. I want your grandchildren to have the same benefit. Together Laura and I will make sure all your grandkids will be educated in the faith, and numbers, reading and music." Now what preacher could ask for more in a son-in-law, I thought to myself.

"We know I'm not going to be the master of the Lee Farm anymore, but I propose to you, maybe it's even better for Laura and me. The farm is supporting so many folks now. We'd do just fine there, but there's too much opportunity in rebuilding our country for me to just chain myself to one place. This whole area's going to rebuild from the War. It's already started and it's gonna be so much better than it ever was. By time I'm thirty, I'm going to have so much more money of my own than I ever could have saved working the farm. I believe in this so much, I'm willing to ask you to make a different agreement. I want you to give me your daughter's hand in Holy Matrimony, at the Sanderson Methodist Church, with you tyin' the knot. And it'll be as soon as I've saved up not two, but *four* hundred dollars, and of course, have a fittin' place for a young couple to live." I found my voice rising, but couldn't help it, "If she's not sixteen yet, I will need you to sign for her, of course."

Jabish chuckled at my sudden combination of brashness and desperation. Having four hundred in the bank in two years or less in those times was unthinkable, especially to a man of the cloth. "You going to tithe your money every week as you go along?"

"Of course I am, sir. The Good Book commands it." My voice still too loud, I was thinking my real answer should have been, "Ooops. I never thought of the tithe, Ouch!" Deciding to up the ante one final time, I added, "And I'll even clean the Sanderson church after Sunday services every Sunday I'm here." Having bid up about as much as I possibly could, and out of words, I blurted out . . . "Please?" Not a real strong closing argument, but I hoped it showed sincerity. And I'd never been more sincere in all my days.

We stood man to man, eye to eye, like two bulls snortin' and pawin', ready to fight over a little calf. The old bull had everything in his favor because he had the most control, but the young bull was loaded with so much determination and was fueled by as true a love as ever existed, and the old bull knew it. The old bull just couldn't make it easy on the young one because his prize-possession in all the earth was at stake.

As they stared, oblivious to any other soul in the room, they heard a voice they both knew as precious coming from behind me. Speaking very softly, Laura said, "Do I matter in this?"

The two bulls slowly, curiously turned their attention to the little she-calf they were fighting over and sheepishly gave Laura the floor.

203

"You two are the men I love, and it irritates me real good to see you negotiating me like I'm some female slave in shackles. Daddy, I will always love and honor you, and you know it. JH, if you want to chase me away, just keep negotiatin' like I'm a sack of potatoes. You know I want to marry you, although you've never asked me. Daddy, JH is right, I'm mature enough to do this, and you know it. Momma and Mrs. Mary Lee taught me right, and I learned their lessons. I'm ready to have young'uns, just ask Momma." Julia blushed and nodded but Laura just kept on, "And I sure know how to keep a house. JH, Daddy's right, you need to get established in your . . . whatever it is you're gonna do. You know I don't mind being poor; remember I was raised by two generations of Methodist ministers. But you need to be able to have things going so you don't worry about me. And I can wait for a while, but if it doesn't work we're going to go back to farming. Those are *my* terms. Do y'all want the deal or not?"

Well, the two bulls just looked at each other, kind of dumbfounded. If there was such a thing as a sheepish bull, the Barnett front porch had two of 'em that day. Jabish said to me, "Four hundred, all tithed up, suitable place to live, plus the church cleaned weekly?"

"You've never seen anybody work as hard as I'm going to work for Laura, Rev. You won't be sorry you made the deal." I held out my right hand and we shook on it, just like it was some kind of business deal.

Mrs. Julia Ann Barnett said her first words of this whole session, "Is that your idea of a proposal to my daughter, Mr. Lee?"

"No, ma'am, *this* is a proposal." I spun around, took a knee and grabbed Laura's tiny right hand in my two big old leathery clubs I called hands. I said, "Laura Augusta Barnett, you'll make me the happiest man in the world if you'll marry me and spend the rest of your life with me, and I will work myself to the bone to make you the happiest girl, er, I mean lady, in the world. Please say yes."

"Now there's a proposal, isn't it Momma?" Laura added, "And I'm going to take your offer and I'm going to turn it right back around to you. I can't wait, and I hope it's tomorrow."

Then she turned to her father, "Daddy?"

"Yeah." he said, kinda choked up.

Then, getting creative as she always was, Laura asked, "Can we rob a bank on Monday to get those four hundred dollars you want us to have?"

We all laughed, but how I wished there was a way we could do just that, and get away with it.

I then asked, "If we fixed up our prison cell real nice, wouldya call it a fittin' place for Laura?"

Jabish smiled, amused at his little girl, then said, "Nope. It's gotta be clean dollars."

After a little celebration I said, "Well time's a-wastin' for me. And I've got to go get started to make it happen. Laura, I may not be able to see you except on Sundays, but I'm going to live up to my bargain and we're gonna get started, and . . . WE'RE . . . GONNA . . . GET . . . MARRIED!" We kissed right in front of her parents. When I caught myself, I looked their way afraid I'd just killed the whole deal, just to see Mrs. Barnett beaming.

Jabish, trying to act disgusted, said, "Ma, quick go get a bucket of water, those two are hotter'n a cheap pistol!" He seemed to enjoy the moment, too.

I headed for the door as Jabish shouted, "How do you plan to do all this anyway?"

"LUMBER!" I shouted back as Laura and I rushed out the door.

Then at the top of his preacher's voice he boomed, "A good name is rather to be chosen than great riches, and loving favor rather than silver or gold." I believe all of Sanderson shook with this pronouncement.

"Yes sir, Proverbs, 22:1, and Laura Barnett is the finest silver and gold this world can offer me. And I aim to make her the happiest gal in the land!"

I kissed her again, mounted Charlie and was on my way to Lake City. "I should be able to tell y'all my plans next time."

She ran up to Charlie, somehow hiked her little foot all the way up to my boot, hoisted her hand up to the saddlehorn, then sprang up and spun herself into her favorite sidesaddle position in front of me. "You're taking me to the edge of town, Mr. JH Lee."

"It might cost ya four hundred dollars, ma'am," I joked.

"How are you going to get four hundred dollars before I'm an old lady, anyway? You know my Daddy never had half as much to his name." Snuggling up a little, she said, "Whenever he got a little savings, he'd always see somebody he thought needed it more'n he did. I respect it in him, but I like your ideas of building something for your family and want to help you however I can."

"You watch me. There's more opportunity in this old beat up land than I can shake a stick at."

Laura added, "You know my uncle, John Tucker, he's done real well down in Orange County and says anybody can make good in cattle in that country. He still calls it Mosquito County, but I hear of lots of folks around here talkin' about moving there."

"Good for him," I said, "But we're staying right here. I heard both my Granddaddies talk about how tough things were here when they settled this land, and I'm pretty sure we want to stay and be part of rebuilding, not building from the ground up."

Then we turned the corner, finally out of sight of the Barnett house. All the way to the edge of town we were silent, unless you count that smackin' sound. I never realized how small Sanderson was. Maybe the good Reverend should move to a big city so the edge of town wouldn't be such a short ride.

The New Business

I knew exactly what I was going to do, but was real glad Jabish didn't cross-examine my plans. I wanted to have a plan in place to inform him rather than ask if my plans were good enough to meet his standards. I figured it'd be harder for him to pick me apart if I presented plans, not just ideas.

I headed to Lake City, and straight to the Cone Brothers farm. They had a workable but kind of rickety sawmill in the back of their farm. During the War, they talked to me about joining them when they fired it up again. They knew there was going to be a boom from all the new houses and businesses rebuilding and starting up. One thing new houses and businesses surely needed was lumber. I was flattered by their overtures but told them my course was already charted. Fortunately, they were still anxious to talk seriously with me and happy my well-charted life's path took a detour. As I approached the Cone Farm, I got really excited for all the possibilities that might come from this meeting.

The brothers, James Barnard Cone, who went by Barnard, and William "Billy" Haddock Cone, were well-known around these parts. Their father was a famous Indian fighter, and the boys made names for themselves during the very brief Third Seminole War, particularly through victories over Seminole Chief Billy Bowlegs. In the Civil War, Barnard, Billy and other brothers were in the Cavalry with us Lees. Prior to the War, they were successful farmers and politicians. Like most mid-Florida farmers, the War left them with slim-pickin's, but they were anxious to try again.

Barnard was a handsome gentleman of thirty-six, tall and with a full, bushy, dark beard but clean shaven sidewhiskers. His eyes were deep-set, dark and probing. He struck a posture similar to Abe Lincoln. A lot of folks said if Abe had been handsome, he'da looked like Barnard Cone. Barnard liked to add, "And if Honest Abe had been honest, I wouldn'ta gone to war against him!"

Barnard was also my uncle because in 1852 he married my Aunt Sarah Lee, John and Ava's third child. Even though he was my uncle, he never let me call him anything other than Barnard.

Billy was the older brother at forty. A dapper dresser with a clean, always trimmed goatee, he became a good friend to Wiley during the War and had an ever-friendly demeanor about him.

While we served together, the Cone Brothers told me I had a standing offer to buy in as a full partner, but I had another idea. I was sure I wanted to be a part of this business, but not yet. I needed money fast so I could claim my prize from Jabish Barnett.

"Here's my deal," I told Barnard and Billy, "I will work for you for room, board and no money per month to start. You take care of all mine and Charlie's expenses, and I will be the salesman you've been looking for. I can live in those empty slave quarters in back of Barnard's house. As soon as I start bringing in sales, I want to earn a commission on my sales. But I don't want it in cash, it goes into my "Partnership Account." I can travel all you want me to, but I will need to be in Lake City on Thursday, Friday and Saturday nights because I'm going to work your new bar, *The Rebel's Rest,* on those nights. I know you need an honest man who's not an alcoholic on those busy nights. Any bar in the South can make good money if it can only find a barkeep who won't either steal or drink up the profits. You know I'm your honest non-drinker, and I know I'm the salesman who can soon be a partner with you in your lumber business. I will save my money from the bar so I can get married. I will only do the bar job until I get my marryin' money, though. My future's not in any bar, but at the sawmill." With the Cone Brothers' strict Baptist background, I thought it odd they were in a bar business, but these times required lots of people to do whatever it took to get by. Just financially speaking, a bar serving Rebel veterans was one fine way of getting by.

I figured I could also help with the timber buying, because every landowner in Middle and East Florida knew my family, but I figured I was going to be the most help in getting this lumber sold. I figured anybody can run a sawmill, but not everybody can sell all they can cut.

I got so excited I nearly ran out of air, but I kept on, "Billy, Barnard, I like your plans for building the sawmill into more than just a board business and your vision to make the high mark-up products like millwork. We can buy the machinery sooner if we can get the mill to running long shifts and six days a week. Once the banks start lending again, they're gonna see we're a real business, not just any old sawmill operation. The sooner they see it, the sooner we'll get the capital to expand. And now you know why I want to work for near-free, so what I don't cost you goes straight into profit. I'm also proposing you both take no money from the operation until the banks will lend us the money to build the big new steam-powered plant we're all dreaming of. If we can be the first in Florida to have a steam-powered band saw, we will be on our way. We'll have plenty of time for drawin' big salaries when the business can easily afford it.

"Furthermore, I've worked the bookkeeping for the Lee farm since I was ten. My Momma taught me to keep the books as part of my lessons. I can save you from having to hire a bookkeeper by doing the books myself on Monday through Wednesday nights unless I'm on a sales trip. Again, every profit we make goes straight to savings - retained earnings, my Momma taught me to call it.

"I know I can't work this pace forever, but we can easily hire folks like bookkeepers once we're doing volume enough to support them. Then I can focus only on my sellin'! You gotta protect me though. I need your help in makin' sure Reverend Barnett doesn't get wind of my second job in the bar . . . If he does, I know he's not going to like it, but I don't know for sure how he'll react. I just hope it doesn't surface. This is the biggest risk I'm taking in this whole thing, and it means everything to me."

Billy spoke up, "I don't see much to dislike about your offer here, JH, but you're sure asking us to put a lot of eggs in your basket, aincha?"

"Uh, not really. I'm just askin' you to put your old sawmill in the basket with a little bit of working capital, then let's not take any eggs out of the basket until the basket's real full. I'm your best shot at realizing your dream of having the finest sawmill in Florida. You both have too much other business to focus on the sawmill. It'll never be anything more'n a dream if you don't let me or someone else just like me run with it. I'm just pompous enough to think there ain't a lot of folks like me around here. If you want to put those plans on hold and go find the other fellow who can and will take over your struggling operation, it's alright with me, but I can sell this same deal to probably four other sawmills around these parts. And you know how lovesick and motivated I am to get going so I can get married. You two Cone Brothers are the best fit for me too, because you're widely known, and we can lever our names together. You've got to work it with me, and I know you've got divided interests with your other businesses, but together, and with me focused on nothing else, I think we're on our way, especially if we can grab the lion's share of the re-building business. If we can quick get to be the biggest and best, we'll prevent a lot of competition."

Barnard chimed in, "You're quite the planner, aren't you, Lee?"

"John Lee taught me 'Failing to plan is same as planning to fail,' so he would take your question as quite a compliment."

At this point, the lumber industry was dead throughout the South because most Southerners were focused on only one thing: survival. Most were still mourning the South's loss, its lost, its wounded and the stagnant business climate, with little hope for improvement in sight.

We agreed once the first season's crops were in the barn, Floridians would begin to see some revenues with spendable dollars. They'd become convinced they weren't going to starve, and within a year they'd start investing in improving their rundown farms. Any lumberyard up, running and ready for this boom would profit mightily. We didn't know if Reconstruction money would flow from the federal government, but we were set up for a boom either way. If the money was to flow as promised, the building boom would be unbelievable.

The Cone Brothers quickly decided to take a chance on me and agreed to my whole plan. My Granddaddy John taught me, "There's never a time so good that somebody ain't losing money, nor is there a time so bad that someone ain't makin' money." We took this as gospel and forged ahead to be the most efficient, lean and productive sawmill in the business, one built to make profits in the fattest or leanest times. It was a big chance for a young buck like me, at twenty-one, to stake my claim in the business world and set my course for good.

I may have been postponing my wedding day some by taking so little up front, but I didn't believe Jabish would allow me to marry Laura before her sixteenth birthday anyway, regardless of our deal. I aimed to get this business going and have the money before then.

You could say I made my deal for my living quarters "sight unseen." I could see them from Barnard's farm office. They looked a little unkempt, not in as good condition as the Lee quarters, but I lived on a trail for almost three years for the CSA, so I figured nothing was going to shock me. I just assumed the inside would be similar to what I was accustomed to.

One first look proved otherwise. When I opened the door, the stench overwhelmed me. It was a combination of soggy rotten thatch, animal waste, dead animal, and piled up garbage. The other contributing smells remain a mystery. I was alright with it, though, 'cause I figured anything could be aired out, but there were no windows and only the skinny door with sagging leather strap hinges would allow air in or out. Even with no windows, I quickly noted by the size of the gaps between the wall boards that I should always be sure to check outside before changing clothes to make sure no one was around. Otherwise, I was gonna be puttin' on a free show.

Well, this wasn't exactly the image I conjured when singing *Home, Sweet Home* around many a soldier's campfire, but I decided to take my first step into my new abode. As I walked in, I saw the instant action of scurrying roaches, probably two hundred of them infesting the garbage pile. I knew I could take care of them in short order. Roaches I could handle, but not . . . FLEAS! Oh no, by time I made it to the middle of my twelve-by-twelve manse, my legs were nearly black with hungry fleas. I went running out, jumpin' and swattin' like a crazy man. I ran to Cone's workshop and found a half-full gallon jug of turpentine. Dousing it on a rag I found, I spread it all over my clothes and exposed skin, then I stripped down and got it over every inch of me, and hoped it would work. I knew I could count on vinegar to control fleas, I just couldn't find any. Turpentine would have to do. And it did.

Next, I had to make my little bit of turpentine spread evenly throughout my new nest and hope it would kill the bugs or at least chase them away. Of course, it wouldn't hurt the stench in there, either, and might just chase away some of the vermin in the roof. I put my clothes back on, found some binder's twine and tied my pants tightly at the cuff to keep the fleas off my legs. I then sparingly put some more of the turpentine on my britches legs and feet to keep more fleas from jumping on me. Then it was back to Chateau Cone for round two of the flea wars.

The four walls were made of only upright one-by-eight rough-hewn pecky cypress boards with no overlap. Originally I thought I would add some overlap boards to better insulate it in the winter, but then I figured I'd better keep all the open gaps between those boards for ventilation. Hard to imagine this space could have housed as many as ten humans.

The floor was hard-packed clay, and once I got all the trash out, it didn't appear to be in bad shape at all.

When Barnard heard of the condition of my, shall we say, accommodations, he came running down, all embarrassed, but laughing. "I hear you're complaining about your room already. Shall I request the innkeeper find another more to your liking?" He said formally and with a huge dose of sarcasm.

"I guess a deal's a deal, and I try not to be a complainer, but it can use some work, Barnard. Unless *Cone Lumber* doesn't mind having the flea-bitten-est salesman in all the South, we might better give it a little tending." We laughed.

What Cone didn't know was I already had my first commission client lined up.

We met at Olustee. He was in Colquitt's Georgia Cavalry. A cooper, a maker of barrels, my friend Jeremiah Tart was from a long line of coopers and after the War was going to follow the family business. He had written me recently to tell me his family was sending him to Lake City to start a new cooperage. I knew he needed a steady supply of high quality white oak barrel-lumber, and I knew Cone Brothers could provide it.

He'd already committed to buy his lumber from us as long as we gave good quality, timely delivery and a competitive price. I was pretty sure we could do all three. The only problem was, to get white oak in the quantity and quality he needed, we had to go to Apalachicola.

Tart's barrels were known far and wide. They were used for dry shipping of grains, nails, tobacco, fruits, vegetables, gunpowder and flour, to name just a few, but I think the booming new citrus industry was the big reason the Tarts wanted to operate in Lake City.

From there, new barrels could be delivered to all the new towns being built around oranges. It was an easy delivery to Hogtown, Orange Lake, Citra, Ocala, Orange Springs and all sorts of other towns booming on the hopes of citrus growing. With faster ships and better rail service, the hardy orange could make it into any number of Northern markets before spoiling. I still had the citrus growing and packing business in my mind for someday, but for the time it was nothing but lumber, lumber, lumber!

Mr. Tart also promised to take me to Valdosta and introduce me around to the lumber users there. They would soon have shortages of wood products because of the huge demand coming in from Atlanta and all the smaller towns and cities between Atlanta and Savannah, all those towns in ol' Sherman's path of destruction, and that was just the beginning!

The most hated man in all the South in those days was General Sherman, but if I were to meet him, I wouldn't know whether to give him a belly full of lead or a hug. He sure created lots of demand for what I had to sell.

Because the market got stronger with every mile closer to Atlanta, we thought we might be able to sell wholesale to lumberyards in Valdosta and Macon. The wholesale buyers would then re-sell it into the Atlanta market. Now we'd rather sell it to a user than wholesale it; but if we developed good wholesale markets, our volume would drive our costs per board-foot down and make us ever more competitive.

It became obvious we needed to tie up as much supply as we could get for as many years as we could. We set out to tie up as much as five years' supply of trees. Once other sawmills got into business, the price of trees was sure to go higher. If we could get guaranteed supply for a few years, we could own the world! Our little mill had a long way to go, but what a promising future.

As you can see, I was entering into one of the busiest and most exciting times of my life. I'd left the farm where I thought life was all laid out for me, and thrust myself into the rough and tumble world of business at a time when the entire South was hobbled. Looked to me like it had nowhere to go but up. I was also trying my hardest to get my family established. Ah, you could just smell opportunity in the air. If Granddaddy John was a young man, I thought, wouldn't he be excited by all the possibilities?

The sawmill building was nothing more than a wide-open pole barn, supported by eight stout cypress logs. It was about thirty feet wide and sixty feet long, with a flat tin roof, slanted just enough to let the rain run off. The burner for the steam engine had a tin smokestack protruding through the roof.

Our machinery was very rickety. The mill was run by a sure enough steam engine, but all the sitting out in the weather it did during the War was not friendly to it. Once it started running again, it quickly had more patches than a crazy quilt.

The big saw could cut in half any tree we could manhandle or mule-handle onto the table. The table was about three feet high and twenty feet long with rollers to aid in sliding the logs into the blade.

There were two other saws, both smaller, for cutting the larger boards into smaller boards. The finer the teeth on the saw blade, the better and smoother the cut was. Then we had the planing station, but planing a board smooth was just a hand operation in those early days. Soon we'd have machines for the job, but at the start fine planing was strictly hand labor. It was done in another barn of about thirty feet by thirty feet. We couldn't wait to get one of those new steam-driven planers.

The steam engine pushed a big piston in and out, which turned a big pulley. It was connected to a much smaller pulley in the rafters by a huge leather belt. The pulley turned a long shaft which was attached to the rafters and ran the length of the mill. Whenever we got a new machine needing power from the steam engine, all we had to do was attach another pulley to the shaft and another belt to the pulley. When that piston was moving we had power.

Our heavy wagons for hauling the logs into the mill were worn out. We could use them for short haul runs, but they were unreliable for the longer runs we planned. We had enough to get started, though, so we were in business. For the time being, we just kept patching up what we had and making it work, but we knew we'd need newer and bigger equipment as the business grew.

The Cones were in charge of getting the equipment back in working shape and I was to go tie up some trees to cut get some lumber orders coming in. We were in business. We were the first lumberyard to re-open after the War, and were committed to being the biggest and best in all of Middle Florida. We were on our way!

In mid-October 1865, Wiley's wedding to Martha Matilda Pennington happened without a hitch. The Lee clan and Martha made their peace. Martha came to grips with her new lot *not* being one of a woman of leisure. Indeed, she had ten of Wiley's children, aged from three to twenty, living at home. About the same number of Ava's and John's were still on the farm, and this new woman who was just beyond childhood herself became step-mother, step-niece, step-aunt, step-sister or step-cousin to the whole clan. It was probably not the life she'd expected when she first set her designs on Wiley, but she really did seem to want to be

Mrs. Wiley Lee, and things looked to be in order. After the wedding I congratulated Wiley, told him I knew he would be happy, and wished him all the best. However, inside me, my head was shaking and my mind just couldn't quite figure out what made those two think they were so right, especially now that the Hamilton County War widows were past their proper mourning stage and were making themselves seen and known. Wiley could have had his pick of the litter. Talk about the spoils of War!

Come to think of it, I coulda taken my own advice and put myself up for highest bid, too. But why hold out for some wealthy planter's daughter when I could have a dirt-poor preacher's daughter named Laura Barnett? Or maybe the saying is true, "There's a Jack for every Jill," and there's just no explaining affairs of the heart.

The first real honeymoon of the Lee clan took place after Wiley's wedding. After Jabish tied the knot under the big oak tree, they had a little celebration around the house then headed to the White Springs Hotel. They stayed there for three nights then came back to the farm to start their lives together. I truly wished them the best, but I felt very sad for this new chapter of much less education and at home. Martha had surely put some spring back in Wiley's step, but this wedding drove home to me how much the Lee Farm and its people missed Momma.

I remained very busy getting my life started and working hard toward my prize of my own new life with Laura. I made a promise to myself to never again wish time away, but I can't tell you how badly I wished I could suddenly add two years to Laura's age to make her marry-able. The time I had to spend to ripen her enough to get Jabish's blessing was harder than any prison sentence I could've imagined.

1866 was a year of making great strides and developing the business. If I hadn't been so busy and so enthralled with building the business, I would have gone crazy wishing Laura's and my lives away to more quickly get to "I do."

She helped me make my slave quarters livable by sewing some curtains to hang over the shutters we made with scraps from the *Cone Brothers Lumberyard*. I went to sleep most nights admiring those fancy curtains and dreaming their creator was there with me. She also found some things to hang on the wall to make it as homey as possible and added an old threadbare throw rug to make the dirt floor look a little less, well, dirty.

Post-War Politics and Reconstruction

I was in love, and I had a golden chance to make something of myself in my own business. I couldn't see anything wrong anywhere I turned; however, real life was a lot more complicated than my rosy view of it at the time.

Political life in Florida in the post-War years could be summarized like this: it was a mess.

The War was over, and business was dead. Throughout the South, the one buyer all farmers had, the CSA, was out of business and bankrupt. All the glorious War left most of us was a whole lot of dead boys, heartbroken wives, children, parents, an economy in a shambles and a bunch of worthless money. At least when the Continental currency went to no value about ninety years ago, we had emerged victorious, not crushed.

With Governor Milton's suicide added to Lincoln's assassination, and Andrew Johnson haplessly groping for a way to lead, Florida was in total chaos for leadership. It didn't matter, though, because soon we were under martial law.

One desperate need for rebuilding the state was the repair of the old bankrupt railroads and construction of new ones, but money and land grants for such big projects were non-existent, and the state was in huge lawsuits over past bungling of the railroad land grant process. These shenanigans would hinder the rebuilding of Florida until the 1880s.

Because of the shortage of capital to build roads and railroads, the St. Johns River shipping industry boomed while big areas not near the rivers or coasts remained in impoverished existence because they couldn't be made available to major shippers of any sort. Places that were hard to get to, and hard to get produce out of, did not prosper in this time.

The shipping boom led to strong development along the St. Johns to the recently Indian-rid lands of South Florida, such as Lake, Orange, and Volusia counties, all parts of the former Mosquito County. This area was good ground for the burgeoning new citrus industry. Even though all the above problems held almost all the South back from its potential, Florida was loaded with possibilities for men who could work land and didn't mind sweating long and hard for a living.

It was planting time, but the slaves were free and there was nowhere close to enough white labor with so many farmers dead or maimed. The farmers were ordered to offer the newly-freed slaves to work on the farms with some kind of compensation, as John Lee and many

215

others had already done. The U.S. government's newly formed Freedmen's Bureau hired federal agents to come around and inspect how the ex-slaves were treated and ensure no farmers were taking advantage of the freed men. While this action might've been understandable, maybe even necessary, it served to disgruntle the farmers who planned to treat the freedmen well whether commanded by law or not; and failed miserably at detecting those who planned to take advantage. The agents also caused unnecessary dissatisfaction among the freedmen as government men poked around and tried to coax unhappy statements out of them.

Not all freedmen, however, found or even looked for work on farms immediately following the War, and thus struggled to benefit from the post emancipation policies. Many former slaves, unready to deal with newfound freedom, rushed away from the plantation exuberant over the realization of freedom which generations of their forebears couldn't dare dream about. Very few had ever learned how to earn or manage money and had no notion of what was required to provide life's basic daily necessities. Y' see, Mr. Lincoln's Emancipation Proclamation and subsequent conquest of the South sure enough freed the slaves, but it gave no thought to how they might make their way in a whole new and frightening world. The gradual approach to freedom, advocated by many for decades, was ignored, and freedom was thrust on them with as much careful consideration as a parent giving a two-year-old a loaded pistol for a toy. The resulting malnutrition and disease roiled the former slave population. Tens of thousands of men women and children quickly died as a result of their "freedom." Some freedmen, of course, did well and even thrived by knowing how to sell their skills and labors or through skillful share-cropping or land-leasing. Others who stayed on the farms saw little change from their previous impoverished existence. While most men agreed slavery had to end one way or another, the sudden and blunt approach to liberty created some winners but many more victims.

Another issue arose during the Reconstruction process stemming from two groups who moved here immediately after the War to take unfair advantage of vanquished Southerners. Carpetbaggers and scalawags, locals who worked in cahoots with carpetbaggers, gained great power through political appointments and grossly crooked elections. Many formerly strong plantation owners were cheated out of their lands by the trickery of these folks. Now not all Yanks were carpetbaggers, most were pouring in for honest opportunity. They certainly knew their dollars would go a very long way here, but they had no intention of taking unfair advantage of us. It was sometimes hard to tell the difference, though.

Local and state politics were a similar mess. Many carpetbaggers and scalawags gained great political power and used it to their benefit. The Ku Klux Klan and Young Men's Democratic Clubs arose out of the frustrations of many white residents to counteract the many obvious ills perpetrated on them. Of course, those efforts got way out of hand, too, as the attempts at vigilante justice brought about atrocities equal or greater than the abuses of the carpetbaggers and scalawags.

These factors were much harsher on the established areas of the state and less prevalent in the new areas. I think the carpetbaggers didn't want just cheap new land they could work and create into productive land; they wanted the good land already developed by the sweat of men before them, and they wanted it very cheap. Hamilton and Columbia counties were in the center of the suffering during Reconstruction.

Throughout the South this period of martial law, which lasted in Florida from 1865 to about 1877, called Reconstruction, was anything but reconstructive to our devastated area. It was crucially important for a good and fair government to administer "justice for all" in the form of rule of law, not the willy-nilly selective justice of various powerful thugs we experienced. In this time, Florida grew in spite of, not because of, its government's policies.

Still in the midst of all this turmoil, I believed the Cone Brothers and I would be able to prosper greatly from one fact alone. No matter how bad our government was, the South needed to rebuild. This would take a lot of wood, and there were very few businesses left to provide the wood needed to do so.

Back to Business

The Cone Brothers' business developed even better than we planned and about as fast as we'd hoped for. Even though the entire South was flat broke, there was so much rebuilding to be done and very little competition to supply the wood for it. The majority of the sawmills, as just little sideline businesses operated by farmers weren't back in operation because the farmers had their hands full getting their farms going again. Lots of the sawmills in Georgia, South and North Carolina, Virginia and Tennessee had been destroyed by invading Yankees. Other viable operations had no one to run them because the War had claimed their previous management. Still others had become rusted-out hulks from sitting idle for too long. Many of these abandoned operations would have to be rebuilt from the ground up. So even though there wasn't a whole lot of business being done, there were very few yards up and running to meet the recovering demand

The Cone Brothers

The small mills had to cut lumber from their own lands because almost none of them had any money other than Confederate dollars, and those were literally not worth the paper they were printed on. A man who had trees, even if he was starving, wouldn't sell to another starving man on only a promise, and mostly-empty promises were all most lumbermen had. Many a landowner thought he was better off keeping his trees than taking a chance on some poor broke Rebel being able to pay him.

Of course the banks were all busted, so even the rare credit-worthy man couldn't get credit because there was none to be had. The banks which had re-opened did little more than just selling safe storage, small check cashing and maybe some very small lending. No real commercial lending was available. We knew this situation would get better, and we wanted to have our foothold on the market before everyone else could get credit, but how to do it?

We found most any landowner would sell us his trees if we could only come up with a deposit of ten percent of a month's estimated yield. If we could make such a deposit, and make good on the rest about a month later, we could buy all the timber in mid-Florida; and we could buy it very cheap; and we could sell for very good prices. Our end-buyers understood they paid cash on-the-barrelhead. We'd be extending credit to large customers later, but we had to find credit so we could offer the growers those ten percent deposits to get us started.

I told the Cones I had an idea and I needed to go and test it out.

Next morning, after a long ride to the Lee Farm, I met with Granddaddy John. After a few pleasantries we got down to business. I described to him the dilemma of anyone trying to do business in this land of no credit, and the desperateness of everyone who had something, like timber, to sell. I congratulated him for his astuteness in buying gold instead of relying on Confederate Dollars. I told him the exchange rate of gold for Yankee dollars was a little less than $200 per "unit," which was about 4.8 oz. Before the War it was $100 per unit in Yankee dollars. Even though the greenback lost some value because of all the War debt and not being convertible to gold, it still bought well more in the capital-starved South than it bought pre-War. John had a double profit because his gold was worth more dollars than when he bought it, and those U.S. Dollars had more buying power, too.

I explained I had an idea of a very good way for him to get his non-earning gold, or at least some of it, back to work for him by converting some of it to Dollars and using it to make timber deposits.

We could assign all our timber contracts to him, so if we defaulted, he would take over our rights to all the timber. Since the deposits were only for ten percent of a month's harvest, he could just take enough wood to get his money back or continue to perform on the timber contracts if he wanted.

We promised five percent annual interest paid monthly, plus ten percent of our net profits on any timber we harvested using his money for the deposit. It was a very fat deal for John, but capital was scarce. I knew he wasn't going to require such a return, but I also knew he was putting us in business in a way our competitors would envy.

In our risky world, I couldn't imagine a safer way for John to use money and get a good return with a good chance of making an outstanding return. He asked how much we needed, and I said, "I really don't know, but let's start with five hundred." When I saw him gulp, I knew I'd pushed too hard, but I was also pretty sure he had it. So I quickly added, "Or let's start with Two-fifty and agree we have intentions to go to a thousand, but only if you're satisfied and comfortable every step of the way, and only if we still need the money. The opportunity here is going to be short-lived because soon everybody's going to have credit, and we'll be competing with more lumberyards and the growers won't need our money as badly as they do now."

We had ourselves a deal. But John said to me, "I'm doing this on one condition. Nobody . . . I mean nobody, is to know the source of your deposit money. I don't want this word spreading and everybody who ever heard of me starts coming to my door with some sort of a scheme. Just like during the War, I don't want anyone knowing I have anything because I don't want our peaceful farm being invaded by robbers and no-good carpetbaggers trying to take what's not theirs. Am I perfectly clear?"

"Yes, sir. Perfectly," was the only answer I could give, and I knew if I didn't say it right, he'd pull out on our deal before the ink dried.

"That means even the Cones. Even though one of 'em is my son-in-law I don't want my business spreadin' through the land. Understand?"

"Yes, sir."

To protect John's privacy, he had me make the deposit in an account in my name in the one Jacksonville bank that survived the War. There would soon be banks springing up throughout Florida again, but at the time this was the only real strong bank. Many landowners wouldn't trust checks from any other bank in those days. We had to give landowners banknotes or greenbacks for their deposits. I felt an awesome responsibility to be a good steward of my grandfather's trust and reliance on my judgment. I knew he didn't yet trust the U.S. dollar and wasn't anxious to convert his jars of gold into cash, but I'd offered him a mighty fine return for his risk.

We shook hands, then he said, "You've turned into a pretty smart boy. I like the way you're thinking, and if you can keep your nose clean and remember your Golden Rule, you're going to go a long way. How'd you get so smart anyway?"

I was humbled by such strong praise from such a strong, quiet-type man. All I could think to say was, "Y'know, my Daddy taught me to work, my Momma taught me to figure and how to trust, and you taught me how to think. Your secret is safe with me, and I will treat every

220

one of your dollars like they're the last dollars left on this earth. Thanks for trusting me, and I'll make sure you won't regret it."

I left with $250 worth of gold hidden in my secret pouch inside my saddle. I was on my way to Jacksonville.

John told me to be sure to stop by and see my new half-brother, Robert Tatum Lee, born to Wiley and Martha just about eleven months after the wedding. I did, and Martha and Dad and I had a nice visit. I told them it felt good to be twenty-five and still meeting new brothers. Little did I know, Tater, as they called him, would be the first of eleven, and I would be having new half-brothers and sisters until I was almost forty five! Isn't it something, my granddaddy sired twenty-three kids into this world, and my Daddy did exactly the same number. I guess Martha was right when she said she made Wiley feel like a young man again. I wondered if I was s'posed to match the siring record of those two men.

Aside from the developing lumber business, I was making real good money in my underground life of bartending. Even though near everybody was still poor, there were plenty of returned veterans who wanted nothing more than to meet with other veterans and spend what little money they had on booze and beer. I really wished it weren't the case, but I was working to win Laura and I was going to win my prize, whatever it took. The hours were long, and the customers very boring after they had a few too many, but this was my opportunity and I was going to make it go.

I had my regrets about the War, too, but there was nothing more insufferable than a drunk old Rebel rehashing his War stories and saying "If theyda put me in charge instead of ol' Robert E. Lee, it woulda come out, hic, different." Well, if I could've had a nickel for every one of those stories I heard, I wouldn't have needed to work so late and so long on top of my main job as lumber salesman. But my savings were growing and I was on my way. My life was good, and with my focus on getting my family started, I didn't need to think back on the War. In fact, I needed very much to put it behind me, forget everything I'd seen and move on with my promising new life. I felt sorry for those chaps, and sometimes I'd try to steer them away from the bar and back to their families or churches. Sometimes, but only rarely, I got results. Short of a miracle, these guys were damaged beyond repair in lots of ways. I made a point to pray for a miracle for all those sad souls while I was serving them and when I was in church.

The Rebel's Rest was nothing more than a rough old shack in Lake City. The creaky board floor supported a rough cypress bar with a very pretty, massive cypress plank bartop. It was planed smooth and polished to a deep luster with many layers of turpentine polish. A few four-legged stools stood at the bar, and crude tables and bowback chairs were strewn throughout the room. The bottles were all hidden, as was the cash drawer, on shelves under the bar and out of sight. A loaded and ready Colt revolver was right next to the cash drawer. The place had that musty, barroom smell of burned tobacco mixed with whiskey and stale beer, mixed with general dirtiness. It was a man's place. There were some women who came, but we didn't feel we needed to gussy up the place for them. They usually knew not to come in, so they hung around outside to make our customers their customers after our customers had their fill at *The Rebel's Rest*.

I knew it was just a matter of time before my future in-laws found out about my second career at *The Rebel's Rest*, but for now the money was just too good, and I was gaining on my goal of having money in the bank to support my bride. I was right on schedule and could see I was getting close. My nest egg was nearing the right amount, but I knew I'd have to spend some to get the "decent place" I'd promised for us. It was getting to the point where I figured any ol' place I could be with my prize was decent enough for me, but I knew Reverend and Mrs. Barnett wouldn't see it exactly my way.

Old Jabish was faithful to take me up on my promise to clean the church after every Sunday service. I really hoped with as hard as I was working he'd say something like, "It's alright, you shouldn't be working on a Sunday anyway, and I can have somebody do it on Monday." He held me to my promise and demanded I make sure Sanderson Methodist Church was spotless every Sunday, whether he was there or on the circuit. I think he enjoyed seeing me work my fingers to the bone to win his daughter. I grew to love my Sunday job, though, because Laura would sneak back in to help me clean. We especially enjoyed cleaning the balcony. Now the balcony was where the darkies sat for services, and I was told I didn't need to clean there, but we could always find a reason to make sure it was in good order. Y'see, from there no one could come into the church without us hearing them first, giving us time to stop our spoonin' and go back to making it look like we were cleaning diligently. What was usually a twenty-minute job for one man could often take Laura and me an hour. I guess you could say we were real thorough!

The Cone brothers were very good about re-investing our profits into more machines to make more and finer lumber. We sold it all, from firewood for the trains, ships and steam generators, to rough logs, to split rails for fencing, to the finest-planed boards and beams to build the best houses, to high grade millwork for furniture and trimming those fine houses. We built a rail siding so railcars could be pulled right up to our mill, where we could load the cars using pulleys, ropes and the muscles of mules and men. Those fine boards would be on their way to Jacksonville or Atlanta and who-knows-where from there. We were quickly the biggest lumberyard in Middle Florida.

The business just kept on growing. Though our contract for the white oak for *Tart's Cooperage* was fairly small in volume, through it I made lots of contacts I figured might be valuable someday for other types of timber. Y'see, I thought my value to the business was going to be from my family being known so well in Hamilton County. As it turned out, I found if a man makes his word his bond, his money's good, and he pays timely, he can do business anywhere he wants. His reputation will go ahead of him, and when a man has a reputation, he's got more than money. If he has his fellow man's trust, he has more than gold. In Apalachicola, Franklin County, nobody'd heard of the Lee family of Hamilton County. I enjoyed knowing my family had a good reputation, but it was a real help to me to know I could build a name for myself in a land where I was a stranger. I remember Jabish shouting to me when I left his house to go into business, "A good name is more to be desired than much gold," and I was learning that age-old lesson in real life.

Because I was one of few timber buyers needing high quality white oak for the special use of barrelmaking, a lot of Apalachicola landowners got to know me real quick-like. I found most any man who had the white oak I needed usually had a whole bunch of all the other oaks, pine, cypress and cedar. If I could perform for him and get him to trust me, I could be first in line to get the rest of his trees. Apalachicola wasn't too far away to get the specialty wood like white oak, but back then it was too far to haul regular, lower-valued logs. I formulated plans to open another mill there someday.

The Cones and I quickly found I was most valuable at buying the timber rather than selling the finished lumber. We agreed the lumber pretty much sold itself in small lots to the locals who needed it for patching up the home places, barns and fences. As business picked up and we developed our wholesale sales, we saw where soon our volume would require we have a strong flow of logs coming from the forests.

The beauty of doing small local sales was they paid cash up front, and the trees we bought from the timber growers we paid for on thirty or sixty day terms. I learned that was called "float," and I loved float. With the huge markup we were getting, and cash sales coming in, and deferred payments going out, we were cash-flowing from the very start. Even better, we had several of our saw mill laborers who were willing to work for nothing but food for their families until we got established, with nothing more than a promise we would reward their loyalty when we could. We knew we could get labor for just food without having to make any future promises in those times, but we knew the other yards would soon be trying to hire our best men away from us. Most of our lumberjacks we wanted to be paid in cash daily. The ones who were good enough managers could wait to be paid weekly. They got paid better than the daily guys and usually turned out to be better workers, too.

We liked to make our growers happy by being sure they were paid ahead of their contractual due dates whenever possible. If our deal was thirty-day terms, we worked real hard to make sure it was paid in twenty, and I enjoyed bringing checks to their doors. We knew word would spread quickly if we had happy growers and make it easier to pick up new supplies of timber. We also knew word would spread quickly if any grower was unhappy, and we knew we didn't want that. Business is great thattaway; a man can make himself rich just by treating his customers the way he'd like to be treated; goes right back to Jacob DeLoach's teachings to young John about the Golden Rule, doesn't it?

Our quick and early success wouldn't have been possible if you-know-who hadn't seen fit to trust the Cone boys and me with a little bit of his gold which he so wisely hoarded during the War. We must never forget it, and my partners must never know who it was. I was told to instruct them not even to try to guess who it was, because if they guessed right I was to return his loan immediately. I was pretty sure the Cones could figure this one out pretty easy-like, but they respected our lender's wishes.

1867 came, and my only two resolutions were to continue building *Cone Brothers Lumber* and most importantly to marry Laura Barnett. December 31, 1866 was a Monday, so I arranged to take off both Sunday and Monday and would be in Lake City on January 1 by late morning. I felt like a real big businessman, taking more than just Sunday off. The New Years party was at the Colonel John Sanderson house. Laura and I were both in kind of a dreamy state. We were exhilarated by the thought and by my promise to her that we might be able to become a family in this new year. We had so much to be thankful for: the War was getting a little further behind us, my nightmares were less frequent and our business was prospering mightily. But enough business talk for now; it was a special night. Laura and I mostly just talked and watched others dance.

As much as my family lived by Methodist doctrine, we really couldn't see the harm in dancing. But the Barnetts, as you might imagine, stood strictly opposed. Colonel Sanderson hired a string quartet from Jacksonville and cleared the furniture so couples could waltz It seemed harmless enough but we knew any kind of public dancing other than a square dance was strictly forbidden. It looked like fun to us but we didn't dare step onto the floor. Because it involved embracing your partner, the waltz could still stir a controversy, even though the world had been waltzing for about 150 years at the time.

If either of the Reverends Barnett, senior or junior, caught wind of their little Laura and her beau dancing, the whole thing might just be called off. With that other risk, the risk of working in a bar, I knew it was best for me not to push my luck.

So as our friends, most of them Methodists and Southern Baptists, twirled around the floor as we watched and smiled. We knew ol' Baptist preacher Wilson called dancing "rape with clothes on," but for the life of me I didn't see anything on the parlor floor remotely resembling my vision of what a rape might look like.

Here's where I had my problem with being Methodist or Southern Baptist. It was fine with me to be plenty strict about plenty of things, like the demon alcohol, hard work, regular Bible study, keeping the Sabbath holy and such, but I felt like if we weren't so condemning and were just a little more accepting, maybe we wouldn't have so many of our flock fall away. I couldn't be too distracted by those thoughts on this night, though, because I was with Laura and we were fixin' to enter the year we both hoped would be our last as singles. We dreamed, we even dared to talk about names for our children, and I said things I never thought I'd say to anyone, but this little adolescent could drag my thoughts out of me like no one I ever met. And now at fifteen, she just kept getting better. I was sure we were ready, and I was almost ready to approach the Reverend.

1867: Marriage Plans Go Awry

In the business, 1867 looked like it would be a year of continued growth. We kept finding opportunities for new markets and new ways to wring more efficiencies out of our costs. We also learned how to do more with the wood so we could add more value as we went along. Our lumber business was doing well.

In early January I called a meeting with the Cone brothers. I thought we should meet away from the mill, so I asked if we could meet on Barnard's front porch. I told them it was time for two things to happen. One was for me to stop working in *The Rebel's Rest* three nights a week. As well as we were doing, I really didn't need to be bothered with bartending to make what I called my dowry money. I would be a lot more benefit to the business by being there full time.

Second, it was time for me to become a full one-third partner and to draw a small salary. We agreed we should still take only what we needed and keep building our business and retained earnings. The Cones could still live off their farm earnings, and I needed only enough to finish raising my $400 and just a little more to set Laura and me up in a fittin' residence. I proposed if Barnard would let us become boarders in his big house, the business could save the money and someday we could build our own truly fine house. This plan would satisfy my commitment to Jabish and keep our company's capital account growing. Momma taught me it was crass to talk about money with strangers, so I'm not telling any numbers, but our business was doing very well. We were prospering and had already paid off John Lee for his deposit money loan and were using our own money to make deposits to the timber growers.

With both Barnard and Billy on board with my proposal, we agreed to have the papers drafted up and stock certificates issued. Within days I was a full partner in the best lumberyard in all of middle Florida. I was bonused one hundred dollars to complete my dowry, and I was ready to claim my prize!

I couldn't wait to tell Laura, and I *really* couldn't wait to tell Jabish. Well, the next Sunday Jabish would be on his appointed rounds; I believe he was in Live Oak that weekend. He wouldn't be home until Monday, and by then I'd be gone to work again.

I had immense respect for Jabish Barnett, and Laura surely loved her Daddy as much as any daughter ever loved any Daddy, but we also loved the weekends he was on the circuit. He watched every move I made when I was around her, and I never knew when he might show up "Just to check on the fireplace," if we were in the parlor. Or if we were on his farm, he'd be by "Just to look at those summer squash. Y'know some bugs have been gettin' after 'em mighty hard lately." If we took a ride to town, here'd come ol' Jabish, "Just to pick up some nails from the General Store." We knew he must be exhausted after each of his weekends at home; of course, we'd be exhausted from trying to lose him so we could do some of the things he wanted to make sure we weren't doing! Mind you, we were proper and were a good Christian couple, but Jabish probably drew the line on what was "proper" in a slightly different place than we did.

Laura assured me Jabish would be home the next weekend, so I set in to telling her what I wanted to tell Jabish. Her eyes got so big, and her smile so wide when I told her I'd met my financial commitment. And not only did I have the cash in the bank, but I was also a full one-third partner with the Cone brothers. I reminded her Jabish promised he would consent for her to marry before sixteen if I could raise such a whoppin' sum of money. All through the last year-and-a-half I told Laura I was making progress, but I was careful to tell her I had less than I really did. I wanted to be real sure I didn't suffer a setback, or have an unexpected expense to dash her hopes. I really wanted to be sure I had the money before I let on I was even close, so I usually quoted her about half of my real balance. She really couldn't believe her ears when I told her we reached our goal.

This was our first weekend Laura wished her Daddy was at home, but we took advantage of his absence anyway. As we sneaked behind the haystack, I joked, "This is the first time I wished your Daddy was here to find us kissin' so I could tell him our news." We laughed and kept on kissin'. What a glorious day! It was hard for me to believe my years-old dream of becoming Laura Barnett's husband was nearing reality.

The next week seemed to be a year. I guess business went smoothly, I don't really remember, and as much as I loved the business we were building, I really couldn't pay it much attention. The Cone boys saw I wasn't good for much and teased me. "Guess we better get you hitched up pretty soon or our bidness gonna go to the dogs," Billy joked.

"You just wait 'til she becomes Laura Lee, fellas, 'cause you ain't seen nothin' yet of what this business can do," I told them. They believed me and I was sure of it myself. Even in spite of the carpetbagger crookedness and general lawlessness throughout the South, Florida was a great place to be a lumberman in 1867. I was real sure it was a great place to be JH Lee, too. I was about to claim my prize.

When Saturday afternoon came, Charlie and I couldn't get to Sanderson fast enough. About 2:00 in the afternoon, I told the office I was gone, and if the Cones wanted me, they could see me Monday. Laura heard me arriving just in time for supper and ran out the front door to greet me. In her usual way, she hiked herself up side-saddle style, grabbed on tight and enjoyed the rest of the ride, all thirty feet of it. I enjoyed it, too. "Sweetie, tonight we tell your Pa, and this means we're real close to making it official. Maybe in about a week! Whaddya think?"

She said, "We gotta wait a week to get hitched?" I liked the way she was thinking.

Now different from all the other Lee romances you've heard, I wasn't nervous in the least. In fact, you could say I reeked of confidence.

When I walked in the house, I first saw Mrs. Julia Barnett and greeted her with a formal but very warm kiss of the hand. Then I offered my usual handshake to Jabish, which he returned, but rather coldly, it seemed. Oh, well, I thought, he can be that way sometimes.

After supper, I asked if we could have one of our front porch meetings, so we all adjourned to my favorite porch in all the world. We hardly sat down when my well-planned, diplomatic speech became a simple sentence. "Reverend, I've got all the money I need according to our deal, and I'm asking your blessing and your services in marrying us."

"How much money you got?" He asked, acting very cold.

"According to my bank ledger, I've got $435 and some odd cents in savings, and I've made arrangements for us to board with Barnard Cone in his house. It's plenty comfortable, and I know Laura will enjoy the company of Sophia." I awaited his reply.

"And it's all tithed up?" He knew the answer, but it was part of the deal, so I was proud to look him straight in the eye with my answer.

"Yes sir, and according to our agreement, the Sanderson Church has never been cleaner than it's been every Sunday since our deal. I believe I've complied with all the terms and conditions, and am ready to ask for your daughter's hand."

"And have you stayed away from the demon alcohol?" His eyes now burning at me accusingly.

"Yes sir, I have."

"You're a stinking LIAR!" he boomed. "Now tell me how you made all your money."

I wasn't only speechless, but breathless, my mind racing. I had no idea what to say. My answer was correct if "staying away" from the demon alcohol meant not drinking it, but I was starting to get the idea what he might have meant.

"DADDY!" Laura shrieked, and bursting into tears all at once. At the same moment, I might as well have been run over by stampeding bulls. "It's not true, tell him JH, it's not true!"

As tough and strong as my beloved was, I knew how much she was hurt by this accusation. I knew she wanted to believe in me, but she clung to her Father's every word as gospel truth. She trusted him and she trusted me. And the two bulls were back to snortin' and pawin' over her again. She looked like she'd just been kicked, and somehow I felt like I'd kicked her.

Trying to remain calm, and with only enough presence of mind to know I wasn't going to snort and paw my way out of this showdown, I calmly said, "Sir, you're not going to find an honest man in the whole Suwannee Valley to tell you I've been drinking since I made my pledge to you. Further, I pledged it to you, to Laura, to the Cone brothers, and to Almighty God himself. I've not had a drink since the War ended."

"Well then, tell me how you made all your money," he demanded once again.

"You know I work for the Cone brothers, and in addition to the money from my work, I've just been made a one-third partner in the sawmill business." Jabish just stared, seeming unimpressed at my profession of business prowess. I was starting to get an idea where his string of questions might be leading, and was finally starting to follow in the long Lee tradition of being very nervous when it came to affairs of the heart.

"Very impressive," he said sarcastically, "how'd you arrange to become a partner so fast?"

Poor Laura was quivering as if it was freezing on this balmy late-February evening, her eyes pleading to know the truth and yet fearing the truth might be unacceptable her father.

"We made an arrangement where none of us would take money out of the business until it was cash-flowing enough to pay us. What I earned, but wasn't paid, was credited to my Partner Account. You know I lived in slave quarters this whole time so I could keep my cost low and build the business. This was exactly how I was going to build a secure life for Laura." I thought I summed it up pretty well. Until . . .

"So how'd you earn the $400?" I now knew he knew the answer to his own question, but I surely didn't know how to answer it. I did know I had to try.

"Tips, mostly," I said.

"Tips? From who?"

"Customers." So far I'd told the truth.

"So, your timber farmers liked your service so much, they let you pay them low prices for their trees, and still gave you tips?" This man shoulda been a lawyer, I thought, but knew better than to say so.

"No, sir." I felt myself backing into a corner, and I felt the prosecuting attorney driving in for the kill.

"Was it the people you sold your lumber to? Did they love your *Cone Brothers* wood so much they'd pay you a little extra? Is money just so free out there nowadays?"

"No, sir."

"So what customers was it who gave you tips?"

"Customers at . . . *The Rebel's Rest*," I said as softly as I could, maybe hoping it wouldn't have as much impact if it was harder to hear.

Laura and poor Julia both gasped, and Laura went to crying; not the loud, bawlin', boo-hooin' kinda cryin', but the quietest, most lady-like, break-your-foolish-heart kinda cryin'. With a soft sniffle here and there and the hanky givin' a soft wipe, I really wished she'd just get up and kick me real hard in the shins. I reached out and softly took her hand and said, "It's alright, I can explain this."

Drawing back her hand gently but sending me no doubt I better not try to touch her again, she said, "I don't see how, but I'm listening."

I prayed silently, and I prayed harder than I'd prayed since bullets were flying around my head in Olustee. Then I tried, "The Cones owned this side-business, and they needed someone they could trust with the money, someone they could trust to not drink up all their profit. I didn't like it, but it was the very best way I could earn the money I needed without being a drain on the lumber business. Again I say I was true to my promise to y'all and the Cones. I didn't touch a drop of their liquor, and I didn't take one dime from their cash drawer other than the little they paid me. The rest was from tips, and that's most of the money I earned, plus the bonus I earned this month when I became partner. I quit the bar this month so I could give all my working efforts to the lumber business. It's going to grow even faster and better now. Laura, I worked some very long and hard hours, lived in slave quarters and traveled most of this state for you, for us. Everything I've done, I've done to try to make you the happiest young lady in Florida. You've gotta know it."

"*The Rebel's Rest?*" she asked. "Of all the places in this world, it's the one Daddy uses when he preaches about the wages of sin and the evils of whiskey. Why did it have to be *The Rebel's*

Rest? Did you know he calls it '*The Rebel's Rest in the Fires of Hell Saloon'?*" I nodded because I knew she knew I'd sat through some of those preachings with her.

I wondered if I should try to redeem myself by telling of the ones, the very few ones, I helped to return to their homes, and the ones I'd encouraged not to waste their lives in that place. Something told me not to even try.

"Let me ask you again, son," said Jabish, "have you stayed away from the demon alcohol?"

"If you mean did I drink, no, sir, I haven't; if you mean have I been in the same room with alcohol, yes, sir, I have." I guessed this was the confession he was looking for. He got his conviction, and in the process his little girl, the apple of his eye, looked like a frail piece of human wreckage. I guessed now all he needed was for the sheriff to come arrest me and carry me away. Maybe he'd just go ahead and shoot me so I wouldn't have to face life without Laura.

"Son," Jabish said slowly like he did when he was winding up for one of his two hour sermons, "you might have kept the letter of our agreement, but you're a smart fellow and you have to know serving alcohol in God's eyes can't be a whole lot different from drinkin' it, can it?" Without waiting for my answer, he proceeded, "I know someone we both know came into your bar, and you'd ask him to make sure I never found out. How could I not hear about it?" Still not caring to wait for my answer, he went on, "Well, you may be happy to hear none of your drunk buddies ever told me themselves, but several of them have God-fearing wives, and they made sure I knew. And you know once the women know, it's known over three counties, don't you? Can't you remember," he piled on, I demanded your marryin' money had to be clean money? How can you call working in a bar, 'clean money'?"

Now he seemed to want an answer. It became obvious I knew he had me because I asked several of my patrons not to let the word get to Jabish. I had to wonder, if I was smart enough to keep it from Jabish, why didn't I know enough to do something other than work in a bar?

No answer seemed to be coming from me but Jabish didn't mind waiting. He and Laura and Julia and I sat on the silent porch. There was no sound but a distant bellowing of some cows and an occasional whippoorwill singing his mournful song. My mind was scrambling, racing to find the right word to say, and every way my brain turned for the right word was met with only a blank. But I had to say something.

"Reverend Barnett, you are correct, I lived to the letter of our agreement but not the spirit of it. I did it, and with every breath I took for almost two years now, I did everything to try to make the best home possible for Laura. I hope you can see this. I surely never meant you,

231

nor Laura, nor Mrs. Barnett, nor anybody the first bit of harm or embarrassment. Every waking moment has been to get me closer to Laura and our goal of being together. I hope you can see, no matter how I might've failed, my intentions were noble and honorable."

Turning toward Laura, I started to speak but was interrupted by Jabish who informed me, "The road to hell is paved with good intentions, son."

I ignored his last shot and continuing to focus on Laura, I was silent for as long as I could be. Looking straight into her eyes, I tried to read her. I knew she would say nothing defiant to her father while I was there, and I knew if she did, I would be forbidden from this house forevermore. But her eyes looked at me with a blend of hurt, betrayal, confusion, and a pretty good dose of anger. Even though I couldn't see a trace of the love and sympathy I was straining to see at this horrible moment, she was still beautiful. She was God's most precious creation, and I had her in my hands and was watching her slip through my fingers for one stupid decision. One decision foolishly made, but made nonetheless out of pure love, was causing me the agony of my whole lifetime.

"Laura, you must know how much I love you. And you must know I've done everything I've done for these incredibly hard years for you and for our family. Yes, I worked at a bar, and I served liquor to people, but my love was always faithful to you. I kept the whole truth from you, and I see now keeping it from you was my biggest sin. My conscience told me it wasn't the right way to go, but my love was driving me to earn all I could as fast as I could so we could be together." Her face was clinging to every word, but her response was one of cold distrust. It was the look of a jilted lover, as if I'd cheated on her with another woman. Her eyes and face were moist from past tears, but they didn't glow. She no longer seemed angry, but she surely seemed hurt.

She gave no response.

Jabish then injected, "JH, I don't see how Laura can trust you. If you can't be faithful in the small things, how can you be faithful in the bigger trials? As her father and your pastor, I can't marry you two together knowing what I know. We all wish you the best in life. I'm sorry it had to be this way."

"Laura, can you walk with me to Charlie? Then I will go," I said, hoping to sound every bit as dejected as I felt.

"I better just walk you to the door," she said, valiantly choking back tears, but strong in her resolve to show me the door and nothing else.

Softly I said, "I'll be back for you," hoping to get some sign from her, some form of an invitation to come back.

Also lowering her voice to barely more than a whisper, she said, "Won't be necessary." The look in her eye told me it was over, and it really, really wouldn't be necessary.

Passing through the door, I had to try one more time. Half turning and half walking forward, I pled, "I still love you, always will."

"Goodnight," she said pleasantly, formally and with finality, just as the door sickeningly clicked.

I stood for just a moment, turned toward Charlie, walked down the steps, then turned to walk back up the steps, to the door and knocked. I heard steps. The door opened. Jabish said, "What do you want? Were we not clear?"

"My bedroll and saddlebag, sir. I think you'll find them in the parlor where I dropped them before supper."

Without a word he turned and returned with my things, dropping them insultingly at my feet, and then I heard the sickening click of the door again.

"And a fine evening to you, too, Reverend," I muttered as I turned toward Charlie.

Feeling a hole in my heart, I mounted my beloved Charlie and we moped on toward the edge of town. I looked back at the house, and just as I did, I saw the curtain to Laura's window quickly fall shut.

The pain stabbed me when we got to the edge of town, right where Laura and I would always stop for a goodbye kiss, as Charlie instinctively came to a stop. "Ain't got nuthin' to kiss tonight, Charles, but thanks for thinkin' of me." I patted his aging neck and gave him a little nudge, and we started our journey, but I didn't know where we were going any more than Charlie did. I didn't want to go halfway to Lake City. Halfway would have us camping at Olustee, which was still too creepy for Charlie and me. I felt kinda like headin' for home to see my family. Family's good at a time like this, but I really didn't want to explain what I'd just been through. I didn't want to see anybody except Laura, and I was sure Jabish would stand between us even if she would see me.

Could it really be happening? After all I've been through to win her, and after her heart was so set on being with me, how could it all be ripped apart and thrown away? Would she go marry another man? Would I ever find someone I delighted in as much as I did Laura? What should I do? How should I get Laura and me back on the right path, the path leading to a wedding altar?

I had a plan. I knew Jabish was on his way real early Sunday to preach at a home church at the Moser family house in Darbyville, only about nine miles east of Sanderson on the main road. I would spend my night on the side of the road, and when he came by about sunrise, I would get a ride with him and we'd be able to talk this out, man to man. I knew Laura and Mrs. Barnett were not coming this Sunday because they'd told me. It seemed like a year ago when my heart skipped a beat because Laura told me her Daddy was going alone, which meant we'd be able to be alone. My life was perfect until just yesterday when it all blew up like an Olustee cannonball.

I found a nice place to camp alongside the road. The live oaks were beginning their annual spring shed, so I just pushed together a nice big pile of leaves and threw my bedroll on it. Charlie and I bedded down, but there was no way I could sleep. I was exhausted, but my mind wouldn't slow down. I was at one of those turning points in my life, and I knew I had to make it just right, and I knew just right meant only one thing: Laura Barnett, no, Laura Barnett *Lee*, right by my side, for life.

I thought and I prayed. I thought of my wonderful mother. I prayed her favorite Bible verse, must've been a thousand times. "Trust in the Lord with your whole heart, lean not on your own understanding. In all your ways acknowledge Him, and He will make your paths straight." Proverbs 3: 5 and 6. I missed Momma, and wondered what advice she would give me. I remembered Laura telling me how much and how specially Momma loved me. I thought of how much Laura wanted to be so much like Mary Lee and how I thought she was such a gift from God for me. I thought of how our love bloomed right when Momma died and how it was such a sign for me. We were meant to be together, and I was not going to let the well-intended but stupid risk I took get in the way. I just had to make one highly principled, and very stubborn man of the cloth understand.

I guess I fell asleep sometime in the night, because I woke up with happy birds singing and a beautiful clear, crisp day, but one groggy head. I felt like I must've slept a total of fifteen minutes, and now I was going to have to be at my very best if I was going to have any hope of winning Jabish over.

I got up and did the usual things a man does when he gets up. I had no way to wash up and make myself presentable for Jabish, who I knew would be all dressed up in his preacher's finery. To him I would probably look like I'd been on a week-long binge, but I couldn't have been more sober, and as weary as I was, I couldn't have been more alert. This meeting was every bit as important to me as being alert on the battlefield.

234

I heard a two-horse wagon coming from the west. From a distance I was pretty sure it was Jabish. As he came closer, sure enough, it was Martin and Luther taking their master on his appointed rounds to do the Lord's work. Jabish was stately in his black parson's outfit, and he was already puffing on his oversized, matching black, curved Sunday pipe. From a distance it almost looked like he was running some sort of steam-powered wagon by all the smoke billowing out of him.

Charlie and I stepped slowly out into the path of the oncoming wagon. Martin and Luther kept bearing down, not slowing a bit. Suddenly it looked as if Jabish was going to run us over! Just as I was about to panic and jump out of the way, he pulled back hard on the reins and those two faithful horses stopped just short of us. I had to tell myself I didn't want to fight Jabish, I wanted his daughter, nothing else.

"You lost out here, boy?" He asked as if he didn't recognize me.

"No, sir. But I need a ride to Darbyville."

"Looks to me like you've got a perfectly good horse there. Why do you need a ride with me?"

"Good question, sir. We have a lot to talk about."

"I think we did all the talking we needed last night. Wasn't I clear?"

"You were real clear, sir," I said as I nervously tried to look confident while helping myself uninvited into the wagon. "But I don't think I was very clear. And I couldn't sleep all night because I still couldn't figure how to make real clear to you my love for Laura, and I dare say she loves me every bit as much." I whistled for Charlie, and he followed as always. With a shake of the reins, Martin and Luther began trotting on their way to Darbyville again.

"So that's why she closed the door on you? Looked to me like it was all over for her. I might have, or had, a lot of respect for you but my daughter's the one I care about when it comes between you two."

"She loves you as much as she loves me, Reverend, and she was hurt, so she followed your lead." I almost panicked when I realized I'd just used a dancing analogy, but Jabish let it go by. "I know with time she'll see how much she loves me and how much she believes God himself is putting us together. The way she was strength for me when Momma died, the way she lights up when I'm around your house. We were meant to be together and I, we, really need for you to forgive my actions so we can move ahead. You taught me about forgiving a man seventy times seven, and how grace is bigger than anything we can do. I need to ask you to dig real deep and find some of that same forgiveness for me."

Jabish was quietly listening. I figured he might be more reasonable with just me alone than he was in front of the two most important women in his life.

"Do you know how much of my life I've spent trying to keep folks off the bottle?"

"Yes, sir," I said as respectfully as I possibly could.

"Don't interrupt. You know I don't need an answer to all my questions. But I've poured myself into Middle Florida trying to help the families have a decent mother and father so we can have a productive, prosperous and Godly society. I've been a laughingstock without knowing it ever since you took your job at *The Rebel's Rest*. I only found out about a month ago because so many people were protecting you, or Laura, or both. So I'm going around here preaching about the ills of alcohol, while you're at the bar serving whiskey to my members. I was so proud of you, and I've gone far and wide telling people how proud I am of JH Lee, and how he's going to make such a fine addition to my family. Meanwhile, unknown to me, JH Lee is tending the bar most nights and leading some of the church's flock straight to hell, all to make a profit, and all to marry *my daughter!* Some of the same men I'm trying to get to stay home are sneaking out to see my son-in-law-to-be so they can hand him their hard-earned money to get drunk.

"Those families will never see a dime of the money those men drank away or tipped your way. Those children will just have to be a little hungrier and their clothes a little rattier because of the decision the pa made to visit *The Rebel's Rest* one night. But it's all real innocent because JH is going to use his tips to buy the preacher's daughter. Sound like clean money to you? Is it what you call an honest living?" Jabish made some pretty good points.

"Not when you put it in those words, sir. I guess I was just paying attention to the best way to make the money I needed, and I thought since it was legal, it was clean. I think I see a difference now."

I continued, "I'm not trying to justify anything now, but I did talk to some of the customers about the same thing, and some of them either quit coming or came in a whole lot less after I talked to 'em. Some of 'em even told me they were going to church with their wives again. But most customers were not talkable. They wanted nothing of any advice I had to offer. All they wanted from me was whiskey."

This discussion continued the rest of the ride to Darbyville. On this ride I gained some new respect for Jabish and his campaign against the bottle. I found he was fully aware of how few of his flock actually practiced the tee-totaling life he promoted. He was even aware many of the wives were hitting the hooch privately in their homes while the men were away working or at the bars. He knew he was fighting a losing battle but nevertheless felt a very strong call to fight it. If this impoverished, downtrodden land of ours was ever going to pull itself up and return to a hint of the prosperity we enjoyed before the War made us all so desperate, we had to change. We must overcome the temptation to continue drowning in the mirage of temporary happiness offered by booze, as it robs the soul from the real happiness of living each day and striving to work out our worldly purpose.

It became clear to me my work plan was a good one only in the eyes of the world, where profit is the Holy Grail. Heck, I'd not only saved up $400, but I'd gained a one-third interest in a profitable and promising business. I'd done way more than I needed, but might have lost everything I was working for in the process.

If we do have a higher purpose and a reason to be on God's earth, we all need to see how each action, or inaction, we take has an impact on those around us, sometimes in ways we never see. Matthew 16 taught me, "For what is a man profited, if he shall gain the whole world, and lose his own soul?" I'd even heard Jabish and his father preach on this verse many a time, but I was usually too busy daydreaming and making my own plans to let the true meaning of the Savior's and the preachers' words sink in to my thick skull.

"JH, I know most of you farmers think us Methodist preachers are crazy as looney birds for the way we push so hard on folks to learn the Word and follow it, but we see so much more to life than just making a pile of money and leaving it here behind us. There's a reason we do what we do and live as poorly as we live, and it's because most of us really do believe this stuff we preach. We're called to do what we can to help a dying world find life." After pausing, he said, "It's so simple but can get so complicated."

I thought it best to keep quiet as he continued, "You know how hard it is around here nowadays, and I know you know there's quick relief from the bottle. But that minute of relief has claimed many lives and destroyed lots of families from north to south, east to west. I know I'm pushing against a mudslide in this fight. I can even tell you of Methodist ministers who're hittin' the hooch on the sly. They know it's wrong to be preachin' agin' it and doin' it at the same time, but it gets its claws in people, even good folks. As long as God above gives me ability, I'm going to do all I can to save just one man, or just one family, especially if it's my own."

My respect for Reverend Barnett and his sincerity deepened that morning. Indeed, I think my life deepened from this very painful ride. I still loved hard work and accomplishments, but I saw in a new way there were lots of other things more important.

As we rode into Darbyville, Jabish asked if I was going to stay for the church service. I said I'd like to, but would he mind if I slipped out early because I figured I still had a commitment to clean a church in Sanderson after Sunday meetings.

Jabish shocked me when he said, "Best I can tell, you've done your commitment to the Sanderson church. I don't think it'll be necessary. You'll probably want to be getting back to Lake City." He sounded so final, after I thought we'd had a real constructive talk. I thought we had come close to an understanding, but here he was, slamming the door on me again. And of course, I couldn't have cared less about cleaning the church, I was most in need of his permission to see Laura.

"I've gotten to kind of enjoyin' the job, sir, so if it's all the same, I'll stay here about a half hour, then excuse myself out the door." I didn't want to take no for an answer.

"Your job is done," said Jabish to my distress. I hoped he was just trying to make me squirm a little, but I couldn't be sure. It sure sounded like he was inviting me to stay away from the Barnett family. I felt like I still stood right where I was the night before when he kicked me out of his house.

Leaving Darbyville for Sanderson, I pushed Charlie a little harder than I should've. I mostly forgot everything Jabish and I talked about, and I was back focused on my prize. I was going back to claim Laura Barnett. Once there, I felt real guilty about Charlie; he was getting older and could still keep a good pace, but I knew I'd pushed him too hard.

Since Sanderson had no preacher that day, the congregation just met for prayer and singing. It would be led by one of the elders and anyone who wanted to share some musical talent. Sometimes these meetings could last all morning just like a full service would. Today there was no dinner on the grounds either, so the whole church and churchyard were still and quiet. It was peaceful. A few scattered azalea bushes were blooming, lighting the whole area with color. The air was crisp, but not cold. What a perfect day for a ride to Ocean Pond for a picnic with Laura.

Opening the church door, I went for my broom and mop. Noticing the mop was wet, I looked around, and someone had already done my job for me, and very efficiently. It was as if I was no longer a part of the church. Was someone just kindly doing my job because I wasn't there, or had I been replaced? The anxiety began again. I walked up to the balcony and saw it was also sparkling clean. I looked at the pews where Laura and I had spent many hours "cleaning." My heart ached to clean with her again. Was it Laura who cleaned this church today? Had someone else accompanied her? Had I already been replaced in her heart as well as at the janitorial job?

Since my job was done for me, I sat down in the front pew and tried to get still so I could figure my best plan. But all I could do was fidget. I couldn't stand to go back to Lake City without seeing Laura, yet I knew I was so nervous I wouldn't be able to speak.

At a total loss for what to do, I simply, out of desperation, decided all I could possibly do was pray. I bowed and just poured my heart out to God, hoping He was listening and hoping He could be more forgiving than the Barnetts. Maybe God could somehow soften their hearts toward me, too. I believed He did all the marvelous miracles I read about in the Bible, but I knew I was asking for a big one.

As I finally got some peace about me, I tried to put myself in Laura's shoes. I realized what a blow this was to her and how she was probably at least as broken over it as I was. I hurt for her having a broken heart, but then I worried for me if she *didn't* have heartbreak. What if she was out cheerfully picnicking with some new boy? I know several in this town who'd love to take their turn with her. Surely she wasn't already entertaining new suitors.

I was a mess, one big emotional mess.

I prayed for inner peace one more time then headed for the Barnett house. My heart was racing about like it was when we were charging the Yanks at Olustee. But at least I knew then I might die. What if she would never see me again and I have to live on? What could be worse? I thought I might rather die.

The Barnett house looked empty, but I knew I had to dismount and knock on the door. I steeled up my nerves, dismounted, walked, opened the little front yard gate, walked to the door . . . then knocked. Nothing.

I knocked again and still nothing. It was clear no one was home. They were probably with another family having an easy Sunday afternoon dinner, but I didn't dare go looking.

Was Laura having a great time? Was she miserable? I discovered I loved her selflessly enough to not want her to be miserable. I also found my love was just selfish enough to not want her having a good time, especially with some new beau. Could the Wilson boy have replaced me this quickly?

I had nothing more to do than to get back on Charlie and head to Lake City. The ride was a miserable stint of misery, heartbreak, second-guessing, what-ifs, shouldas and couldas. But none of them made any difference now. How could any Lord's day, planned to be so perfect, turn out so perfectly rotten?

Tomorrow started a new week in the timber business, and I had a job to do and employees, customers and growers depending on me. I had a lot of people I needed to make happy, and the one I wished I could make happiest was very unhappy with me. Charlie and I rode away. Once we turned toward Lake City, Charlie knew the way. I let him set his own pace, which was noticeably slower than normal.

When I was a horse soldier, Sunday afternoons were my most lonely time. My mind would wander home and I'd feel so empty for missing the happy Sunday goings-on at the farm. This day was lonelier than any day I ever had as a cavalryman. Not only was I missing all my family at Swift Creek, but my new family in Sanderson had just made clear I wasn't part of it anymore. I felt I'd just had a hole shot in my heart.

I have no idea just how slow Charlie was going, but the trip would have normally taken me only four hours, yet I was well past dark getting to my quarters at the Cone house. As it was a pretty dark night, I had to ride extra carefully and be alert for my last leg of the trip.

Arriving and dismounting, I realized I hadn't eaten anything all day and had hardly even taken a drink, of water, of course. It wasn't like me to miss out on vittles for a whole day, but I really didn't care. I tended to Charlie, put him up in the stable and fell in my bed. I was alone and miserable.

I woke up mid-night as usual and did some anxious, worried praying. It was mostly about Laura. I must admit my prayers were much more manipulative than submissive; I was much more concerned with the desires of my heart than "Thy will be done" at this crisis point of my life. I must have figured if I could petition Almighty God hard enough, maybe His all-knowing, all-seeing, all-present will could somehow be bent to the point He might see things my way. Jabish himself once taught me, "If you want to make God laugh, just tell Him your plans!" Well the heavens must've been roaring with God's belly laughs right then because I was pretty sure, fine salesman as I was, I could get God Himself to see how my plans were a masterful fit into His plan for mankind.

Winning Her Back

I don't know when I drifted back to sleep, but I could tell I'd been up far too long in my mid-night wake. I was groggy and pretty sure I wasn't in much condition to be making decisions.

At the sawmill, everything seemed to be cranking up for a new week and all seemed in order. I was glad, but couldn't really care. This place was my entire future, but my mind and my heart got left three towns away with a half-pint child of a woman who I was real sure I couldn't live without. I'd always been as comfortable around Laura as I was with my own sisters, but now the thought of her made my stomach churn with anxiety. I was right at my twenty-third birthday, she was only fifteen. I was a tough horse -soldier, who'd fought real battles and was building a real business, she a preacher's daughter with no more world experience than a spring chicken. What was wrong with my mind?

After pretending to work a little at the sawmill, I mounted Charlie and headed toward the telegraph office. At a total loss to know what to do, I ordered a telegram to Laura. It read, "Missed you yesterday, can see Saturday?" I was determined to try and try again until I won my prize.

As I dug for cash to pay, the operator told me not to worry about paying for this personal note because the sawmill was such a good customer. "We're happy to help," he said. Even though the price of a short telegram had come way down to $1.00 by now, I considered this quite a favor from the telegraph company. I thanked him and turned to leave as he unknowingly joked, "Looks like your love is in full bloom now, JH."

"Yeah, I reckon it is," I said at a loss for any better words. Preoccupied and not feeling like my usual social self, I kept on walking.

The week ground on in misery. I guess some business was done, but I don't remember a bit of it.

The worst part of the week was the anxiety of hearing nothing back from my pitiful plea of a telegram to see Miss Barnett again, until finally, late on Thursday, a telegram came to the sawmill for me from Sanderson Station. It had to be my response from Laura. I nervously grabbed it and took it to a bench we had under a spreading oak by our horse watering trough and hitching post.

I fumbled to tear it open. Knowing it would be brief because telegrams cost by the word, my mind was going wild imagining what my response might be. Might it be, "Please come?" A simple "Yes" would do just fine, or maybe a more playful "Can't wait" would be her response?

Ripping the envelope to get into it, I quickly saw the answer was just as brief as I thought it would be, but the content couldn't be more different than I imagined. The response was . . . "No need. Laura."

My week just went from bad to horrible. My life fell apart. With three terrible words, she cut me down like a sharpshooter's bullet. My heart was lying in the dirt in front of me and no longer had the will to beat. I couldn't imagine loving anyone else, much less living my life with any other woman in the world. I'd heard the saying, "Time heals all wounds" all my life, but reading Laura's response to my plea to see her again was more of a mortal wound. And as I saw first-hand during the War, time doesn't heal those wounds. The mortally wounded quickly go into rot, infection, decay, gangrene, maybe a little hemorrhaging, then death. I think I just suffered one of those unhealable mortal wounds.

I was thinking, "Maybe I should just become the best darn customer *The Rebel's Rest* ever had." The only thing to keep me away was the thought there still might be a chance, even if only a slim one, to redeem myself and win back my love. I knew if it got back to Jabish or Laura I was now frequenting the institution at the center of my newly failed love, there would be no patching things back together.

On Friday morning, I told the Cone brothers I needed to miss Saturday work and go home to the farm to see Granddaddy John. They understood but used this time to pry into what was obviously bothering me. Barnard started with, "JH, something ain't quite right with ya this week, is it? I didn't wanna butt into yer business but I'm guessin' maybe it didn't go so well with yer girl's folks last weekend?"

I laughed a little for the first time in a week. "Barnard, I guess we don't need Pinkerton's detectives around here now, do we? It went a whole lot worse than not-so-well, and not just with her folks, but with Laura, too." I then explained the whole sad story, including the part where the Cones' bar played a starring role in the sad saga. They felt bad for me and agreed I might be best to take off and try to let a little of John's wisdom soak in to me.

I realized this was the first time all week I'd talked to anyone about my problem. Momma often told me I needed to talk things out rather than just stewing over troubles and trying to conquer them all alone. I knew she was right, but pride, embarrassment and fear, mostly pride, was always there to keep me from getting right on top of my problems when it might only take a little wise counsel from a sure-enough wise person. I had a lot of those kind of folks in my life, but the one I could listen to the most was my Granddaddy John.

Billy chimed in, "JH, we got our ducks in a pretty good row here right now, so why don't you head on over to Lee farm and surprise everybody? Take a couple days, talk it out with yer Granddaddy, and maybe yer sister Sadie, too. She's younger'n you but she probably understands yer honey better'n anybody else. Sometimes yer right to ask for help, and sometimes yer right to keep yer problems to yerseff. I think this'ns got you in way over yer head and the sooner ya ask, the sooner somebody's gonna throw you a rope. Get gone and let's see you back here in workin' condition on Monday."

Then he chuckled, "Besides, you ain't been worth shootin' 'round here all week!"

"We're glad to know it's just woman troubles," Barnard said. "Those are always fixable one way or another. We were worried you had some kinda real troubles."

We laughed. I took them up on their offer and was gone before they could think again. We weren't big on taking time off at *Cone Brothers Lumber*, and I'd already taken a half a Saturday just the week before. I didn't want to push my luck too much.

I told them I needed to do a little prospecting around Jasper, so I could head up there Monday morning and be back to Lake City by late day Tuesday.

It was late morning by time I left the sawmill office (I forgot to tell you we built ourselves a real office and I had my own desk, made of beautifully polished *Cone Brothers* cypress, in a corner of the Owners' Office). I quickly loaded my saddlebag and was gone with Charlie. It was early March, and a beautiful time to be on a ride in mid-Florida. The day was neither hot nor cold but had a beautiful breeze and gloriously happy sun. Spring was well on its way, and my own outlook was the best it had been since the previous Saturday's massacre. Charlie must've felt it, too, because he had a little more spring in his step than he had all week; or maybe he could tell I'd come just a little out of my darkness.

The family was well surprised to see me before supper time on a Friday. The Lee farm was back to full strength, meaning it was once again no problem to just show up un-announced at suppertime. There was plenty for one or several extra plates at the table just as it used to be.

It had been a long time since I was home on a weekend that wasn't a Barnett visitation weekend. Sister Sadie came running out to see me just like Laura did when I returned home after the Battle of Olustee. Thanks to my talk with the Cone boys, I was in a much better mood and enjoyed joking around with the family and being at the old table. It was good to see prosperity at the farm again. Even though prices for our crops remained low due to manipulation by the carpetbaggers and scalawags, we could feed ourselves well.

It didn't even bother me when Sadie said, "We didn't think we'd ever see hide 'nor hair of you again 'cept on those weekends Laura and the Rev were here." Everybody had a good laugh at my expense, including me. Then she said, "We all think it's wonderful how you've become such a disciple of the good Reverend Barnett and his fascinating sermons! Why, we're half expectin' you to announce you're gettin' out of timber and goin' to the seminary school." The whole family roared.

I just blushed and brushed it all aside with, "I'm prospecting some timber owners up 'round Jasper Monday, so thought I'd get a head start on my trip. Figured y'all might benefit a little from my good influence this weekend," and we laughed again. It was good to be happy and at home again. I didn't let on how miserable I was inside.

The Lees were well-fed again because we could grow all we needed. John mostly made sure we grew just enough of the fiber crops, like hemp and cotton, to meet our own needs. We also grew an abundance of animal feed crops for our own animals, with a little surplus for selling into the market. The rest of the land was dedicated to human food crops which we could can or preserve. We sold these through the meat market, which was also prospering again. The hotels in White Springs were re-opening, and the Northern tourists were anxious to come back after five frigid winters of not being able to come South.

The farm animals were fattening up nicely, and we had plenty to feed them. The Lee boys and girls were all plump-cheeked again and in good spirits. It wasn't easy to see how hard life was during Reconstruction; life didn't look so hard by looking at the Lee Farm because it was once again self-sufficient. With special thanks to John for his foresight in hoarding gold, we were able to buy anything we had to have, but he made very sure we *had* to have it before he'd part with another ounce of his precious yellow metal. We were very fortunate we weren't relying on crop prices to sustain us. John had enough staying power to outlast any carpetbagger taxes or the crazy policies of our Reconstruction government. Sadly, not all our neighbors were able to endure, and every now and then, another one of our nearby families would have to move out, and a carpetbagger family would move in. When they did, the new family's property taxes would miraculously go down, and they would be off and running on their new farm. It was hard to warm up to these new neighbors, especially the ones who took over the Pennington Farm.

After a great supper with my family, I asked Sadie to take a quick ride with me. As dark was falling, she learned the full story. I told her just how my heart had been breaking. We got no farther than the swimmin' hole before we dismounted. Sitting on the bank, I poured my heart out to Laura's best friend, my sister. I told her of my poor choice, Jabish's over-reaction, and my resulting pain.

After listening patiently and wide-eyed to my woeful tale, all Sadie could say was, "All this time I thought you were smart. How could you think Reverend Barnett wouldn't catch wind of you working at *The Rebel's Rest?* What were you thinking? It mighta been a good plan for money, but how would a Methodist preacher look at this brilliant idea?"

"Well, I ..."

"You know you don't need to answer all my questions," she interrupted. "Let's figure how to make it work out just right. It's gettin' late, and I've got no answers right away. Let's talk tomorrow or Sunday."

"It's a deal, Sadie, and thank you. Just like your good friend, you're a lot smarter than your age. You'll make a great catch for somebody . . . someday," I said trying to sound as sage as a big brother who'd just admitted his stupidity could.

"You know I'm marryin' age now, JH, if you can find a man out here who can read, write, work, have Christian standards, and is lookin' for someone who'll raise kids right, you just let me know."

"Oh, come, Sadie, you're not ready for marryin'. You know what all it means," I said as I realized how stupid I sounded yet again.

"JH Lee, who do you think you are tellin' me I'm not ready for marryin' when you're hotter'n a cat on a hot tin roof to marry somebody a year and a half younger'n me?" Maybe my little sister had a point.

Trying to recover, I said, "You might just be right, there, and I tell you what, I will sweep this whole Suwannee Valley for the best catch, and I will snag him for you. You help me catch Laura and I'll be more than happy to return the favor." We shook hands to seal our deal.

What I was really thinking was how was my poor sister ever going to get a man? She was certainly a good catch, good at all the duties to be expected of a farmwife, a good Christian young lady, educated and fully able to educate all the children she could produce, and from a great family, too. Our state just lost five thousand of our boys and men, though, and maybe the same number more were maimed and mangled beyond recognition. They certainly were out of commission to be husbands and providers. Another big batch of them was so addled by the War they could never hold a job or be any value to a girl like Sadie. Then I figured a pretty big piece of the ones that came through the War unharmed were spending way too much of their productive time and treasure at places like *The Rebel's Rest*. I could hear Jabish's accusing voice yet again.

I figure there must've been ten eligible young ladies competing for every young and middle-aged man worth his salt. I remembered braggingly telling John Harley and Wiley both about their newfound value in the romance market, but I hurt for my poor sister when I looked at the same situation from her side of the aisle. What a horrible situation. I loved all my sisters, but I vowed to do my best for this special one.

Sadie vowed to help me. We conjured up a plan. Jabish was scheduled to come to Swift Creek in two weeks, and Laura was almost sure to be with him.

The rest of the weekend I spent with Granddaddy John seeking his best advice for how to patch up the ties I'd so stupidly broken. In short, he let me know just how foolish I'd been, and I heard a lot about knowing what risks are worth taking and which ones aren't. Wisely, I decided I would never again work in a bar to get money to marry a Methodist minister's daughter.

The next two weeks came and went painfully slowly. My orders from Sadie were to be sure to have absolutely no contact with Laura, to let her wonder what I was doing and thinking. If she still cared at all, it would drive her crazy not knowing. If she didn't care, it didn't matter anyway. We'd soon know. My job was to throw myself into my job and keep the business growing, and I did my job well.

When the time came, Sadie had me come to the farm but stay away from the farmhouse. Laura usually arrived mid-day Saturday, and I was to be nowhere near. I was camping and waiting at the swimmin' hole. Sadie would be working Laura and sending messages through my younger sisters, Mary, Martha or Frances, when there was something to report. The youngest, Alice Ann, didn't participate because she wasn't quite four yet. My job was to wait at the swimmin' hole.

While waiting, I kept myself busy cleaning my dirty clothes, giving Charlie a bath, giving me a bath, and just sitting still with my thoughts. My main thought, of course, was how much I hoped to redeem myself and patch things up with Laura.

The messages came far too slowly for my liking. The best news was Sadie thought she could manipulate Laura into taking a buggy ride in the early afternoon. Finally Frances came running as fast as her eight-year-old-legs and bare feet would take her. Breathlessly she shouted, "They're coming, they're coming!" It was my cue to be me at my very best ever, and I suddenly didn't know how exactly to do it. I didn't know if she'd want me to act desperate, which I was, or be aloof, not caring if she saw me or not, or somewhere in between. I figured the honest approach was best, which meant I was desperate. So I won't tell you what was said because I don't have to embarrass myself if I don't want to, but I believe my performance was somewhere between a helpless puppy and a blithering fool.

She never looked better. When I saw her riding up with Sadie, I knew there could be no other one for me, and I would never need another woman. While she started out kind of stiff and formal, she slowly warmed up and we were able to talk again and reason it all out between us. I asked her not to scold me for my stupid moneymaking plan because everyone else in the county already had.

Somehow, a miracle happened that day. It must've meant she loved me anyway, in spite of my misdeeds, mistakes and bumbling appeals. The only important thing to me was Laura Barnett ended up in my arms again! I was happy, and guessin' from her tears, I think she was too. I thought all my onlooking sisters would never stop crying. Me, I just couldn't quit grinnin'! I never knew so much happy could be in any one place as right then and there at the ol' swimmin' hole.

We took a ride on Charlie. I got a little chill because my clothes were still damp from the washing. I know I felt cold and clammy to Laura, but she didn't seem to care.

She asked me, "If you missed me so much, why didn't you just write me?"

Confused, I said, "Of course I wrote you. If you missed me, why'd you answer my telegram with 'No need'?"

To that, we locked eyes, staring quizzingly and of course, lovingly. It took about a split second until she exclaimed, "DADDY!"

Laura squealed, "Of course he intercepted your message, and of course he did what a good father would do and answered for me. Then it just 'slipped his mind' to tell me." We laughed. How stupid of me to expect otherwise, knowing every piece of mail to the house went first through him."

We discussed how we'd handle the Jabish situation and agreed we really didn't care. We'd love his blessing and would work hard for it, but I committed I'd wait until she was a full adult if I had to. We were sure. For the time, I would continue camping at the swimmin' hole and wait until church the next day to show myself to Jabish.

Then we continued our ride on this farm I loved. I told her memory after memory of growing up there. The stories flowed, and I regaled her with all the silly, funny, crazy and sad tales of my youth on the Lee Farm. I even told her of my surprise visit with Wiley and Martha at the swimming hole. Then I dared to tell her ever since that night, I dreamed it would someday be us swimming together there. She knew a fitting and proper single young lady shouldn't approve of such a suggestion, but her blush and smile gave all the response I needed.

Next morning as we assembled, we began by singing the great new hymn, "Shall we Gather at the River?" Published in 1865, it spread like wildfire through the country, mostly carried from church to church by the circuit riders. It seemed a fitting tonic for the thirsty soul of America, and the congregation of Swift Creek Methodist Church loved it;

> Shall we gather at the river,
> Where bright angel feet have trod,
> With its crystal tide forever,
> Flowing by the throne of God?
> Yes, we'll gather at the river,
> The beautiful, the beautiful river;
> Gather with the saints at the river
> That flows by the throne of God.

It would be hard to know how much this simple hymn soothed American believers in the painful post-War period. And at the time it was calming my nervous self miraculously, at least until the fourth verse when Jabish walked in through the side door to take his place in the preacher's chair.

While seating himself, he looked across the congregation and saw me sitting in the back with his little girl. I thought he was going to spit nails. Laura leaned toward me and whispered, "Don't worry, I warned him you'd be here. I decided it shouldn't be a surprise." But if Jabish was giving me a look of an un-surprised man, I was sure glad he was prepared to see me.

Many of the congregation had been told the day's message was about "The Grace of God," which I was happy to hear, but apparently my presence inspired him to change, because we were treated to the most rousing and strident message on the ills of the demon alcohol ever delivered. In it, he even got so riled up as to mention he was aware of a place in Lake City called *The Rebel's Rest*, but this time he proposed it be re-named *The Rebel's Torture in the Eternal Flames and Damnation of Hell!* As he did, Laura had the presence of mind to reach over and hold my hand real firmly, but well out of Jabish's sight. This was one sermon I just had to endure.

Jabish's sermon itself was a full two hours of railing and raving, and on this pleasant spring morning he was sweating harder than a plowboy in the July sun. Every time he slapped his Good Book or waved his arms, the faithful in the front row got their own little baptism with Jabish's own alcohol-free holy water sweat. I knew he meant what he preached. At his core, I knew this wasn't just country theater he was delivering, but his very heartfelt concern for a real problem taking its toll on our land. And he was honestly worried it might soon threaten his own family. It was my challenge to allay his fears for his family.

In the rare moments Jabish wasn't staring our way, she would whisper things to me like, "Don't worry, this too shall pass." She gave me the confidence to stay and absorb the verbal poison arrows which half the gathered faithful knew were aimed straight at me.

When he finally staggered back to his preacher's chair, he was wringing wet. As the congregation sang the closing hymn, "Holy, Holy, Holy," he began to towel himself off with his handkerchief, which was quickly just as wet as he was. The more he wiped, I thought he was just smearing it around on himself. I was afraid he was going to have a heart attack, and I was going to be the cause. I felt guilty, angry, frustrated and scared all at the same time. While I understood I had it coming, I didn't think he needed to spend his entire message making me squirm.

Laura and I let everyone else process out of church so we'd be last to see him. I figured I had to see Jabish and attempt to make things right between us. I had no idea what I'd say, but I knew it had to be sincere or else my chance would be gone again. I thought Laura would marry me anyway, but I sure didn't want to start our lives together by coming in between her and the father she admired so much. A house is always happier if things are fittin' and proper between a man and his father-in-law.

I told him I agreed with every word he spoke, and asked if he wanted me to act as the biblical Jacob in pursuit of his beloved Rachel. Did he want to play Rachel's father, Laban, and have me work for him for seven years to earn her hand? If this is what he wanted, I told him I was willing because we wanted his blessing and we wanted him to officiate.

Though moved by my offer, Jabish remained in full bluster all day, especially if anyone else was around to hear. Laura told me I just had to tolerate it for a while. Sure enough, when I showed up at his house uninvited the next Saturday afternoon, he was a different man, but he still fell short of giving his blessing and agreeing to officiate our service. This standoff continued for months with no word of his blessing or consent.

Finally, in mid-July, I told him we needed him to bless us or tell us where we stood with him. Laura told him in no uncertain terms she was soon going to be sixteen, and if he wouldn't honor us and our plans now, we would elope on her birthday in late October. She said Wiley was a Justice of the Peace, and he would have no problem doing the job for us. Besides, Laura told her father, "Wiley thinks all the to-do over alcohol is foolishness and overblown anyway. He says lots of men drink but don't let it control them or ruin their families."

She was strong, yet choking back tears, as she told her beloved father she was ready to dishonor and disobey him in order to do what she knew was her calling in life. I remained amazed at this tiny yet powerful young person and gloried in how she loved me enough and how our love had grown so much for her to be willing to leave her family to start a life with me.

At this ultimatum, Jabish said, "You know I am a man of my word, and I swore to Almighty God I would never perform the service of matrimony for my daughter to you, JH Lee, after the dirty way you raised your money to satisfy our agreement." Then his eyes twinkled just a tiny bit as he gruffly said, "But, I may have a solution to which we can all agree."

The Wedding and New Life

"What Gaaawd hath brought together, let no man put asunder," Reverend Barnett's voice reverberated. Though somewhat raspy from age, he could still summon his rich bellow so typical of the Southern evangelical orators of his day. You see, this was the Rev. Thomas Robinson Barnett, not William Jabish, who figured he could still keep his word to not marry us, yet we could still be married by Reverend Barnett if his father would do the service. It was easy for Thomas, even though he was every bit as strident against the ills of alcohol as his son. Maybe we could say he'd mellowed with age, or maybe his granddaughter just had him wrapped around her little finger. Thomas was real fond of me and couldn't bear to see his granddaughter in pain. Jabish, too, sat beaming as a member of the congregation, finally giving us his full approval and blessing. He was able to remain firm on his word, yet didn't have to break his daughter's heart over his stubborn, but righteous, commitment to principle. My life with Laura began on July 28, 1867, and I was a better man for the painful test of fire Jabish put me through.

James H. & Laura Lee

It was a quiet family service, so the church was loaded with Lees. Barnetts were few, with Laura being the only child and all. Since it was a Sunday, we just stayed in church after the regular service. Of course, sister Sadie stood with Laura as her maid of honor, and Wiley was my best man. I wore my new business suit which the Cones nearly coerced me to buy. Laura surprised me by wearing a brand new snow-white wedding dress she and Mrs. Barnett made. Everyone else wore whatever were their best clothes and made real sure to be very clean. We sang a few songs Laura requested, but I can't remember a single thing except the look on her face. Once it was done, we joined the rest of the congregation at the Sunday dinner on the grounds. We were off and running on our new life together.

I asked her how she made such a fine dress in the mere two weeks since Jabish gave his blessing. She gave a sly smile and whispered, "We've been working on it for a couple of months."

On Monday we went to work. Since Laura didn't have much to do to maintain our little room at the Cone house, it was agreed she could come to the lumber office and work on billing and collecting from the customers and paying the employees and growers. It was a great help to have her there. We knew we could trust her with the company's money, and her careful figuring would have all bills and payments spot accurate.

Though she appreciated her upbringing in the poverty of a preacher's house, Laura was excited to be in the world of business, and she was good at it. She got to know the customers quickly and made sure they were happy, something we might have taken for granted before.

I was busier than ever and Florida was growing like never before. In spite of the crookedness and ugliness of the Reconstruction era and the Reconstruction government, Florida couldn't help but grow, and our lumber business was one fine way to take advantage of it.

White Springs had several new hotels planned; roads, railroads and bridges were being built and improved; farmhouses and barns were sprouting; wagons and implements of all kinds were being created, and steam had to be generated to power all these things. And every one of those things caused demand for wood, wood and more wood!

We continued buying trees from large and small landowners and from government lands. There was lots of land and lots of trees, but even in this early stage of development, we already noticed our trees were coming in from farther and farther away. We concentrated on buying timber near railroads and near the Suwannee or any of its tributaries. We could count on the trains, rivers or maybe a combination of both to bring us the trees for sawing into lumber. Of course, the trains were becoming the most important way to transport our lumber if the order was of any great size or had to travel any distance at all.

The trains were not only getting more reliable but were gaining speed. The new iron rails had mostly replaced the old wooden ones. Not only did iron rails make slightly faster speeds possible, but they were much more durable and breakdowns of the rails much less likely. The locomotives could still break and leave us stranded, but it was becoming less common. The ever-larger steam engines, they could carry ever-larger loads, too. The new trains were making as much as seven to eight miles per hour, but they still had to stop all too often to restock with wood and water.

Despite all the improvement, there was still the ever-present risk of a boiler mishap. Too often a steam line would break, or maybe the entire boiler would blow. People were regularly burned or killed by either the explosion or from the escaping scalding hot water. If a breakdown happened out in the middle of nowhere, the passengers, cargo and crew would just have to wait until another train came along to offer assistance. Even with all its dangers, though, steam made transportation and industry better than ever.

Like the finest racehorse, the early years of marriage and business flew by quickly. After about a year and a half, Laura delighted me with the news we knew was bound to come soon. A baby was on the way! Doctor Curlee was worried because of her young age and small size, but he forgot to figure in her strength, determination and strong constitution. Laura handled her pregnancy just fine, and on August 25, 1869, she presented me my first son, William Wiley Lee. Boy, was I proud, and boy, was I busy.

The young Lee family had outgrown its little room in the Cone house. Laura didn't want to move because she greatly enjoyed the company of Sophia, whose help and experience were greatly appreciated, and I really loved the cost. The Cones claimed hearing a baby cry in the wee hours was no bother to them, saying it made them feel young again, but a move to larger quarters was becoming necessary.

Little Wiley was a good baby and sure didn't take much room. We emptied the bottom drawer of a chest of drawers, put in a soft blanket, and li'l Wiley had himself a bed. Surely he'd be just fine there until he got big enough to pull himself out of the drawer. Then we'd need to make him a real crib. I promised I would make one. I didn't know how I was going to find the time in the next three months to do all I'd promised at home and work, but I was young and I was going to do it all or die trying!

I'm pretty sure Reverend Barnett wouldn't have approved, but the only time I found for building Wiley's crib was on Sunday afternoons. I had a woodworker at the sawmill make all the pieces according to my drawings. Then all I had to do was put them together. It only took a few hours.

While putting together the crib, I realized another great need we had. My poor young wife was a momma without a rocking chair. Now, I didn't mind either of us going without, but because she was so short, there wasn't a chair in the house she could sit straight in and touch the floor at the same time. This chair situation posed us no problem as long as we were childless because whenever she was in a chair, I normally preferred she be in my lap anyway.

And if her feet couldn't touch ground, so much the better for me! It was real uncomfortable for her to try to rock a baby in a chair made for someone half again her size, but never was heard a complaint from Laura.

Before I was even finished with the crib, I designed and ordered the wood for a rocker made just for Laura. It was simple enough, but it was going to be the best piece of furniture I would ever make. I hand-picked every piece of the white oak from our stock. I designed it and watched as each piece was cut. The rockers were perfectly and identically bent.

On purpose, I made the chair too small for most any adult to use because this was Laura's chair. It was intended for her and her young'uns to have rocking time and for their Momma's magic to soothe whatever ailed them at the time. When the pieces were done, I couldn't wait to put it together. Another Sunday afternoon was not kept holy by the definition of the day, but I felt I was doing as close to the Lord's work as I ever had by making this simple, beautiful little rocker for the love of my life and our children.

I said the chair was small, but I mean it was really small. From the floor to the top of the back was 32 inches, the seat was only 14 inches from the floor, and measured only about 15 inches by 16 inches. It had a caned seat to soften it a little for those long and late nights. No normal-sized person would be comfortable using it for very long, but it was just right for tiny Laura. It was light because it was so small, but it was very strong. I bolted, screwed, pegged, nailed and glued the thing together so it would surely last through all Laura's and my babies. I really hoped it would serve all my children and their children when the time came for them to need rocking. I wasn't in the habit of praying for furniture, but I prayed for this little piece of wood to serve generations of Lees and for it to do its part in building the mother and child bond in that special way only a rocking chair can do.

Once I put it together and sanded it smooth, I couldn't wait to show it to Laura. Polishing the wood would just have to wait.

I loaded it into the wagon, and off I went to the house to present it. When I saw Laura I started running with it to show her. How beautiful she looked as she looked it over. I felt like a king who'd just given his queen the finest jewel in all the land. I put it in front of her and begged her to give it a whirl. I ran to wake Wiley from his afternoon nap to make sure I could watch him and his Ma take their maiden voyage together.

When she rocked, it had a very soothing, rhythmic creak. And with her soothing voice, she was able to use the creaking to keep time to the hymns and lullabies she sang to all her young'uns.

I knew if I was still a baby in my Momma's arms, I would fall contentedly asleep at the first little creak. While watching Laura rock Wiley, I thought of my own Momma and how proud she'd be of William Wiley Lee. Laura and I guessed she'd even be proud of me! We were a start of a real family. Nothing unusual about us, but to us we were the three most important people on earth. I wouldn't have changed a thing about our lives together.

The Chance of a Lifetime

I was so busy with my work, and it seemed it just kept getting better by the month. Laura and I saw each other at the mill more than we did at home. We were both committed to making a go of our business and our family. We talked of the days to come when we would have more time for ourselves and for Wiley, but at the time we just had too much to do.

When I came home one beautiful April day in 1870, as I walked in our room, Laura and Wiley were enjoying a rocking chair ride together. Her pretty smile never failed to make me feel welcome home, but this one was extra . . . glowy. Then I noticed the bucket next to her by the rocker. When she noticed me noticin' the bucket, she jumped out of her chair and squealed, "We're havin' another!" Then all the excitement apparently caused her innards to revolt again. Quickly she handed Wiley to me, grabbed the bucket and set off on a hurling session to wake the dead, laughing all the time!

"Aren't you miserable?" I asked.

"Of course I am," she replied patiently, "But I couldn't be happier to know Wiley's going to have a playmate and our family's gonna grow. A little sickness isn't going to rob me of the joy of our family! Maybe it'll be another boy and you'll have two partners for your lumber business."

I just stood amazed then said something silly to Wiley. He had no possible way of understanding, but he thought I was the funniest man on earth, so he just sat there cackling.

Well, soon Laura got to feeling better again and seventeen months to the day after we had Wiley, on January 25, 1871, here came John Theodore Lee. We couldn't have been happier.

The next morning, the Cone brothers sat down with me. They had an offer for me.

"JH," Billy said, "you've done a fine job of building this company, and it's time you had it all to yourself."

Surprised, I asked, "What do you mean?"

"It means we think you've built this business, you still want to work it like a slave, and you still don't want to take anything out of it. We appreciate all you've done, but we feel we're dead weight, and we've gotten to the point where we want to take something home. We can use the money to buy more farmland, or build better houses or buy our wives each a real fancy new carriage, maybe even a real fine suit of clothes." It sounded like Billy wanted out for sure, and Barnard's silent nodding indicated he was right there with him.

Barnard finally spoke up, "Y' know ol' Roy McAlpin over near Live Oak doesn't have half the business you do, and he paid himself four thousand dollars last year. The three of us could'a each made as much. Now we never complained 'cause you were building it, and you were sacrificin' more'n we were all day every day. You've built a fine business, and we think you should have it all. Think of your family. If you can keep this thing growing, you can have a business what could keep a big family busy for generations. It's not what we want, though."

I guess I never slowed down enough to think of what the brothers wanted, because they were so supportive of my idea to keep plowing into the business. It never dawned on me they might have wanted to enjoy some of the fruits of their labors. It wasn't my nature, and it wasn't the nature of my father or his father.

"What's it worth?" Not having any idea myself, I thought I should let them show me their cards before I ventured into the bidding.

Billy said, "We think $10,000 a piece to me and Barnard is real fair for us and you, too. With you still workin' it, it should earn you back even more in a hurry."

My next comment naturally jumped from my mouth. "Where can I get $20,000? That's a mountain of money."

"Easy," they told me, "just get half from the bank and pay us the rest over time, with reasonable interest, of course. You let the business buy itself." They then explained how easy it was. Since they believed in me so, I could pledge the whole business to a bank, and they would let their obligation be junior to the bank's. I would pay both back out of operating profits. Since the business was growing at a clip of about fifty percent a year, it should be able to pay off all the bank and Cone debt in a very short time. It should also be able to start paying me more for my efforts and could put Laura into a house more fittin' for a beautiful young mom. They sure made good points.

I still saw no reason to slow down when there was such huge potential here in Middle Florida. I was pretty sure I needed to strike while the iron was hot to make our timber operation, lumberyard and mill works the biggest and best for miles around.

"JH," Billy said, "We should also tell ya we're not sure this business is going to stay as good as what we see today. Sure, Florida's gonna grow, but it might just have some ups and downs. If you do nothin' but grow the business, it's like you're doubling down on every hand you play. As long as you never have a losing hand, you get real rich real fast. But we're not sure the world works thatta way. But if you want it, it's yours for a very reasonable price, a price you can easily service over time. You go talk to your banker friend. I bet he has you approved for this deal faster than greased lightnin'."

I knew they made wise and cautious points, but I was pretty sure we were about to finally settle out the Reconstruction government. Once Florida was finally governing itself again, it seemed obvious the carpetbaggers and scalawags would have to move on. They'd find themselves another place where they could suck the lifeblood out of a new group of local folks with a whole new scam. I thought when Reconstruction was over, we'd see a Florida boom the likes of which we'd never seen!

Laura and I talked excitedly about the prospects of owning this business ourselves. Together, we'd buy out the Cone brothers, the business would provide capital to keep growing and the Cones would have money to start taking life a little easier. We loved the plan. Before committing, though, I met with my friend Richard Rowe at the First National Bank of Lake City. In addition to the acquisition debt, Mr. Rowe was happy to extend us a line of credit for up to $4,000 against the property and all the business assets for expansion and financing receivables, etc. As the business performed, he said the line would be able to increase. Laura was plenty nervous about borrowing such sums of money, but she trusted me to do the right thing, and she agreed it seemed to be a once-in-a-lifetime opportunity.

Before we knew it, we had cash from the bank of $10,000 to be split between the Cones as their first installment, $5,000 per Cone. Our goal was to use plowed-back profits, not the credit line, for expansion, but we were not to be afraid of using it for those great opportunities as they come along. I was only twenty-seven years old and in full control of one of the most modern saw mill businesses in the recovering, still-new state of Florida. And Laura, not quite twenty, had a hand in the business, and a hand rocking the cradles of two year old Wiley and newborn John Theodore Lee. Our potential was limited only by how hard we wanted to work.

I was very proud to tell Grandpa John of my deal and my plans to make this business go. Close to eighty years old now, he'd long since left the farm totally in Wiley's hands and the butcher shop under the management of one of my cousins. He built himself a fine house in White Springs and was enjoying his old age. Though he was no longer active in business, he kept a keen interest in both his businesses and the ventures of his many children and grandchildren.

He surprised me, though, when he expressed strong concern about the size of operation I was planning to build. "You're talking about big dollars goin' in and out of this operation, son. If you don't keep track of every dime, it can break you before you know it." I thought he was either beginning to show his age or was being too cautious because he couldn't believe the future our great state had ahead of it. He gave examples of local families sunk by borrowing too much and how their lives were turned upside down by the ruin brought on when debt came due without cash flow available to service it.

Even as concerned as he was, he finally told me, "I know you know your business, and I know how hard and how smart you're willing to work. I just hope you won't be bitin' off more'n you can chew. If you'll promise me you'll pay off that bank debt ahead of schedule, and if business will keep on hotter'n a branding iron like it is now, I think you'll make a go of it. You have all my best wishes, but you sure have my worries, too, son."

I left there thinking John really didn't understand how much momentum there was in the wood business and how every new railroad, road and town meant more and more need for the good things we get from trees. I thought he also had never lived in a time when money circulated so freely as it was in growing areas like ours. The folks who wintered in Florida were beginning to bring their money with them and were investing in our state. This was causing the big banks from up North to begin investing in our smaller banks. The little local banks, which used to be limited to loaning the meager deposits of the local folks, suddenly had money being pushed at them and were under pressure to get it invested into land and businesses in Florida. Other than our continuing concerns with the Reconstruction government, the business climate couldn't have been more perfect than it was.

I appreciated John's caution. I always appreciated his advice and encouragement. I left his house thinking about getting the debt paid off ahead of schedule and vowed I would do so.

Laura and I made plans quickly. We found a decent little house we could buy for four hundred dollars. It was perfectly suitable for us at the time. Since we thought it would be unwise to reduce our cash reserves by paying cash to buy it, we asked Mr. Rowe for another three hundred dollars against the house. He was happy to lend it. Our business was good, our credit was very good, and our family was prospering. I thought we owned the world.

Again we remembered John's advice and pledged to ourselves we would make sure to pay all this new debt as soon as we possibly could. We would take no part of lavish spending and all the niceties of the booming social life in towns all over Florida. We would spend very carefully, and every spare penny would go into the business. No fancy living for us, just build, build, build!

To keep our operation going and growing, we added several large cutting crews working larger tracts than before. With bigger property, we could get contracts we could work on for years rather than just weeks or months. The extra volume allowed us to build roads into the land to make wood more accessible and removal less laborious. We built some wagon roads and even tram roads, which were small rail lines pulled by animals or small locomotives. With every improvement we made, we were focused on producing more wood with less effort. Our new operation was all about efficiency.

The new system saved man- and mule-power and kept the mill running daylight to dark. We figured our modern mill would produce about half again the per-day run of board-feet with about the same number of men. We added gas lights to the mill so we could start a little earlier and run a little later each day. We employed maintenance men to keep the machines in top order and the saws at peak sharpness. With the lights they could work all night if need be, and the daylight hours could be one hundred percent devoted to production except for breakdown times, which became more and more rare due to the excellent maintenance we gave the machines.

We were surprised to find we were becoming one of our own best customers because the firewood required to create the steam to make the new plant run would keep one log-splitter busy several hours of each day the plant ran. We also found the railroad to which we were paying huge sums was paying us back large amounts for its incessant need for firewood to keep those trains rolling.

We broke the logging function into three divisions: Procurement (Buying), Timbering, and Transportation. The mill was divided into Lumber, Millwork, Firewood, and Sales divisions. Under this new type of business structure our business could grow to include multiple locations and massive operations. We planned to grow it gradually to cover most of the state and to be the biggest lumber operation in all of Florida.

Most of our vendors gave us some time to pay, but rail service was a big exception. We spent a lot on rail freight, and it was strictly pay-in-advance. Our lumber was treated just like a passenger who had to buy his ticket before he took a ride. The railroad was crucial, though, because it was the key to making it possible for us to open up the timber business in this still-remote area. As careful as we were to plan our cash flows, we'd neglected to consider how much the advance-paid shipping costs would impact our liquid cash. We weren't surprised, though, when we found Mr. Rowe was there to lend us the shipping fees using the receivable for the load of lumber itself as collateral.

He now had pledges from us on our mill, personal stock certificates, receivables, inventory, and even our timber leases. Oh yes, and our home. Our debt, including the Cone brothers, quickly totaled up to about $30,000, a king's ransom and then some, but it was all backed by one fine lumber business and rock solid receivables from some of the most rock solid customers we could dream of.

We got to where we weren't sure we had anything left to pledge. I jokingly offered Rowe a lien on my horse, Charlie, to which he jokingly responded, "He's too old, so all I could offer for him is his horseflesh value, and that ain't much!"

We knew we were using every bit of borrowed money we possibly could. But John Lee told me many times, "Never bet on anything but yourself." We were very sure we were betting everything on ourselves and on the future of fabulous Florida. One of the smartest and most prudent bankers in the state believed in us and seemed ready to loan us even more as we continued expanding. Of course, all those liens were no restriction on us as long as we paid on time and the cash continued to flow, but we knew we would be skating on thin ice if we got tight and struggled to make our payments for any reason. We figured we only had to operate at our new level for about four years, then our whole operation would be paid off and we'd be free of debt. I promised Laura then we'd start planning our fine house. The whole plan required we keep our own living costs at the pauper level, but we had no doubt we'd someday be paid well for our sacrifice.

It started off smoothly. Receivables mounted as volume increased, and since our customers were doing well, the receivables were getting paid right on time with very few slow-pay customers. The main difficulty I had was in realizing the company was twice its old size so we had twice the number of problems. Wherever I was, usually the problems were somewhere else. It was hammered in to me the importance of having good people managing each of the divisions. Hiring only the best workers, and paying them well, is the only way to run the kind of business where the owner can't have his eye on everything every minute; true then, and ever truer today.

A Change in the Air

We religiously followed John's advice to obsessively pay down our bank debt as soon as we could. By mid-1872 we'd shaved the balance down to about $15,000, and our cash flow was hitting stride so we believed we'd be able to accelerate the pay down and be free and clear by early- or mid-1875. At least it was possible as long as we didn't see any new expansion opportunities or suffer any major setbacks. It always seemed every time we pared down a little debt, another big capital project came along to make us draw it up again.

At mid-year, we began to get word of an equine flu running wild in the workhorses of the Northeast. The big Northern newspapers were running panic stories on it, and our local papers were telling of it. We figured there'd be little chance of it coming to Florida so we kept on working. By October we were getting stories of supply disruptions all over the Northeast due to the widespread illness and increasing death in the horse population. Coal deliveries were being disrupted to many cities trying to build their supplies for winter. All kinds of goods normally moved around the country by train were disappearing from the shelves. Even though trains still ran just fine, it took horses to get the goods to and pick them up from the trains. It even took horses to get wood or coal to the trains so they could operate.

The infection rate for the horse population was running near 100% in some areas, but still it stayed confined in the Northeast. Where the infection rate was high, the death rate was generally less than 10%, but when owners tried to force the horses to work through the illness, the death rate of those herds soared. The disease usually lasted about fourteen days for each infected horse. If the horse was worked while sick, the illness could easily linger double that amount of time.

In the cities, all kinds of delivery services were delayed. For example, milk was souring at dairies because the delivery horses were out of service and grocery stores weren't able to receive deliveries needed to keep their shelves stocked. One of the worst impacts was a major interruption of garbage collection, which was brought to a near standstill in the Northeastern cities. The experts were worrying the resulting filth in the streets could cause a human epidemic even worse than the equine flu.

We were already seeing a slight slowdown in our lumber orders when the disease started to show in Florida in mid-September. Since it was thought to be a mosquito-borne disease, we could only guess it would be even harder to eradicate in Florida if or when it did come our way.

The very worst impact of the equine flu was in Boston on November 9th and 10th. There was a downtown fire. It was an ordinary fire and should have been taken care of with fairly minimal losses, as most city fires go when tended properly. However, the fire horses were sick, and not enough of them could be mustered to get enough equipment to the site before the fire got out of control. The result was almost seven hundred buildings destroyed. The devastation was shocking.

Part of the Devastation in Boston

The better livestock managers studied to see what ways were best to try to save our animals when the flu came. We began keeping our horses apart. We didn't allow sharing feed or water troughs, and we kept our horses in separate pens or tied up outside away from each other where they couldn't be in contact. We'd never put a saddle or a bit on one horse after it had been on another. We decided to quit using any of our two-horse wagons. If one healthy horse could pull it, we would still use the wagon as long as we loaded it light. We worked our horses shorter days. The efficiency loss was small compared to the risk of having our horses spread the disease among themselves. The main preventative seemed to be to watch the herd. At the first sign of illness, we needed to let it be known far and wide, and keep the sick animal under strict quarantine.

Well, as you might guess, the equine flu was soon spread throughout Florida, and almost every horse got it. The work slowdown took our production down at least fifty percent, and our orders were down about the same amount. We knew the Boston fire was going to bring new business to all the big Florida sawmills, and we'd have liked to have had inventories built up for it, but it would've been very foolish to try to run at full capacity now if it meant gutting our horse fleet. We had to wait it out.

At the start of the flu, our cash flow actually increased as production dropped off because customers were still paying bills but not ordering new lumber, so our operating expenses went down as our revenue temporarily continued. We knew not to celebrate this seeming bonanza because it certainly wasn't good news. We carefully shepherded our cash flow; one way to do so was by no longer making early payments against our debt, we continued to pay on time, but nothing early.

The biggest tragedy of the horse flu outbreak for me was watching my old best friend, Charlie, suffer. He was getting old and weak anyway, but he still seemed to love to carry me on my rounds. We had been through a War, a courtship, and building a family and a business together. I'd watched lots of farm animals die. I knew they were here to serve us, and I could get quite fond of any good animal, but in my whole life, I knew there would only be one Charlie. I still miss him. When he lay down in his stall, in weakness and pain, I knew he was through and knew what I had to do. I also knew no one could do this but me. It was my duty.

Poor, well-intended Luke, our stable boy, saw my pain and offered to do the tough job for me. "Mr. Lee, I can do this for you," he offered.

"I will fire your ass if I don't shoot you first," I cruelly shouted at him as I took out my frustration and pain on a kind young man who'd only tried to help. I cried out loud as I loaded my revolver. It was one of the ones Charlie and I carried at Olustee. I sat down on the dirty stable floor with Charlie, in his horse flu-infested waste. I gently placed his fever-hot head into my lap. Having never before told a horse I loved him, I wondered why I hadn't in our many one-sided conversations. I stroked his mane and petted his head for a little while. His near-lifeless eyes seemed contented, even relaxed, as he looked up at me. Then, I slowly stood up, cocked then rapidly unloaded my revolver straight into his brain through his right ear. I wanted to make sure his suffering was over.

"Rest in peace, Charlie . . . You're a friend I will never replace."

Then I apologized to Luke and asked him to dispose of Charlie for me.

Winter came, the mosquitoes went away, and the equine flu was gone. The rest of our horses recovered fully.

I was glad Laura watched our cash so carefully. Once the horse flu was past, our coffers were getting about as skinny as I was at the end of the War. Our receivables were paid down since the downturn, and our operating costs were about to ramp up again. We knew we had to manage our business like we'd never managed before. It was a pretty big monster and could gobble cash if we let it.

We got some sizeable orders for the rebuilding of Boston. We treasured them, filled them quickly and shipped them just as quick as fast as we could. We never shipped an order unless it was signed by the Buyer and covered by insurance or letters of credit from Boston bankers. We lost some business by doing so, because lots of the other sawmills were hungry enough, or foolish enough, to take the business and just ship the lumber cash-on-delivery. We knew those folks were risking having lumber in Boston with nobody to pay for it. It would be worth about ten cents on the dollar if it got stranded at the port there. We were going to cover ourselves best we could.

We received a total of about $50,000 of new business from Boston, with every stick of it covered by insurance or bank guarantees. We would agree to the orders by telegraph, but we wouldn't ship until all the documents were put in the hands of our agent in Boston. Once he telegraphed all was in order, we shipped. It wasn't smart business, just plain necessary.

Not only was volume suddenly back up to snuff, but since the Boston builders knew they needed lots of supply, they didn't quibble over price either. They just wanted to be sure they'd get delivery. Winter was coming on fast, and little construction could be done before cold weather shut it all down. The builders were racing to amass stockpiles of supply before winter so they could go to work rebuilding Boston at the first hint of spring. There was $56 million of total insurance coverage on the destroyed properties, and suppliers far and wide were getting a piece of it.

We didn't rejoice in the tragedy of those folks in Boston, but we were mighty thankful to have this business come our way. We put our mill back in full tilt and loaded traincar after traincar bound for Boston. We noticed orders from our usual customers were kind of skinny, but at the time, we were real busy filling the biggest batch of orders we'd ever seen. If we managed well, we figured, the Boston orders alone should give us the staying power to make up for our business lost to the horse flu and bridge us until our local business picked back up.

Isn't it funny how business works sometimes? Business across the nation was definitely hurt by the horse flu. The Boston fire was indirectly caused by the horse flu, and now, because of the flu, our Boston orders were going to more than make up for our lost work. We planned on clearing at least $10,000 net profit on our fire business by time all was said and done.

Well, orders flowed in and lumber flowed out. Our plant performed beautifully. You shoulda seen those train cars rolling out of our yard to the Jacksonville port to be loaded on ships headed North. It was a beautiful sight. The first few orders got paid right on time. We felt confident in this business because up North the customer couldn't leave the shipyard with our lumber unless our agent there released it, and he wouldn't release it unless the insurance guarantee or bank letter of credit was safely deposited in his hands. It was a beautiful system.

What we failed to anticipate was the fire bankrupted about twenty Boston insurance companies and near-bankrupted a whole bunch more. Of course it took them several months to declare it. At first, we thought it must just be a little cash pinch for the payors, and surely given some time, they could sell their portfolios and make good on all the claims. When the first company declared bankruptcy, it brought a whole chain of them down. A number of banks followed suit. Only about a quarter of our loads to Boston were paid as agreed. The rest became a very big problem.

Now, once we delivered lumber and had the insurance company go bust on us, we figured we had three options. First, we could get in line and hope to get paid. This might take years. Second, we could bust the deal and sell the lumber on the open market. The local Boston market, as you can imagine, had collapsed because of so much product shipped to bankrupt insurance companies. Or third, we could have the wood reloaded onto the next ship home or another market like New York and try to resell it.

We did some of option one and some of option two, but none of option three. Reloading and reshipping required us to invest more cash in a load which was already a loser for us. We chose not to take the risk of losing even more. John Lee called it, "Throwin' good money after bad."

Of the option one wood, we rarely got our full price, and it took months or years to settle. Option two was quick money, but the Boston price of lumber quickly fell to ten percent of our contract prices. We just about got our shipping cost out of those loads, but little more. Option three wood, distressed product shipped to another port, also suffered brutal discounts. Speculators from New York got in the act and bought huge volumes of supplies to resell when the market healed. If we'd been more liquid, we'd have done the same thing by warehousing our wood and waiting out the market.

Because of the time required to settle out these messes, it would take years to know what our real losses would be. But we knew our immediate loss to our cash flow was about $17,000. What we recovered over time would help, but we needed cash flow right then. As you know, our reserves were already stretched thin by the work slowdown due to the equine flu. We were taking our first real blow in our business, and it was a big'n.

No matter how well a man prepares and covers his risks, things just sometimes go wrong. Our business took its first big losses in the Boston market, but our banker was good to work with us. He let us pay interest only for a year and even cut our interest rate in half. We were deeply appreciative and told him we were loyal customers as long as he wanted us. As gracious as he'd been to us, we knew it was still gonna be a struggle just making those half payments of interest.

Back home, orders were creeping back toward normal by early spring of '73. Our operations were smooth again, but we just couldn't sell the volume we once could. We had a feeling the equine flu had done some lingering damage to the market. Laura was uneasy, but I said we just needed to keep our chins up and look real hard for the business others might be missing. Some smaller mills closed during the horse flu and appeared they wouldn't open back up. It was a great time for an operator with cash to buy equipment and businesses on the cheap.

By mid-year 1873, we were optimistically talking with another timber man about doing a future partnership to build a sawmill on the Suwannee near White Springs. We would buy our trees upriver and near the river. They would be cut and hauled to the water, then lashed together, and raft men would ride the gentle current, steering the rafts with poles downriver to the mill. What a fine source to help us meet the growing demand for boards for all the new construction on the drawing boards in Middle Florida. Mr. Rowe would surely have first chance at our banking business on any expansion we did.

We agreed we'd pursue these plans hard as soon as business volume and cash flow got back to normal. We figured it'd just be a few months 'til we'd be pushing ahead with our second sawmill operation. Surely a horse flu couldn't affect the lumber market for very long, could it?

For the first time, we found ourselves having to jockey our receivables and payables, making promises to folks we owed money to, then staying awake all night wondering how we'd make good on those promises and how we'd collect the money owed us.

In late September, we got word of a New York investment giant named Jay Cooke who was having some troubles. We'd heard of this man and his company before because he was one of the North's principal financiers of the War Between the States. After huge success at selling War bonds, he rolled right in to selling railroad bonds and was the single largest source of funding for the 35,000 miles of rail laid in our country since the War. In fact, the railroad industry, including the folks building and those operating the railroads, had overnight become the largest employer in the country. Cooke went bankrupt in one of the most spectacular business failures in America's history.

Wall Street is known for having its panics. Sometimes those panics stay right up there on Manhattan Island, but sometimes they spread far and wide. We could tell real early which type of panic this was going to be.

Lots of the Southern businessmen were guffawing and chest-thumping about Cooke's demise, saying he finally got his comeuppance for financing the Yankee devils. But Grandpa John told me those men might just be dancing on their own graves. "Sure he financed our enemy, but he was also financing the recovery. All those new rail lines were makin' lots of folks rich who didn't have anything to do with rail other than getting benefits from using it. If Cooke's gone down, there's no telling how many more will go down with him, and there's no telling where the ripples from this crash are gonna go," John advised. "I've been through these before, and anybody who's not hunkered down when it starts is gonna have a real hard time getting' through it, pure and simple." I knew he was talking straight to me. I appreciated how he never wagged a finger or said he'd told me so; he was too fine a man for such arrogance. I knew what he thought, but I was also sure Laura and I would get through it. We were too good at what we did, and our plant was the best around. We had a great team and a fine reputation from Florida all the way to Maine.

Well, the ripples began coming in. Railroads were going belly-up. At first I was relieved. As a user of the rails I thought it was good that most of the lines weren't shutting down, they were just changing owners. Soon bondholders were in control of nearly one-third of the railroads in the country. I thought not much would change for the customers. Surely bondholders would continue operating the lines in the most efficient way they could. In his wisdom, though, Grandpa John taught me the way things really worked. "No, sir!" He exclaimed, "Don't let 'em fool you, those rail lines now owned by bondholders are really being run by lawyers and accountants. Do you think they know anything about running a railroad? The answer's NO!" John always got real excited when he thought he had an important point to make.

I had to ask then, "What makes you think so? People are rational, aren't they?"

"You gotta look beyond your nose, son. Of course, people are rational, but the bondholders can't put on conductor suits and go run the rails. They put people in charge. And if it's going

268

to process through Wall Street, it's going to end up in the hands of lawyers. All those bonds were sold through Wall Street, so Wall Street lawyers are going to be the receivers of these businesses. Using your theory now, are lawyers rational?"

"I guess so," I said.

"Good. Now we're gettin' somewhere. What does a rational lawyer think about? Is it service? Is it being competitive? Is it investing corporate capital to build the business to make more money for the bondholders over the long run? What is it a bigshot New York lawyer's goin' to look for when he's put in charge of a multi-million-dollar business?"

"I think you're lookin' for me to say all he cares about is big fees for himself." I retorted.

"You just jumped to the front of the line, son," John said waving his arms sarcastically. "JH, there's no hope for a good while now, and here's why: this panic just started and it's a big'n this time. The major rail lines are going to run, but they're going to be run into the ground by short-sighted klutzes who want only to look like they're running the railroads. They'll be raising prices and cutting services, and short term it might work, but it's going to put a chokehold on commerce. You know how you make yourself more money every time you wring another efficiency out of your operation? These men are not tuned to think that way. They will manage railroads in Florida from Wall Street. They'll tickle the ears of their bondholder clients, and use all their big Wall Street words to make sure everyone thinks these are the smartest guys ever. And they are smart, but they're only smart in a very self-serving, self-centered way."

Pausing to catch his breath and take another pull on his pipe, he asked, "Now those bondholders, what do they want?"

"I never thought about it, but I guess all they want is their bond money back with some interest."

"You're close," he confided, "but they've already given up on being made whole. Nowadays they're waking up at night having dreamt of getting 70 cents on the dollar. Or they might wake up in a sweat for fear all they're gonna get is 20 cents. But you can sure see they're not gonna worry about your service or your freight cost or investing more capital to make the railroad better. They want as much as they can get as fast as they can get it, and they trust the lawyers and accountants to get it for them more than they do the operators. You don't even need to get me started on the accountants. They may all be good folks, but see my point? They have no reason to care about what their railroad business is doing out here in Florida. You need to look for freight rates to go up big, and rail traffic is going down by more than the rates will go up. But the bondholders will sheepishly think the lawyers are doin' 'em a great job, son." Then he said, pointing his pipe at me, "Commerce is fixin' to grind to a halt. And the government hasn't even had a chance yet to wake up from its nap to see there's a railroad crisis going on. When it does, what do you think will get done?"

Trying hard to think like John, I said, "The government's going to point fingers trying to make sure the people don't think it's the government's fault."

John smiled and asked, "How'd you get so smart?"

"Frankly, I'm not so smart, I've just gotten kinda good at knowin' how you think." We both laughed. "Grandpa, what if the government can't fix it?"

"Son, there's no *if* about it. The government *can't* fix it. Federal government can't fix anything. More important, it shouldn't." I could tell John was just getting started. "Be watching. If, or when, you see the government trying to look like it's solving the problem, you will know for sure this thing is going to last a long time. Every time some windbag powerful senator stands up and talks about solutions, you know he's just trying to get votes to keep his fat self in his seat because sure as fire he doesn't have the ability to make it in business on his own. If you see the government keeping out of it and letting the problem sort itself out, then you'll know it's going to be a sharp but short panic."

He paused while I tried to absorb it, then the old fox asked, "Which do you think it will be this time?"

"I don't know which way it'll be, but I know you're right. I'm going to be watching. I'm not at all ready if it's going to be a bad one. I was too busy investing to be the best possible timberman I could. I guess I wasn't watching my backside."

John quietly said, "JH, I think you were doin' the right thing but at the wrong time. I'm sorry you have to go through this at your age, son. I went through it in my folly of the War of 1812. I was young, and I lost nothin', but only 'cause I had nothin' to lose. I got spanked real good and had to run back to Georgia with my tail 'tween m' legs. And I was better for it. Don't lose sight that you can come through this a better man, but win or lose, I know you have a tough time ahead. You're gonna come through it broke, but you don't have to come out broken. Do you see the difference?"

"Yes, sir, I see it real clear. I'm going to learn everything I can and resolve to come out of it better and stronger than before, one way or another."

"I hope I'm just a doddering ol' fool and you'll have no troubles, but I know you will," he said reluctantly. "You're in a boom-and-bust business, and it's bustin' big right now. The important thing for you is to learn lessons from it, but don't you let it break your spirit.

There's a reason our wise Founding Fathers taught us not to trust government - because it's not trustworthy. It's going to try to make itself look trustworthy now, and people are scared, so they are going to want to trust government to make things better. I've lived through nation-wide panics in 1819, 1837 and 1857, not to mention the post-War calamity of the South. Every time it's what government does or doesn't do that determines how long the hard times last, and you should never, *never* count on your politicians to do right. There's certainly some good men up there, but there's way too many who're nothin' more'n cheap politicians, and that's a real problem for the country. They'll find someone to blame, throw a few folks in jail, pass some laws, and surely raise a new tariff here or there and expect us to appreciate all they do for us.

"It's like ol' Jacob DeLoach taught me, 'Beware of government, it has neither soul to save, nor *ass to kick!*'" It was one of John's favorite lines, and I'd heard it many times. In the past, we'd share a good laugh over it. This time I laughed alone, but quickly sobered up when I saw just how dead serious he was. John closed the meeting by saying, "JH, I was told years ago, 'Experience is what you get when you don't get what you want,' and I believe you're fixin' to get yourself a lifetime's worth of experience."

As quickly as I could I called a meeting with Richard Rowe. I told him I needed his straight take on how our business was going to be affected by the Panic.

My friend the banker said, "We get special reports from Washington and New York, and the reports are telling us we could have a couple quarters of slower growth, maybe even a down quarter, and then we'll be back to rebuilding. We still have a lot to do to rebuild from the War, and there's still lots of railroads we can build all over the country. JH, the outlook's really pretty good once we get through this rough spot." It was quickly clear to me these special reports were packaged for high falutin' subscribers who wanted to have their ears tickled with news of how we'd all be alright in the long run. It was an awfully different take on the days ahead than John gave me. Funny, John had no fancy degrees, but I was pretty sure his sixth-grade education and loads of common sense made him better educated than most of Wall Street.

"So, how do you think my business is going to be impacted?" I asked Richard as candidly as I knew how.

"Here at First Bank of Lake City, we think you had such a great year in '72, we think worst case, you may have to give back what you made then, but you should recover from there, and we're confident you'll continue building your fine business," Richard said optimistically.

"Thanks, Richard. I will take those results right now if you can guarantee them. I hate to tell my banker this, but I'm just not quite so optimistic." I left thinking those were probably not smart things to say to my banker. Maybe I shoulda been as optimistic as he was. But it dawned on me he was similar to John's take on bondholders. He really just wanted to be able to tell his board the Lee loan would be just fine. He really didn't want to lose any sleep over it. He was a trusted friend and cared about my business more than most bankers would. But at times like those, when things got really messy, a businessman was gonna find himself very alone.

I called an employees' meeting. These men were co-workers and friends. They relied on me for their family support, and their labors over recent years built wealth for my family. The employees felt as long as I was worried about things they would be all right. They wanted their weekly pay, and they liked me as long as I could provide it.

I told them I thought I saw dark clouds ahead for the foreseeable future. They didn't understand. The only thing they were going to understand was a job and a paycheck. This I understood. I cut the payroll to the bone. I asked everyone to take cuts in pay. If they could get better jobs elsewhere, please go to it, I recommended. Not one man left. I took it as part a display of devotion, and part a sign of just how little work there was to be had elsewhere in our corner of the world.

Laura and I weren't sure what we were going to do. For our years of doing the right thing by plowing all surpluses back into the business, we had nothing to show. We had no personal savings, no bags of gold under the bed. Our business was our savings and our future. We had taken enough for our bare necessities. That was all. We had done the right thing to build a business, but howdy, did we leave ourselves exposed to a bad downturn!

With our reserves gone, our payables and receivables just about matched on paper. There was just one big difference: our receivables were getting' real doubtful, but the payables remained a sure thing. We cut our overhead as much as we could, but our biggest overhead item was the bank loan. We found once you've borrowed money, there ain't much you can do to un-borrow it except to pay it back, and don't forget to pay the interest. If you're out of cash and out of cash flow, your goose is cooked.

By early '74, the orders dried up all the way. They just disappeared. It seemed everyone got hurt just enough in the equine flu epidemic to pull in their horns just a little. Then the Panic of '73 hurt some folks a lot, and was enough to cause the spirit of fear to overtake everyone's spending plans. Just as rebuilding the country had people thinking up and looking forward, the Panic of '73 killed all optimism. People were suddenly focused only on survival.

The bank was once again gracious to us to give us another year of paying only half of the agreed interest. It was a much appreciated lifeline, but I knew what I needed was some sort of miracle.

Come April, we had most of our tree growers paid to within sixty days, but the bank was still owed about $12,000. We were out of money. We had lots of good equipment, a strong fleet of horses and rolling stock, a list of loyal suppliers and a wonderful book of customers, all at a time when nobody put any value on those things. We only had a little food left in our pantry from our garden and Laura's canning. She said every time she canned anything she still remembered my Momma. I was glad Momma couldn't see her boy at this time. Or I guess I mean I'm glad I couldn't see Momma seeing me right then, because I'd hate to have to tell her of my failure.

Laura said, "JH, I know exactly what she'd say to you."

"What would that be, Laura," I snapped kind of disgustedly.

"First . . . she'd call you 'Jimmy' like nobody but your Momma dared, and only when she knew you needed a Momma. Then she'd say, 'Just try again. Don't give up. You're too good to give up. You're young. You're smart. You know how to scrap for what you want or what you need. Together, you and your family can get through anything.'"

Then Laura added, "And you know it, too, don't you . . . Jimmy?"

I didn't answer. I couldn't answer, but I tried to give her a look to say I appreciated what she was trying to do, and more, I appreciated . . . her. Once again, I felt my tiny young wife giving strength to me in the same way Momma did since I was a baby. When a man knows his woman believes in him, any man worth his salt will have strength to move whatever mountain gets in his way.

I'd heard the saying, "He's got the weight of the world on his shoulders," and now I knew I was that man. The only thing had me puttin' one foot in front of the other was believing Laura believed in me just as Momma believed in me in my youth. I knew I was up against long odds, but I was going to fight it to the end.

And the end wouldn't take long.

I met with all my growers. Timbermen, of course, were hurting badly by this time. They needed cash flow, and I needed them to give me credit. I went to each of my accounts, asked them to trust me with small lots of their wood, and I would pay them a fair market price, but only after I received payment. I was no longer to be their buyer, but a partner. To the growers who could afford to do without cash flow, I recommended they save their trees for better times and prices. To the ones who needed cash, I offered a better-than-market price, but only after we got paid, *if* we got paid. I had to get the bank to agree to my scheme because all sales proceeds were assigned to the bank before I could pay anyone. The bank had full control of my checkbook and full rights to grab every dime I deposited, but once again, the bank, and Richard Rowe himself, did everything possible to help my flailing operation survive.

I missed the April half-interest payment. Then May rolled around. It was officially hopeless.

I continued plodding. What little business came in was enough to keep a skeleton crew working about half time. It wasn't enough for any worker to feed his family and make all his obligations. The ones who had a good-sized garden or small farm plot could survive. I don't know how the rest of them got by. Most of them were illiterate, but they were all smart enough to demand I pay them daily.

My friends were telling me I needed to watch out for myself and my family. I should've had some savings from all the good days. I should have some cash in the bank and some hidden somewhere. I had none of it. I had plowed everything right back into the business I believed in so much. Like John said, I did the right thing at the wrong time.

After three months of the scaled-down operation, no half-interest payments made, and no prospects for catching them up, I surrendered. Laura and I had two dollars and some change between us. The business had about twelve dollars in the cash drawer. Taking it, I vowed to Laura somehow we'd find a way to get started in a new business, and someday, somehow, we would be stronger than ever. But for now, we hoped only to survive.

We closed the plant and sent word to our friend and banker, Mr. Rowe, and told him we'd be coming to his bank and were prepared to sign everything over. We loaded up a sorry old two-wheeled, one-horse cart with our food, our farming tools, Laura's spinning wheel and loom, and whatever personal belongings we could fit. Now it was a big wagon for just a two-wheeler, but it wasn't much for holding all our worldly possessions. Laura insisted on only one thing: her little rocker was to go with us. I tried to talk sense to her, told her it was just a simple little piece of wood and I could make her a better one as soon as we re-settled, but she would hear none of it. She said if her rocker stayed, she stayed. When I lovingly told her how foolish she was being, she looked me square in the eye and said, "All three of my babies rocked in this chair, and if you think you might want anything to do with having more babies in this place you're taking us, you just might want to pack up m' chair, Mr. Lee." I didn't know if she meant it or not, but the stakes were too high for me to risk it, so I loaded the rocker.

I knew Laura could easily leave me. She could go home to her folks. They could declare me a fool and an embarrassment, and she could live out her life as the homebody preacher's daughter. The community would believe I'd been unfaithful or something. Surely tongues would wag. She could raise our children under the Barnett roof. I knew the Lake City Baptist preacher, Alderman Wilson, would have loved to arrange for his boy and my Laura to be man and wife. And I knew Jabish thought pretty well of the idea way back before I showed interest. Laura and the Wilson boy were the same age, so he'd been too young 'til just about now. He was a decent fellow and was following in his Daddy's footsteps. I was happy Laura never let on to having any thoughts for him and never wanted anything to do with moving back to her parents' house. I couldn't blame her if she did. How much could any young lady take? In the midst of all my loss, debt and disaster, I knew I was a blessed man and still had so much to live and work for.

With the bank's approval, we took two young, strong horses from the barn and a saddle for each of them. L'il Wiley, now five, could already ride. He would make our trip in the saddle. John Theodore, Theo we called him, was only three-and-a-half. He thought he could ride like a cowboy, too, but we figured he'd do best beside Laura, who rode on the wagon's bench seat in the tiny space we had for her, holding our latest addition, infant Julia Kate. With no room left in the wagon, I mostly walked alongside the hitched horse with a loose rein in hand and a small buggy whip for the unlikely time I might need to speed up the journey. Part of the time I rode on one of the horses, but I walked as much as I could to spare the extra weight on either the horses' backs or in the wagon they pulled.

The horses we chose were a pair we named Prince and Duchess. They were both strong and spirited but gentle. We hoped they could be a breeding pair for us someday.

We closed the mill. We said our good-byes, hitched one horse to the wagon and started our trip to the Lee Farm in Hamilton County to work the harvest before we made our journey to our Promised Land, wherever it was. The good wishes our former employees gave us as we left gave me about the most heartwarming feeling I'd ever had. Heartwarming *and* humbling, I should say.

I felt like the biblical Prodigal Son returning to his father's farm after squandering his fortune.

We could only count on making about ten miles in a long day, and maybe about fifteen miles on our best travel days with our little gang. Not only was the cart slow and bumpy, but someone was always crying, needing changing or falling asleep in the saddle, or hungry, or needing a Mommy, or needing carried by Daddy. I gotta admit, it was the most carefree time I'd had in two years. Even though I was worn out, this little trip gave me the confidence our little family was going to be alright. I think it was the only time in my life I wasn't in a hurry 'cause I knew the more I hurried, the more frustrated I was gonna get.

Before leaving Lake City, we stopped at the bank to do what we had to do. When I first saw Richard Rowe, I knew one thing I just had to do. I reached in my pocket and pulled out my twelve dollars of cash from the mill's cash drawer. I carefully laid it on the desk and said, "This belongs to the bank." Then I signed the papers giving the bank every other possession I had left, including the complete sawmill, receivables, timber contracts, wagons, axes, all the equipment and animals that had served me so well in a different day. I knew I was short of what I owed, but it would be months before the bank could get it all sold and I could know just how short I was.

When finished, Mr. Rowe insisted we come to his house for the noon dinner. His wife fed us well and we sat on the porch a couple more hours talking about what we'd been through. He told me how worried he was for his bank, and I told him how sorry I was for my role in his troubles. He said he, likewise, felt sorry for his role in our troubles. When I looked at him shocked, he said, "Think about it, if I hadn't loaned you the money, you'd not have to pay it back, and you coulda just hunkered down and weathered the storm 'til business got better. You wouldn't have gotten the fine, high volume operation, quite so soon, but you'da sure been more solid to weather this storm. Us bankers call it lendin' a man the rope to hang himself with, and a banker doesn't know if that's what he's doing until it's too late."

I responded that I couldn't remember him ever holding a gun to my head to make me take the money. We laughed and decided two fools had just caused each other a lot of trouble.

I asked him, "Richard, you know somehow I'm going to make good on what you lost on me, don't you?"

"I know you will," Rowe said, "but I don't even know if it'll matter. I'm not sure the bank's going to be here much longer, seems those fancy reports we got from up North were a little on the rosy side. Every day it seems another customer comes in to say he can't pay us anymore, and the losses we're taking when we sell the collateral are eating up our capital. If we get illiquid, we'll have a run on the bank and our doors will shut and that'll be all she wrote."

He was so matter-of-fact about what he was facing. It never dawned on me the bank was having troubles, too, but now it made perfect sense. I really hadn't taken much time to think of other folks and their problems. Mine were so enormous I thought I was all alone, but now I was beginning to understand the depth and severity of our nation's problems and John's wisdom in being able to see it coming.

We left the Rowe's and made a few miles before setting camp. We needed to get far enough so we'd know we could make it to the Lee Farm the next day with our slow cart and young'uns.

The next day was special because it was the day Julia Kate learned to say "Mommy," or something like "Mommy." To make Theo feel important, we gave him the job of teaching Julia Kate to speak, and he relished his professorial role. Toward the middle of the day, Theo was holding class. He started with "Where's Mommy?" To which she pointed straight to Laura. Then he said, as he had for we-don't-know- how-many-times, "Can you say Mommy?"

She'd usually just gurgle something back at Theo, but this time the little student whispered, "Gommy."

We stopped the horses to make a big deal over her and over her teacher, too. When Theo asked her again, she said it a little more surely, "Gommy." Once she realized she was the center of attention, she started shouting, *"GOMMY, GOMMY, GOMMY,"* while laughing uncontrollably at herself.

Theo was frustrated. Because she wasn't saying it right he thought he'd failed as a teacher, so I counseled him to be patient and she'd get the hang of it, to which Laura said, "I think I like it. I'd like Gommy to be my name. We're gonna be moving to a new land, I might as well have myself a new name, and it's one everybody can call me, young and old!"

And Gommy became her name forevermore. The boys adopted the new name right away, but for me it was a bit tougher. For a while her name coming from my lips was "L-Gommy." But this old dog really could learn new tricks, and eventually not only her family, but her whole world got to know Laura Barnett Lee as simply Gommy.

Back at the Farm and Making New Plans

Once at the farm, I went to meet with old Wiley to ask if he needed a farmhand. He simply said "Yes. You know you're welcome here anytime."

I spent the afternoon with Granddaddy John. When he asked me to tell him what happened, I just said, "The best I can tell is I thought I had all my ducks in a row, then somebody opened fire on my dad-gummed ducks." We'd have normally had a good laugh at such a line, but he knew how much it hurt and knew I wasn't trying to be funny. He just listened as I told him more of how it all unfolded and I lost everything. He was most happy when I told him I had no worries about Laura's faith in me, or us, wavering. It was good to tell my whole story to another man who I knew could listen to it all and never say a judgmental word. That was John.

Wiley Lee (left) John Lee (right)

We moved in to the Lee Farm in late July of '74. The family welcomed back Laura, William Wiley, John Theodore, five-month-old Julia Kate, and myself. I insisted we move into labor quarters.

It was a good time to be back. There were never too many hands in the summer time and early fall. Little Wiley was put to work doing some chores. He fed livestock, shelled peas, pulled weeds, washed porches and more. He could learn to work at a young age at the farm. We planned to put him to work young at the sawmill, but not as young as we could at a farm because of the danger in all the heavy equipment, saws and lumber swinging around.

278

He, Theo and Julia Kate loved all their cousins, aunts and uncles and loved life on the farm. Wiley and Martha were still making babies just as fast as Martha could spit 'em out. Together they'd had seven with one on the way. Unbelievable, but this next one would make Wiley's total record just three young'uns shy of his Daddy's record of twenty-three!

There were more mouths to feed than ever at the farm. It was great to be home, but even in spite of my failure, I was glad I'd left to build my own life. I wasn't there a week before I knew I had to move on again, and soon. Nothing was wrong here, mind you; I just knew I needed to go out and try again to build my own life.

I was only here to help out with the harvest, and it was a good one. I was working from before dawn to after dark six days every week. I was dog-weary, but it was a very good weary, the kind you get from good, honest hard work, not the kind you get from worryin' and figurin' and negotiatin'. I was coming home tired from just plain ol' workin', and it was doing me good. As my Daddy taught, "It's good for a man to come to the table hungry and go to bed sleepy."

Laura and I were real sure to spend plenty of time talking about where we saw our family going from here. We made it known we were going to leave by the first of November. We just weren't real sure yet where we were goin'.

I was sure I didn't need to go back into the timber business. It was a good business, but it was a boom-and-bust affair, probably more than any other line of work I could think of. I knew the people and sure knew the ropes, but I got burned so badly I wanted no part of it anymore. In fact, my new joke was "If you find somebody you hate a whole lot, just give him a sawmill!"

Laura again mentioned her uncle John Tucker and how well she heard he was doing in the cow business in Orange County. Because of the politics of the day, lots of folks left Hamilton and Columbia Counties and went to Orange, Lake and Volusia Counties. I didn't think I was too interested in the cow business, but there was one thing I was for sure interested in down there.

Florida's peninsula had an attraction to me because it was quickly becoming the heart of the citrus growing region. It had a mixture of well-drained, sandy soils and lots of lakes, swamps and rivers to provide natural cold protection. The winters were milder and much more suited for a semi-tropical tree like orange, grapefruit or tangerine. There were stories of trees in those counties which came through the very hard freeze of 1835 in very good shape, while every citrus tree from Ocala north was killed to the ground. If you settled in a spot where the freezes were rare, and the hard, killing freezes almost never, I believed it was possible to make a very good living growing citrus.

Citrus trees will grow well on the well-drained, sandy soils. It's best to have a deep sandy topsoil with some clay content below it. The sand lets the tree grow a big, strong root system, while the clay in the lower soil profile gives it some water retention ability so the trees don't suffer as badly in the occasional droughts. Normally, Orange County gets about fifty inches of rain a year, and that's aplenty, but it doesn't all come just when you want it. There's times you have way too much, like most summers, and that's when you need the well-drained sandy topsoil so your trees don't get "wet feet." Then there was times you'd have far too little rain, like many an April and May, and that's when the clay subsoil holds water to keep your tree from gettin' too thirsty.

You always want to plant your grove on a nice, sloping hill so cold air can drain off of it, and you need to be on the south or southeast side of a lake. You could even be several miles south of a really big lake like Lake Apopka and still get cold protection from it. But even if it's a small lake, you get good warmth if you plant right on the southeast shore.

Orange County also had abundant, rich bottomland soils. It was only a little over a hundred miles south of Columbia County, but that was far enough to have a much longer growing season. On the really cold nights, Orange would be generally about ten degrees warmer than Hamilton - a big difference. You could have something growing just about year-round. How could any farmer not be interested in Orange County?

I only hesitated when I thought how wild South Florida must be, and how much we'd be leaving behind in this highly-developed part of the state. Did you know at this point most of the road from Jacksonville clear to Lake City was wide enough for two wagons to pass without one having to pull off the road? Much of the road was clay-based, and several stretches were paved with bricks. Only the bridges were still mostly one-at-a-time affairs.

I knew I could rebuild my life in Orange County and hold my head up even with my business failure. Even though my business ended with my inability to pay all I owed, no one said I cheated them. I may have fallen short, and I hated it, but I knew I fell short honestly. I didn't have to leave my homeland because my lumber business collapsed, but for some reason I felt the same yearning Grandpa John said he felt when he had to leave the peace and security of St. Marys to risk it all in the wilderness of Hamilton County.

I didn't know exactly what would await me, but I knew I was in for a much tougher life than if I stayed. The Lee clan had grown huge, and Hamilton was the home of it. I didn't understand my wanderlust, but I knew it was in my blood, and sometimes a man just can't fight his own blood!

I think more than anything it was my fascination with oranges calling me south. I loved those few, poor trees we had on the farm. Even though they would get freeze damage most every year, I knew freeze damage would be much less frequent and severe in Orange County. I was sure I needed to make the move, and Laura was all behind it.

I talked to John about it, and he said he wouldn't wish a move into the frontier on his worst enemy, not after what he'd put himself through almost fifty years prior. But if I felt the urge to go, he wasn't about to hold me back. Knowing the state of my finances, John warned me how I didn't want to turn out like those neighbors of ours who came to Hamilton County penniless. They failed at a much higher rate than the ones who brought money with them, even just a little money.

I appreciated his straight talk, but I was sure I had assets I could turn into money over time. Those were my education, ability to work, knowledge of farming and all the business experience I'd gained in my young years. All my life experiences taught me those were things no one could take, and no matter what happened to my financial fortune, I could survive and thrive with those basic skills.

The next day, John gave me one hundred dollars in five-dollar bills. He called it my "survival money" and said, "I won't tell you what to do with it, all I can advise is stretch it as far as it'll go. Treat it like it's the last money on earth, and someday, I hope it's someday soon, it will treat you right." There's all he said before he choked up just a little and said, "God be with you, boy. You and your young family go into this new land, prosper and grow. And be sure to let us folks back home hear from you now and again." Then he turned, mumbled something about needing a nap, and left me standing in his fine downstairs parlor.

I protested, "Granddaddy, NO! You don't owe me this money, and I know I can make it down there in time."

He shuffled away a little slower while saying, "It's the money the farm owes you for working the harvest for us. You did more work than any of our hired hands."

"Yes sir, but the farm fed and housed my family all this time. You'd call room and board fair pay for fair work if I was any other migrant worker."

He stopped shuffling, turned and looked straight into my eyes. "Maybe so, but you aren't just any vagabond worker, either, are you? Take the money and stretch it hard; it's going to be real hard to get established if you got no money. If your pride's a-swellin' up now, just swallow it and take the money. You're in for a long hard run, and not just the journey there. It's gonna be hard getting established in new land. Don't take it for yourself, keep it for your family, and go with my blessing."

I was struck by his generosity. It was a lot of money. I also knew it could slip through my fingers in no time flat. "Thanks," I said, "you can bet I'm going to take really good care of this money. I will never forget your generosity."

Laura and I agreed we would make the trip and land in Orange County with a hundred still in hand. We would only use it when we had to, and whatever we absolutely had to spend, we'd refill the coffers by picking up jobs along the way. It would be our seed money to get us started in whatever we found to do in our new lives in Orange County.

We discussed me going ahead, getting established, then sending for the family to come after I had some stable earnings. This plan made all the sense in the world to me, but Laura would hear nothing of it. She said we were in this together, just like we had been in the lumber business together. She said if she couldn't be beside me to support me in the thin times, she'd never feel she had a rightful place to stand beside me when good times came again. I admired her spunk but was afraid she didn't know what she was getting herself and our three young'uns into. When Laura planted her feet, though, I knew there was nothing I could do to change her, so I might as well not try.

We planned our move.

Leaving the Farm and Starting the Big Move

October came, and we knew it was time to go. I can tell you I still had the same enthusiasm for moving to South Florida, but somehow I added a pretty good slug of nervousness along with it.

Now the easy way to go from Hamilton to Orange County was simple. You just take the train to Jacksonville, put your horses, wagon and belongings in the cargo hold of a steamer ship, then you jump aboard. You get your family a deluxe cabin and enjoy the ride. The whole trip won't take you any more 'n about three days.

This plan had only one problem: it was expensive. With our family of five and our horses, cart and possessions, we'd put a pretty good hole in our scant wealth. I figured altogether the trip would cost us at least fifteen dollars for passengers and freight. It would leave us with little money for getting started in our new life.

Our only option was to ride the cart the entire way on the roads and trails traversing Florida. We could camp along the trails or stay with friends. We could pick up work along the way, thus preserving our precious dollars. This route would take weeks counting our work-stops. We decided getting to Orange County in a hurry wasn't important compared to arriving with all our capital. Once we arrived in our new home, I would have plenty of time to get back in a hurry to rebuild my life, but for the time being, slow and easy was how it would have to be. Laura agreed. When I look back on it, I had no idea why she agreed, what with two young boys and a baby girl under her care but that's Laura. With all I'd put her through already, she was still agreeing to uproot her little family and go with me on a hundred-some-mile cart ride through some of the wildest parts of our country.

Sunday, October 18, was a beautiful, cool morning; a fine day for a sendoff service at the Swift Creek church. Laura's father and grandfather came to team-preach. And if you think team preaching means each preacher only speaks half as long as usual, you'd be sadly mistaken. Surely it was a beautiful sermon by two giants of the Methodist church, but most of the congregation became so mind-numbed by the long-windedness of these two gentlemen we could scarce remember a word, or even a point of the sermon. The whole reason of having both Barnetts to preach was to give Laura and her little family the best possible send-off.

Laura's mother, Julia Ann Tucker Barnett, didn't care how long the service took because she happily made herself in charge of her namesake, Julia Kate Lee. The two of them had a great time in the pew, neither one caring how long the two windbag preachers carried on. In fact, old Julia was seen holding onto young Julia like she was the only baby left in the world, for she knew once we left, she may never see this child again. Not only did Julia recognize her own aging, she was painfully aware how hard the journey was between the old and new Floridas. She knew she could never make the trip by road because the roads weren't even good trails. On their preacher's stipend, they wouldn't afford themselves to make the easy comfortable steamboat trip up the St. Johns River. It would seem a waste of the eight dollars it might cost for the two of them to make the round trip. Surely the Lord could use that money for higher cause than luxury travel. We could see those sweet old Julia eyes drinking in every feature of the new Julia, and we could see her laying her hands on the baby, praying for this young life, this piece of her which could go on in this world for many decades after she was gone.

The boys called Laura's mother "Granny Judy" ever since young Wiley learned to talk. She liked her name just fine, and for the last days of our time in North Florida (as it's now called), every time she heard "Granny Judy" from her only grandsons, you could see her let loose with a winsome smile as she fought back tears. I thought I must be the world's biggest heel for ripping these youngsters away from this sweet, aging lady.

Granny Judy never complained, though, and she said how happy she was we'd be living somewhere near her brother, John Tucker. He left when Laura was a little girl, but she knew he'd watch out for her and be a big help to us in getting settled into our new life.

As we processed out of the church, Aunt Nancy, though getting a little older, could still make the old piano sing. She played and we sang the ancient, wonderful hymn, "Oh God Our Help in Ages Past." Laura and I adopted it as our hymn to cover us and our family as we went through the dark valley which had been our lives for these last couple of years. We often remarked how we loved the hymn for being more than two centuries old. We just knew it stirred the hearts of our forebears as they went through worldly tribulations, and so it likewise inspired us to believe there was a way to get through our trials in those modern days of 1874. It's a grand hymn:

> O God our help in ages past,
> Our hope for years to come,
> Our shelter from the stormy blast,
> And our eternal home.
>
> Under the shadow of Thy throne
> Thy saints have dwelt secure;
> Sufficient is Thine arm alone,

And our defense is sure.

Before the hills in order stood,
Or earth received her frame,
From everlasting Thou art God,
To endless years the same.

A thousand ages in Thy sight
Are like an evening gone;
Short as the watch that ends the night
Before the rising sun.

Time, like an ever rolling stream,
Bears all its sons away;
They fly, forgotten, as a dream
Flies at the break of day.

O God our help in ages past,
Our hope for years to come,
Be Thou our God while life shall last,
And our eternal home.

When the hymn was done, Laura, the children and I walked to the church graveyard to say our good-byes to all the Lees gone before us. I had special words with my sweet mother, Mary McDonald Lee. I thought this might be my last graveyard visit with her. I gained so much solace, hope and inspiration from our little church and graveyard during my life. My eyes welled up and my vision got real blurry when I thought yet again of the rich family heritage I was leaving. Momma's parents, James Hiram and Mary McDonald, both passed away in recent years, and were buried right near the Lee plot. Also at the site was young Robert, the four-year-old son Wiley and Martha lost just two years ago to pneumonia. He was a sweet boy.

Our last night was restless. I wrestled with a combination of worry and excitement over both the trip ahead and our new lives in South Florida (as Peninsular Florida was then called). When I found Laura was sleepless, too, we sat up talking. She did a fabulous job of hiding her own fears and shared the burden with me in a way no one else could. She knew me better than I knew myself.

She even got a little playful some time in the wee hours of the morning. She said, "You remember when you told me about coming up on Wiley and Martha at the swimmin' hole?"

285

"Yeah, of course I do. I was the happiest man in the world when I told you of it because I had just won you back."

Then she asked, "Do you remember telling me how you wished it could be you and me there all alone?"

"Yeah."

"Well, I feel real bad I never made good on your wish. Seems we got so busy making a life for ourselves, we forgot to have a little fun." She now had command of my full attention.

"Woulda been fun, huh?" I said wistfully.

Then she said, "Still not too late, but time's a-wastin', ain't it?"

I sprang out of bed almost roaring, "And there's no bigger waste than a waste of time, is there?"

She laughed and shushed me, reminding me the whole thing would be ruined if we woke the children.

We hurried out of the house in our bedclothes and stirred up one of the horses. I mounted him bareback style, and just like I did so many times when Laura and I were just flirty young friends, I reached down to her as she grabbed my hand then sprung up to land side-saddle in front of me. Off we went just as fast as we dared, with nothing to hang on to but each other. I pushed that horse as fast as I could without bouncing both of us clean off and into the field.

At the swimmin' hole, we dismounted, disrobed and raced into the water, splashing and laughing like silly children. I commented how funny it would be if Daddy Wiley rode up on us this time. We laughed. We swam. We kissed. We had a good time. We splashed some more, then we just found ourselves locked in an embrace. Holding tight, we laughed some more, cried, and hoped, but mostly we just held on. The night was so silent, it was like all the critters in the world turned away to give us our little time together.

So many women wouldn't have been able to handle the losses a man like me had just put my Laura through. I was very aware she'd married a rising young business-star who had success written all over him. And in seven short years, I'd taken her from great promises of owning the world to destitution. So many women would've lashed out at the man who'd cost her all her worldly security. I figured if Laura had treated me that way, I'd've deserved it. But she never did. I vowed right there to spend the rest of my life building the best life I could for her, the love of my life.

286

Before we left the swimmin' hole and so many memories, and after creating my favorite memory there, Laura suggested we take some time to sit on the bank and pray about our trip and new life. We sat at the water's edge, and there we were, just Laura, me and our God. We were thankful and we were fearful. We cast our fears on the water. We told our Savior we'd rely on him. We told each other we'd rely on us. We promised God and each other we'd always "Gather at the river" of life together and we'd share our worries and allow God almighty to take those worries from us, just as He promised He'd do. We prayed for our children, their children, their children's children, and all the folks we'd be leaving behind in North Florida. We reflected on how our path had gone in directions we never could have predicted for a homegrown farmboy and a homebody preacher's daughter. We promised God we'd listen to His voice, go where He led and do what He commanded. Again, we prayed for our children - the ones going on the journey with us, and the ones we didn't yet know. We prayed we could build a home for them and future generations, just as John Lee had so wonderfully done. We prayed the ancient hymn, *our* hymn, "O God our Help in Ages Past," and recited all the verses.

The time flew.

We remounted our horse and rode back home, this time slowly but still holding on tight to each other. We knew we were all we really had, but I knew with her beside me, I had all we needed to find our way. I told her so. I loved her so.

As we rode up to our quarters, the eastern sky was beginning to leak in just a little of the first morning light. We'd been at the swimmin' hole most of the night! I'da said we'd been there about an hour and a half. It was time to be up and feeding and readying to leave the farm, and we hadn't slept a wink. I wasn't tired at all, at least not yet.

Our wagon was loaded the day before. It was full of mostly food staples like corn, oats, grits, sugar, molasses, some lard and jars of pickled and preserved fruits and vegetables the women of the family put up during harvest. Our provisions were topped off with about ten pounds of beef jerky. It was all we had for meat, but it was sure to make the trip without spoiling. We had enough food to get us to Fort Christmas if we didn't find a thing to eat along the way. But our goal was to arrive with as much of our starting food supply as possible, because we had no idea what supplies awaited us when we got there, and we aimed to use our cash to start our business, not to buy food. If necessary we could use our money to feed us, but we wouldn't last long if we did. I worried about Granddaddy John's warnings about the farmers who tried to homestead undercapitalized in Hamilton County. I knew we were underfunded, but I thought as long as we were careful with our resources, and very resourceful, we'd be able to manage.

Aside from all the food we could cram on the little two-wheel cart, we had our little bit of clothes, hand farming tools, Laura's sewing and weaving equipment and, of course, her rocking chair. Pots, pans and water buckets hung on hooks outside the cart. We had a bedroll for each of us, except Julia Kate. She'd share her Momma's bedroll.

I loaded all the farm tools I could fit. I figured the more tools I had, the better chance my tools and I had of finding work on the journey. We had a couple of tanned cowhides we could use for all kinds of repairs and a couple of beeswaxed canvas sheets for rain protection.

I packed my four revolvers, the same Colt 1851s that got me through the Civil War, but now they'd been modernized with a loading gate conversion. They were no longer muzzle-loaders, and boy, couldn't I have used those ready-to-shoot cartridges back in the War days! At least one of the Colts was going to be on my side at all times while we traveled. We hoped the sight of it would be enough of a deterrent so we wouldn't need it for defense.

For rifles, we had my Sharps Carbine for hunting and a new Winchester 1866 "Yellow Boy" rifle for defense. The Yellow Boy could hold fifteen rounds in the magazine tube, and it could be ready in seconds if trouble appeared. We were well armed.

Our money was spread around and hidden in the wagon at several different places. We might get held up, and a thief might be able to get some of our money, but he'd have to take the cart apart to find all of it.

As I've already said, In order to arrive with our full hundred, we had to pick up jobs and spend nights with friends along the way, and we needed to hunt and forage for food as we went. Every time we dipped into our supplies, we felt like we were losing ground against the forces wanting us to fail. Every penny we spent felt just the same. To save money and supplies was why we weren't just taking the train to Jacksonville and the riverboat to Orange County. Fort Christmas could wait, but we must arrive with plenty of supplies and resources to get started.

We left early Monday on the first leg of our journey, which was to Sanderson and the Barnett house for a two-night stay. I was gettin' itchy to get going, but Laura wanted to say goodbye to her parents in their home, and who was I to tell her no? This young lady was following me to the ends of the earth; in fact, she was pushing me to make the move. It was no sacrifice to have one more comfortable day with my in-laws before striking out into whatever awaited us out there in the wild new Florida. Laura and the kids rode with the Barnetts in their swift wagon while I plodded along behind them with the cart. The loaded wagon was slow, so they waited for me in Lake City the first night and we spent the night with Barnard and Sophia Cone in the fine new house he built after I bought the sawmill from him and Billy.

Barnard, Billly and I spent a good while talking on the porch about things, like how far we'd risen and how much we'd lost. They were in full support of me and my new endeavor. We talked of the future and how bright it might be as soon as Florida could get out from under the crooked Reconstruction government and back to self-rule. I still owed them some money from my failed acquisition of their business, but they insisted they would refuse any payment of it.

They asked if I thought I might get back into the sawmill business once I got on my feet down South. I don't think they believed me, but I told them I'd be a timberman again just as soon as I saw newspaper headlines proclaiming pigs had learned to fly. We laughed and talked more, but I had to excuse myself and retire early since I'd gotten no sleep the night before.

The next morning the family was up and gone before first light. Again, they rode ahead with Jabish and Julia in their fine wagon, which could make the twenty-mile run in an easy day. For me, it was a day and a half of solid plodding. The horses and I trudged along alone in the family wagon loaded with all our worldly possessions. It was the most alone time I was going to have for some time as we trekked Florida. It was good for me.

I camped at the Olustee battlefield. This place was still eerie for me, but it was a real good spot to water the horses and rest them overnight. I tied them up and took a short walk over the killing field. It no more showed signs of the pain and death it hosted a mere decade ago. Sure, you could rummage around and find all kinds of remnants of the conflict, like wagon wheels, belt buckles and buttons, but from a distance it was just another placid field of pines and underbrush.

As I walked I prayed for all my friends who'd fought with me there; those who'd lived and those who didn't; some I still knew, and some I'd never see again. I even prayed for the Yankee bastards we fought and slaughtered there and for the folks they left behind.

The night was cool, not cold. It was very pleasant weather and was the exact reason we decided to make our trip at this time of year. We would have plenty of miseries, but at least we expected the weather would be pretty good overall. This time of year in Florida was typically mild, with normally no big rains but just passing cool front storms. Daddy taught me "Only fools and Yankees predict the weather," but we had to pick a time and take our chances. With the exception of the slim chance of a hurricane, this time of year was a good one to bet on for the most comfortable weather.

Just a month prior we'd had a hurricane come from the Gulf to Cedar Key to Gainesville and on to Jacksonville, Fernandina, then along the Atlantic Coast into New England. We hoped our chances of a repeat performance were not very strong, but you just never know with hurricanes. We worried that some of the trails we planned to take might still be strewn with hurricane trash, like downed trees and such, but we had to go on.

I trudged on from Olustee to Sanderson the next morning, arriving early afternoon. The family was happy to see me, all except for Julia Barnett. She knew my appearance meant it would soon be time for her only three grandchildren to leave her life after just one more night. She never blamed me for any of the mess we were in, but she was having a real hard time saying goodbye to those young'uns and her only daughter.

When morning came again we had to say farewell. Laura almost asked me, and I almost suggested we scrap these crazy plans, and just stay and scrape a living out of the land somehow. Our eyes locked for a minute, and for the first time I saw fear in her. She was hugging onto Granny Judy with her face toward me. Granny Judy was sobbing torrents, apologizing all the while. "I know I'm not helping you any, but I'm going to miss y'all so," she said pathetically.

I overheard them once in the cook shed, mother and daughter. Laura was weeping, telling her mother she thought she'd have her mother around to help her in raising her kids, and she wasn't at all confident she was going to be able to do the mothering job on her own without Julia's guidance. Julia, likewise, was crying and saying how those grandchildren were the light of her life, and she couldn't imagine herself growing old without Laura and them around.

Laura worried about her parents growing old without their only child around to help them, but Julia said she needn't worry because they were well cared for by all the good Methodists of the area. Nonetheless, she would sorely miss Laura, the children, and even me.

Then, at leaving time, and almost miraculously in their country way, the two women straightened up, wiped their faces with Granny Judy's apron, and looked up smiling as Laura chirped, "Come on kids, we gotta go. We're gonna take an adventure you'll NEVER forget! We're gonna go meet your Uncle John Tucker in Christmas, Florida!"

Wiley Junior's ears perked up, "CHRISTMAS! Is it Christmas every day there?"

"Oh no," Laura said, "but it's a real special place and we gotta get goin', don't we Granny Judy?"

"Yes you sure do," said the heart-broken grandmother with the most cheerful smile you ever saw. It was obvious, she wanted to be sure if Wiley could remember her when he got older, he'd remember her happy with her big smile. She picked up Wiley, gave him a big bear hug and said, "Young man, when you get to Christmas, I want you to find ol' Saint Nick and give him this big hug for Granny Judy, will you?"

Wiley hugged her right back and said, "You bet I will, Granny Judy, I'm gonna hug him just like *this*," as he squeezed her neck as hard as he could.

We all laughed, and Jabish just had to tickle each one of his grandchildren one last time. He and I had a long warm, handshake. It turned into a rare hug, and he gave me a benediction I will never forget. "God's peace be with you and your family. May you find the prosperity you seek, and may that prosperity never come between you and the God of ages; and may this little family grow in stature, grace, numbers and most importantly, in the knowledge and love of our Savior. Godspeed, young man!" He hugged his little girl, Laura, and escorted her to the wagon, smiling all the way; then he took Julia Kate from Granny Judy and placed her in her Momma's arms. By then Theo had climbed aboard the bench seat, Wiley on the resting horse. I was ready to walk, so Jabish went to the horse, slapped his flank, and let out a great big, guttural "HEEEYAAHHHH!!! Get gone horse, GET GONE!" And we began our journey waving and laughing.

Into the Wild

We stayed real busy on our journey, laughing and singing silly songs just to make sure our kids didn't get nervous about our excursion and to convince ourselves, too.

It was about eighteen miles of good road to Lake Butler where we hoped to spend our first night. Laura knew lots of folks there because Jabish was a frequent preacher at the Union church. The Union churches were how most of the small towns got their churches started. Once a congregation got too big for home church, all the Methodists, Baptists, and whatever Presbyterians and Episcopalians the town had would pitch in to build a building, and the circuit riders would take turns at the pulpit. The church building would be a different denomination every week, and so would the congregation. If the townfolk wanted to hear a preachin' and have a dinner on the grounds, they'd best show up at the Union church and support whatever denomination was available on any given Sunday.

Jabish had already arranged for us to stay with the Prevatt family for just one night before heading on to Gainesville.

Gainesville was a pretty stout two-day run from Lake Butler. It was thirty miles and included a ferry crossing of the Santa Fe River. It cost us fifty cents to ferry us and all our stuff because we had to divide our load into two trips. This crossing was expensive and time consuming, but we had to do it. The toll was going to have to be borrowed from our reserves because I hadn't stopped for any jobs yet.

All the trails we'd traveled so far were familiar to me from my cavalry days. I reflected how different it was to be driving the trails in a cart with wife and three children than as a young horse soldier. Even though I'd lost so much, this trip made me aware of how much I'd gained since my Army days.

It was quickly obvious to Laura how long this trip was going to be in our two-wheeled-cart. Y'see, it had no springs in its undercarriage and no cushions on its seat, and I should mention it only had a smooth one-by-eight board for a lower back support. Laura never complained, but I could only imagine what she thought when we were be passed by one of the swift carriages or stagecoaches. They not only looked good, but they could make at least twice our speed because they had leaf springs on all four wheels, and nicely upholstered seating for the passengers. They were made for going long distances. Even though our horses were strong and good, our cart was not; any sort of pothole, big root or rock in the trail could send passengers and cargo flying, and each bump sent bone-jarring jolts straight from the wooden wheels into the poor passenger. Even Laura's parents, in their preacher's poverty, had a fine carriage with a very comfortable ride. It was a gift by one of Jabish's congregations and was an immense help to him in covering all the miles between his churches.

The stagecoaches were the deluxe way to travel. The best ones had teams of four horses and would change horse-teams at most of their stopping points so there'd always be a fresh set pulling the coach. The downside to the stagecoach was it drew plenty of attention. Its passengers were likely to be important people, and its cargo high value, so it was a magnet for robberies. No one could say my two-wheel cart held any attraction for thieves, at least not smart thieves. Nobody sizing us up would give us a second thought as candidates for robbery. We figured we were about as shabby a crew as the Florida backwoods had ever seen.

Our traveling days involved lots of stops. The youngsters needed frequent tending, and I was so very afraid of spending any of my money on things like food. It wasn't unusual for us to make ten stops in a day to gather some sort of food, or shoot or catch some meat, or tend to the young'uns.

We were on constant lookout for edible things on the way. We had no shortage of meat animals to shoot, but gathering the plants for eating would be a different story. A mainstay of our diet would be swamp cabbage, also known as palm hearts. It was plentiful and you could harvest it in fairly large pieces, but it was a lot of work. We kept some on the wagon at all times. The fruit of the cabbage palm was edible, too. It was a berry growing on long stalks, and there was plenty of it around in the fall, except where the critters have already stripped them clean.

The wild beauty berry was also mature this time of year. It didn't taste like a whole lot, but you could eat the deep blue berries right off the stalk, or gather up enough and make a pie, or mix it in with bread, grits or hotcakes to add a little flavor.

Even sandspurs were edible. And the great thing about sandspurs was you didn't have to go out lookin' for 'em because they find you! You could lightly singe the barbs off 'em, then eat the hull and seed, or you could rub 'em between two pieces of animal skin to make the seed fall out. You could eat them raw or make them into flour for bread or hotcakes.

Of course, our favorite find was oranges. The farther south we traveled, the more plentiful the wild orange, grapefruit and tangerine trees were. It was still early in the season, so the fruit we got was on the tangy side, but it was still good, and it was something we could stock up on because it would travel well and supply us on those days we couldn't find much in our foraging.

The Spanish Bayonet was a very useful plant, but not for eating. It was our source of needles and thread. If you carefully cut a thin strand down the length of the fibrous leaf up to and including the needle, you ended up with a very passable needle and thread ready to go into service to put together a new pair of moccasins (I could wear one out in just a few days), or sew up clothes. I had one good pair of work boots in the wagon, but I wasn't about to use them up on this trip. They were going to be for me to use when I got real paying jobs in Orange County. On this trip I would sometimes wear my home-made moccasins but mostly went barefoot.

For meat, it would be the rare day we couldn't find a raccoon, 'possum, gopher turtle or other small critter to feed us, but we preferred to bag a deer, turkey or gator to get a stock of meat for several days. We had frequent chances to drop a line in a creek or lake for fresh fish. Meat was not a problem in the Florida wild lands, and we had plenty of uses for the skins. At most all times of our trip the cart had a gator, deer or some other kind of hide stretched out on top of it, salted and curing in the sun.

We arrived in Gainesville on Saturday October 24, right on schedule even though we had no schedule. I was surprised what a mess the town still was from the hurricane. We stayed with the Ingram family, who had a large farm and sawmill in the Hogtown area just north of Gainesville. We had lots of laughs together about how cruel things had been, and we wondered if the timber business would ever reach its former glory.

As luck would have it, work was plentiful in Gainesville because of the aftermath of the hurricane I was so worried about. Ingram told me it'd be best to spend a few days working there. There were still lots of folks who hadn't been able to dig out from the hurricane yet, and all the farmhands were busy trying, mostly in vain, to salvage what they could of the crops.

I signed on with Ingram. He was happy to have me. He put me in charge of a crew of men, fed my family and paid me a dollar-fifty a day for my labors and the work of my horses and cart. Meanwhile, the roads were drying out a little more with every day of working and earning. We stayed in some converted slave quarters behind the Ingram house, but it was luxury compared to riding the cart all day and camping on the trail. Laura helped around the house as part of our deal. After a week there, we needed to move on even though Gainesville was very welcoming to us and our hosts tried to get us to stay. It was very attractive, with its booming new citrus industry, plenty of work and friendly folks, but we were sure we were headed to Fort Christmas in Orange County.

While in Gainesville, I had to firm up our route. I was torn between the eastern route to Palatka, crossing the St. Johns, then heading south on the good ridge roads between the river to the west and the ocean to the east. I knew there were good trails, but I would have to pay to ferry us across the St. Johns twice, which I really didn't want to do.

The western route had less developed trails, but on it, we'd never have to pay our way across the big river, a savings of at least one dollar. It would take us down to Ocala, then Leesburg, then to settlements called Tavares, Eustis, Mrs. Drawdy's homestead on Lake Dora, Apopka, Fort Maitland, then on to Fort Christmas. I talked with folks at the General Store who were getting news of road conditions all around South Florida. It seemed the swamps in the western route were full from the effects of a pretty wet summer season with a hurricane piled on top. Parts of those roads really weren't anything but old Indian trails and weren't handling the high water very well. It was mostly advised I should take the eastern route.

They also advised the western route had longer stretches of unsettled land, which only meant danger to a young family. Even though I always had a pistol strapped to me and Laura always had my carbine loaded and ready at her side, we could easily be outgunned by a mean enough gang, especially if they took us by surprise. The better travelled routes would be not entirely safe, but safer from outlaws.

One old fella hanging out at the General Store got real blunt with me. "Mister," he said, "Yore just nuthin' but a damned ol' fool for takin' the pretty lady and young family of yor'n onto these backwood trails with the river cruiser makin' the trip safe, comfterble and faster than wut yer doin."

I responded, "I see your point, Mister, and I appreciate your advice, but I'm outa money. This cart is the only way I can get to Orange County so I can make a new start." Even though he did make me feel like a fool, I wanted it known everywhere I was broke. If word got out I was sportin' a hundred dollars around on my horse cart, somebody would make sure to relieve me of it before the trip was done. Maybe he was right and I was a fool, but I was committed.

The east route meant crossing the St. Johns by ferry from west to east bank in Pilatka, which had recently changed its name to Palatka for some reason. It was an active port town, so we just might find work there for a few days. After crossing the St. Johns then the Crescent River just a few miles later, there was a good ridge with a decent road going to Welaka, Barber's settlement, Pierson, DeLeon Springs and on to Enterprise. There we'd have to cross the big river again at Lake Monroe to arrive in Orange County at Fort Mellon.

Against all good advice, I decided to take a middlepath. I would head down to Ocala. The road to Ocala was decent, and there was a man there I wanted to see. From there we would head east on the old soldier's trail through the Big Scrub and cross the St. Johns on a new ferry boat I'd just heard about.

We left Gainesville with full bellies and full pockets. We got twelve dollars for the work of my horses and me, a well-fed family for Laura's efforts, and some good new friends. I was thinking if we could just get a few days more work along the way, we may have all the travel money we'd need to make our destination without disturbing our real money.

We were on our way to Ocala. We'd already sent ahead and told Capt. J.J. Dickison we were heading his way and would like to call on him as we passed through. We hoped he knew we meant we'd love to stay with him, but we hadn't heard back from him by time we left Gainesville. If he wouldn't receive us, surely we could camp in the back of his farm or beside his place or somewhere. All we really needed any given night was enough fresh water to drink, cook and clean, water the horses and take care of Julia Kate's constant supply of dirty diapers.

Fortunately, Captain Dickison was happy to see us and took us in. He never knew me well during the War, but he and my Daddy were good friends. Since I was just a lowly private, he and I didn't have much interaction during my service.

Now Dickison was one of the legends of Florida's Home Guard in the Civil War. Widely known as the "Swamp Fox" of Florida, he somehow managed to get himself into all the major incidents in our state. He and his Company H, 2nd Cavalry, were in the very first Florida skirmish up in Fernandina. They fought both battles of Gainesville. He led the Florida Cavalry at Olustee, was in charge of the legendary sinking of the Yankee steamer *Columbine* on the St. Johns River, and again commanded the cavalry in the battle of Natural Bridge. He was a legend in our state. Because of his reputation, the carpetbaggers and scalawags gave him wide berth. They were real sure to find out who his friends were around Ocala, too, because they sorely didn't want to rile the old Swamp Fox.

Dickison turned out to be quite a gracious host. He had a nice home and insisted we stay in his guest quarters. He was anxious to hear of my father Wiley and really took a shine to young Wiley. He wanted to get my reflection on the Civil War since we were almost ten years past it. He wouldn't allow me to work in his home or on his farm. Even when I told him my predicament, he boomed, "No War hero guest of mine will ever be seen laboring on my premises! We've been through too much together for me to be hiring you for odd jobs or getting you hired out around town."

It was then he told me he'd written young A.D. Cone and me up for "Coolness during the engagement" in his written report to President Davis after Olustee. I never knew it, and if Olustee had happened sometime earlier in the War I'da gotten some sort of a medal for my display of valor during the fight. But as late as it was and as broke as the Confederacy was, I never even got wind of my special commendation. The medal wouldn't have done me any good, but the news of it did make me figure maybe he knew me better'n I thought he did.

He was mighty gracious to put us up and not allow us to work, but I don't think the dear Captain quite understood how broke we were and how badly we needed the work if we were going to make our trip without spending any of our reserves. So Ocala ended as a mighty nice two-day break for us, but not as we planned.

What Dickison did do for me was to write a "To whom it may concern" letter of recommendation I could show to anyone who needed a reference for my abilities and work ethic. He was happy to help find me work everywhere else on my journey, but just wasn't going to have me as a laborer while under his roof. As he handed me the letter, he laughed and said, "You might not want to show this to the Captain of the *Columbine* or a few other folks I tangled with during the War," he joked. "My recommendation may not help your cause with some of those folks from the other side, but if it can help you, I'm real pleased for you to use it however you like."

Everywhere we stopped, the boys found something new to fall in love with. Each time we'd pack up to move, they'd be protesting they were sure this was the place for us. However, Laura and I were resolved we were going to move on and weren't going to stop until we reached Orange County in South Florida.

Crossing the Ocklawaha and the Big Scrub

We headed east on our way to a new settlement called Manhattan. On the west bank of the St. Johns, it was being developed by a Mr. William Astor of New York City. The Astor family was one of the wealthiest in the world, and William was determined to make Manhattan, Florida an important tourist destination, shipping hub and industry and farming center. It was right in a spot where a wealthy Jewish man, Moses Levy, had tried to build a huge sugar cane and citrus plantation starting over fifty years before. He'd failed due to Indian wars, pestilence and disease, but Mr. Astor was pretty sure the new steamships, less Indians and new labor supply would make it a lot less remote, and he could get his produce to market a whole lot faster. Astor was pretty sure Moses Levy was on the right track, but just a few decades early.

Manhattan was located at a rare place in the river with good riverbanks on both sides. The eastside St. Johns bank at that point was Volusia settlement, the oldest inland white settlement in Florida. From Lake George south it seemed wherever you found a high bank on one side, usually the east, it was swampy on the other. Manhattan was a rare exception, with workable banks, dry but not so high as to be inaccessible, on both sides. Astor said someday he was gonna build a bridge and this place would become a major river crossing point for east-to-west movement in our state. To start, he just improved the crossing with a self-propelled, side-wheeler steam ferry, the likes of which you'd have to go to New York City to see. This spot was the first south of Lake George where the banks were good for crossing, and to the south the river couldn't be crossed again for at least twenty miles. I think Mr. Astor was on to something big.

I heard a lot of us cracker boys grumbling about all the Yankees bringing their money down here and trying to make something of our state. "Who do they think they are," they'd grumble. I even heard an ol' chap one day say, "We'll show them they can't build anything decent in our town!" He was serious and never stopped to think how stupid he sounded.

How stupid can a man be? I was always amazed when I'd hear that kind of talk. It made me realize the only way Florida was going to grow and let us make anything of ourselves was if the newcomers found prosperity, too. If they made money, more and more Northerners would want to take part in it. I decided again, the horrible Civil War was over for me. I wanted the honest Yankees to make their money grow like they'd struck gold, and I wanted to prosper right along with them. Now I'm not making excuses for carpetbaggers, y'know, but I found most of the Northerners moving in here just wanted to earn an honest living like the rest of us. The ones coming down here just to take advantage of our misfortune could hang from the highest tree as far as I cared, but we shouldn't make life tougher for the good ones, especially the good ones with money.

On our way to Manhattan, we stopped for a while at Silver Springs. It had to be one of the prettiest spots in the world. The settlers around the spring were real friendly. Mr. Howse, the owner of the spring, told us there were big plans for a tourist hotel. He invited us to stay, but we figured we needed to get a few miles east to the Ocklawaha River, where we were told there was a ferry. It was a free one, so I wouldn't have to part with any of my precious cash. The ferry crossing was short, but sometimes the water was pretty swift. Because there hadn't been much rain since the hurricane, I figured it would be pretty passable for us.

One of my fears became reality at the Ocklawaha crossing as I looked to see the barge and the rowboat both waiting for me . . . on the other side. Any user was responsible to make sure he left the barge on one side and the rowboat on the other. That way, the next traveler had a way to cross no matter which side he came from. Even if the boat you wanted was on the opposite bank, you had a way to get to it. You'd then, say, row to the other side, beach the rowboat, board the barge, take it back and pick up your people or cargo. After ferrying them across, you'd tie the boats together, row them both back, leave one, then return to your family or payload with the remaining boat, thus leaving the crossing with a means of transport on both sides. It was a good system when folks used it right.

Every now and then a traveler of lesser character, shall we say, would just leave with both boats on one side. Therefore, a traveler who came to the river on the non-boated side would either have to wait until someone came to cross from the other direction, or he would have to swim across, tie his horse, then row the barge back to pick up the rest of his belongings or family, or maybe he'd have to swim himself across, risking gator or moccasin attack. It was cumbersome. If you came up to a ford with both barge and rowboat on the other side, it gave you fair warning of who, or what, might be ahead of you. People with any civility didn't leave both on one side of the river. It was a code of honor among travelers.

Not only did my fear become reality at the crossing, but the barge itself was way too small. This crossing was only about 150 feet wide, but it was deep, and it was going to take me several trips once I got my hands on the barge. Since the barge was so small, I was going to have to bring my horses, wagon, family, and all belongings across in separate trips for each. If I overloaded the barge, it might capsize and sink. We would lose most or all of our meager belongings. Or worse yet, we might lose one or more of us.

I'd been accused of taking foolish risks with my family on this trip, but this was no time for ridiculously foolish risks. It was going to take us a long time to get across, and I had to be in no hurry. First, we'd camp on the west bank overnight, hoping someone would come along from the east to relieve our problem of both boats being over there.

We set camp under a scrub oak thicket. It was real close to the crossing, and I was able to take the horses and wagon about twenty yards more into the woods where they couldn't be detected by unsavory types traveling by night. As long as the young'uns stayed asleep, and Julia Kate didn't wake up crying for her Momma or 'cause she was a mess, we should be alright.

I stayed up all night nervously watching for signs of life. I was hoping for helpful folks who might lend a hand with the crossing, and, of course, I'd return the favor for them; but I was praying hard against malevolent folks who might cause us all kinds of trouble. I had firepower enough to take care of several bad men, but if it was a big gang, like the legendary Murrell gang of North Florida, I would have my hands full and then some.

Well, it was a good thing no bad men showed during the night, but it was a bad thing no good folks came along either. The sun rose, I hadn't slept a wink, and I had a big job to do.

First, Laura gave the boys some hard biscuits from our supplies, then she gave Julia Kate her morning vittles as only a mommy can do. While they ate, I hitched the wagon to Prince and he pulled it the short trip to the edge of the river. I then jumped onto Duchess and she and I swam the river to the other side.

The current was pretty strong that morning. I tied Duchess then decided to take the rowboat back first and get the feel of the current. I'd be sure to bring my human cargo across first while I was as strong as I was going to be the whole day.

With the family loaded, we rowed across the black water of the Ocklawaha River. I had to row sideways like a crab into the current in order for our boat to take us straight across to the east bank. This first leg of the journey happened without incident, but I was quietly getting worried.

I untied the barge, then called for Wiley to ride back with me. He liked being the big man when I needed him, and little did he know how much I was afraid I really needed him that day 'cause he was the closest thing I had to another man for miles around. I was able to pole the empty barge while Wiley manned the tiller in a vain effort to give us some direction against the current. It looked hopeless to get the barge across with a load, but I had an idea.

When we got back to the west side, I put Wiley on Duchess, then I tied my two one-hundred-foot ropes together and tied one end onto Duchess' saddle horn. Wiley was a pretty experienced horseman for his mere five years, but I was fixin' to put him to the test . . . and his Momma, too. He knew how to ford a horse, so I shouldn't have been worried, but I knew if anything happened to make him fall off, I would have a devil of a time finding him in the pitch-black Ocklawaha water. I was glad Wiley didn't know the risk he was taking and prayed Laura didn't know either. I figured the horse would have firm footing on river bottom about the first third and last third of the crossing, but I knew she'd be swimming with my boy on her back for the middle third, and that was when things could go wrong. If something happened to spook the horse, like a gator, or she hit an unexpected submerged log, or who knows what, this trip could turn bad. Thankfully, it didn't, and they got the rope to the other side and hitched it to a real stout cypress knee.

I tied my end of the rope to a young cypress tree on my side, and then was able to pull the loaded barge across on the rope without having to pole it alone. If there had been two men, we could have easily poled it across, but with just me, the little flat-bottomed barge woulda gone sailing down the river if we hadn't been able to rig up the rope to pull it across. I was real proud of my boy Wiley for his help. Now I had two horses and all my people on the other side, I just had to move our stuff from one riverbank to the other.

It took three trips on the little barge to get our few belongings across, leaving only the empty wagon on the west shore. My next challenge was to get the wagon across. It was too big to go on the barge, but it could straddle it. What I didn't know was how far it could go on the barge without capsizing it. If it capsized, I reckoned we were in a bad way because I would never be able to pull it to the other side against the current. I only had one choice.

I took the rope from the cypress tree and tied it real snug to the front of the wagon. I then started to roll the wagon slowly down the gentle slope to the water. I yelled to Laura to take both horses, tighten both their cinch straps as tight as she could, then with Wiley holding them close together, Laura was to string the rope through their cinch straps and tie them together.

While three-year-old Theo took care of his infant sister, Wiley and Laura each mounted one horse, when I hollered "GO," they were to gee the horses down the trail as swiftly and smoothly as they could. My job was to squat in the back of the cart and shift my weight from side to side to balance it and keep it from flipping, which was easy as long as the wheels were on riverbottom, but real soon I could tell we were floating. All we had was the speed of the cart over the water and my balance to make sure we'd reach the other side in upright position. If it rolled over I knew I had my work cut out to right it without breaking something on it or something in me. I had no idea how my plan was going to work, but I can tell you, when I felt the wheels starting to bump and lurch as they found bottom on the other side, I was one relieved fool. I yelled for the horses to slow down. My wheels were back on solid ground and I knew our wagon was safe. My new worry was if I hit a big pothole, root or a submerged log too fast, I could break an axle or a wheel, and we'd have a whole new set of problems.

With the horses slowed down, the wagon and I emerged from the mighty Ocklawaha River. All we had to do was load up our wagon and we were on our way again. We were giddy with our unlikely success. "Daddy, that looked like fun," Wiley exclaimed about my wild ride across the river.

"Well, it was fun, son, because I knew I had a steady hand running the horses for me. I knew I had my number one son driving those horses, so I had no doubt the job was gonna be done right." Theo joined in and let out a yelp. He had no idea what all the excitement was about, but boy was he happy! And li'l Julia Kate, she just sat up on her blanket and squealed. Laura told me I looked like a big wet rat. I told her she looked like a big piece of cheese and started chasing her while the boys followed. It was a merry time right in the midst of some real tough times.

We re-loaded our wagon and headed on to the east as far as we could before dark. I strapped on two revolvers for this leg of the journey. Laura looked at me kinda curious-like but didn't say anything. A couple of miles from the Ocklawaha we came into the Big Scrub. It was mile after mile of just about nothing except those short-needle, or sand pines and sorry old blackjack oaks. both of 'em good for nothin' but firewood. There wasn't much settlin' goin' on here because there wasn't much way to make a living out of this super-sandy soil and this sorry type of pine tree. They grew so thick, tall and flimsy that they were always falling or shedding big ol' branches across the road, if we could call it a road. Horsemen, of course, could usually step over or almost always ride around a fallen tree, but a wagon driver had to either get the tree out of the way or see if he could navigate his cart around it and just start a new road. It was most unusual for a wagon man to make this run from Silver Springs to Manhattan without having to cut up and haul off at least two trees or create a detour or two. The road was originally cut by soldiers, I s'pose. It was once a fairly true east-west line from Fort King across the Ocklawaha, the St. Johns, and on to the King's Highway, which ran up and down the state just a little landward of the east coastline. By this time, though, it wasn't much more than a zig-zagging mess.

Goin' up the hills, the sand would get so deep a horse with just a rider would struggle by time he got to the top. Pulling a wagon made the incline near impossible. Every time a horse would pull a load up the hill, he'd make it worse for the next traveler; because this ground was such bottomless sand, each horse digging in to climb the road would have to dig deeper than the one before, causing the sand to get looser and looser. We hitched both horses for this stretch of road. Even then, several times we had to unload about half the wagon at the bottom of a hill and make those poor horses go up, unload, go back down, reload and climb again. Now this was Florida, so it wasn't like any of these hills were anything to impress a mountain-man, but the deep sand made them very hard to travel.

I would station Laura and the children at top of the hill while I fought to get our load up the hill. They'd hide off the side of the road, Laura with the carbine and one loaded revolver. I'd been told here was where we'd have our biggest chance of running into trouble, and mostly at night. Fortunately, we didn't see too many people of any kind. Not yet, anyway.

We stopped at one of the frequent lakes along the trail and decided it would be our camping spot for the night. We pulled well off the path, and I forbade a fire the whole night, using the excuse I was just too tired to fool with it, I never let on to the family how worried I was about this stretch of our trip. From Silver Springs all the way to Manhattan was a long stretch with very little population, and we were in the thick of it. Even Captain Dickison had real concerns about us on this leg of our trip.

Although the shade of the thick sand pines made us comfortable, they allowed very little groundcover underneath, so there wasn't much for the horses to graze on. We broke into our corn and oats to feed them for the first time since we'd left home. I knew it wasn't bad to use some of our supplies, but I felt real possessive of all the food and feed we'd brought. The better we could stretch our supplies, the better off we were.

We bedded down for the night. I made palmetto beds for each of us. They worked so well we really couldn't tell we weren't in some fine hotel. I made them by cutting palmetto sticks - big, stiff ones for myself and smaller, more flexible ones for each of my smaller family members. Then I lashed 'em together using strips of palmetto frond in four-to-five inch spacings onto two long, straight oak poles laid parallel about two to three feet apart. Next, I dug each of us a little trench to fit the size of our bodies. When you lay the frames over the trench, you'd find you're not sleeping on the hard ground anymore, but suspended over your trench, with a couple layers of blankets, clothes, or Spanish moss on top of the frame. The beds were comfortable. Come morning, we'd load our palmetto racks on the wagon, and off we'd go on our new day's sojourn.

Next morning, we set out early in hopes of making it all the way to Manhattan, which I figured to be a fifteen-mile run. With all the soft sand, our going might be real slow. I knew it was going to be a hard day.

Laura started each day with a morning hymn. The day's selection was "When Morning Gilds the Skies." Wiley knew most of it and Theo knew a word here and there, so they'd sing along with us as best they could. Julia Kate just squealed. Our morning song time was a big help to start us off in a happy mood. The boys knew if they sang along well, it could lead us into silly song time, and singing could help melt away those tedious hours.

We had many favorite silly songs. The boys loved "Oh! Susanna,"

> Rained so hard the day I left,
> The weather it was dry,
> The sun so hot,
> I froze to death,
> Susanna don't you cry.

It was written by Stephen Foster, the same fellow who wrote "De Camp Town Ladies" and "Old Folks at Home." We understood he'd never seen the Suwannee River, but he sure wrote a pretty song about it.

What fun when we'd break into one like "Ol' Dan Tucker,"

> Ol' Dan Tucker was a fine ol' man
> Washed his face in a fryin' pan,
> Combed his hair with a wagon wheel,
> Died with a toothache in his heel.
> Git out da way, old Dan Tucker,
> Git out da way, old Dan Tucker,
> Git out da way, old Dan Tucker,
> You're too late to git yer supper."

And "Polly Wolly Doodle" had to be everyone's favorite, except for me, of course. By time our trip was over I was pretty sure I didn't care if I never heard ol' "Polly" ever again. But I must admit when the kids got scared or just plain cranky, we could roll right into their favorite silly song and the whole mood would change!

And if those seem silly to you, you shoulda heard some of the ones we made up as we went. We must've had a hundred little songs to sing as we rode along.

After we watered the horses at a pretty little lake, we came to our biggest hill yet. This one was a fairly easy climb, though, because it was a very gradual slope up from the lake and the soils were a bit heavier than the last hills, so it didn't become too rutted-up until we got almost to the top.

At the top of the hill, I could see our trail well ahead in the distance. I saw some movement just about as far away as I could see. I made a clear mark in my mind of where I saw them; it looked like four horsemen. They'd disappeared just as quickly as they'd shown up, probably because they saw us. They were probably up to no good.

About a hundred yards before we got to the spot where we saw 'em, I stopped us.

I checked Laura's Winchester. It was fully loaded with fifteen rounds. I cycled the lever action, checked to make sure the hammer cocked itself, and handed it carefully back to her. I put Wiley on the wagon seat next to Laura with the carbine. It was cocked and ready, too. I told him, "Now don't start shootin' unless I shoot first. And remember it's a hair trigger."

"Yes sir," he replied, not knowing whether to be giddy with excitement or to cry in fear.

"You're my big boy there, son, just hold it nice and steady and listen for me to tell you what to do. I'm proud of you and I know you can do just fine. Remember what we practiced."

I put the two spare revolvers between Laura and Wiley so if she used up her fifteen rifle rounds, she had another twelve shots ready to go. We spread a blanket over their laps to hide the weapons.

I un-holstered my two revolvers and carried them down at my sides so I would be at least as ready to fire as the bad men were. I walked beside the wagon on the left side with my pistols low and out of sight. Laura sat on the right side of the bench seat with Wiley on the left in between us.

We put Theo and Julia Kate right behind the seat between some feed barrels. We told Theo he needed to be the big brother now and make sure his little sister stayed still and didn't cry.

When I first saw the horsemen from the top of the hill, I'd noted a scrub oak tree arching over the trail just a little ways ahead of where they'd disappeared, so I knew about where to expect them to be lurking. I still had no idea what we were up against, but was real glad I saw them so far in advance. I think they saw me, too, but couldn't be sure. I could only hope four of them was all there was.

I got us singing again. This time all joined in for a rousing chorus of a brand new song I'd just learned, called "She'll Be Comin' 'Round the Mountain." I figured the merrier we sounded the more surprised they'd be since they thought they were surprising us. Maybe, just maybe, our merriment would be disarming to them.

We headed down the road as alert as we could possibly be while striving to sound carefree as a family of bluebirds. As we got close, I looked real carefully up into that scrub oak tree to see if there was a bandit waiting in ambush for us. It seemed clean, and most of the rest of the trees around here were un-climb-able sand pines. We were ready, and all our weapons were ready to go into service, if needed, and we were singin' all the while.

Just a few steps past the tree, I saw them. The four of them stepped out of a scrub oak thicket on horseback, right smack in the middle of the road about twenty paces ahead of us.

"She shore is perty, Boss," one of them said. With that I knew for sure this was no social call.

"Mornin'," I said, not wishing to make engaging conversation, but trying to give the impression I had no concern about them.

"What brings y'all out this way?" The biggest of them asked.

"Goin' to Manhattan."

"What business you got there?" He asked again.

"I reckon it's none of your business," I said, trying to get them to the point.

He let out a little laugh. "What's yer names?"

"M'name's Pa, and this here's Ma," I said. Don't ever give a criminal your real name.

Big Feller continued, "Well, if'n yer not the friendly kind, I guess I'll jest get to my bidness. I'm the roadkeeper here, and you need to pay us a little toll to get through on yore way to Manhattan."

I walked to the front of the wagon and lifted my pistols up into plain view. With this cue, Laura and Wiley uncovered their rifles so our new friends could get a good look at how out-prepared they were.

"You're one sorry-ass roadkeeper then, 'cause this here's the worstest road I've seen in mah life. Besides, ah don't pay no tolls." (My Momma woulda washed my mouth with lye soap for the grammar I used, but I figgered real fast I wanted to sound just as plain and uneducated as they were. I surely didn't want to lead 'em on that we might have anything of value onboard.) I was feeling a little bold because we had four weapons at the ready while theirs were still holstered. I knew I had the advantage unless they had some surprise reinforcements hidden in the bushes.

"You need to give us yer money," he said, still seeming not real convinced he should take this well-armed family of silly-song singers seriously. I guess we were s'posed to be easy pickins.

"Got no money. There's twenty-seven cent on me. That's all, and if'n you don't want Captain J.J. Dickison comin' out here after you, you probably wanna just git outa the way. Just day 'fore yestiddy ol' J.J. told me he was gettin' itchy to do something 'cause he ain't, shall we say, turned in any bad guys lately. Ah'm not reel sher wut he meant by turnin' 'em in, 'cause I been ridin' a long time wif ol' J.J. and I ain't yet seen 'im turn in nobody he din't like. But he might like you fellers just fine. Ah rightly don't know. But ah do know for sure he jest shoots common roadside robbers and leaves 'em fer the buzzards to pick clean. Not real sure how he cottons to . . . 'roadkeepers.'" I knew these varmints knew Dickison's name, and I invoked it because it was likely the only name they'd fear.

Not giving up easily, he said, "Well, just give us some of what's in the wagon."

"The wagon's only got food for my family and my horses. Yer not gittin' it. You gotta get through us to take our food. I think you can tell we're ready fer you, and yer not real ready fer us. Ma here, she's got you sighted in, Big Feller, and I'm full ready to take yer next two goons. Junior here, he's got the scrawny one on the end." I said all that not to try to entertain my guests, but to give instructions to my troops, so all of us were real clear on who we were gonna shoot. It'd be a waste for each of us to be aimed at the same feller, don'cha know?

I pointed to Wiley, "Junior here, he's young and all, so y'know he just might miss, but Ma and I will have ol' Scrawny gone before he can draw on us. Through all that, one of y'all might jest git a shot off before you hit the ground. I recommend ya aim fer me, 'cuz I can fill the air with lead when me and my Colts get a-'goin'. You might even git me, but you look like smart fellers to me, and I don't think y'all wanna be takin' that kind of chance, now do ya?"

Then I decided to scoop up a little more fear. "Hey, Junior, ya gotta good bead on ol' Scrawny there?"

"Yes, sir, Pa."

"Hey Scrawny, how's it look from yer angle there. Is he lookin' down the barrel all proper-like?"

Now Scrawny was gettin' real nervous, and I could tell he was starting to shake. "I asked you a question, Scrawny, does m'boy have that carbine aimed clear through the middle of yer chest?"

"Y-y-yesss, sssirrr, he surely does, don't let 'im shoot me, Mister. That thing ain't really loaded, is it?"

"Not a risk you wanna take, Scrawny. I'm glad to hear he's aimin' true. Y'all know how proud a pa gets when he knows his first boy can aim straight, doncha? Now he knows that thar rifle has a hair trigger, but wit him bein' so young and all, I'm agonna 'pologize in advance that he might hit ya afore I'm good 'n ready fer him too, Scrawny. That's 'c uz of bein' young and all, he's a mite excited right now, an' if'n any one of you worthless misfits so much as moves, his trigger finger's likely to twitch, and that's agonna ruin yer day. So I felt it fittin' and proper fer me to 'pologize now, 'cuz you ain't agonna be 'round fer no 'pology if a mistake happens."

Big Feller interjected, "If Junior shoots, that rifle'll put yore boy on his ass in the back o' yer waggin."

To which I replied, "Beggin' to differ, sir, if'n you'll look real close-like, y'might notice he's got the butt propped against that thar sugar barrel behind him so's 'twon't happen. But y'might be right. If'n that happens, Scrawny's prob'ly not a-gonna catch the round in his chest where Junior's aimin'. Likely the rifle will rise with the recoil, meanin' the round'll go clean through ol' Scrawny's head. So while I'm pickin' my boy up from the floor of my waggin, you'll be pickin' Scrawny's pieces up from out o' yonder trees behind ya, that is, if you can find any of the pieces. But I forgot, you won't be doin' nun o' that 'cuz yer agonna be swimmin' in a pool o' yer own blood under yer horse right thar. Yer horse is gonna finish y'off when he stomps ya tryin' to git the hell away fum here."

By now Scrawny'd gone from tremblin' to outright cryin', while Wiley kept starin' that poor critter down right through the barrel of his rifle. "Pleeeeease, Mister, call him off."

"I don't reckon ya' need to worry too much, Scrawny, 'cuz him and me, we practice on scarecrows, and he usually don't shoot 'til I give 'im the word. Of course, der was a few scarecrows met an unfortunate and early demise, but Junior got better wit' practice."

"And Ma here, after her first shot, she's got fourteen more rounds in her Winchester and two more Colts sittin' loaded and ready by her side. We made us a deal if'n we have to open fire on anybody, we ain't agonna stop 'til we're all outta bullets. I di'nt introduce ya, but Ma's got two more young'uns behind her, and Ma may be little, but she's kinda like a momma bear when it comes to her cubs, and I think she thinks you fellers might pose a threat to her litter."

I might shoulda been shuttin' up about there, but I heaped on just a little more. "Judgin' from appearances, y'all'er sum perty pore and hungry bastards, but if'n you know how to judge from appearances, y'might be thinkin' same thing 'bout us'ns, and you'd be right. If'n you'll take sum advice, I recommend ya try holdin' up folks wut gots money. Thattaway yore more'n likely to have a better chance of gittin' more than just a bullitt in the gut out of yore robbery dealins out here."

I continued, "Fellas, I think you can see we're just not the kind of customers yer lookin' fer today. Now y'all just head west real slow-like right now, and pass real wide and reeeal slow around my wagon, then listen fer further instructions. I'm watching y'all 'til I see you go over that hill. Then I'm on my way to Manhattan. If I see you again I . . . will . . . shoot . . . you . . . . on sight. No questions asked. Ever'body keeps his hands on his reins. If'n ya got an itch, my advice is just suffer with it 'til after ya clear the top o' yonder hill. We're all keepin' a bead on ya, and anythin' looks close to a reach for a gun, yer chest'll explode from behind, just like that. Nuthin' personal, I hope y'all knows, I jest cain't take nary a chance, I dun hear tell of sum pretty bad fellers out here, y'know wut ah mean?"

I concluded my performance with, "Don't follow us, y' understand?"

Scrawny cried out his understanding better 'n Julia Kate could, and by then his britches were wetter than one of my baby girl's diapers!

I got no answer from Big Fella, but with a nod and a defiant spit, he nudged his horse to comply with my very reasonable request, then the other three carefully followed. They trudged on as instructed, with not a one of them getting out of step.

When they'd just cleared the wagon I fell in behind them jabberin' all the way so they'd know I was there. When they'd gotten past the wagon about twenty paces, I shouted, "HALT NOW."

Those men and horses froze in their tracks as I gave some new instructions. "Scrawny, you slowly drop yer pistols. Don't dare turn around, and don't look over yer shoulder. Just DO WHUT I SAY." Scrawny complied again, quite willingly it seemed.

After holding them dead still for just a moment while Wiley had time to turn his rifle and re-aim it onto Scrawny, I said, "Next in line, it's yer turn. Sorry I di'nt give you a name. If'n we meet agin it'll be Dead Man. You other feller thar, yer name'll be Headless, but only if'n I see

309

ya again. So you two go ahead an' drap yer pistols too." It was amazing how much tamer these fellas were ever-since we'd reached an . . . understanding.

"Big Fella, yer next. Drop yer pistols, no turning around, just drop 'em on the ground." That didn't take long, so I continued, "Good. Now Big Fella, drop that rifle o' yer'n. And your ammo fer it, too."

After a rifle and a bag hit the ground, I said, "Anybody else got a rifle, or any other kinda weapon?"

"NO SIR," they all reported.

"Alrighty, then everybody drop yer holsters, all together, but don't forget we still got beads on y'all." As holsters hit, I shouted, "Junior, you still got a bead on ol' Scrawny, doncha?"

"Yes sir, Pa," at which we could see Scrawny flinch. By then, I couldn't tell which was wetter, his face or his britches.

"It's not getting' too heavy for ya, is it son?"

"No, sir, Pa. Not too bad at least." He was perfect!

"Okay, ever'body go forward slowly 'til I say stop again." Once again, they complied.

I motioned for Gommy to quickly jump from the wagon and re-fix her aim on the big one. When I stopped them, I said, "Now, Big Fella and Scrawny, dismount slowly. You other two, stay mounted." Then I said "I'm sure you fellas won't mind, but I can really use a couple extra horses for our trip. This deep sand's got my two plum-tuckered out. You two double up with yer buddies there, and you just keep on a-ridin'. Remember, now, if'n I sees any funny bidness goin' on, these rifles will put a hole right through two of you at a time now that yer all doubled up. So just keep goin' nice and steady. Looks to me now like I can kill four worthless critters with just two shots. And don't turn around to check on us, I can guarantee ya we're watchin'."

The one whose horse Scrawny was trying to mount shouted, "Mister, cain't you just make him walk? Cain'tcha see he's all nasty?"

I couldn't resist havin' just a little more fun. "It's all right, you'll jest git yersef a little warm feelin'. Besides, I know you four are mighty good friends, so what'll it matter? Get on up there, Scrawny, and try to control yerseff a li'l better next time a five-year-old has his rifle aimed at yer gizzard. It ain't very becomin' to the ladies, y'know."

Then I overheard Big Fella say to Scrawny, "You know that kid's rifle ain't loaded, why'd you have to get so fool whiny?"

I looked at Wiley, and told him, "Son, turn yer rifle toward that tree," while gesturing toward a young sand pine about twenty feet ahead of the horsemen and just five feet off the path.

After Wiley moved his aim from Scrawny, I calmly said, "Fire at will."

Wiley's finger barely touched the hair-trigger, then a great explosion, and the tree snapped and the top fell off like it'd been hit by a Texas tornado! Scrawny screamed again, flinching so hard he kicked the horse. The horse panicked, jumping into the air like an unbroken bronco. Scrawny flew off the back, landing on his tail-bone, unhurt by the soft sand but smack in the middle of a sandspur patch! He jumped up with his wet pants all loaded down with sand and sandspurs to see his comrades barrelling away just as fast as they could. Last we saw, poor ol' Scrawny was still runnin', squealin', holdin' up about ten pounds of wet, sandy, sandspurred britches and cussin' up a storm at his partners!

I'd taken the rifle from Gommy and tried my best to keep a bead on them as they fled like scolded pups, but I was laughing so hard I could hardly see straight. Gommy took the pistols, but she was quaking so hard she could hardly lift 'em. Good thing we didn't need to make a shot 'cause we couldn't hit the broad side of a barn by then.

When we finally put down our guns, we took just a minute to laugh nervously and hug and squeeze each of the young'uns. Then we picked up our new pistols, holsters and rifle and grabbed the reins of our new horses. We figured these new members of our herd just had to be named "Big Fella" and, of course, "Scrawny."

We turned toward the wagon as I said, "Let's get out of here. They should be harmless now, but if they have a cache of weapons and horses nearby, they might just be fool enough to come back."

"And we might not be lucky enough to see them before they see us this second time around," Gommy wisely observed.

We hitched our new horses to the wagon to give 'em a try and to give ours a break. I tied Prince to the back of the wagon to follow along. Even if the new ones were weak, we'd still make better time the rest of the trip because we wouldn't have to stop to rest our only two horses so often, we could just change teams and keep going.

The best thing for me was it looked like my walking days were finally over for this trip. Gommy told me I was back to being just about as skinny as I was at the end of the War. She was hoping to get some meat back on my bones real quick.

We were only mid-morning by this time, and we were just a few miles away from Juniper Springs. I'd not planned to stop there, but after what we'd all been through, we scrapped our plans for a long run to Manhattan and figured a short day on the road would suit us just fine.

After posting Wiley on the sugar barrel as our sentry to watch the road behind us, I mounted Prince, and the wagon sprung into motion.

As we began rolling, Gommy scolded me with, "You know your Momma would have your hide if she coulda heard your language and your grammar, and swearing right here in front of the children!" I sensed she wasn't teasing me. We then rode in awkward silence for seemed like an hour.

Then Wiley broke the ice at just the wrong time by asking, "Daddy . . . what's a bastard?"

Juniper Springs to Manhattan, Florida

As I groped for an answer to Wiley's innocent question, Laura brilliantly piped in with, "That's a word you *never* call anybody unless you're fixin' to shoot him." That settled Wiley's curiosity but didn't stop Gommy from giving me another tongue lashing for using such language in front of the children. After apologizing, I explained I needed to talk at the bad men's level so I could make sure they understood me. I dealt with varmints like them when I was working the woods during the War. I knew if they got an idea I had any education they'd be more likely to suspect I had money hidden in our cart.

Juniper Springs was a small settlement of three or four squatter families at the time. It had some good farmland in the lower ground around it, plenty to support a few families, but not enough to run a real commercial farm. Nowhere did you get more than a hundred yards from the spring without being right back in the big scrub with all its worthless sugar sand.

The settlers at Juniper Springs were always happy to see strangers so they could get news and exchange stories of the outside world. Our kids played with the Juniper kids, and we visited with some good folks. The spring itself was just a small hole in the ground with the cool clear water gushing out into the Juniper Run, which made its way downstream about six or seven miles through swamps to Lake George. Wildlife was abundant at the spring. It was the watering hole for large and small critters from near and far, just like the swimmin' hole at the Lee Farm.

We gave our new friends warning of what we'd just experienced. They'd heard of those bandits and said we were the first they knew of to get away from them without losing something. They laughed when we told how we ended up being the robbers instead of them. I knew how fortunate I was to see them before they saw us. If we hadn't been cocked and ready when we came up on them, the outcome would've been a lot different. I vowed then, for the rest of our trip through Big Scrub, I would have one pistol in my hand and one in the holster, Laura would have her rifle in her lap, and anytime we were in thicker woods with low range of sight, the guns would be at ready.

The Juniper folks told us we shouldn't have much more trouble heading east, especially after we crossed the intersection of the Eustis-to-Palatka road, which was only a few miles east of Juniper. We were happy this part of the journey would quickly be behind us.

During our short stay we shot a couple of squirrels and Wiley caught some small bass a ways down Juniper Run. Supper was good. Laura took advantage of this unexpected stop to give a real thorough wash to our clothes right at the mouth of the spring.

The next morning was another early start. We moved the two youngest up into their spots in the wagon and let them keep on sleeping. Wiley woke up as usual ready to help as soon as I was moving. He'd load our palmetto beds and any pots or pans we may have left out by last night's fire. Or he'd help his Momma gather up the laundry she left hanging to dry overnight. He was so helpful, and we still marveled at how well he handled the robber situation.

If Theo woke up he'd help, too, at least as much as any three-year-old can help.

Gommy gave us each a little biscuit and some of the left over fish and squirrel from supper. She'd kept it in a bucket hung high up in a tree so the Florida black bears couldn't get it. I was kind of hoping one would come to our camp for it because I'd like to have a bear hide, but no such luck yet.

Gommy's morning song for the day was, "Guide Me, O Thou Great Jehovah," which seemed very fitting for where we were and what we'd just come through:

Guide me O, Thou great Jehovah, Pilgrim in this barren land,
I am weak, but Thou art mighty, Hold me with Thy powerful hand;
Bread of heaven, bread of heaven,
Feed me 'til I want no more,
Feed me 'til I want no more.

If we weren't a family of pilgrims in a barren land, weak and being fed by His providence, I don't know who was. I thought of yesterday's episode and marveled how we came out of a robbery attempt with two extra horses and sorry saddles, four pistols, four holsters, one rifle and a fair stock of ammunition. It could have gone real badly. We could've been robbed of most or all our belongings, or one of us hurt or killed in that wasteland called Big Scrub. We believed God saw fit to shine His providence on us in a real big way.

Well, the road from Juniper Springs started out real tough with the deepest sand we'd seen so far. I was real glad we had two horse teams now. Our horses were better on account of they'd been better fed and cared for, but the bandit horses weren't all bad. With a little better treatment, they just might make us some pretty good farm animals in our new home.

After we crossed the intersection of the Eustis-to-Palatka road, the land firmed up and flattened out a little. The soil still wasn't good for growing anything but those short needle pines and sorry blackjack oaks, but it could do a fine job of that. We even made up a silly song for sand pines, too.

We were told we'd come to Wildcat Lake real soon, and sure enough, the trail took us right alongside a beautiful big lake. It had a nice sandy beach and sandy bottom out as far as you could see, with crystal clear water. We led the horses to the water, then waded in ourselves for a little break.

With only about five miles left to Manhattan, we were anxious to get going, so we switched out the horses and were back on the trail. The rest of the ride was uneventful, and we arrived mid-afternoon. I guess because it was Mr. Astor's project, I was expecting to see a whole lot more than we found. Turns out, though, his experts had been planning the new town for several years, but it didn't amount to much yet. He just finished his house and office here earlier this year, and he brought in a lot of labor to plant his groves and build his port. The hotel and the rest of the town were still on the drawing board.

While it looked like we'd be able to pick up some work here, we'd made such a windfall with our new horses and guns that I decided we'd go on and make our crossing and camp on the east side of the river in the old settlement of Volusia. If I had to tell you the whole truth, though, I think I was really just excited about crossing the river on the new and beautiful, powerful ferry.

We stepped in to Astor's office to meet his manager, Mr. Nelson, and give Captain. Dickison's regards. Nelson had been one of Dickison's key lieutenants over on the East Coast during the War, and now he ran the development of a whole new city for Astor. I knew who he was, but he had no idea who this lowly private was, though he did know my father. I showed him my work reference letter, just in case he came up with some too-good-to-be-true offer. While there, I wrote a letter to Captain Dickison informing him of those nice fellows we met in the Big Scrub. The rest I left in the Captain's capable hands.

Nelson was a talkative chap. When I gave him my answer to his "Where ya headin'" question, he just started laughing. "Why you goin' to so much trouble when you can get there from here so much quicker on the river? Don't put your pretty family through all the trouble, man. Why, on the boat you could be enjoyin' beautiful Blue Springs by tomorrow afternoon, but it's a three or four day hard slog with yer cart and horses. On the boat, you'd likely spend tomorrow night in Enterprise."

"I've priced steamer fares, and I just can't afford it," I insisted with a prove-it-to-me sort of tone.

"Well, sir, whatcha might not know is these boats get emptier as they go further upriver. The smart captains know they're better off to fill a seat at any price than to run the last leg to Lake Monroe empty. Dead-headin' they call it. What I'm tryin' to tell you is I think you can bargain with 'em. I'm a ticket agent for all these steamer lines, and I might just be able to get you a special price."

I thanked Mr. Nelson but told him my plans were set and I should be able to make my final destination in a week to ten days, unless I found some really good work along the way.

"Well, sir," Mr. Nelson said, "I hope ya makes a million pickin' up jobs on the way, but yore surely doin' things the hard way. And yore still runnin' risk of getting robbed again and the next gang you encounter may not be quite as lame as the goons you met up with in the Big Scrub. If'n 'twas my perty wife and young family, we'd be on the boat. But I guess it's none o' my bidness."

"Thank you, Mr. Nelson, I appreciate your help." What I was really thinking was, "This chap just made me feel like a fool. Maybe he was on to something."

"Pleasure's mine, son. If'n ya change yer mind, just come back and see me. I do think I'd protect yer family a little better if'n I was you. There's still a lot of rough territory down here. The world's wide open for you to build whatever you want here or down South, but yer family's gonna pay part of the price. If ya must go on, though, here's a pass for a free ride on the ferry for you, your family and all yer belongin's."

"Thanks again," I said. "My pleasure meeting you."

At the ferry dock, I saw a cart full of black rocks; curious things, they were. At first I wondered why somebody would be shipping black rocks, then it dawned on me. I saw a dock boy and asked, "Izzat coal?"

"Yes sir," the dock boy answered. "Mr. Astor is aiming to make this the biggest coaling depot on the St. Johns. He says pert' near every ship in New York burns coal now, and 'twont be long 'til it'll be the same here. You can go farther for cheaper on a ton of coal than a ton of wood, and it takes a lot less room. It don't rot, and it's a lot easier to clean up, but, boy, it sher is sooty!"

He continued, "Mr. Astor sez if we don't change over our ships and trains to coal, we're someday gonna burn up every tree in the country, then what'll we do? With coal, all we gotta do is dig it out of the ground, and it seems there's enough to last forever."

I thanked him and walked over to the family. "Remember this, Wiley. You're fixin' to take your first ride in a coal-powered steamboat. Pretty soon almost all the steam engines almost everywhere are going to be powered by coal. It's a big advance. Coal may just be the very best form of power man has ever or will ever have." I'd read before how coal was coming, but it had a deep effect on me to see it in person and know it was really happening.

Then, there it was, the one big improvement Astor had already accomplished. He had commissioned a beautiful new coal powered steam ferry boat brought down from New York, and it was here to take us on our two-hundred-yard journey across the river. After our last river crossing over the Ocklawaha, I almost fell to my knees to thank the Lord above. I could just drive my whole family, wagon and four horses onto the thing, and enjoy a quick ride across the big river! Another couple of families and their wagons could have fit on this thing with us.

I told Gommy, "I woulda been real happy to part with twenty-five cents to have the same kind of crossing at Ocklawaha." I felt like I was Mr. Astor himself!

She quickly retorted with, "NO! Mr. Lee, if there was a ferry like this at Oklawaha, you'da told the ferryman there was no way he'd get a dime from JH Lee for such a short trip. You'da said 'I'll do it myself and keep my pennies, thank you very much,' now wouldn't you?" She turned and walked away with Julia Kate to show her a pair of fish hawks in a nest high in a cypress tree, fussin' up a storm at each other; the fish hawks kinda reminded me of us. Oh, the wonders of this beautiful spot! Gommy and I had a way of friendly sparring, and she had another way that was meant to put me in my place. I kinda knew which this last exchange was.

I realized she might've been right, and I had to wonder if I'd spent this whole trip being penny wise and pound foolish. So far we hadn't paid too dear a price for my tightwaddedness, but was I tempting fate by pressing on?

The St. Johns River was simply beautiful. I'd seen it before, but none of the kids had. The pitch-black water, which Wiley said looked just like molasses, was rolling north with such resolve, and the tropical foliage framed the banks. What a place! I loved showing new things to my brood, and they were fascinated with the river. But what I really loved was my free ferry pass. I complimented the ferry captain on his fine craft, and he just laughed. "Back in N'Yawk, this one's too small to be in service anymore. Mr. Astor's already said if we can keep the ferries busy, he'll send us more, bigger and better ones. Someday he's goin' to build us a bridge, and it'll be a drawbridge on a big turntable so it can open up for even the biggest rivership to go through. This man's got great ideas for this place. I tell you Manhattan, Florida, might just rival that other Manhattan someday! And Mr. Astor tells me I'm his ambassador for Manhattan. He says we're the ones what make or break this place, and we're to make it attractive to everybody."

With his short spiel, we'd already met our destination at the Volusia dock, and off we rolled into the oldest inland settlement in the state. Here were olive trees left from the days when the Padres first brought them from St. Augustine. Beautiful orange trees clung halfway up the riverbank, showing off their bountiful crops like decorated Christmas trees. The rich soil and plentiful water made this place look like a Garden of Eden, a true tropical paradise. Ladyfinger bananas were putting out the last of their bounty for the year. I'd never seen the likes of it. We traveled northward along a riverfront trail looking for the best place to set up camp, which we found in just a few hundred feet.

We were sure we could build a great life in this place. Gommy asked why we didn't go back and get a job with Mr. Astor and take part in building what looked a sure bet to become one of Florida's best cities. I listened, but I told them if they loved this place, they would surely love Orange County even more.

After supper the boys ran and played 'til their legs were just about to fall off. As dark came and the fire died down, and as fast as we could dig their trenches and lay down their palmetto beds, they were fast asleep. Julia Kate was likewise.

Gommy and I stayed up long after, which was unusual since most of our days were so exhausting. This place was enchanting to her; she knew we could build a life here. I reminded her everything we saw there was what we heard there was even more of in Orange County, so let's push on. We'd made it this far, why not go all the way?

I propped up our bedrolls against an orange tree, and Gommy nestled up to me. She slowly, dreamily, fell asleep, and I just held her close. As tired as I was, and as peaceful as the setting was, I couldn't sleep. My mind was racing with the risks I'd taken with the lives under my care. I was excited about what awaited us, and I was weary from the roadtrip we'd taken so far, yet it had been a great experience for us. I musta slept some that night, but it seemed every whippoorwill, hoot owl, bullfrog, cricket and bull gator was singing some curious song just for me, and I didn't miss a note all night long. Every mullet jumping in the river was trying to tell me something, but I was clueless as to what it was.

As dawn finally came, I told Gommy to feed the family and have a good time, and I would be back. I had some business back in Manhattan. She knew not to ask because she could tell I had something on my mind. She also knew I wouldn't be satisfied 'til I'd gotten my answers.

I walked over to the ferry station and stepped aboard. The ferryman saw me reaching for a nickel to pay the crossing fee and said, "Just keep yer dime. Mr. Astor told us we're not to make a profit on this ferry. The ferry will make us money by bringing people to Mr. Astor's city."

"Thank you, sir," I said as I bounded off on the Manhattan side and headed for Mr. Nelson's office. Nelson wouldn't be in for a while, but I wanted to be sure to be the first to see him. While waiting in a rocker on his porch, I admired the banana trees, kumquats, Japanese plums, pomegranates, oranges, grapefruit, lemons, limes and even pineapples growing on the grounds around the office. This place was a paradise, and I was told it would get even better as we progressed farther south.

When he arrived, I accosted him. "Mr. Nelson, I need you to tell me how to get the really cheap fares on the riverboats. I thought about it last night, and you're right. I need to be gettin' on down to Orange County so we can get our lives started, and I don't want to waste any more time, but I don't have much money."

"Whoa, now, Mr. Lee," said Nelson, "you may just have to wait and let a few boats go by before you find a skipper who's hungry enough for a discount customer. I suggest you bring your family and the wagon back over here and have 'em waiting and ready to jump on the ship as soon as I can strike a deal for you 'cause he ain't gonna wait on you. Your cart and horses might have to go separate on a cargo ship."

"When's the next one coming in?" I was anxious.

Nelson replied, "They kinda come in when they come in, but we should have a morning ship or two. Some spend the night at Silver Glen Springs off of Lake George. They get here early morning. Some come down from Palatka, they'll be 'bout noon. Some just run straight through, stopping only to pick up wood for the burners, let passengers on and off, then go on up the river. If we can get you on an express line, it'll be your best price, but you won't get to see the sights as well as you might like. You definitely want to show your family Blue Springs. DeLeon Springs is nice, and some of the boats go up there, but it's a little out of your way."

"With all respect, sir, I don't mind too terribly if we see something along the way, but my interest is in getting there and doin' so real cheap." I'd about been won over to the idea of taking a boat, but I was real sure I wasn't going to make a vacation of it. I didn't care if it took a month if it was the cheapest way there. He looked at me like a pitiful waif, and I knew I gave that image; but I didn't care. I didn't see how anyone who'd hit bottom as hard as I did could bear to part with a nickel unless absolutely necessary.

319

Nelson informed, "Cabins on these boats are usually a dollar a day per person, and to get to Lake Jesup should take two, maybe two and a half days since ya gotta change into a smaller boat at Fort Mellon.

"Pardon me," I interrupted, "If it's gonna be anywhere near five dollars a day plus my cargo, I better get back on my cart and be on my way. Besides, do I have to have a cabin?"

"Well no, you don't have to have a cabin, but with your pretty young wife, I didn't think . . ."

"I'd love the cabin, but I just can't afford it." I wasn't in the habit of interrupting 'cause I'd been taught it was rude, but I was in shock at the idea of paying so much money just to get us moved upriver, then have nothing to show for it. I also desperately didn't want to subject my family to the dangers of the trail again. I knew I might not be as lucky next time.

"Let's see what we can do when the ships come in," Nelson said with a sigh.

"Thank you," I said. "If any of the boats need any help along the way, I'll be happy to work to help pay my way. I've never worked on a ship, but I'm expert at runnin' and maintainin' steam engines. And my wife can cook and clean like nobody's bidness."

"I'll see what I can do for you," said Mr. Nelson. "But tell me again how much to tell the captain he should pay you to ride on his boat?" We laughed and I thanked him in advance for his help. He said, "If you hadn't waved that letter from J. J. Dickison at me, I woulda kicked you out of my office. Son, you're either poor as a church mouse, or else you're so tight you squeak when you walk. I suspect yer just tight as a tick, but at any rate, I'm bettin" someday you're gonna own whatever town it is you settle in. So I'm happy to help you now, and I hope you remember me someday when you're richer than Mr. Astor. But don't forget, if you'll be as tight with his money as you are with your own, Mr. Astor can use someone with your talents. I can't tell you how many grabby folks come in here just wantin' to rub elbows with the man, hopin' some easy money falls their way or thinkin' they can take advantage of him."

I thanked him again and laughed a little nervous laugh. Did he think I might have some money? Did others think the same?

I ferried back (free!) and got the family. We started our ragtag caravan back toward the ferry and crossed the St. Johns yet again to wait on a boat to take us from Manhattan to Orange County.

Well, I spent a real pleasant morning watching the river and the hustle and bustle every time a ship came in, with the passengers and cargo loading and unloading. There were rows of goods, mostly in barrels or wooden boxes, some covered in burlap; all waiting to be shipped somewhere or waiting for some local recipient to come claim his goods.

I read the labels to the boys and did my best to tell them something about the destination city of each item, or we'd speculate what might be in the boxes waiting for pickup by local folks. Maybe some Momma was getting some fine new furniture or her dream dress. Maybe some daddy was getting a new farm tool he couldn't make for himself. That tool might let him do twice the work with half the effort. Maybe a new business was getting a new safe, or maybe a rifle was coming to a proud new owner.

There were several rows of barrels of citrus bound for the Northland. They would surely go to Jacksonville, then change ships, and head to the New York markets on one of the big new ocean-going freighters with maybe only one stop in Charleston for fueling and provisioning.

Didn't they know none of this fruit was quite ripe yet? Maybe Yankees liked their oranges a little on the sour side. I figured maybe they had to be picked this early so the fruit could make it to their new home up North before it rotted. It's a fact a riper, softer orange won't ship as well as a greener one would. There were loads of goods neatly lined up on the pier. A fellow on the dock told me, it doesn't matter what time of year it is, if that orange has "broken color" from the deep green to the first bit of orange in the peel, there were folks up North who'd buy whatever we could ship 'em. I was fascinated.

"Well, what about all the new groves I've seen on my trip? Startin' about Gainesville, it seemed like I saw more young citrus trees with every mile I passed, 'cept in the Big Scrub, I guess."

He smiled and said, "Mister, if'n yore goin' on south frum here, you ain't seen nuthin' yet. We may see the day we've done planted too many trees, but I'm told there's lots o' Yankees ain't eaten their first orange yet. And the more they pile those folks up in those big cities o' their'n, the more oranges, grapefruit and tangerines they's a wantin'! I tell you what, I think the more we grow, the more they're agonna want."

He sounded half like my Grandfather McDonald and half like a plain ol' farm hand. I asked, "When did ya get here from Scotland?"

"Bin here near forty years now, came as a li'l lad, but guess I jest cain't hide my bloodlines, can I?"

"Nuthin' t' be 'shamed of, sir, my Momma's folks were Scottish; McDonald was their name."

"Ah, fine name," he opined, "mighty big clan. I'm a McBride m'self."

"Are you an orange grower y'self?"

"Yes sir, I got ten acres 'bout two miles east o' here on the road to Barber's settlement. It's about five acres of grove, my homestead, and a few acres of cypress head. The grove's ten years old this year. I got out of President Davis's service in '64, and I grew most of 'em from seeds that year. It's been a struggle, but they're producin' now. I had to raise food for m' family in between the trees before they were producin'. But they seemed to love when I planted peanuts or beans between 'em. Those leaves would green up and get so plump, you could tell them were sum happy trees! They only give a piddlin' amount of fruit early on, but come year seven, they orta be doin' jes' fine fer ya. Mine's been producin' good crops three years now, and I'm doin' good. My wife and four kids oughta be just fine from here on out. And if'n sumpthin' happens to me, my wife orta be able to manage jes' fine without me. Ain't many women can do that with a cotton farm now, is they?

"Me and my two boys, we do everything. We don't have to hire nobody fer nuthin', and we like it thattaway. We can even pick the whole grove all by ourselves on account of oranges get ripe and stay ripe on the tree about three months. Grapefruit's ripe pert near a half a year! Now the tangerines, you gotta little less time for them 'cause they'll get soft on you, but you still got some time. Y' gotta pick 'em pretty much between now and New Year's.

"I'm a-figgerin' this year's crop'll be worth 'bout $2,000, and we ain't got hardly a dime of cash expense comin' outa that. We just bought another plot of ten acres, this'n's all high and dry. My boys and me, we're gonna plant it and it's agonna be their'n. I wanna do same for m' two other brood, the girls. That should make 'em real attractive to some young man someday, y'know what I mean?"

"Yes sir," I said, "Yer makin' 'em look powerful perty to me, and I already got my own wife and kids!"

McBride laughed so hard I thought he was gonna fall off'n the dock, but that friendly ol' fella gave me a lot to think about. We talked for over two hours about nothing but citrus. He told me not everybody got results as good as he did, but he and his boys babied every tree; some folks thought they could just leave 'em alone, and come out to pick 'em come harvest time, but they come up short every year.

He continued, "I think yer smart as a whip to be goin' as far south as y' are. Volusia here was way south when I settled. Most of us have forgotten 'bout the freeze of 1835, but it wiped out almost all the trees around here. Most of the older trees you see 'round here came back from the roots 'cause the whole trunk and top of the tree was killed to the ground that

322

winter. Took 'em three seasons to produce again when they had to grow back from the ground up. The thing you gotta watch out for down there, though, is the land gets thinner, lots more sand and lots less beef to the soil. Bottom land's good and rich, but y' don't wanna plant citrus trees there; they don't like wet feet. But when you kin find a patch of good ground, y'know, well-drained but still has a little loam and a little clay in it, and find it on the south side of one of the lakes, and there's lakes everywhere there, you've found yerse'f sumpthin' to hold on to.

"Yessir, that big freeze of '35 seems a long time ago now, and it's been forgotten by most growers, but when we have another sho 'nuff freeze, lots of us are gonna be hurt bad. We've had several little freezes since the big one, and these guys'll moan about losin' a crop or a half a crop, but brother, if'n you can't afford to lose a crop, ya' better not be in this bidness. But I'm not real sure jest wut I'd do if'n I lost m' whole grove and had to start all over again. I don't think yer gonna hafta worry about that if'n you gotta sho -'nuff good Orange County grove. Oh sure, you'll take a punch now and again, but you'll come right back. I'm afeared a lot of us 'round here'll be starting all over. And when ya get rich in this bidness is when you have a crop the year *after* the freeze. If you've got recoverin' trees and even jest a half a crop, you'll make more'n you ever dreamed a bumper crop could be worth. We're findin' the Yankees will pay what they hafta to get our oranges, and if we're short, they'll pay real long for what we do have. Some think we're due for another granddaddy freeze, but others think 'twon't ever happen again.

"M' boys take turns comin' down here t' the dock startin' November one. They'll bring a box of oranges fer juicin', a box fer sellin' whole oranges, an' a half box o' tangerines. They'll sell a small glass of juice fer a nickel, whole oranges two fer a nickel, grapefruit and tangerines a nickel a piece. That gives 'em the money they're planning to put into their own grove. They can clear five dollars on a real good day, sumtimes more, just sellin' oranges and juice to travelers on the dock. They even sell the peels to horse owners fer a couple o' pennies a bucketful! The horses kinda git to expectin' it when they get to the dock. And we grow some sour oranges, too. We make marmalade out of 'em, and the boys sell it at the dock, too.

"Yes sir, you can't beat the citrus bidness. It's a great way to raise yer boys, too. The work's hard, but it's not as dull and backbreakin' as row-croppin'. And you and yer wife don't need to have two dozen kids just to git all the farm work done."

I heard a man hollerin' in the background, but I wasn't payin' it any mind. I was very interested in this man's tale of how well my family could do with such a small plot of citrus. I was already formulating ideas for how I could use what I just learned. Then I realized the hollerin' was for me.

323

"LEE, LEE, are you deaf, or what?" I now recognized Mr. Nelson's voice. I said my good-byes and best wishes to Mr. McBride and ran over to the porch of the office.

"Yes, sir, Mr. Nelson."

Nelson told me he had the best deal he was gonna get for us to ride to Fort Mellon. We'd spend the night at Enterprise and cross Lake Monroe to Fort Mellon next morning. A captain was severely short-handed on his ship, the *Hattie Brock*, because his fireman had taken ill and he had his cabin boy acting as fireman. He well knew the risk of having a novice fireman at his engines and desperately needed somebody who knew steam engines to fill in. I had a job! He said he'd give me a cabin for the family and carry my wagon, horses and load for just $4.00. At the end of the run, if I proved to be worth my salt, he promised he'd refund $3.00, with $1.00 kept for feeding and cleaning up after the horses. I was confident enough in my own abilities to manage a steam engine, so I saw it as making a bet on myself, and I said "You're on!" We were going to get to our new home quicker than we thought, I got a cabin for my much-deserving wife and children, and I had a job to keep me busy and make the trip near-free. Nothing could've been better.

If we'd been paying regular fare for ourselves, the cost would've been only $1.00 a head, recently discounted from $2.00, plus the freight charge for the animals, cart and the load. The competition for customers had gotten so great anyone could travel almost free. The steamer lines counted on making much more than the fare through food and bar sales and especially gun rental and ammunition sales for the sporting going on up on the top deck. St. Johns cruise customers tended to be a pretty free-spending lot. I wondered if the captain figured he'd end up making money on us, not knowing what tee-totaling Methodists we were, or if he really did need a fireman so desperately.

Nelson asked, "You got the four dollars?" I assured him I could scrape it together, and he just replied, "I figured you could."

I thanked Mr. Nelson for his help and the special interest he'd taken in us. He said, "We're always happy to be of service around here to any traveler. But you got a little special attention due to your note from Captain Dickison. I don't know if it'll have the same value where you're goin', but I'd hang on to it. A letter from ol' J.J. is a mighty good introduction piece around here, and probably will be down there, too."

I was relieved to not have to dip into my savings for this trip. Even though I knew my horses and weapons bounty from the Big Scrub hold-up would pay for our trip many times, I'd been advised horses and weapons would be worth more in Orange County than up here in civilization. As McBride told me, "Ever'thin's in short supply down there. If'n ya kin find somebuddy whut's gots money, he'll be glad to pay you a good price for yer things. Only problem is, ain't many where yer goin' got two nickels to rub together."

The Hattie Brock

The *Hattie* was a solid vessel of just over 130 feet in length and 25 feet of beam. Due to being the fall of the year, she was only about half full. In about a month, Nelson said, she'd be chock full as the snowbirds come down in droves. *Hattie* was a side-wheeler with separate steam engines for each side, which made her much more maneuverable than the stern-wheelers. She had a large cargo hold and plenty of deck space for the horses. The wagon would barely fit in the hold, and our stack of cargo above the sides of the wagon would have to be packed separately in a big burlap blanket courtesy of Mr. Nelson.

After we removed a sack full of our canned goods, jerky and biscuits to feed ourselves during the trip, we covered the cart over and tied it down real good to make sure none of the contents spilled out in transit. We also hoped to discourage sticky fingers from helping themselves to our things during the trip.

We boarded about noon and were shown to our cabin. To say it was small wouldn't describe it. It was called a "cabin for two," but it was only about four feet wide and seven feet long. It featured a bench seat along the left wall. The seat of the bench made a bed for one real skinny person, and the back was hinged to the wall. It would swing up, and was held up by straps from the ceiling to hold it flat, which gave a second tiny bunk bed. In the far corner of the room opposite the bench was a tiny washbasin with a pitcher of water and a honeypot in case any of us needed to do our business at night.

Julia Kate and Laura would sleep on the bottom bunk. I set Wiley up in the top and Theo slept on the floor next to the bunks. Now Gommy and I didn't mind at all being close, but this was real close. I joked with her it was such tight quarters I'd have to step outside just to change my mind! We decided we'd all be better off if I slept in one of the deck chairs on the topside of the ship when the time came.

From inside the cabin, you could hear the lapping of the river water on the hull of the boat. It had such a soothing sound. Even though it was a cool day, all the cabins were stinkin' hot from the heat of the steam engine. I threw open the tiny porthole window hoping it would cool the cabin once we got underway. We left the hot room and headed for the open air of the main deck, where the captain recommended the women and children ride. We were warned some of the passengers on the top deck had been drinking since the crack of dawn in Palatka, and that part of the boat wasn't much of a place for kids. I left my family on the main deck to report for duty at my new job in the engine room.

On the River

Captain Charles Brock showed me the equipment. He was the son of Jacob Brock, the legendary St. John's River captain and owner of several riverships. I was very familiar with every piece of this machine from my sawmill days, except for the running gear that drove the big paddlewheels. All I had to do was to grease all the fittings and make sure all moving parts had good oil supplies. The lubricants on this ship were petroleum products. Back home, we still used turpentine resins because it was so available. We only used horribly expensive whale oil when we needed very high quality lubricants. Here on the river, though, Mr. Rockefeller's oil products were becoming available, reliable and cheap for any machine with moving parts. The whaling industry was feeling quite a squeeze due to the tough competition of cheaper and more efficient petroleum products.

Since the fire had been untended for about thirty minutes at Manhattan station, it had cooled down to mostly coals. I checked the water tank, and pumped in raw river water to fill it up. I threw in a couple pieces of lighter pine and pumped the bellows briskly. This burst of fresh air caused the sappy "fat wood" to almost instantly burst into flames, so I pitched in some of the oak wood and soon had a roaring fire. I watched as the steam pressure rose and looked over to Captain Brock, who just nodded and said, "I think you'll do just fine. We try to get about ten miles out of every cord of wood," he shouted as he turned and headed to his command bridge.

One long blow from *Hattie's* steam whistle told the passengers they'd best be loading up. Then, as the steam pressure reached full power, Captain Brock let out three shorter whistles. The cabin boy hollered "ALL ABOARD THE *HATTIE BROCK*," and began working to pull up the starboard-side gangplank as the dockmaster began untying the bow line from the cleat. The dock boy then untied the stern line and tossed it on board. Using a long pole called a boathook, the dockmaster easily nudged the big, heavy bow out into the oncoming river current. As soon as the captain felt the current swinging the bow out into the river channel, he slipped his control gauges, both port and starboard, into forward. In turn, a dial in my engine room told me to engage both forward. The engines let out a mighty hiss as the pistons resumed their long day of nothing but back and forth, back and forth. Next, the paddlewheels lumbered into action. Slowly at first, then quickly the swooshing sound of those massive paddles being powered through the water propelled our big heavy craft forward. We were on our way!

I'da done this job for free, and here I was gettin' paid for something I loved. It all seemed too good to be true. And I had so much to think about from my discussions with McBride. I loved my afternoon working like a slave in blistering heat, doing a simple but crucial job and being all alone with my thoughts. I thought I could find myself loving the citrus business as much as he did. I loved my little one-day job, but I was getting' real antsy to get started on my new life.

Being a fireman in the belly of a ship was very similar to running a steam engine in a sawmill. You were constantly watching the water temperature and the pressure. If the water wasn't hot enough to make the pressure high enough, you lost speed. It's the controlled escaping of the steam into the pistons which causes the shaft to oscillate back and forth to turn the paddlewheels. And it took lots of steam to drive those big side wheels. When the pressure started to drop, and before it dropped too much, you'd have to stoke it first with the bellows, and then add more wood

Of course, if the temperature and pressure got too high, every life on the ship was at risk of explosion, burning by steam or fire, and maybe sinking and drowning; which happened all too often. When the pressure was getting too high, I'd close the baffles to cut down or cut off the air supply so the pressure could settle back down. I had an emergency valve I could open to let a large amount of steam escape quickly if the pressure got dangerously high. A good steam operator tried hard not to use the emergency valve because it was a waste of a great amount of precious steam.

There was only one big difference between running a steam engine at a sawmill and on a boat. I thought the sawmill job was a hot one, and it was; but doing the same job in the bowels of a ship was nothing but brutally hot. At least at the sawmill, you could catch whatever breeze came along. In the ship, it was just you, your tight little quarters, and lots of heat. My only relief came from the porthole windows lining the engine room. I had those wide open, but they couldn't let in near the amount of cool air as the heat the wood eating monster created. I'd sneak a quick look at the scenery through the windows every now and then too and heard the sounds of the passengers on the decks. I guessed those men on top were enjoying the view more than I was but they weren't getting paid like I was. As they lounged, drank and caroused, I worked. Things were just the way I liked 'em.

I believed what the captain said about the gentlemen hitting their whiskey early, judging from the rowdy hoots and the gunshots sounding from the top deck. It had become quite a sport to shoot at whatever wildlife moved as the ship progressed upriver. They particularly enjoyed blowing holes in the many fish hawk and eagle nests lining the river. It was disgusting. I had no problem shooting animals, but I couldn't believe the waste they were creating by just blowing up any old thing they could with no intention of ever retrieving it for meat or hides. Most farmboys got over those destructive drives by about age eight. The big prize, of course, was to shoot a big alligator. On bright days like today, gators would lazily sun themselves on the banks, making easy targets for our drunken sharpshooters. The banks of the river were strewn with corpses of dead gators, deer, and the occasional bear in all stages of decay; evidence of past drunken cruise boat revelers. The only ones to benefit from this carnage were the buzzards, at least the ones that didn't get shot.

These uncouth Yankees saw no shame in this ridiculous waste. The captains mostly hated it, but none prohibited the practice because it was the best part of the ride for the men passengers, so tolerance ruled and profits flowed as the steamer lines rented guns and sold ammunition and booze to these gun-crazed pismires. What a racket!

Up and down the river, carcasses of herons, egrets, fish hawks, eagles and all types of waterfowl floated along, all of them senselessly killed by these unthinking idiots.

I thought it a shame because no self-respecting lady, much less the children, could go on the top deck with those miscreants, and what a wonderful place to enjoy a beautiful day in such a beautiful spot. The barmaid was half-lit herself, a middle-aged gal getting passed around up there from one man to the other and thinking she was the Belle of the ball on the rivership *Hattie Brock*. To me, she looked more like the floozy of Florida with too many parts hangin' out of her outfit! I'd been around enough of that in my days at *The Rebel's Rest* and couldn't see anything attractive about spending scarce money on anything so sure to be nothin' but trouble. Most of those men had wives one deck below them.

Despite the ruckus and debauchery on the top deck, my day on the *Hattie* was beautiful. I'd seen a lot of Florida during the Civil War and there were many beautiful places in this state; but I couldn't imagine a place anywhere prettier than the St. Johns River.

We spent the afternoon winding to the port, then winding back starboard as captain Brock navigated skillfully up this graceful, meandering river. We progressed through narrows and wide spots as we chugged relentlessly upriver.

Hattie had two ways to steer herself. First she had a steering wheel to control two big rudders submerged under the hull at the stern of the boat. Second, she could aid the rudder by controlling the steam power going from the boiler to the separate engines. If captain wanted to steer right, he'd signal me to reduce the throttle to the right engine. To steer left he'd power up the port side. For really tight places, he'd have me working the two engines opposite each other, one forward, the other reverse at the same time. The two engines working against each other made the big boat turn on a dime! The *Hattie Brock* was a true marvel to me, but as one of the older ships on the river, it was outclassed by the newer, sleeker liners.

By about mid-afternoon, we edged up to the bank at the point where Blue Springs Run converges into the St. Johns. In the deep, crystal-clear water of the run you could see schools of bass, bream, speckled perch, mullet, and the occasional alligator lazily moving up or down stream. Brock nudged our craft up to the beach. When he felt the bow touch the shore, he carefully poured on more steam and the wheels pushed furiously as we edged forward just a few feet. As we felt the bow rise up toward hard ground, he quickly cut the power and dropped the engines into neutral. The big wheels quickly came to a stop and the wildly whirling waters astern of the boat went calm again. The captain then dropped a gangplank straight off the bow so his passengers could easily disembark. At most of our stops we hoped to take only ten minutes before getting back underway, but since the passengers loved Blue Springs, we made a bit longer stop here so they could walk the trail to the spring or just enjoy this placid, inviting spot.

Brock announced we had a half hour but told me he usually stayed about forty-five minutes while the passengers enjoyed the stop. This passenger, though, had lots of work to do. It was my job to replenish our wood supply, re-lubricate every moving part of the engine and drive assembly, and keep the fire going at a medium level so I could easily stoke it back to full power when the time came.

With about five minutes to go on our Blue Springs excursion, the captain came down to me and said, "I recommend you go jump in Blue Springs Run and real quick-like take yourself a cooling-off break. It's gonna be a hot afternoon down here." I happily took his advice. With child-like joy, I jumped off the stern of the *Hattie*. I swam underwater chasing after the big schools of mullet and bass and marveled as they parted away from me, always just out of my reach. What a beautiful world! Swimming to the shore, I walked out of the river and climbed up onto the bank feeling like a new man. After sweating so much in the engine room and getting' just about worn out, I felt like I could have at it once again. I didn't care if my clothes were soaked because I figured my hothouse of a workplace would get them plenty dry in no time. Then my sweat would make them plenty wet again, plenty quick. I was right.

The captain blasted his steam whistle message to his passengers, again signaling time to go, then after calling, "All aboard *Hattie Brock* for Enterprise," he paused for those last stragglers. The cabin boy drew the bow gangplank from the bank of the beautiful Blue Springs Run.

With some new wood and another round of bellows blowing, the steam pressure quickly built up. Captain Brock sent me the reverse signal, then full reverse. The engines powered up, but the *Hattie* didn't budge. We were beached. Unruffled, the captain left his pilot house and yelled down to me, "Keep the steam pressure up." Then he and the cabin boy went to the bow and asked all passengers to please move to the stern of the boat. He next went to the middle deck and walking briskkly down the hall, knocking on each door shouting, "All passengers please go to the stern, we need to get underway." Then he looked up to the men on the upper deck, and hollered, "All passengers move astern, please."

Once he was satisfied he'd gotten enough weight onto the back of the boat and sufficiently lightened the bow, he re-assumed his powerful post. On command, I threw the big machines into reverse gear, then powered up to full reverse throttle. With a mighty rush of water and fearsome slapping of the paddles, I felt the big hulk of a boat slowly moving, first one inch, then another, then it quickly sped up as it slid off the bank like a lazy gator sliding into the river after a pleasant sunbath. The big boat quickly lunged backward and straight toward the middle of the river channel. Brock quickly commanded both engines throttled down and into neutral. After we glided backward with the spring's current toward the middle of the river channel, he put the port side into forward half power. Once the bow started to slide to the starboard, he deftly shifted the starboard engine back into reverse. As *Hattie* pivoted towards her new course, he signaled starboard neutral and the bow continued rotating, He then ordered "all forward full steam" and we were back on our way up the St. Johns. The passengers cheered. What a marvel these newfangled twin-paddlewheel machines were! I quietly thought what trust he put in me, a rookie at engine controls, to follow his commands promptly as he ordered them. A sleeping engine man could easily put a ship on shoals long before the captain had any ability to change course with his mere rudder controls. The ability to steer this monster by working the paddlewheels in opposition to each other was extremely powerful when done right, yet disastrous if done wrong. When I had my sawmill, I'd sometimes take a moment to watch the steam-powered saws doing their work. It was quite a sight, but it paled next to the majesty of the mighty riverships, moving the massive floating palace effortlessly up the river in absolute grand style.

I could feel the big wheels turn up to full speed, and we were on our way to Enterprise. The afternoon trip was uneventful, with a couple of ten-minute stops along the way and only one incident. Our starboard wheel hit a submerged log or something and caused about three of the paddles to break. The captain quickly slid both engines into neutral, and told me to release my excess steam and choke the fire down.

Dropping anchor, he quickly brought out some replacement paddles and reinstalled them as best he could. The metal frame of the wheel was bent enough so none of the new paddles fit perfectly, but he was skilled at getting them secured well enough so they'd stay on. We resumed our travels with a delay of only about an hour. Meanwhile the patrons on the top deck kept drinking away and blasting away at anything that moved in the air, on the banks or in the water. Captain looked at me, then glanced up at the gentlemen gunslingers and said, "These repair stops are the most profitable time of any trip. Whenever we have a breakdown I'm sure to beat my quota on that run! Some captains have even been known to stage a breakdown, just to get one last chance to goose their booze and ammunition sales," he laughed.

As Captain Brock began working on his last replacement paddle, he told me to quit helping him and get the boiler stoked again. By time he was finished repairing the wheel and lifting the anchor, we were at full pressure and ready to roll. And we did, all the way to the town of Enterprise on the north bank of Lake Monroe.

Lake Monroe is one of the largest lakes in South Florida. The river went through it on an east - west alignment about ten miles long, and it was about seven miles across at its widest point. Enterprise was on the north side, settled around a high Indian mound. The Brocks built a grand hotel, named Brock House, in 1855 about a mile west of the original settlement. It was the finest hotel on the river. The larger riverboats used to terminate their trips at the Brock House, but when Mellonville, just up the river and across Lake Monroe, opened its fine long pier the big boats could terminate there, but most still stop first in Enterprise.

The big spenders loved the Brock House, and even though dinner was twice as much as the on-board fare, many would go there that night. Some would even rent a room even though they had perfectly good cabins paid-for on the *Hattie*. Us Lees, of course, we had our canned vegetables, hard biscuits and jerky to eat. I heard Ava's sweet voice saying, "Waste not, want not."

As Gommy was digging through our gunnysack choosing our supper, Captain Brock kindly invited us to eat with him at his table for dinner. When I thanked him and declined, he said, "Well, your family has to eat, don't it?"

"Yes, sir," I replied, "but we brought our own so we could save the money."

His brow furrowed as he registered his displeasure. "Don't you know that's strictly forbidden?"

I wasn't terribly surprised, but I hadn't been told it directly. "No, sir, I didn't. I thought poor folks like us were allowed to supply our own vittles."

Brock explained the ship line had to make some money and surely wasn't doing it on $1.00 fares. The ticket agent was supposed to explain ships rules, and we could be evicted at the nearest port if we were found feeding ourselves.

332

"I'm sorry, I didn't know. We've had a good time on your ship and hope we don't get kicked off, Captain."

"I don't think you're in much danger of getting kicked off. You kept my engines humming like an expert today. I tell you what you can do. If you and your brood will have dinner with me tonight at my table, at my expense, we'll call it even. Is it a deal?"

"I think it's a deal we can't turn down." Then I asked, "It's not gonna spoil our young'uns, though, is it?"

"Oh no, just the opposite; it's good for 'em to experience the finer things every now and then so they'll know how to act when they're grown."

We had a fabulous meal with the captain. It surely would've cost us $2.00 if we had to pay, and that was with Julia Kate eating free. During dinner, Brock told us he loved his work, but he got real tired of the drunks and watching them so recklessly killing things and acting so obnoxiously. He pointed up to the hotel and told us, "Most of the passengers off the *Hattie* don't have any business going up to the fancy hotel fer their fancy dinner, but they're a-gonna, and they're gonna eat real big and keep on drinking just as hard as they've done all day. This river's beautiful, but there's something about it brings out the drunk in lots of men." Then he added, "Most of them drunks up there ain't got a nickel left to their names, and when I drop 'em off in Mellonville tomorrow, several of 'em are gonna slink away and try to find odd-jobs around there to earn themselves the fare home. Or if they're aiming to start a new life here, they's dun wasted all their savings on eatin' and drinkin' and'll hafta start again at the very bottom of the ladder just to feed themselves. I guess they had themselves a good time, though, on the *Hattie*. They each got to play the big man, and my Daddy got a little richer by hostin' 'em on his ship. I reckon ever'body's happy thattaway."

He asked our plans, and I told him of our dream to grow citrus and build a growing, packing and shipping business for any of our family to work in if they wanted to. I was going to start by hiring out my farm skills and equipment. Eventually I would buy land, plant, grow and manage it for absentee owners and for myself.

Brock was all ears. He seemed surprised to learn his down-and-out fireman had big dreams and he was real excited to hear more. We told him of our plans to move near Laura's uncle in Christmas. He said we needed to stay right near Lake Jesup, just a little ways south of Lake Monroe if we really wanted to grow citrus. The soil was better and deeper there, and it got far more cold protection from the lakes and swamps than Christmas had. He told me Christmas was a cowboy place, not so much a farming and citrus place.

He told us the big boats didn't service the settlements around Lake Jesup because the river was usually too shallow between there and Lake Monroe. That was why we would have to get off *Hattie* in Fort Mellon, then take a small, flat-bottom barge to one of the wharves on the south side of Lake Jesup, or just go by land. Until the river gets dredged the big boats woouldn't go past Mellonville. Shipping fruit from the warmer, more southern location would be inconvenient but the extra freeze protection should be well worth it.

With the shipping advantage, it seemed to me Fort Mellon might be the perfect place. I told him I knew General Finegan, who owned thousands of acres west of Mellonville. Maybe I could buy some of his land and be much closer to a deep port.

He said, "I guess you haven't heard. Finegan sold all his land down here. He had to sell it to get money to protect his homeplace near Jacksonville. Seemed the crooked Reconstruction government had been torturing him with taxes and all kinds of roadblocks because he was such an effective General and had so much to lose here in Florida. Well, looks like the thievin' carpetbaggers and scalawags have won this one. Poor ol' buzzard, even though he got somethin' like $14,000 for the Mellonville land, he lost his house and plantation in Jacksonville anyway."

He went on, "A Yankee feller name of Henry Sanford bought up all Finegan's Orange County land 'ceptin' a little patch around Fort Mellon, and he's planning a great city there named after himself. He calls himself 'General,' but it's a title he bought somehow or another. He's traveling all over the North and even Europe now promotin' it. Lots of folks think it's the big city of the future. Quite the promoter he is! He's plannin' to bring in lots of European labo, and wants to make it a farming, shipping and culture center. Says he wants to make it the 'Gateway to South Florida'," Brock said with a grand flourish. "I think he's got a good shot at it, but he's got a long way to go. He's got the same kind of plans ol' Bill Astor has for Manhattan, and he's got lots of money, but he ain't got Astor's kinda money. We'll just have to wait and see."

I felt sick about what happened to Finegan. "Yankee carpetbaggers!" I shouted. "There's plenty down here for everybody without having to take land from anybody. Whatever happened to the 'Charity for all and malice toward none' Mr. Lincoln was talking about? Looks like they're not gonna be happy 'til every poor rebel gets buried in debt and loses his land on the court house steps. This news hit me personally, because I fought under General Finegan. I risked my life under him along with lots of other stupid boys. Many didn't come out alive. Now, those lowlifes were killing Finegan financially out of vengeance for a war that's been over almost ten years!"

Captain Brock said he agreed but was pretty sure we could do nothing about it and all us ol' Rebels needed to learn the War was over.

I knew he was right, and apologized for my tirade. He said he sure understood because the Yanks had taken *Hattie* from him during the War, but he said life just had to go on. He inspired me to vow to quit expressing my anger so loudly. Lots of the Northerners were only trying to make a living, just like the rest of us. There certainly were some carpetbaggers who took unfair advantage of the War's devastation in the South, but sometimes it was hard to tell one from the other.

I knew if I wanted to get ahead I'd better treat everyone with human respect until I had real strong reason not to. The War just wasn't quite over yet for a whole lot of folks, and no matter how much I might think their way, I decided for me it was done and settled. I was getting on with my life, and I didn't want to let my bitterness show. Life was better that way. I made a vow to speak only good things of a man. I struggled to keep my vow the rest of my life; I failed many a time, but it still helped me more than I can tell to strive to speak well of a man or hold my tongue. I remembered my Momma admonishing me, "If you can't find something good to say, say nothing at all." This lesson would re-visit me throughout my life.

After dinner I escorted my family to the cabin and left to take my sleeping place on an upper deck chair. I hoped the drunken revelers wouldn't come back aboard and resume their drunken dissipation. I was reminded of Reverend Barnett and his futile quest to influence better behavior from men like these. I remembered my Daddy and his admonition about hooting with the owls and soaring with eagles. I missed those men and their wisdom already. I prayed Laura would slip out of the cabin and come see me under the stars on the observation deck. My prayer was answered and we held each other close and talked excitedly about the new life awaiting us on the other side of the big lake.

Orange County, Our New Home

The next morning came bright and early. I was up at 4:30 to begin prepping the engines for their day's labor. My duties included emptying out all the cold ash from yesterday's wood, oiling every moving part on the steam engines, boiler and running gear, and building up the new fire. The heat from the fire was welcome at first because it was a chilly, damp morning down in the hold of the *Hattie*. I was quickly plenty warm and knew very soon I'd be welcoming the opportunity to get out of the hot boiler room into fresh air again. It was a very exciting day for me.

Promptly at first light, we pushed off from the Enterprise pier. Across the river, the dawn haze lifted just enough to reveal a faint outline of the pier at Fort Mellon. Very soon I would make my first footprint in Orange County, Florida! I was pretty sure I could make this place my new home. I hoped and prayed Laura would like it after all I'd put her through to get here.

Once we were halfway across Lake Monroe, Captain Brock invited me up to the command bridge for a very brief view from above. Since we were only going across the lake, I wouldn't need to keep building the fire. It had all the heat it needed to get us the rest of the way across the lake, and my only remaining job was to run the throttles and transmission as we docked, then dampen the fire down once we docked at Fort Mellon. In this last leg of the trip, he told me I'd done a good job as his fireman and he happily refunded three of the four dollars I'd paid for our cargo. He told me the Brock Company was always in the market for good folks to run the equipment. He said I could easily keep my current job and pretty quickly become captain of my own ship. I thanked him and said farming was in my blood and I just had to give citrus growing a shot before I did anything else. He said he understood, but he made clear he didn't understand why I couldn't see steamships were the real future of this land. He told me he was sure I could make my fortune a lot sooner and a whole lot pleasanter at the helm of a riverboat than behind a mule.

Then he gave me some more of the same advice McBride had already given. "Well, then, I don't think you wanna be nowheres 'round Fort Christmas. That there's cow country, and you don't wanna try growin' no orange trees around so many cows. You'll never get a tree to grow up there without some cowman runnin' his herd through yer grove and tramplin' yer trees before you can ever get 'em to bearin' size. I'm guessin' you otta be lookin' at the new settlement of Oviedo or Clifton Springs. I can give you a letter like the one you got from Dickison, and it should hep ya get settled. Take it to my friend up at Clifton Springs, I know he's always alookin' for decent help on his docks or in his orange grove. If you get a toe-hold around there, you'll quickly learn the lay of the land and you, yer horses and yer tools should be able to pick up enough work to get you goin'." I thanked Brock and told him I thought I'd be taking his advice.

I just had to ask, though, "Why don't I just put up a fence and keep the cows out of my grove?" It seemed a logical question to me.

"Those cowboys'll tear yer fence down just as soon as you put it up," he told me, "an' ain't a blessed thing you can do about it. It's free range country roun' here, just like all of Florida, but 'round Christmas the herds are huge and the cowmen run the place. You'll never get your trees started down there."

We were silent while I spent a moment staring forward at Fort Mellon as it grew larger. I saw its strong pier, with rails for a mule-drawn rail-cart to come out to meet us to carry our cargo the couple hundred yards to dry land. At the base of the pier were several storage buildings and a few scrappy houses. Beyond them, the old fort I'd heard so much about all my growing up years; beyond the fort, not much else. My gaze was fixed on this settlement, and I guess my mind must've wandered, because next thing I knew, Brock was barking at me curtly, saying, "I need you below. Fort Mellon's coming up fast." Bounding to my engine room, I saw he'd already moved the controller to 'forward idle,' so I quickly adjusted the steam so the giant paddlewheels were barely turning. *Hattie* lazily entered into her last port of call before turning around to head back downriver all the way to Jacksonville. I briefly wondered if Captain Brock or even *Hattie* herself ever got tired of the St. Johns River, but couldn't imagine how.

When I saw the command to go into neutral, I quickly complied, then said a quick prayer for my family and me as together we started our newest adventure. As *Hattie* angled into the dock, I braced myself for the now-familiar bump you'd feel as her bow gently nudged the pier. I will never forget the excitement and the feeling of coming home to a place I'd never been!

A starboard bow line was thrown and tied to the big cleat on the dock. Captain Brock sent me the command for port engine reverse idle, which slowly pulled against the rope to lay *Hattie* neatly dockside. A quick tie of stern line to another cleat and we were moored.

My new friend Captain Brock scratched out his recommendation letter and handed it to me. I thanked him, and we agreed we'd enjoy meeting up again. By then our horses and cart were being unloaded, so we took our leave of a most enjoyable ride on a most beautiful river.

Then I did it. Stepping off the *Hattie*, with Julia Kate in one arm, the other arm around my beloved Gommy, and the boys at our sides, we walked together down the long pier to take our first steps onto Orange County soil. Then, very farmer like, I just had to touch it. Instinctively, I bent over and took a handful of the wet, grainy shoreline soil, and rolled it around in my palm. Then I gently put it right back where it came from, where it seemed to belong.

I was in a strange place, but I knew I was home. Though we still had a ways to go, and still didn't really know exactly where we were going, we knew we were home. Home, in Orange County, Florida!

James Hiram Lee with Orange Tree

END OF VOLUME I

Please look for Volume II, hopefully available in late 2014

Bibliography

Adams, Charles, *When in the Course of Human Events, Arguing the Case For Southern Secession*, Rowman & Littlefield Publishers, Inc, Lanham, MD, 2000

Best, Christine Kinlaw, *The History of Fort Mellon,* Sanford Historical Society, Inc., 2003

Black, Robert C. III, *The Railroads of the Confederacy*, University of North Carolina Press, Chapel Hill, NC, 1998

Brown, Canter, Jr., *Florida's Peace River Frontier, University of Central Florida Press*, Orlando, FL, 1991

Brown, Canter, Jr., *Ossian Bingley Hart, Florida's Loyalist Reconstruction Governor,* Louisiana State University Press, Baton Rouge, LA, 1997

Clonts, Thelma Lee, *Lee Family History*, Compiled 1992

Denham, James M., *A Rogue's Paradise, Crime and Punishment in Antebellum Florida*, 1821-1861,The University of Alabama Press, 1997

Dickison, J. J., *Conferate Military History Florida*, eBooksOnDisk.com, Gulf Breeze, FL, 2002

Doudney, Alfred, Try and Try Again, The Loves of Two Youths Who Became Clergymen of the Church of England, W. Macintosh, London, 1864

Gannon, Michael, *The New History of Florida, University Press of Florida*, Gainesville, FL, 1996

Gramling, Lee, *Riders of the Suwannee, a Cracker Western*, Pineapple Press, Inc., Sarasota, FL, 1993

John, John E., Florida During the civil War, Iniversity of Florida Press, Gainesville, FL, 1963

Jones, John Paul, *Cold Before Morning*, Father and Son Pubishing, Tallahassee, FL 1992

Oppel, Frank & Meisel, Tony, *Tales of Old Florida,* Castle, A Division of Book Sales, Inc. Edison, NJ, 1987

Pratt, Theodore, *The Barefoot Mailman*, By Arrangement with R. Bemis Publishing , Inc., 1993, Florida Classics Library, Port Salerno, FL

Shearhart, Mary Ida Bass Barber, *Florida's Frontier, The Way Hit Wuz,* Florida Historical Society Press, Cocoa, FL, 2010

Smith, Patrick, Forever Island and Allapattah, Pineapple Press, Inc., Englewood, FL, 1973

Taylor, Paul, *Discovering the Civil War in Florida*, Pineapple Press, Sarasota, FL, 2001

Wallace, John, *Carpet Bag Rule in Florida. The Inside Workings of the Reconstruction of Civil Government in Florida,* Da Costa Printing and Publishing House, Jacksonville, FL 1888, Reprinted and Copyrighted by Bibliolife, LLC, Charleston, SC, 2012.

List of Illustrations

Title Page A Cracker Cowboy Remington, Frederic, 1861-1909. Title:. Publication info: New York : Harper & Brothers , 1895.This work is in the public domain in the United States, and those countries with a copyright term of life of the author plus 100 years or less.This file has been identified as being free of known restrictions under copyright law, including all related and neighboring rights.

Opportunity Strikes and Young Love Jean Lafitte. Note: This is an artist's conception of Lafitte's appearance some 80 years later. While there is no reason to assume it is necessarily more accurate than more recent and more widely circulated artist's conception of Lafitte, it is at least now in the public domain. Date 1895 Source Engraving from 1895 book "New Orleans: The Place and the People" by Grace King, via online copy Not signed, possibly Frances Jones. This is in the public domain in the United States. This applies to U.S. works where the copyright has expired, often because its first publication occurred prior to January 1, 1923

Olustee Cavalry fight, Harper's Weekly, November 29, 1862. This work is in the public domain in the United States, and those countries with a copyright term of life of the author plus 100 years or less.

Back to Business The Cone Brothers. Photograph circa 1860. . This work is in the public domain in the United States, and those countries with a copyright term of life of the author plus 100 years or less.

The Wedding and New Life James Hiram Lee and Laura Barnett Lee wedding photo, private collection. Used by permission.

A Change in the Air Aftermath of Boston Fire, November 9th & 10th, 1872. Digitally enhanced (colors adjusted & tear partially hidden) by Dave Pape. Library of Congress Prints and Photographs Division. http://hdl.loc.gov/loc.pnp/pan.6a06305. Smith, Joshua, copyright claimant Original photo is public domain (U.S. pre-1923). Modified version released to public domain by Dave Pape.

Back at the Farm and Making New Plans. John Robert Lee and Wiley Lee photo. Private collection. Used by permission. Original photographs have been cropped and enhanced for this publication.

Juniper Springs to Manhattan, Florida Steamboat Hattie Brock.

Orange County, Our New Home James Hiram Lee photo, private collection. Used by permission.

Front Cover:
Horse pulling plow hand-held by man. Author-Unknown. Department of the Interior. Bureau of Indian Affairs. Aberdeen Area Office. Cheyenne River Agency. (1949 -) Wikimedia Commons. No source information or the image has been tagged as being under a free license, but information required by the license (or to verify the status) is missing. NARA's Central Plains Region (Kansas City) (NREA), 400 West Pershing Road, Kansas City, MO, 64108.

Unidentified Steamboat on St. John's River ca 1880

Steam powered sawmill at Landmark Heritage Centre This is capable of doing a proper day's work - it's not just a twee visitor attraction. It's driven by a large Marshall overtype portable engine. 30 October 2005. This image was taken from the Geograph project collection. See this photograph's page on the Geograph website for the photographer's contact details. The copyright on this image is owned by Chris Allen and is licensed for reuse under the Creative Commons Attribution-ShareAlike 2.0 license. The copyright owner does not support or endorse the book, Try and Trya Again.

Whitney's Florida Pathfinder, A Guide to Florida, Information for the Tourise, Traveler, and Invalid. Publsihed Annually by John P. Whitney – Season 1880-1881. Project Guttenburg. Document in public domain.

Behind the Confederate lines Reenactor's depict the Confederate advance. Olustee Battlefield, 2 miles east of Olustee on U.S. Route 90 in the Osceola National Forest Olustee. 7 September 2013, 22:31:37. Author Robert W. Mann. Camera location 30° 12' 46.00" N, 82° 23' 21.00" W On February 20, 1864, more than 11,000 cavalry, infantry and artillery troops fought a five-hour battle in a pine forest near a railroad station called Olustee, Florida. The four hour battle ended in defeat for the Union troops and preserved Confederate control of the interior and the capital of Florida until the war ended. Tallahassee was the only Confederate capital east of the Mississippi River not taken by the Federal Armies

$12.99

ISBN 978-0-9899696-0-4

51299>

9 780989 969604

CPSIA information can be obtained at www.ICGtesting.com
Printed in the USA
LVOW11s0116011013

354853LV00001B/1/P